Financial Models and Tools for Managing Lean Manufacturing

SUPPLY CHAIN INTEGRATION SERIES
Modeling, Optimization, and Applications

Sameer Kumar, Series Advisor
University of St. Thomas, Minneapolis, MN

Supply Chain Cost Control Using Activity-Based Management
Sameer Kumar and Mathew Zander
ISBN: 0-8493-8215-7

Financial Models and Tools for Managing Lean Manufacturing
Sameer Kumar and David Meade
ISBN: 0-8493-9185-7

Additional Titles in
RESOURCE MANAGEMENT SERIES

Financial Models and Tools for Managing Lean Manufacturing

Sameer Kumar · David Meade

Auerbach Publications
Taylor & Francis Group
Boca Raton   New York

Auerbach Publications is an imprint of the
Taylor & Francis Group, an informa business

Auerbach Publications
Taylor & Francis Group
6000 Broken Sound Parkway NW, Suite 300
Boca Raton, FL 33487-2742

International Standard Book Number-10: 0-8493-9185-7 (Hardcover)
International Standard Book Number-13: 978-0-8493-9185-9 (Hardcover)

Library of Congress Cataloging-in-Publication Data

Kumar, Sameer.
    Financial models and tools for managing lean manufacturing / Sameer Kumar and David Meade.
        p. cm. -- (Supply chain integration--modeling, optimization and applications ; no. 1:2)
    Includes bibliographical references and index.
    ISBN-13: 978-0-8493-9185-9 (alk. paper)
    ISBN-10: 0-8493-9185-7 (alk. paper)
    1. Business logistics. 2. Production management. I. Meade, David.
    II. Title. III. Series.

HD38.5.K849 2006
658.5--dc22
                                                            2006008335

Visit the Taylor & Francis Web site at
http://www.taylorandfrancis.com

and the Auerbach Web site at
http://www.auerbach-publications.com

Dedication

To our families,

thank you so much for all your tireless support.

Contents

Appendices

Key Features of This Book

The aim of the book is to elevate the level of understanding of the impact that traditional accounting practices have on operational improvement programs that lead to a rapid lowering of any or all inventories. Without a thorough understanding of the dynamics of the impact on the profit and loss statements, existing accounting practices can have a stifling effect on improvement programs that, if allowed to continue, would lead to improved firm competitiveness.

In summary, this book explains how existing accounting practices have a tendency to report the results of operational improvement programs in a negative light. Other authors have identified this issue but have not attempted to quantify the impact to a firm's profit and loss nor have they shown the impact over a period of reporting periods.

The key selling points of this book that distinguish it from others on the topic include:

- It supports lean manufacturing efforts and programs.
- It provides information to operations management and finance that will enable them to successfully manage operational improvement programs.
- It provides data that will enable firm management to predict the impact to the profit-and-loss statement that will result from a lean manufacturing implementation effort.
- It identifies issues with traditional accounting practices used in the United States leading to poor operational decisions with respect to improved international competitiveness.

Organization of the Book

Chapter 1 — Introduction

A brief review of the issues surrounding the reason to analyze the problem is presented. It includes the historical background of the problem, objectives of the analysis, questions to be answered, and the importance of this analysis.

Chapter 2 — Impact of Management Accounting Methods on Lean Implementation

The interactions of various management accounting systems with the dominant production planning systems are the focus of this chapter. In particular, this chapter provides a detailed overview of (1) the origin and the intended purpose of management accounting, (2) the transition in the focus of financial reporting from internal to the business to external, (3) the difficulties presented to operations management, in regard to making operational improvements, by the current forms of financial reporting, and (4) the concepts and attributes of just-in-time (JIT) and lean manufacturing practices.

Chapter 3 — Multi-Period Simulation Model of a Factory with Lean Manufacturing

This chapter provides a description of the tools, methods, and assumptions employed in the development of a simulated repetitive manufacturing environment used to conduct this analysis.

Chapter 4 — Analytical Findings from Lean Manufacturing Factory Operation

This chapter reviews the analysis of the dataset created using the modeling tools. The analysis is designed to answer the research questions posed in Chapter 3 by providing the essential analysis to test a series of research hypotheses.

Chapter 5 — Conclusions and Implications from Lean Manufacturing Factory Operation

In this chapter, the results of the statistical analysis of Chapter 3 and Chapter 4 are interpreted in terms of the application to real-world manufacturing operations. Limitations of business analysis and suggestions for future work are also highlighted.

Chapter 6 — Impact of the Pareto Distribution on Product Cost Calculations

This chapter identifies and evaluates a new allocation base that is better matched to the consumption rate of the indirect costs being allocated. Using multi-period simulation, the relationship between allocated cost categories and production or sales order activity through the operations is explored. Results show that at the aggregate reporting level (e.g., income statement), the use of sales order or production order activity as an allocation base track closely with performance levels experienced using other traditional bases. This approach toward cost calculation would be equal to other enterprise resource planning systems–based solutions in terms of simplicity of maintenance while offering more accurate costs than ABC systems requiring substantially more resources for maintenance.

References

A comprehensive list of up-to-date references on the chapter topic is included at the end of each chapter.

Appendices

Appendix 1 through Appendix 3 contain a complete 35-replication dataset for each of the five accounting systems under evaluation. Appendix data was created under an environment of moderate sales stochasticity. Appendix 4 contains sample income statements for each of the five accounting systems under evaluation.

Preface

Lean manufacturing principles have been revolutionizing American manufacturing for more than 20 years. The principles, born in the days of Henry Ford and perfected by Toyota's Taiichi Ohno in post–World War II Japan, call for the relentless pursuit of the elimination of waste throughout the manufacturing operation.

Roadblocks to lean manufacturing, introduced by the accounting methods employed in American accounting practice, have only recently come under scrutiny in the realm of applied research. Unfortunately, past studies have failed to quantify the significance of the problem in terms of the short- and long-term impact to a firm's profitability.

The results of a multi-month analysis of the impact on a firm's reported profit, stemming from the implementation of lean manufacturing strategies, enable us to address these issues. Armed with this knowledge, a lean program manager will be in a position to defend the lean program through the months when the income statements indicate a decline in profitability. The analysis identifies how the decline in income is the result of past poor manufacturing practices that are being "cleaned-up" by the operational improvements brought by the lean program.

In summary, this book evaluates issues with accounting practices that have been in use in the United States since the early 1900s. At present, there is no indication that these practices will be changing in the foreseeable future. In addition, lean manufacturing practices are being adopted at an ever-increasing rate in the United States as the threat of foreign competition increases. The indication is that the information contained in this book will be valid for explaining profitability problems in a firm's profit-and-loss reports for many years to come, 10 to 20 years conservatively.

Preface

Acknowledgments

The authors would like to thank all those who helped bring this book to publication. First and foremost, we have greatly benefited from the wealth of a vast array of published material on the subjects of management accounting, cost accounting, lean manufacturing, and simulation of manufacturing environments. Second in importance are our experiences with various industries regarding the negative impact of different management accounting methods on reported profits as inventories are being reduced as part of lean manufacturing program implementation.

We would like to thank the reviewers of the manuscript of the book. The contents of this book have benefited immensely from their valued insights, comments, and suggestions.

Both authors are indebted to their families, parents, and friends for their support.

Finally, we wish to thank our editor, Raymond O'Connell, and the entire production team of the Taylor & Francis Auerbach group for their assistance and guidance in the successful completion of this book.

About the Authors

Sameer Kumar, Ph.D., is a professor and Qwest Endowed Chair in Global Communications and Technology Management at the College of Business at the University of St. Thomas, Minneapolis, Minnesota. Prior to this position, he was a professor of engineering and technology management at the University of St. Thomas. Before joining the University of St. Thomas, Dr. Kumar was a professor of industrial engineering in the Department of Industrial Management, University of Wisconsin–Stout.

Dr. Kumar's major research areas include optimization concepts applied to design and operational management of production and service systems. He has been actively involved in a wide variety of challenging industry projects for more than 25 years in the United States and India. He has published in various research journals and presented papers at numerous conferences. He is a registered professional engineer, certified manufacturing technologist, certified manufacturing engineer, and certified plant engineer.

Dr. Kumar has master's degrees in mathematics (University of Delhi), computer science (University of Nebraska), and industrial engineering and operations research (University of Minnesota). He received his Ph.D. in industrial engineering from the University of Minnesota.

David Meade, Ph.D., is an assistant professor of manufacturing engineering at Western Michigan University. He has nearly 20 years of direct industrial experience. He spent 16 years as an employee of General Motors, Frigidaire, Hoffman Engineering (a subsidiary of Pentair Corporation), and Rittal Corporation, the U.S. entity of Rittal GmbH. He has held positions as a field service engineer, controls engineer, project manager, engineering manager, as well as the director of operations.

Dr. Meade's interests include facility planning and design, computer simulation techniques for both physical operations and operational financial performance, product costing system development and evaluation, manufacturing planning and controls systems from the front office to the machine level, and finishing system design, implementation, and optimization. His recent research includes the evaluation of the discontinuities between operational improvements and financial reporting practices and improvements to generally accepted product costing methods for the allocation of overhead.

Dr. Meade earned his B.S. in robotics engineering technology (Lake Superior State University), his M.S. in manufacturing systems engineering (University of St. Thomas), and his Ph.D. in industrial engineering from Western Michigan University.

Contribution of This Book

In September 2005, more than 300 accounting professionals, educators, consultants, and business leaders attended the first annual Lean Accounting Summit held in Detroit, Michigan. Icons of accounting literature such as H. Thomas Johnson, Robyn Cooper, and Brian Maskell delivered presentations at this inaugural event. What were the attendees seeking? What led the sponsors to organize such an event? The answer to both questions is this: accounting practices of the past 100 years are inadequate in today's manufacturing environment where lean manufacturing is a do-or-die proposition. One presenter offered a more appropriate name for the event: he suggested "Accounting for Lean," which is at the heart of the issue. Current accounting practices do an inadequate job of accounting for the improvements brought by a lean program until months or years after the gains have been realized. As companies move to a leaner form of operation, through the adaptation of various lean principles, the accounting systems begin to send erroneous signals indicating that things are getting worse. This book explores one of the fundamental problems in this area: that of falling gross and net profit figures while experiencing a reduction in inventories. Identified here is the magnitude of the impact on reported profit levels as well as the quantification of the duration of the reported downturn, which has been left out of previous works addressing this issue. Any company or project leader charged with the implementation of lean principles within his or her company should be armed with the knowledge contained within this book before the financial reports begin to reflect the inevitable and the program is stifled due to ignorance.

Chapter 1

Introduction

Lean manufacturing implementation efforts are being met with resistance due to misleading performance measures. This is a confounding situation because *lean manufacturing* is defined as the elimination of waste, which should be desirable within a manufacturing operation (Merchant et al., 2005). Accepted accounting practices, most of them developed around the turn of the 20th century, provide an inaccurate view of the operational improvements realized through the implementation of lean strategies. Many researchers have identified the negative impact that accounting methods have on reported profits as inventories are being reduced (Johnson and Kaplan, 1987; Cooper and Kaplan, 1988; Kaplan, 1994; Garrison and Noreen, 1994; Drury and Tayles, 1997; Lere, 2001; Womack and Jones, 2003; Cunningham and Fiume, 2003; Soloman, 2003). Using simulation, this research explores the magnitude and duration of the negative impact on reported profits experienced during a lean manufacturing implementation.

The problem is addressed through a multi-period simulation model. The model is designed to emulate the operation of a manufacturing facility through a series of months of operation. Material requirements planning (MRP) functionality is employed through the incorporation of production planning and control functionality, as a means of controlling finished goods inventory levels through the series of simulated periods.

This book documents the details of the methods and tools employed in the development and execution of the model manufacturing operation. Also discussed are the data evaluation methods and subsequent results of the study.

Historical Background of the Problem

The accounting function within the manufacturing environment came under criticism in the 1980s when H. Thomas Johnson and Robert S. Kaplan published their book, *Relevance Lost: The Rise and Fall of Managerial Accounting* (1987). This book chronicled the history of the development of modern day accounting practices as they pertain to manufacturing. The two areas of accounting in this category are namely managerial accounting and financial accounting. The second is primarily concerned with the processing of data and information for external reporting, that is reporting to investors and the government. Managerial accounting is concerned with the management of the internal operations of the business. External reporting is governed by law and, therefore, must be supported on an ongoing basis. Noncompliance is not an option. However, external forces do not govern support of the manufacturing operations with financial information in addition to that required for external reporting. Companies must decide if they are willing to support a financial reporting system in addition to that required by law to provide information relevant to operations for decision support. Per Johnson and Kaplan (1987), many companies have opted to rely on financial accounting information, which is prepared for external reporting and for managerial decision support. In effect, managerial accounting has become subservient to financial accounting. The unfortunate result of this development is that the financial information required for external reporting lacks the accuracy required for internal decision support. Lacking the appropriate information for decision support, the operations management team has attempted to interpret where profit is being lost using the available financial reports. These reports often provide a misleading picture of what the current dynamics are in terms of the financial performance of the firm. This is due to several factors; cost allocation schemes and timing for the recognition of operational expenditures are two issues among these factors. As a result, lean manufacturing programs are being viewed as failures due to the effect they are having on the profit and loss statements in the early months of implementation (Womack and Jones, 2003; Cunningham and Fiume, 2003; Soloman, 2003). In fact, the more successful the lean manufacturing program, the more damaging it can be on the financial statements. However, this phenomenon is only temporary and has no relevance to the true current operational performance. The length of time it will take the traditional financial reports to reflect the improvements depends on how poorly the operation was doing in terms of inventory management prior to the initiation of the lean effort. It is hypothesized that through the application of simulation modeling, the dynamics of this phenomenon can be better understood. The results of this study will lead to a superior ability to predict the effects on the financial statements resulting from the initiation of a lean program. In turn, this knowledge will lead to the avoidance of surprises that impede progress with the implementation of lean strategies.

The problems that are created by traditional financial accounting practices are several. First, due to the need to account for indirect costs, costs that cannot be directly attributed to the product, such as direct labor or direct materials, allocation schemes must be used. These schemes attach a portion of the overhead costs to the final product in an effort to "recognize" these costs in the reporting of financial results. Sales price targets can then be calculated by using the derived cost information. However, in reality, the market usually determines the sales price that must be met to compete. The problem with allocation schemes are that they are, at best, estimates. The basis for application of a dollar amount is based on direct labor hours required to produce the product in 68 to 73 percent of manufacturing operations (Drury and Tayles, 1997). This assumes that all the indirect costs necessary to support the production of a particular product are proportional to the amount of direct labor required to produce that product. Many scenarios can be envisioned where this is clearly not sound logic. For instance, a part that has been in production for years may have a lower level of automated operations leading to a higher content of direct labor. A new part in the same operation, with a high level of automation, would have lower direct labor content. The new part requires new capital equipment with a higher depreciation value than the old part. In addition, it is typical that in the early months or years of manufacture that a product requires much more support from departments other than production than does a product that has been manufactured for years. In a costing system that relies on allocations, the old part would be carrying a greater portion of the indirect burden than the new product, in essence carrying some of the overhead costs of the new product. Using product cost information such as this to identify profitable products from those that are unprofitable can lead to incorrect conclusions. When these cost accounting practices were developed, direct labor in the United States constituted about 60 percent of the total product cost. Today, direct labor in the United States accounts for 4 to 10 percent of the total product cost (Boothroyd

Dewhurst, 2005; Cunningham and Fiume, 2003). This transition has only exacerbated the inaccuracies inherent to this method of determining product cost. This problem is investigated further in Chapter 6.

A second issue created by traditional accounting practices comes from the concept of cost attachment and the handling of these "attached" costs. This is the primary issue causing the misrepresentation of performance improvements from lean manufacturing programs. In accounting terms, the cost attachment process has the effect of deferring the efforts (expenses) of producing a product until the accomplishment (revenue) is recognized. In other words, what attachment does is postpone the recognition of an expense until a later date. For instance, material and labor plus overhead required to produce a product are actually shown on the profit and loss statement in the period when the product is sold or otherwise removed from the finished goods inventory. This means that labor and materials that were expended and paid during the current month may possibly not show up on the income statement this month and perhaps not for several months to come. Once the material has been converted into finished goods, the cost is transferred to the balance sheet as an asset. When the item is sold, the expenses are recognized on the income statement as a cost of goods sold. Therefore, if a lean program results in the lowering of finished goods inventories, which should be the case, the costs from prior production periods will begin to show up on the income statement without the corresponding transaction to the balance sheet that previously postponed the recognition of current period labor, material, and overhead expenses. Without a corresponding offsetting transaction, a reduction in period indirect labor or salaries, for instance, the income statement results move in a less favorable direction, i.e., lower gross and net profits. This will continue to occur until the finished goods inventories stabilize. In some operations, this could continue for a considerable length of time. As mentioned, a reduction in period costs would offset the effect of liberating the attached costs; however, this is a difficult option to manage. It is true that production will likely decrease for a time while inventories are being depleted. However, these reductions will most likely be across all product lines, making it difficult to remove a specific group of production workers and supporting staff. In addition, once the inventories have been lowered to the desired level, production will return to the prelean level, presumably requiring all or most of the production workers that were part of the operation at the onset of the lean program. The labor pool most affected by lean initiatives is indirect labor: those activities associated with moving material while in process or after completion. When material is eliminated from the operation, the indirect activities associated with its movement are also eliminated. These savings begin to build over time in terms of their contribution to the income statement, but do not occur during a timeframe sufficient to offset the initial negative impact from inventory reduction.

Objectives of the Study

The primary focus is to study the impact on key external operational financial measures, as reported by various financial accounting methods, which result from the implementation of lean manufacturing practices. The analysis is conducted under several cost accounting environments. The traditional method of full absorption costing is used as a baseline and is important to this study as it is the method with the longest history and is most often used in industry (Drury and Tayles, 1997). It is also the method accepted by the Internal Revenue Service (IRS) and Securities and Exchange Commission (SEC) for calculation of externally reported financial results. Other known methods evaluated include direct costing, activity-based costing, and throughput costing (TPC). These methods have arisen out of a desire to develop a cost accounting method that removes or diminishes some of the negative aspects of cost accounting systems described earlier. A fifth method is introduced that has not yet been discussed in published literature. This method is the order activity costing method and is based on the premise that overhead costs are not volume related but rather are the result of transactional activity that products cause in a manufacturing operation. The intent is to better understand how the external reported figures are affected under the various systems.

Previous research has chosen to evaluate which combination of manufacturing environment and management accounting system results in superior firm performance (Lea, 1998; Boyd, 1999). The study documented here is not concerned with the evaluation of manufacturing methods, such as MRP, TPC, or just-in-time (JIT), in an effort to determine the one best method. It is extremely difficult to identify the best manufacturing environment in terms of short- or long-term profit. MRP or batch may be superior to JIT in ship building, for instance, but TPC or theory of constraints may be superior to JIT and MRP in industries with very high capital equipment costs. Lean strategies, on the other hand, can be defended in nearly any manufacturing environment. It is true that lean strategies would be most closely aligned with a JIT method of manufacturing, but aspects of lean manufacturing could be applied to any manufacturing environment. If the strategies implemented had the effect of reducing on-hand inventories, then the impact on the income statement as previously discussed would be present. A base assumption of this study assumes that the benefits to a firm, which will come as the result of the adaptation of lean strategies, are evident and that lean has been accepted as the improvement strategy of choice. Additionally, this study accepts the fact that financial accounting methods required for the external reporting of operation performance will not soon change and, therefore, the problem of ineffective reporting will continue into the foreseeable future.

Important Questions for the Study

Because the various cost accounting methods differ in their handling of the recognition of the various components of cost, which lead to variations between gross and net profit, the major questions that arise are divided as follows:

- Within a given cost accounting method, does rate of inventory reduction have an effect on reported gross profit?
- Within a given cost accounting method, does rate of inventory reduction have an effect on reported net profit?
- Within a given inventory reduction policy, does the cost accounting method have an effect on reported gross profit?
- Within a given inventory reduction policy, does the cost accounting method have an effect on reported net profit?
- For a given inventory reduction policy, does the cost accounting method used have an effect on reported gross profit?
- For a given inventory reduction policy, does the cost accounting method used have an effect on reported net profit?
- How does the rate of inventory reduction affect the customer service level, measured by stock outages, under the production and market environment modeled in this study?
- How does forecast accuracy affect gross and net profit under the production and market environment modeled in this study?
- How does forecast accuracy affect the customer service level, measured in terms of stock outages, under the production and market environment modeled in this study?

Importance of This Study

Hoffer (1994) presents four reasons for conducting explorative study:

1. The issue or topic has not been studied before.
2. The frequency with which the issue is observed in the real world is increasing.
3. Theory on the topic is nonexistent, incomplete, internally inconsistent, or inconsistent with empirical observations.
4. The issue is very important to successful management practices.

In reference to this study, the above points can be answered thus:

1. Past professional literature on this subject includes accounting texts, journal articles, popular books on operations management, and research dissertations. These publications have identified the negative effect on gross and net profit that occurs when inventory is "moved" from the balance sheet to the income statement. What has been lacking in the literature is a longer-term perspective of the problem. What needs to be better understood is how significant is the impact and how long does it last? This study attempts to expand the level of understanding of this problem in regard to these questions.
2. The movement toward the acceptance and application of lean manufacturing strategies has been gaining speed for the past 20 or more years. Large manufacturers were the early adapters, for instance, industries like automotive and appliance. However, much of American manufacturing is still in the early stages of implementation of these strategies. As more and more publicly held, or heavily financed, companies begin to embrace the philosophies of lean manufacturing, the issues identified in this study will lead to an increasing number of failed implementations.
3. Regarding the theory on this topic, the level of understanding of the impact on the financial measures is high within the accounting community. This understanding has given rise to some of the other methods of cost accounting previously identified. However, the level of understanding of the problems researched in this study diminishes rapidly outside of the accounting circle. The weight given to the reported results for gross and net profit by stakeholders external to a corporation can have a devastating impact on the firm. It is in this community that the issue is not understood and where the expectation for positive operational results is quarter by quarter. This study will

show that a short-term perspective of this nature will have a stifling effect on the implementation of lean strategies.

4. The economic environment has also been changing significantly over the past 20 or so years. The sophistication level of investors and their access to within the hour information regarding the performance of corporations has contributed to a culture that has an extremely short-term perspective in regard to firm performance. As a result, managers are under pressure to focus on the short-term implications of any program that impacts operational performance. Because the negative impact experienced in the reported financial measures resulting from a lean program will surely span several quarters, the incentive for managers is to avoid the implementation of lean manufacturing practices or take a cautious stance and not move rapidly or aggressively. For firms in financial difficulties, this may be a formula for bankruptcy.

References

Boothroyd Dewhurst, Inc. (2005). DFMA Overview, http://www.dfma.com/.

Boyd, L. H. (1999). Production Planning and Control and Cost Accounting Systems: Effects on Management Decision Making and Firm Performance, Ph.D. dissertation, UMI Co., Ann Arbor, MI.

Cooper, R. and Kaplan, R. S. (1988). How cost accounting distorts product costs, *Management Accounting*, 69(10), 2027.

Cunningham, J. and Fiume, O. (2003). *Real Numbers: Management Accounting in a Lean Organization*, Managing Times Press, Durham, NC.

Drury, C. and Tayles, M. (1997). Evidence on the financial accounting mentality debate: a research note, *British Accounting Review*, 29, 263–276.

Garrison, R. H. and Noreen, E. W. (1994). *Managerial Accounting*, Irwin, Inc., Burr Ridge, IL.

Hoffer, C. W. (1994). MAN class handout, University of Georgia, Athens, GA, Winter.

Johnson, H. T. and Kaplan, R. S. (1987). *Relevance Lost: The Rise and Fall of Management Accounting*, Harvard Business School Press, Boston, MA.

Kaplan, R. S. (1994). Management accounting (1984–1994): development of new practice and theory, *Management Accounting Research*, 5, 247–260.

Lea, B.-R. (1998). The Impact of Management Accounting Alternatives in Different Manufacturing Environments, Ph.D. dissertation, Clemson University, Clemson, SC, UMI Co., Ann Arbor, MI.

Lere, J. C. (2001). Your product-costing system seems to be broken: now what? *Industrial Marketing Management*, 30, 587–598.

Merchant, M. E., Dornfeld, D. A., and Wright, P. K. (2005). Manufacturing — its evolution and future, *Transactions of NAMRI/SME*, 33, 211–218.

Soloman, J. M. (2003). *Who's Counting?* WCM Associates, Fort Wayne, IN.

Womak, J. and Jones, D. (2003). *Lean Thinking: Banish Waste and Create Wealth in Your Corporation*, The Free Press, New York.

Chapter 2

Impact of Management Accounting Methods on Lean Implementation

This chapter reviews professional literature pertinent to this explorative study which describes (1) the origin and intended purpose of management accounting, (2) the transition in the focus of financial reporting from internal to the business to external, (3) the difficulties presented to operations management, in regard to making operational improvements, by the current forms of financial reporting, and (4) literature defining the concepts and attributes of JIT and lean manufacturing. Also pertinent to this study is a review of recent research activities in the area of the interactions of various management accounting systems with the dominant production planning systems.

Management Accounting

Prior to the Industrial Revolution, accounting was primarily record keeping of external transactions between businesses (Scott, 1931). During the period prior to the Industrial Revolution, manufacturing was essentially a system of artisans exchanging their output, or product, on an open market. It was not until the advent of the factory, where several manufacturing processes became linked, that measurement systems were developed to monitor exchange between units of an enterprise. Management accounting grew out of the need of large, integrated enterprises to track financial data between business units for purposes of administrative control. Johnson and Kaplan (1987) use the examples of the textile, steel, and railroad industries to further identify the evolution of managerial accounting practices. During the period of the Industrial Revolution, manufacturing management transitioned from a system of buying goods on the open market to one that employed internal contractors to supply manufacturing labor to employing the laborers directly. The driving force behind this transition was the belief, of the owners of these single-activity enterprises, that greater profits could be realized through integration of processes. This transition brought about many new challenges in regard to monitoring performance of the organization. The key issue was that of tracking worker performance, i.e., efficiency. In the market-based piece-rate system, prices for intermediate output were unambiguous purchase prices. In the integrated system, the cost for the intermediate output was now dependent on labor content and, therefore, not as evident as in the market-based system. To ensure increased profits, owners created entirely new managerial accounting procedures to monitor and evaluate the performance of internally managed processes.

The earliest record of the systems developed to support the integrated manufacturing processes were in the textile industry. Detailed records were kept of the efficiency of the use of cotton, labor, and general overhead. This information was used to determine the cost of intermediate output and ultimately the finished product cost. Product cost information was used to evaluate the performance of workers. Worker performance was evaluated between employees in the same period and on the same process, as well as across several periods for the same worker on the same process. It is important to note that the cost information provided by these systems was intended to focus managers' attention inwardly on the operations of the business, not outwardly on performance in the market (Johnson and Kaplan, 1987).

The steel industry cost management systems developed in a similar way to that of the textile industry. What was unique to the steel industry was the introduction of the "voucher" system to job tracking (Chandler, 1977). The voucher system was a system of tracking that had been in use in the railroad industry but had not been widely seen in factories. The voucher system is analogous to "job-cost" systems of today whereby the direct manufacturing related costs to complete a specific job, labor and direct materials, are recorded on a cost sheet or "voucher," one per job. Utilizing historical records of cost sheets, steel manufacturers could evaluate performance on a job-by-job basis. These cost sheets were the primary control mechanism for the administration and oversight of managers, foremen, and workers. In addition, the information in the cost sheets was used for quality checks for a mix of raw materials, to direct process and product improvements, and for decision making pertaining to the development of by-products. Again, in the steel industry, as in textile, the focus of the information was internal for the purposes of bringing about improvement.

Johnson and Kaplan (1987) further explain the origin and evolution of management accounting with a discussion on "scientific management." Between 1880 and 1910, engineer-managers in American metal working firms developed systems used to evaluate task productivity and to analyze profit by product in the more complex manufacturing segments. These segments included the manufacture of reapers, sewing machines, locks, firearms, pumps, typewriters, and the machines used to produce these products. Tracking performance of the processes utilized in the manufacture of these goods was no longer enough for the owners and managers of these businesses for adequate management as they attempted to increase profits. As a result, targets for productivity were established using engineering standards developed through the application of scientific management techniques. The practitioners of this science were engineers. Their focus was on identifying the "one best way" to use labor and material resources. Again, the focus was on internal process and product improvements. Martin-Vega (2001) credits industrial engineering pioneers such as Fredrick Taylor and the husband and wife team of Frank and Lillian Gilbreth with the development of the early systems and tools applied to manufacturing for human performance measurement for the purposes of efficiency improvement.

An important point that Johnson and Kaplan (1987) make, is that during the time frame previously discussed, inventory valuation was not viewed as an important aspect of an accounting system. At times when inventory value was reported, in audited or unaudited financial reports, market price was frequently used for valuation purposes. Additionally, capital management was not a component of the accounting process. Depreciation was not tracked in any form and, therefore, was not included in the product costing process. These are both important components of a 20th and 21st century cost accounting system.

Garrison and Noreen (1994) describe management accounting as that which is concerned with providing information to managers inside the organization. Specifically, this means those who are charged with directing and controlling the operation. They contrast this with financial accounting, which is concerned with external reporting to stockholders, creditors, and others such as the SEC and the government. They also identify eight major differences between management accounting and financial accounting. Management accounting (1) focuses on providing data for internal uses by the manager, (2) places more emphasis on the future, (3) emphasizes the relevance and flexibility of the data, (4) places less emphasis on precision and more emphasis on the nonmonetary data, (5) emphasizes the segments of a corporation rather than just looking at the organization as a whole, (6) draws heavily from other disciplines, (7) is not governed by generally accepted accounting principles (GAAP), and (8) is not mandatory. In contrast to the previous authors, Hartley (1983) chooses not to distinguish between the two functions stating that the two areas do not have clear territorial boundaries. He does, however, note that those who view management accounting differently from financial accounting make their distinction in the target uses of the information; internal to the operation versus external, respectively. Horngren (1995) identifies that management accounting has two simultaneous missions: (1) transmission of information to help reach wise economic decisions, and (2) motivation of users toward organizational goals. Again, the target of the information is internal to the corporation. He further states that management accounting systems must meet the cost-benefit criteria. Elaborate systems are a large expense in both money to purchase and time to support. Therefore, decisions to implement these systems must be weighed carefully with the potential benefits.

Transition in Focus from Internal to External

Johnson and Kaplan (1987) explain how, until the 1920s, managers invariably relied on information about the underlying processes, transactions, and events that produced financial numbers. By the 1960s and 1970s, however, managers relied commonly on the financial numbers alone. They explain this transition as being the result of two forces. First, as companies transitioned from single purpose operations whose focus was economy of scale, to vertically integrated operations whose focus was economy of scope, performance tracking became more complex. In the vertically integrated environment, tracking the consumption of indirect resources at the unit level became too cumbersome. It was felt that the benefit received was not worth the expense necessary to collect the data required to cost the product adequately at the unit level for a diverse product line. This was somewhat due to the labor intensiveness of the tracking systems available at that time. Second, after 1900, new requirements were placed on corporate enterprises by capital markets, regulatory bodies, and the federal government for external reporting. Included in these demands was the need for externally audited financial reports by independent public accountants. This requirement led to the development of well-defined standard procedures for corporate financial reporting. Among these procedures was a process for valuing inventories, both finished and in-process. In order to value inventories, auditors needed to add to the available material and labor information a portion of the overhead costs of the operation. For their purposes, the costing methods developed by engineers after 1880 were too cumbersome and confusing. They instead developed a simple system of distributing the overhead cost by utilizing a common base, such as direct labor hours or direct labor cost. This was adequate for external reporting purposes as the inaccuracies inherent to the system were offsetting. In aggregate, the financial reports were accurate and acceptable. Differences in accuracy between the engineers' product cost system and the auditors' inventory cost system ensued. The engineering system, not having the necessary support from the accountants or regulatory entities, was replaced by the auditors' system. There is general agreement in the literature that the unit product costs information resulting from allocation methods is inappropriate for managerial purposes, i.e., internal decision support of product pricing, product profitability determination, or process change decisions (Cooper and Kaplan, 1988; Johnson and Kaplan, 1987; Kaplan, 1994; Garrison and Noreen, 1994; Drury and Tayles, 1997; Lere, 2001; Nachtmann and Needy, 2003).

Two of Garrison and Noreen's (1994) points in reference to management accounting, (7) is not governed by GAAP and (8) is not mandatory, identify an important issue that impacts the level of interest to support a management accounting system. External reporting is required by the IRS and the SEC, among others, and requires a financial accounting system. Unfortunately, most companies are unwilling to support dual systems (Johnson and Kaplan, 1987). Drury and Tayles (1997) substantiated Johnson's claim with survey results that indicated that 79 percent of respondents "often/always" use product costs derived from stock valuations for decision making and only 9 percent claiming that they "never/rarely" did so. Systems to address the issue of inaccurate product costs, due to inaccurate allocation of overhead costs, have been developed and introduced over time. Three of these systems are direct costing, activity-based costing, and TPC. External financial reporting regulations require that stocks be valued at "full production cost" to include the indirect costs of running the operation (Drury and Tayles, 1997). Because direct costing and TPC do not allocate indirect costs for product valuation, neither system is acceptable for external reporting purposes. Therefore, if either of these improved management accounting systems was to be used, it would necessarily need to be in addition to a system that provided full product costs, including the allocated costs, again leading to dual systems.

Drury and Tayles (1997) conducted a survey with the purpose of investigating the claims of Johnson and Kaplan, that management accounting has become subservient to financial accounting. They found that 73 percent of the nonautomated and 68 percent of the automated manufacturers used labor hours or direct labor cost as the base for allocations, even though other systems, with claims of better accuracy exist. Only 4 percent of the surveyed companies had implemented ABC costing with another 9 percent indicating that they had intentions to do so. Their conclusion is that simplistic methods are being widely used for decision making. These are methods that have been primarily designed for meeting financial accounting requirements. Their survey findings indicated that many companies use the same information for both internal and external purposes, even when conventional wisdom suggests that they should not. They concluded that Johnson's and Kaplan's claims, that management accounting had become subservient to financial accounting, could not be disputed. Elnicki (1971) found that since the 1950s, corporate management has "managed by the numbers," using data compiled for external financial reporting.

Difficulties Presented by the Current Forms of Financial Reporting

Lere (2001) identifies several issues with the use of product costs derived using a common allocation base for market decisions. The inaccuracies introduced by the allocation process can lead to product costs that are over or under actual costs. This can (1) lead to sales focusing on sales efforts of the wrong products while forgoing efforts to sell the right products, (2) cause sales to enter and exit the wrong markets, and (3) set prices that are too high or too low. He references a hydraulic valve manufacturing company that, through a change in accounting systems, identified that they were losing money on 75 percent of their product line. One specific example was a valve that reportedly had a gross margin of 47 percent when in fact its gross margin was –258 percent. In his survey of 500 U.S. companies, the most common allocation base identified was direct labor (either hours or cost). Lere states that the drawback in using a direct labor measure as the overhead rate denominator assumes that the use of manufacturing capacity is proportionate to direct labor consumption. He further states that in labor-intensive manufacturing environments that may be the case, but in other manufacturing environments it may not.

Traditional cost accounting practices tend to influence overproduction (Womack and Jones, 2003). The need to absorb overhead allocations cause managers to maximize the standard labor hours or machine hours over which the overhead needs to be spread. Through experience, managers learn that by increasing run quantities and minimizing downtime from start-up or set-up activities this is more easily accomplished. Womack and Jones (2003) believe that to influence managers to do the right things, standard cost and variance analysis systems need to be abandoned.

Cunningham and Fiume (2003) suggest that as companies begin the transition from batch to lean, trouble will ensue with the product costing system. These authors suggest that the role of the cost accountant must change to cost management. The attempt to identify costs precisely, at the item level, results in irrelevant information due to necessary inaccuracies. Instead, managing financial matters at the aggregate level should be their concern. These authors advocate that "plain English" management financial statements be developed by the accounting function to replace the standard profit and loss statements used for external reporting. The information conveyed by the new financial statements will allow the reader to easily evaluate the results of changes that are being made because of a lean manufacturing program.

The practice of cost attachment, whereby labor and overhead costs become "attached" to the finished product, is identified repeatedly in the literature as problematic for management accounting decision support (Hartley, 1983; Drury and Tayles, 1997; Cunningham and Fiume, 2003). The issue here is that overproduction, resulting in an increase in finished goods, becomes stored on the balance sheet as a capital asset. The costs resulting from the production of these items are not recognized on the income statement until the items are sold, which could be some time into the future. Therefore, overproduction will result in an increase in the capital assets of the company, capitalizing labor and overhead costs in the process. Gross profit will increase for the current period because of these capitalized costs, including labor and overhead, being moved to the balance sheet where they are not recognized as a period cost. When the reverse occurs, more products sold than produced resulting in an inventory reduction, the result is a lowering of the gross profit as these stored costs are liberated. During the implementation of JIT or lean manufacturing, inventory reduction is certain to occur. The mechanics of this issue are best explained with a sample income statement from before and during a lean/JIT program, see Figure 2.1.

JIT and Lean Manufacturing Practices

There is formidable consensus in the literature as to the origin of JIT manufacturing and lean manufacturing practices. These formal systems were clearly developed by Japanese manufacturers with aspects of these disciplines having been birthed in the United States (Pine, 1993; Womack and Jones, 2003; Schonberger, 1982a). Wantuck (1989) uses the example of the Ford automobile plant in Dearborn, MI, where iron ore was unloaded from a ship and converted into a complete automobile within 48 hours prior to 1926. This process was documented in a book, authored by Henry Ford, entitled *Today and Tomorrow,* published in 1926. Strangely, the book was not sold in America. It was however converted to Japanese and was still available to purchase in Tokyo until the mid 1980s.

Shah and Ward (2003) identify JIT manufacturing techniques as a subset of lean manufacturing. It is described as a "bundle" of interrelated practices, one of four bundles that encompass the aspects of lean manufacturing. The remaining three are total quality management (TQM), total preventive maintenance (TPM), and human resource management (HRM). JIT is described as a manufacturing program with the primary goal of continuously reducing and ultimately eliminating all waste (Sugimori et al., 1977). Work-in-process (WIP) inventories and delays are cited as two of the major forms of waste that JIT focuses on eliminating. The tools and techniques used to accomplish the improvement are (1) lot size reduction, (2) cycle time reduction,

	Before lean	During lean
Net Sales	100,000	100,000
Cost of Sales		
Purchases	35,000	23,000
Inventory material: (+) −	(6,000)	6,000
Total Material Cost	29,000	29,000
Processing Cost		
Factory wages	11,000	11,000
Factory salary	2,000	2,000
Factory benefits	5,000	5,000
Services & supp.	2,500	2,500
Depreciation	2,000	2,000
Scrap	2,000	2,000
Total Processing Cost	24,500	24,500
Occupancy Cost		
Building dep.	200	200
Building svrc.	2,000	2,000
Total Occupancy Cost	2,200	2,200
Total Manufacturing Cost	55,700	55,700
Inventory-labor, Overhead (inc) dec	(4,000)	4,000
Cost of Sales	51,700	59,700
Gross Profit	48,300	40,300
Gross Profit %	48.3%	40.3%

Figure 2.1   Impact on gross profit due to cost attachment. (From Womack, J. and Jones, D. (2003). *Lean Thinking: Banish Waste and Create Wealth in Your Corporation,* **The Free Press, New York, NY. With permission.)**

(3) quick changeover techniques, (4) cellular process layout, (5) reengineering production processes, and (6) bottleneck removal. In contrast, lean is described as a multidimensional approach that encompasses a variety of management practices including JIT, quality systems, teams, and supplier management working together in an integrated system. The core objective of lean is to create a streamlined, high quality system that produces the product at a pace equal to the demands of the customer.

Not evident in the list of lean practices, but certainly implied, is the benefit of reduced inventories. Schonberger (1982b) in an article exposing the beneficial impact of JIT on inventory reduction indicated that, although the focus of the article was mainly on WIP inventories, the concepts also applied to finished goods inventories and their flow from manufacturing to distribution. He states that by extending JIT forward, pressure is exerted on the factory to match daily output to daily sales. Listed as the benefits of reductions in inventory are a lowering of inventory carrying costs, scrap/quality improvement, and productivity increases.

Fullerton and McWatters (2001) have identified that the implementation rates of JIT in U.S. firms has been relatively slow despite awareness of its purported benefits. The reasons identified for the resistance of firms to adopt these practices were (i) resistance to change, (ii) lack of understanding of JIT methods, (iii) incompatible workforce and workplace environment, (iv) nonsupportive suppliers, and (v) inadequate performance measurement and incentive systems. Their survey examined the benefits resulting from the implementation of JIT in six operational measures: (1) quality benefits, (2) time-based benefits, (3) employee flexibility, (4) accounting simplification, (5) firm profitability, and (6) changes in inventory. Most notable in their findings were that time-based benefits, the reduction of nonvalue added activities, and the shortening of manufacturing cycle time were significantly improved by JIT implementation. Additionally, reductions in WIP and raw material inventories were substantial. However, the results indicated little difference in finished goods inventories following the implementation of JIT practices. Noted also in the study was that several studies have examined the production benefits resulting from JIT, but there is limited and conflicting evidence on the effect on financial performance measures resulting from the implementation of JIT. Their study did show a significant correlation between the perceived increases in financial performance of the respondents and financial improvements reported externally by those firms.

Related Studies and Missing Elements

Recent studies in this area have focused on the identification of the most profitable combination of accounting method and production planning systems (Lea, 1998; Boyd, 1999). These studies couple various cost accounting systems with several manufacturing environments and test the performance of all combinations by comparing income and total income, i.e., the sum over some period. Both authors take the stance that to maximize profit, a firm must select a managerial accounting method that is well aligned with the manufacturing environment that exists. A baseline premise in both studies is that demand exceeds production capacity. A further assumption ingrained in the two studies is that the firm is at liberty to choose which products they will manufacture. This criterion creates a simulated manufacturing environment where product mix is used to maximize profits. Profit by product varies under the various management accounting methods due to the differences in the way overhead is calculated and distributed. In these two studies, the researchers used the profit by product information as calculated by a variety of cost accounting methods for a number of products to determine what to produce based on profit maximization. Simulation was used to simulate manufacturing environments for a number of differing methods of manufacturing to determine when to produce the various products. Running the simulation allowed these researchers to determine what would actually be produced. By following this procedure with all combinations of the cost accounting method and the manufacturing operation, they were able to identify which combination produced the maximum return, short- and long-term, based on the other assumptions built into their models. The studies produced differing results, which is an indication that they were operating under differing assumptions. This also gives an indication of the difficulty that exists in attempting to prove the theory that profit maximization can be achieved as the result of the correct selection of cost accounting method and production system.

In Boyd's (1999) study, the accounting methods chosen were traditional (full absorption), TPC, activity-based costing (ABC), and direct costing. The production philosophies studied were reorder point, MRP, JIT, and theory of constraints (TOC). Boyd's conclusion was that the TPC–TOC combination performed as well, if not better, than all other combinations tested. However, the TPC method of accounting is not approved by regulatory agencies for inventory costing and, therefore, would not provide a single system of accounting that has been pursued to satisfy managerial as well as financial accounting issues.

Lea (1998) chose full-absorption costing, TPC, and ABC for cost accounting methods under MRP, TPC, and JIT manufacturing environments. Her conclusion was that the ABC method was superior as well as being more sensitive in the presence of environmental uncertainty. She noted, however, that given an appropriate allocation rate, traditional costing methods preformed nearly as well. Many authors have identified ABC methods as another method of determining allocations (Kaplan, 1994; Womack and Jones, 2003; Drury and Tayles, 1997).

Therefore, as the allocation method of the traditional system is modified to more closely align with that of an ABC system, the reported results would logically merge.

The researchers for the studies just described did not include operational improvement in the focus of their analysis. The studies were limited to evaluating firm performance under a number of pre-determined operational conditions and management accounting methods. The studies did not identify, or attempt to quantify, the short- or long-term effects on reported net profit or total net profit that would result from an operational improvement effort that led to a lowering in on-hand inventories, labor reductions, facility space savings, etc. A second issue with these studies is that the evaluation of performance of the various combinations of accounting method and manufacturing environment were quantified by using profit figures derived from product standards. The standard costs that were used were developed using machine hours as the allocation base for the distribution of overhead costs. As has been previously stated, the need to allocate indirect costs is at the root of the issue with accounting reports providing irrelevant data for the purpose of profit determination (Johnson and Kaplan, 1987; Kaplan, 1994; Drury and Tayles, 1997; Womack and Jones, 2003; Cunningham and Fume, 2003; Soloman, 2003). Therefore, according to substantial agreement in the literature, the assessment of which combination of accounting method and manufacturing environment demonstrated superior performance was based on flawed data.

It has been identified, in previous sections of this chapter, that a common belief in manufacturing is that JIT offers numerous operational improvements to manufacturers, with the most noted benefits being (1) reduced cycle time, leading to better customer service levels, and (2) inventory reductions in the area of raw and WIP inventories. Many authors have also identified that finished goods inventories should be significantly reduced through the implementation of lean methods; however, survey results do not indicate that this is always the case (Fullerton and McWatters, 2001). Also identified, by this review of literature, is that the dominant accounting practices in use today in the United States and the United Kingdom, specifically full-absorption costing and the concept of cost attachment, are suspect in their ability to provide meaningful information for decision support in terms of operational decisions. Further, these practices are known to confound decisions when accurate product cost information is required or when manufacturing inventories, raw material, WIP, and finished goods, are changed significantly between reporting periods. An additional complication of cost attachment is the effect this practice has on the value of capital assets of a company as reported on the balance sheet.

Problems with Previous Studies

We have identified three problems with previous studies:

1. The simulation models tested have presumed, as a base assumption, that demand for product is unlimited and that a firm is at liberty to produce only the products it chooses. This unfortunately is often not the situation on a sustained basis. Even in a situation where sales have outstripped manufacturing capacity for a product, manufacturers are often required to produce complementary products to support the sales volume.
2. From an external reporting standpoint, an approved accounting system must be in use at a manufacturing operation to satisfy compliance issues. Any planning method that does not utilize either full-absorption costing or ABC would have to be in addition to one of these, implying a need to support a dual system of accounting.
3. None of the work so far has addressed the phenomenon of falling gross or net profit as a company becomes more "lean" with any level of actual research and analysis.

Contributions of This Study

Simulation has been used to model the dynamics of the phenomenon identified in point 3 above. The model was designed to accomplish the following:

- Identify the duration of the reduction in the reported gross profit based on the starting inventory positions and the rate of reduction of inventories.
- Predict the magnitude of the impact on the reported gross profit based on the starting inventory positions and the rate of reduction of inventories.

This study expands the current body of knowledge in the area of lean manufacturing. The understandings gained from the output of this study allow inferences to be made in regard to the above points. Such inferences include the ability to predict outcomes of a lean effort, with sufficient accuracy, to provide credibility for lean implementation efforts. Preselling of a lean program to management and investors could include the recognition of this phenomenon as well as predictions as to the impact, short-term and long-term, on gross and net profit. Achievement of such predictions would provide encouragement to stakeholders rather than being a cause for alarm.

References

Boyd, L. H. (1999). Production Planning and Control and Cost Accounting Systems: Effects on Management Decision Making and Firm Performance, Ph.D. dissertation, University of Georgia, Athens, GA, UMI Co., Ann Arbor, MI.

Chandler, A. (1977). *The Visible Hand: The Management Revolution in American Business,* Harvard University Press, Cambridge, MA.

Cooper, R. and Kaplan, R. S. (1988). How cost accounting distorts product costs, *Management Accounting,* 69(10), 2027.

Cunningham, J. and Fiume, O. (2003). *Real Numbers: Management Accounting in a Lean Organization,* Managing Times Press, Durham, NC.

Drury, C. and Tayles, M. (1997). Evidence on the financial accounting mentality debate: a research note, *British Accounting Review,* 29, 263–276.

Elnicki, R. A. (1971). The genesis of management accounting, *Management Accounting,* 16.

Fullerton, R. R. and McWatters, C. S. (2001). The production performance benefits from JIT implementation, *Journal of Operations Management,* 19, 81–96.

Garrison, R. H. and Noreen, E. W. (1994). *Managerial Accounting,* Irwin, Inc., Burr Ridge, IL.

Hartley, R. V. (1983). *Cost and Managerial Accounting,* Allyn and Bacon, Inc., Newton, MA.

Horngren, C. T. (1995). Management accounting: this century and beyond, *Management Accounting Research,* 6, 281–286.

Johnson, H. T. and Kaplan, R. S. (1987). *Relevance Lost: The Rise and Fall of Management Accounting,* Harvard Business School Press, Boston, MA.

Kaplan, R. S. (1994). Management accounting (1984–1994): development of new practice and theory, *Management Accounting Research,* 5, 247–260.

Lea, B.-R. (1998). The Impact of Management Accounting Alternatives in Different Manufacturing Environments, Ph.D. dissertation, Clemson University, Clemson, SC, UMI Co., Ann Arbor, MI.

Lere, J. C. (2001). Your product-costing system seems to be broken: Now what? *Industrial Marketing Management,* 30, 587–598.

Martin-Vega, L. A. (2001). *Maynard's Industrial Engineering Handbook*, 5th ed., McGraw Hill, New York, NY.

Nachtmann, H. and Needy, K. (2003) Methods for handling uncertainty in activity based costing systems, *The Engineering Economist*, 48(3), 259–282.

Pine, B. J. (1993). *Mass Customization: The New Frontier in Business Competition,* Harvard Business School Press, Boston, MA.

Schonberger, R. J. (1982a). *Japanese Manufacturing Techniques: Nine Hidden Lessons in Simplicity,* The Free Press, New York, NY.

Schonberger, R. J. (1982b). Some observations on the advantages and implementation issues of just-in-time production systems, *Journal of Operations Management*, 3(1), 1.

Scott, D. R. (1931). *The Cultural Significance of Accounts,* Henry Holt, New York, NY.

Shah, R. and Ward, P. T. (2003). Lean manufacturing: context, practice bundles, and performance, *Journal of Operations Management*, 21, 129–149.

Soloman, J. M. (2003). *Who's Counting?* WCM Associates, Fort Wayne, IN.

Sugimori, Y., Kusunoki, F., Cho, F, and Uchikawa, S. (1977). Toyota production and Kanban system: materialization of just-in-time and respect for human systems, *International Journal of Production Research*, 15, 553–564.

Wantuck, K. A. (1989). *Just in Time for America: A Common Sense Production Strategy*, KWA Media, Southfield, MI.

Womack, J. and Jones, D. (2003). *Lean Thinking: Banish Waste and Create Wealth in Your Corporation,* The Free Press, New York, NY.

Chapter 3

Multi-Period Simulation Model of a Factory with Lean Manufacturing

This chapter describes the methods and tools employed in the development of a model manufacturing operation used to answer the following three questions, which were presented in Chapter 1:

1. What are the effects on operational performance, as determined by standard financial reports, resulting from the implementation of a lean manufacturing program?
2. How do varying accounting systems differ in their reporting of the identified effects?
3. What is the trend of operational performance over a 12-month period based on the inventory reduction policy chosen?

The simulated factory models a build-to-stock, repetitive manufacturing environment. ProModel Simulation Software from ProModel Corporation, Orem, UT, was used for the development and operation of the simulation model. Excel® spreadsheet software from Microsoft® Corporation was used for production planning and financial reporting functions and Visual Basic® for Applications (VBA) was used to automate the execution process and provide a user interface and prompting during execution.

Experimental Design, Statistical Hypotheses, and Data Analysis

This section describes the statistical model that uses analysis of variance (ANOVA) to test the hypotheses along with Tukey's all pairwise comparison method to determine which factor levels have the greatest effect on the measurements of interest. A brief overview of the analysis of the data describes the usage of the proposed model.

Experimental Design

The experimental design, used to address the proposed questions, includes three experimental factors. They are three levels of inventory policy, five levels of management accounting system, and three levels of sales volume per replication. The experimental design is a $3 \times 5 \times 3$ full factorial experiment in a randomized block design and 35 replications. This is accomplished by fixing a unit sales level for 1 complete data generation cycle of 36 iterations, which provides 1 year of data for each of the 3 inventory policies. Inventory policy is fixed for one 12-month cycle, completing 1 year of profit and loss data for 1 inventory policy. This is repeated for all inventory policies prior to the next replication, requiring a change of sales volume data. The five management accounting systems then use the resulting data to determine gross and net profit levels and percentages. The preceding process is followed for 35 replications under each of 3 sales volume stochasticity scenarios. Sales volume data is randomly changed within a range following a normal distribution based on a forecast value for each of the 30 parts to be produced prior to each replicated run. The values used for standard deviation for the three sales levels are 10, 25, and 40 percent of the mean value.

The mathematical model for this experiment is

$$Y_{ijkm} = \mu + S_i + IP_j + MA_k \qquad \text{(main effect)}$$

$$+ SIP_{ij} + SMA_{ik} + IPMA_{jk} \quad \text{(two-way interactions)}$$

$$+ SIPMA_{ijk} \qquad \text{(three-way interactions)}$$

$$+ \varepsilon_{m(ijk)},$$

where

Y_{ijk} = gross and net profit
μ = the true mean of the population
S_i = the sales volume effect where i = 1, 2, or 3
IP_j = the inventory policy effect where j = 1, 2, or 3
MA_k = the management accounting system effect where k = 1, 2, 3, 4, or 5
$\varepsilon_{m(ijk)}$ = the random error in the experiment where m = 1 through 35

Proposed Hypotheses

The following hypotheses are explored using the simulation model:

H_1: Within a given management accounting method, does the rate of inventory reduction have an effect on reported gross profit?

$H_{1,0}$: Policy$_i$ = 0 for gross profit.

H_2: Within a given management accounting method, does the rate of inventory reduction have an effect on reported net profit?

$H_{2,0}$: Policy$_i$ = 0 for net profit.

H_3: Within a given inventory reduction policy, does the management accounting method have an effect on reported gross profit?

$H_{3,0}$: Acct$_j$ = 0 for gross profit.

H_4: Within a given inventory reduction policy, does the management accounting method have an effect on reported net profit?

$H_{4,0}$: Acct$_j$ = 0 for net profit.

H_5: Do various combinations of inventory reduction policy and management accounting method have an effect on reported gross profit?

$H_{5,0}$: Policy$_i$ × Acct$_j$ = 0 for gross profit.

H_6: Do various combinations of inventory reduction policy and management accounting method used have an effect on reported net profit?

$H_{6,0}$: Policy$_i$ × Acct$_j$ = 0 for net profit.

H_7: Does inventory reduction policy have an effect on the customer service level, measured by stock-outs, under the production and market environment modeled in this study?

$H_{7,0}$: Policy$_i$ = 0.

H$_8$:   Does volatility in the sales demand have an effect on reported gross and net profit under the production and market environment modeled in this study?

H$_{8,0}$: Sales$_i$ = 0.

H$_9$:   Does volatility in the sales demand have an effect on the customer service level, measured by stock-outs, under the production and market environment modeled in this study?

H$_{9,0}$: Sales$_i$ = 0.

Data Analysis

The study described above combines fixed effect and random effect factors. Inventory policy is limited to three levels. Management accounting system is limited to five levels. Unit sales level has three factor levels that impact the stochasticity of the value used by the model. This model parameter is allowed to take on any value, with such values following a normal distribution with the mean equal to the forecast and the standard deviation equal to 10, 25, or 40 percent of the forecast based on the factor level being modeled. The hypotheses will be tested using ANOVA for all factors and interactions.

Methods Diagrams

Figure 3.1 graphically represents the data generation process through the use of a flow chart. From this diagram, it can be seen that the process follows that of a real-world manufacturing operation where a schedule is established based on a forecast and current inventory position. The plant attempts to satisfy the schedule, at times falling short. At the conclusion of the month, profit and loss statements are produced based on the results of the period including actual sales. Then the cycle starts again with the creation of next month's production schedule, again based on a forecast and current inventory position.

The mechanics of the data generation process are depicted in Figure 3.2. This diagram details the interfaces between the software packages employed in this research. VBA was utilized to aid in the replication process by automating many of the steps required for spreadsheet data update, data transfer between software packages, and data archiving between replications.

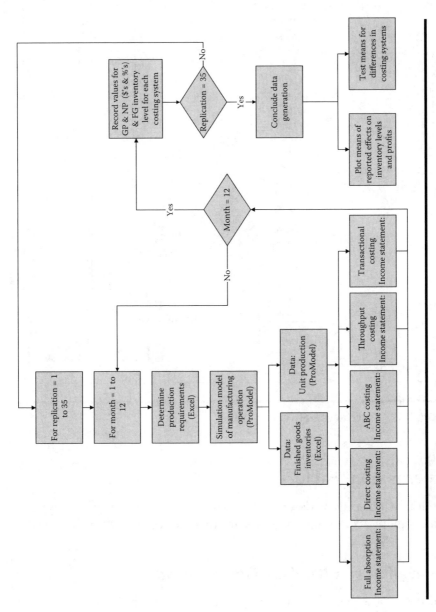

Figure 3.1 Data generation flow chart.

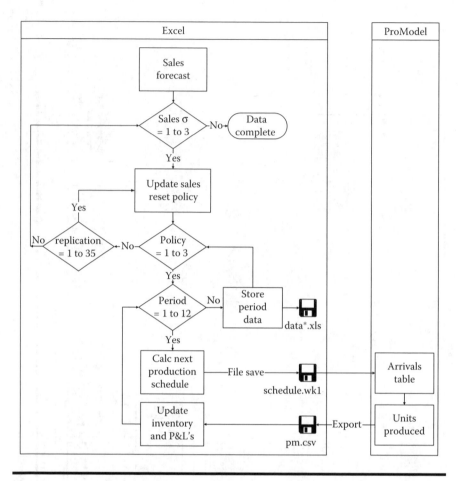

Figure 3.2   Interfaces between systems.

Experimental Factors

The following sections describe how sales volume, inventory policy, and management accounting methods are made operational for this study.

Generation of a Random Sales Demand

The entry of a sales forecast, by part and by month, for the period to be modeled is provided through a series of cells in an Excel spreadsheet. The modeled period was 12 months for this study. Forecast values are arbitrary based on the designed capacity of the model plant.

To emulate the effects of forecast error (the difference between actual demand and forecasted demand), simulated sales values were computed using the following procedure. Actual sales volumes by part and by month were generated through the utilization of a formula adopted from Hillier and Lieberman (2001) that provided a random number, approximately normally distributed, with a mean value equal to the forecasted value and a standard deviation of 10 percent, 25 percent, or 40 percent of the forecasted value. This procedure provides for three levels of stochasticity in the sales demand of the model. In the case of the 25 percent setting the actual demand used in the simulation becomes a number that is ± 25 percent of the forecast value 68.3 percent of the time, 25–50 percent below or above the forecast value 27.1 percent of the time, 50–75 percent below or above the forecast 4.3 percent of the time and greater than 75 percent above or below the forecast 0.3 percent of the time. The formula used to accomplish this was

$$= [RAND() + RAND() + RAND() + RAND() + RAND() + RAND() + RAND() + RAND() + RAND() + RAND() + RAND() + RAND()]^*control\_sheet_{d9}^*forecast!_{ij} + forecast!_{ij} - 6^*control\_sheet_{d9}^*forecast!_{ij}$$

where $forecast!_{ij}$ is the cell reference to the appropriate cell on the forecast sheet that corresponds to the part for which sales data is being calculated and $control\_sheet_{d9}$ is the reference to the cell containing the current setting for sales stochasticity. This formula is contained in the various cells on the "sales_simulation" sheet that provide for the calculation of 12 months of sales demand by part. Recalculation of new sales figures is accomplished by initiating a recalculation on the "sales_simulation" sheet. Once calculated, the numbers are rounded to whole units and copied to the sales sheet using the copy values command. This step stores the values in a state that will not change during further model execution. The values are in a sense frozen so that they can be used by the scheduling logic throughout the 12-month simulation cycle. VBA was employed to automate the process of updating the sales values following the completion of the 36th iteration of the production update sequence between Excel and ProModel.

Inventory Policy

Inventory policy is defined in this study as the reduction targets for finished goods over a stated period of months. The three scenarios examined in the study are (1) no reduction over the 12-month simulated period (baseline), (2) 50 percent reduction in on-hand inventory over the 12-month period, and (3) 50 percent reduction in the first 6 months of the 12-month period and no further reduction in the remaining 6 months.

The rate of reduction of inventory has a significant effect on the reported financial results of the firm. This is primarily due to the movement, on paper, of assets. Using the concept of cost attachment, a business essentially stores the manufacturing costs of the finished goods inventory produced in excess of what is needed in the current period. The labor, material, and factory overhead costs are virtually moved to the balance sheet where they are recognized as an asset. Physically the product is stored in a warehouse facility until disposed of. These costs are not included in the current period's income statement; instead, they are recognized in a future period when they are removed from inventory, either as a result of a sale or as a result of being scrapped as obsolete or otherwise unacceptable inventory. The chosen levels of inventory policy will allow the effect of these accounting practices to be measured and compared.

Management Accounting Method

Financial reports using five different management accounting methods are used to compare the differences in reported results between systems. The five systems are (1) full-absorption, (2) direct, (3) ABC, (4) TPC, and (5) order-activity (transactional).

Full Absorption

This method of accounting is the most accepted and most widely used method of cost accounting (Cooper and Kaplan, 1988; Govindarajan and Anthony, 1983) and is used in more than 60 percent of industries surveyed by Hendricks (1988). This method is characterized by the use of an allocation base to apply overhead costs to products. Some common bases include direct labor, direct materials, and machine time, among others, with the most common base being direct labor (Drury and Tayles, 1997). This method of product costing is characterized by the inclusion of all variable and fixed manufacturing costs being "attached" to the product in inventory. When production is greater than sales in a given period, these costs are capitalized on the balance sheet.

The profit and loss statement for the full-absorption method in this study utilizes standard labor as the allocation base. Standard labor and materials plus the allocated costs are used in the calculation of gross profit.

Direct (Variable)

In the direct method of product costing, allocations of overhead costs are not made at the product level. Instead, these fixed costs are quantified for the given reporting periods and are included or assigned to the profit and loss for that period regardless of the sales volume. This prevents the storage and later recognition of these costs as products are taken from inventory to satisfy the current period's sales.

The profit and loss statement for direct costing in this study utilizes standards for labor and material to determine product cost, which are then used in the determination of gross profit. Allocated costs are distributed evenly across the 12-month period and included in the calculation for monthly net profit.

ABC

The ABC method of product costing arose, similar to direct costing, out of a desire to create a more accurate method for assigning allocated costs. Many authors agree on the issues related to the inaccuracies introduced in product costing by the use of allocation bases such as direct labor, machine time, plant square footage, etc. (Johnson and Kaplan, 1987, 1994; Drury and Tayles, 1997; Horngren, 1995). These bases may have little or no relationship to the proportion of allocated resources consumed by a particular item of production. ABC attempts to correct the inequitable distribution of these costs by identifying what cost generating activities, referred to as cost drivers, are caused by a particular family or group of products. Using this information, the pool of costs can be distributed in a fashion that relates more closely to the real world.

This method of costing is simulated in this study by allowing the assignment of allocated costs to vary based on product family. The three families are A, B, and C. The model allows allocated costs to be adjusted independently for each family in the "costs_ABC" spreadsheet, thus simulating the effects of ABC costing and the resulting impact on gross and net profit.

TPC

Throughput costing is an outgrowth of a method of plant performance improvement called "the theory of constraints" popularized by Goldratt and Cox in their book, *The Goal* (1982). In this method of product costing, the only relevant cost is the material cost. Therefore, all other costs, including labor, are considered fixed period costs and are expensed at the end of each period. Using this method, gross profit is determined using material costs only. Material costs are taken from standard.

Order Activity

The order-activity method of cost accounting is currently being researched as an alternative method to others previously discussed. This cost accounting method uses a new approach to address the issue of an appropriate allocation base. As mentioned earlier, the traditional approach of full-absorption costing uses direct labor, direct materials, machine time, or plant square footage, among other bases to apportion overhead costs. The full-absorption method of costing has been under attack in the literature for many years. ABC attempts to improve on this method by identifying cost drivers by product family for the equitable distribution of costs. The ABC method is an improvement over full absorption but still has two primary drawbacks:

1. The system is costly to maintain as the drivers and apportionment are determined through interviews and will change over time requiring continued follow-up interviews to make adjustments.
2. For purposes of efficiency, products are grouped into families and overhead costs factors are then applied by family. Not all products within a family will necessarily consume activities in the same apportionment as others in the family.

The order-activity method addresses the issue of cost allocation based on unit production volumes. The types of costs that are being distributed through allocations have among them engineering, purchasing, accounting, maintenance, shipping, and receiving, and others, many of which are influenced by transactions. This is to say that many of the allocated costs are equal for an order of 1 or 1000 products. When direct labor is used as the base, the total direct labor for the order is factored to identify the allocated portion. When the order is for 1 versus 1000 then the allocated amount is 1/1000th of the order for 1000, although the support from engineering, purchasing, accounting, shipping, and receiving will often be the same for either case. In this situation, the high volume product is penalized disproportionately. The order-activity method attempts to correct this by setting allocations based on transactions. One measure for transactions is number of sales orders. This is a simple number to retrieve from a sales order entry system, eliminating the high maintenance costs of ABC. The factoring for allocation is based on the following equations:

$$transaction\_per\_product = \frac{\sum_{month=1}^{12} sales\_orders\_by\_product}{\sum_{month=1}^{12} units\_produced\_by\_product}$$

$$transaction\_cost = \frac{annual\_budgeted\_fixed\_costs}{\sum_{all\_products} annual\_sales\_orders}$$

$$product\_cost = direct\_labor + direct\_material +$$

$$(transaction\_per\_product * transaction\_cost).$$

Using this method for applying the allocated costs produces a product cost that presumably is closer to reality.

Detailed Description of Data Generation Process

The following section steps through the data generation process, as briefly as possible, in an effort to allow future readers to replicate the tools for further research purposes. The following example of the data generation process will reference Figure 3.3 extensively. References to actions such as recalculation of sheets, cutting and pasting of data, and opening and closing of computer files throughout this description are actions preformed by the VBA data bridge unless otherwise noted.

The data generation process begins with the establishment of a forecast to be used for the duration of the 35-replication process [process (1) in Figure 3.3]. Table 3.1 shows an excerpt from the "forecast" sheet from the Excel-based production planning and control

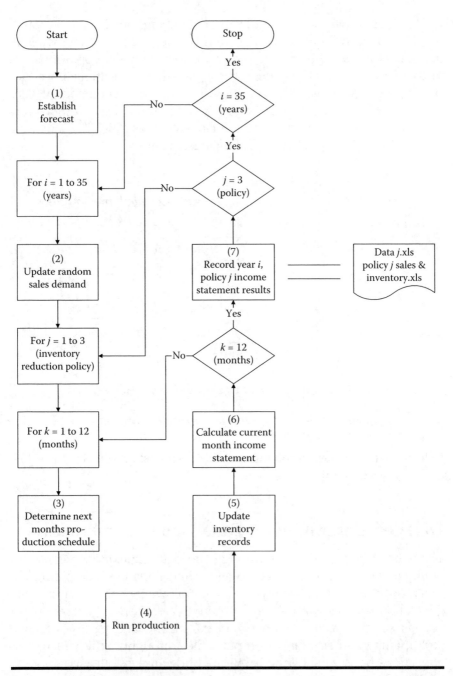

Figure 3.3   Execution process.

Table 3.1 "Forecast" Sheet of Excel Production Planning Simulation Tool

		January	February	March	April	May	June
Sales Forecast	Family A	5885	5885	5885	5885	5885	5885
	Family B	1422	1422	1422	1422	1422	1422
	Family C	2091	2091	2091	2091	2091	2091
Family distribution (Pareto) factors		0.5	0.36	0.04	0.03	0.02	0.015

Units (part)	Month	January	February	March	April	May	June
A1		2943	2943	2943	2943	2943	2943
A2		2119	2119	2119	2119	2119	2119
A3		236	236	236	236	236	236
A4		177	177	177	177	177	177
A5		118	118	118	118	118	118
A6		89	89	89	89	89	89
A7		74	74	74	74	74	74
A8		59	59	59	59	59	59
A9		45	45	45	45	45	45
A10		30	30	30	30	30	30

simulation tool. The monthly forecast quantities for January through June are shown in the top three rows. These are family forecast quantities with each family consisting of ten individual products. The values used for this study were near the capacity of the ProModel simulation model and were established using a trial and error process to seek out the demonstrated capacity of the system. The fourth row contains the factors used to convert the family forecast quantities to individual unit quantities; only the first six factors are shown. The bottom rows of Table 3.1 show the unit forecast quantities, which are the result of multiplying the Pareto factor by the family forecast quantity. Therefore, unit quantities will automatically be updated when family forecast quantities are changed.

Table 3.2   "Sales_Simulation" Sheet of Excel Production Planning Simulation Tool

Sales Actual (Stochastic Calculation)						
Part No.	January	February	March	April	May	June
A1	2042.82	2729.32	2937.66	2354.57	1050.76	3210.29
A2	1488.18	2157.40	2189.51	2229.23	1662.00	2141.65
A3	207.05	231.09	268.75	254.35	110.07	272.57
A4	201.84	166.22	147.06	190.96	160.45	164.76
A5	101.01	63.47	120.86	133.39	177.19	127.34
A6	123.42	60.16	103.98	53.66	90.77	109.28
A7	82.32	65.26	53.51	77.38	91.76	81.12
A8	60.52	75.21	86.18	104.36	42.73	60.41
A9	49.76	44.46	62.52	21.44	27.85	45.50
A10	40.11	16.91	35.49	33.29	20.84	28.39
Total	**4397.02**	**5609.49**	**6005.51**	**5452.63**	**3434.43**	**6241.31**
B1	960.04	558.51	556.82	349.02	902.59	493.46
B2	403.45	760.24	470.89	639.49	764.04	486.75
B3	53.24	63.42	79.80	68.67	57.71	45.02
B4	53.56	47.82	58.75	24.54	44.91	49.73
B5	28.35	48.00	32.95	23.46	24.10	25.36

With the forecast set, the process continues by establishing the random sales values that will be used throughout the first year of simulated operation [process (2) in Figure 3.3]. Table 3.2 shows the "sales_simulation" page of the Excel tool. The unit values shown in Table 3.2 reflect the effect of the application of the equation described earlier under random sales demand. The cells in this sheet reference the values in the "forecast" sheet, again allowing automatic updating when the forecast values are updated. The values in the "sales_simulation" sheet are rounded to whole numbers and saved as values, not formulas, in the "sales" sheet of the Excel tool where the numbers are prevented from changing as the model execution progresses through the 12-month process. In this way, the random sales values for all 12 months are established prior to initiation of the replication process.

With the actual sales volumes established, the simulation process is set to begin. The inventory reduction policy is selected based on the current cycle through a for–next loop. The loop starts with policy 1 and ends with policy 3. The cycle starts by calculating the schedule for the coming month [process (3) in Figure 3.3]. ProModel will use this schedule to emulate the operation of a manufacturing process. The production schedule is calculated by subtracting the forecast demand and the safety stock target level from the current inventory quantity. Table 3.3 shows an excerpt from the production schedule sheet in the Excel tool. The values in the various cells of Table 3.3 show the result of this calculation. Inventory levels were equal to safety stock target level as part of the initial conditions of the model. In the top row of Table 3.3, the factors used to control inventory reduction policy can be seen. Factors for only the first six months are shown here. These factors are referenced in the cell equations and used to factor the safety stock target level. The safety stock target level is multiplied by the factor in the cell above the month for which the schedule is being calculated. In Table 3.3, the factors for inventory reduction policy 3 are shown. In this policy, the safety stock target level is reduced to 50 percent of the initial target value within a six-month period. In this example, the schedule value for part A1 in June would be calculated by the following equation:

$$Schedule = Current\ inventory\ level\ for\ A1\ -$$
$$[5886\ (safety\ stock\ target) \times 0.5\ (reduction\ factor)] -$$
$$2943\ (forecast\ for\ June).$$

Inventory reduction factors are stored in the "inventory_policy" sheet of the Excel tool. These factors are automatically updated in the "production_schedule" sheet to coincide with the current inventory reduction policy being modeled. Unit quantity data in the "production_schedule" sheet is then reformatted by the "to_ProModel" sheet, in preparation for transfer to ProModel. Reformatting is required to provide the level of detail required by the simulation model. The simulation model requires the arrival of several subcomponents to create a completed part. The "schedule.wk1" file is opened and the column in the "to_ProModel" sheet corresponding to the coming month's production requirements is copied to the appropriate column in the schedule file, and the file is closed. At this point, the user is prompted

Table 3.3 **"Production_Schedule" Sheet of Excel Production Planning Simulation Tool**

Schedule (Minimum Orders)							
Inventory reduction factors		0.917	0.833	0.750	0.667	0.583	0.500
Part	Safety Stock	January	February	March	April	May	June
A1	5886	2453.0	1364.0	2045.0	2724.0	3286.0	1248.0
A2	4238	1766.0	2905.0	1739.0	1977.0	861.0	2462.0
A3	472	197.0	147.0	215.0	206.0	179.0	269.0
A4	354	148.0	118.0	226.0	152.0	120.0	107.0
A5	236	98.0	66.0	54.0	73.0	158.0	93.0
A6	356	59.0	48.0	67.0	54.0	60.0	44.0
A7	296	49.0	64.0	17.0	45.0	12.0	62.0
A8	236	39.0	52.0	47.0	44.0	34.0	34.0
A9	180	30.0	46.0	25.0	19.0	33.0	14.0
A10	120	20.0	26.0	4.0	10.0	37.0	24.0
B1	1422	593.0	786.0	792.0	404.0	233.0	676.0
B2	1024	427.0	620.0	442.0	497.0	150.0	472.0
B3	114	48.0	48.0	20.0	30.0	53.0	46.0
B4	86	36.0	41.0	40.0	24.0	40.0	27.0
B5	58	24.0	20.0	31.0	15.0	23.0	23.0

by a pop-up user window to "Run the simulation model, export the entity activity report, then click OK" [process (4) in Figure 3.3]. At this point, manual intervention is required to start the simulation model execution. The model will open the "schedule.wk1" file and copy the schedule information into the "arrivals" table in ProModel. The model runs to termination and the user is prompted by a pop-up user window that asks, "Do you want to see the results?" Selecting "Yes" opens the report module within ProModel. The user selects the tab for "Entity Activity," and under the "File" pull-down menu selects "Export" to provide the completion information, in a data file, to the Excel tool. At this point, production results have been stored in a location accessible by the Excel tool.

The user then selects "OK" in the window that initiated the manual activity. This starts an update cycle that opens the data file, copies the column corresponding to the last month's production counts, pastes the values in the appropriate month column in the "from_ProModel" sheet in the Excel tool, and closes the completion data file [process (5) in Figure 3.3]. The new data is formatted for use elsewhere within the Excel tool by the "production" sheet in the tool. This sheet strips off information pertaining to subcomponent activity and reports only unit production. Inventory records are updated in the "inventory" sheet of the Excel tool through the use of a formula in the cells that track ending inventory levels (Table 3.4). The equation adds the new production from the "production" sheet to the ending inventory level from the previous month then subtracts the unit quantity sold from the "sales" sheet. If this calculation results in a negative number, then zero is entered in the ending balance cell indicating a stock-out situation. The unit sales information is adjusted in the "revenue" sheet to reflect the lost sales due to the stock-out situation.

Process (6) in Figure 3.3 compiles information from a number of sheets to calculate the month end profit or loss. Table 3.5 shows an excerpt from the income statement for the full-absorption costing method. COGM refers to the cost of goods manufactured. The values in the cells for each month come from the "costs_method" sheets where *method* refers to the accounting method, full absorption in this example. An excerpt from the "costs_FA&D" sheet is shown in Table 3.6. The components of COGM can be seen to include direct labor, direct material, and manufacturing overhead. The next component in the income statement is COGS, which refers to cost of goods sold. This is the key area that drives the confusion with the recognition of operational improvements, resulting from a lean effort, that lead to inventory reduction. The cost of goods sold is the COGM minus the increase in finished goods inventory. If inventory decreases, then the COGS is the COGM plus the inventory decrease. The income statement shown in Table 3.5 shows what happens during a period of rapid finished goods inventory reduction. This income statement displays the results from inventory reduction policy 3. As can be seen, the change in finished goods inventory is negative each month, indicating a steadily decreasing inventory level. The cells in the sales row reference values calculated in the "revenue" sheet. An excerpt of the

Table 3.4 "Inventory" Sheet of Excel Production Planning Simulation Tool

Part No.		Initial	January	February	March	April	May	June
			Inventory (FG)					
A1	Beginning		5886	6484	5313	4143	3091	4638
	End	5886	6484	5313	4143	3091	4638	3718
A2	Beginning		4238	2746	3559	2967	3730	1776
	End	4238	2746	3559	2967	3730	1776	2950
A3	Beginning		472	482	375	345	332	203
	End	472	482	375	345	332	203	231
A4	Beginning		354	354	217	261	264	247
	End	354	354	217	261	264	247	73
A5	Beginning		236	249	241	202	98	143
	End	236	249	241	202	98	143	165
A6	Beginning		356	338	289	272	237	223
	End	356	338	289	272	237	223	200
A7	Beginning		296	257	279	226	235	160
	End	296	257	279	226	235	160	126
A8	Beginning		236	204	189	172	163	143
	End	236	204	189	172	163	143	115
A9	Beginning		180	149	155	146	117	121
	End	180	149	155	146	117	121	74
A10	Beginning		120	104	116	100	63	66
	End	120	104	116	100	63	66	72

"revenue" sheet is shown in Table 3.7. Sales values are the result of multiplying the sales quantity times the selling price. The remainder of the income statement is subtracting COGS from sales to calculate gross profit and subtracting inventory-carrying costs from gross profit to calculate net profit. This is a greatly simplified income statement; it includes only the cost and revenue components of interest to this study. The items that are not included are considered constant under

Table 3.5   "P&L FA" Sheet of Excel Production Planning Simulation Tool, Income Statement for Full-Absorption Costing Method

	Income Statement (Full Absorption)					
	January	*February*	*March*	*April*	*May*	*June*
COGM						
Total COGM	521,374	598,934	536,497	443,451	549,242	541,923
COGS						
Finished goods +/–	–120,467	–68,915	–11,298	–45,831	–100,653	–47,206
Total COGS	641,841	667,848	547,795	489,282	649,894	589,129
Sales	649,487	680,155	593,852	526,295	613,620	591,213
Less COGS	641,841	667,848	547,795	489,282	649,894	589,129
Gross profit	7,646	12,307	46,058	37,013	–36,275	2,085
Gross profit percent	0.0118	0.0181	0.0776	0.0703	–0.0591	0.0035
Interest expense	14,000	12,337	12,061	11,536	9,192	8,159
Net profit	–6,354	–31	33,997	25,477	–45,467	–6,074
Net profit percent	–0.00978	–0.00004	0.05725	0.04841	–0.07410	–0.01027

all inventory reduction scenarios. The remaining four income statements, representing the results of the four other accounting methods, are updated simultaneously using the same methods and working from the same production data.

The process just described continues for a period of 12 months, as shown in Figure 3.3. When the 12th month is completed, the information from the 5 income statements is logged [process (7) in Figure 3.3]. The information of interest for later analysis is gross profit dollars and percent, net profit dollars and percent, as well as inventory states by month and sales volumes by month. This information is saved in a series of Excel files: data1.xls, data2.xls. data3.xls, policy1 sales & inventory, policy2 sales & inventory and, policy3 sales and inventory. The digit on the file indicates what inventory reduction policy the data pertains to. With the data logging complete, the cycle reverts to the initial month using the next inventory reduction policy. When all three

Table 3.6 "P&L FA" Sheet of Excel Production Planning Simulation Tool, Cost of Goods Manufactured Calculations for Full-Absorption Costing Method

Manufacturing Costs—Full Absorption

Full-absorption overhead rate = 200%

Part	Cost Component	Amount	January	February	March	April	May	June
A1	Direct labor	3.7167	6,894.417	9,421.75	11,949.08	14,034.13	6,463.283	8,057.733
	Direct materials	25.0000	46,375	63,375	80,375	94,400	43,475	54,200
	Overhead	7.4333	13,788.83	18,843.5	23,898.17	28,068.27	12,926.57	16,115.47
	Total	36.1500	67,058.25	91,640.25	116,222.3	136,502.4	62,864.85	78,373.2
A2	Direct labor	3.7167	12,108.9	7,775.267	8,663.55	4,512.033	10,462.42	4,787.067
	Direct materials	25.0000	81,450	52,300	58,275	30,350	70,375	32,200
	Overhead	7.4333	24,217.8	15,550.53	17,327.1	9,024.067	20,924.83	9,574.133
	Total	36.1500	117,776.7	75,625.8	84,265.65	43,886.1	101,762.3	46,561.2
A3	Direct labor	3.3000	617.1	838.2	808.5	722.7	1,016.4	795.3
	Direct material	15.0000	2,805	3,810	3,675	3,285	4,620	3,615
	Overhead	6.6000	1,234.2	1,676.4	1,617	1,445.4	2,032.8	1,590.6

	Total	24.9000	4,656.3	6,324.6	6,100.5	5,453.1	7,669.2	6,000.9
A4	Direct labor	3.3000	488.4	841.5	600.6	491.7	452.1	927.3
	Direct materials	15.0000	2,220	3,825	2,730	2,235	2,055	4,215
	Overhead	6.6000	976.8	1,683	1,201.2	983.4	904.2	1,854.6
	Total	24.9000	3,685.2	6,349.5	4,531.8	3,710.1	3,411.3	6,996.9
A5	Direct labor	3.3000	280.5	244.2	306.9	584.1	372.9	234.3
	Direct materials	15.0000	1,275	1,110	1,395	2,655	1,695	1,065
	Overhead	6.6000	561	488.4	613.8	1,168.2	745.8	468.6
	Total	24.9000	2,116.5	1,842.6	2,315.7	4,407.3	2,813.7	1,767.9
Labor			65,583	78,218	68,191	55,760	71,354	71,821
Material			324,625	364,280	331,925	276,170	335,180	326,460
Overhead			131,166	156,436	136,381	111,521	142,708	143,642
Overhead variance			0	0	0	0	0	0
Total (FA)			521,374	598,934	536,497	443,451	549,242	541,923

Table 3.7 "Revenue" Sheet of Excel Production Planning Simulation Tool

	Revenue						
	Selling Price	January	February	March	April	May	June
A1	45.19	83,823	114,550	145,278	170,628	78,581	97,967
A2	45.19	147,221	94,532	105,332	54,858	127,203	58,202
A3	31.13	5,820	7,906	7,626	6,816	9,587	7,501
A4	31.13	4,607	7,937	5,665	4,638	4,264	8,746
A5	31.13	2,646	2,303	2,895	5,509	3,517	2,210
A6	45.19	3,479	4,383	3,796	4,022	3,344	3,028
A7	45.19	3,977	1,898	3,163	1,627	3,931	4,338
A8	61.94	4,398	4,150	3,964	3,283	3,345	3,840
A9	61.94	3,778	2,478	2,106	2,973	1,796	3,778
A10	61.94	2,230	867	1,239	2,911	2,106	1,115
B1	92.71	83,901	84,365	48,486	32,541	73,703	68,233
B2	92.71	65,452	48,857	53,956	21,879	51,639	61,002
B3	69.17	4,012	2,006	2,767	4,288	3,873	3,528
B4	69.17	3,320	3,251	2,213	3,251	2,352	2,421
B5	69.17	1,729	2,421	1,383	1,937	1,937	1,522
Monthly Total		649,487	680,155	593,852	526,295	613,620	591,213

inventory policies have been completed, using the current sales volume demand data, the program recalculates the sales volume demand data and begins the process again with inventory reduction policy 1. This continues until 35 replications of 12 months of data have been created and logged for each of 3 levels of sales stochasticity.

Simulation Model Design

The following discussion describes the logic and execution process for the simulation tool, which was developed to address the previously stated research questions.

Simulated Factory Parameters

In an effort to be consistent with previous studies, Lea (1998), Ramasesh (1990), Cochran et al. (2002), and Krajewski et al. (1987), the following list of assumptions were used for model design:

- No preemption of orders: orders ran to completion or terminated due to lack of available production time.
- No alternative routings.
- No back orders: demand that is not filled is lost.
- The first operation was never starved for work if there were remaining orders in the schedule.

Model Manufacturing Operation

The model factory employs three repetitive manufacturing cells configured as in-line flow cells. Each cell is designed to accommodate the fabrication and assembly of a given family of products. The families are designated A, B, and C. Between fabrication and assembly is a shared painting operation that all three cells utilize. The product families are composed of ten unique products per family. Ten products allowed a relatively simple application of the Pareto principle for production volume distribution within the given family. This distribution, whereby 20 percent of the part numbers contribute to 80 percent of the unit sales, is a pattern that is prevalent across many industries (Kensinger, 2004). Each part within a family has an identical routing to other parts within the family but different processing times. Standard times are used in the model as mean processing times in each operation with the actual modeled cycle time being a normally distributed random number with the mean equal to the engineered standard and a standard deviation of 10 to 20 percent depending on the operation. The standards are displayed in Table 3.8, Table 3.9, and Table 3.10.

The model operates as a collection of repetitive manufacturing cells. This is characterized by a flow of material through each cell as the various operations take place. One-piece flow, first-come first-served, is utilized throughout the model including the paint process. Several queues are utilized in operations where the simulated operation would require the parts to stage for a given period to cure prior to being consumed by the next process. Raw material enters the system in batches at the beginning of each line. The arrival process is not sequenced by time; instead, the arrival file contains all orders for the

Table 3.8 Standard Operation Times for Family A (Time in Seconds)

Item	A1	A2	A3	A4	A5	A6	A7	A8	A9	A10
Category	Medium	Medium	Small	Small	Small	Medium	Medium	Large	Large	Large
Operation										
A_cover_blanks	15	15	15	15	15	15	15	15	15	15
A_cover_flange	27	27	27	27	27	27	27	36	36	36
A_cover_form	36	36	36	36	36	36	36	45	45	45
A_corner_weld	30	30	30	30	30	30	30	36	36	36
A_grinder_cover	36	36	36	36	36	36	36	48	48	48
A_hinge_to_cover	24	24	18	18	18	24	24	36	36	36
A_body_blanks	15	15	15	15	15	15	15	15	15	15
A_body_form	54	54	48	48	48	54	54	72	72	72
A_auto_welder_body	60	60	48	48	48	60	60	78	78	78
A_grinder_body	30	30	30	30	30	30	30	45	45	45
A_mounting_feet	45	45	45	45	45	45	45	54	54	54

A_panel_studs	54	54	54	45	45	45	45	45	45	45
A_cover_to_body	36	36	36	24	24	24	24	24	24	24
A_load_paint	24	24	24	18	18	18	18	18	18	18
Paint										
A_gasket	54	54	54	30	30	24	24	24	30	30
A_gasket_queue										
A_assy_1	90	90	90	60	60	30	30	30	60	60
A_assy_2	45	45	45	45	45	45	45	45	45	45
Packaging	90	90	90	75	75	60	60	60	75	75
Finished_goods										
Total direct labor (sec)	873	873	873	669	669	594	594	594	669	669
Total direct labor (min)	14.55	14.55	14.55	11.15	11.15	9.9	9.9	9.9	11.15	11.15

Table 3.9 Standard Operation Times for Family B (Time in Seconds)

Item	B1	B2	B3	B4	B5	B6	B7	B8	B9	B10
Size	Medium	Medium	Small	Small	Small	Medium	Medium	Large	Large	Large
Operation										
B_body_blanks	30	30	30	30	30	30	30	45	45	45
B_punch_corner_notch	120	120	120	120	120	120	120	180	180	180
B_panel_nut_weld	120	120	100	100	100	120	120	220	220	220
B_body_brake	240	240	160	160	160	240	240	400	400	400
B_manual_weld	360	360	240	240	240	360	360	600	600	600
B_hinge_hole_punch	120	120	120	120	120	120	120	200	200	200
B_door_blanks	15	15	15	15	15	15	15	25	25	25
B_door_form	60	60	60	60	60	60	60	75	75	75
B_corner_form_trim	60	60	60	60	60	60	60	75	75	75

B_hinge_barrel_weld	75	75	75	75	75	75	75	100	100	100	100
B_stiffener_weld	75	75	75	75	75	75	75	100	100	100	100
B_load_paint	25	25	25	25	25	25	25	45	45	45	45
B_gasket	60	60	50	50	50	60	60	90	90	90	90
B_gasket_queue											
B_assy_1	120	120	120	120	120	120	120	200	200	200	200
B_assy_2	150	150	150	150	150	150	150	300	300	300	300
B_package	120	120	120	120	120	120	120	240	240	240	240
Finished_goods											
Total direct labor (sec)	1,750	1,750	1,520	1,520	1,520	1,750	1,750	2,895	2,895	2,895	2,895
Total direct labor (min)	29.16	29.16	25.33	25.33	25.33	29.16	29.16	48.25	48.25	48.25	48.25

Table 3.10 Standard Operation times for Family C (Time in Seconds)

Item	C1	C2	C3	C4	C5	C6	C7	C8	C9	C10
Size	Medium	Medium	Small	Small	Small	Medium	Medium	Large	Large	Large
Operation										
C_wrapper_blanks	20	20	20	20	20	20	20	30	30	30
C_end_wall_blanks	20	20	20	20	20	20	20	30	30	30
C_offset_brake	40	40	40	40	40	40	40	60	60	60
C_body_brake	60	60	60	60	60	60	60	90	90	90
C_endwall_brake	40	40	40	40	40	40	40	40	40	40
C_panel_studs	60	60	40	40	40	40	40	80	80	80
C_body_weld	480	480	360	360	360	360	360	720	720	720
C_body_grind	480	480	360	360	360	360	360	720	720	720
C_body_hardware	150	150	120	120	120	120	120	180	180	180
C_cover_blanks	20	20	20	20	20	20	20	30	30	30
C_cover_hemm_form	45	45	30	30	30	30	30	60	60	60
C_cover_weld	60	60	60	60	60	60	60	120	120	120

C_cover_grind	60	60	60	60	60	60	60	60	120	120	120
C_hinge_to_cover	60	60	45	45	45	45	45	45	90	90	90
C_door_stiffeners	60	60	0	0	0	0	0	0	90	90	90
C_load_paint	20	20	20	20	20	20	20	20	40	40	40
C_gasket	75	75	60	60	60	60	60	60	90	90	90
C_gasket_queue											
C_assy_1	180	180	180	180	180	180	180	180	360	360	360
C_assy_2	120	120	120	120	120	120	120	120	180	180	180
C_assy_3	180	180	180	180	180	180	180	180	360	360	360
C_package	240	240	220	220	220	220	220	220	300	300	300
Finished_goods											
Total direct labor (sec)	2,290	2,290	1,875	1,875	1,875	1,875	1,875	1,875	3,540	3,540	3,540
Total direct labor (min)	38.16	38.16	31.25	31.25	31.25	31.25	31.25	31.25	59	59	59

Table 3.11   Setup Times

Family/Part	Mean	Standard Deviation
A/cover	20 min	2 min
A/body	20 min	2 min
B/cover	20 min	2 min
B/body	30 min	3 min
C/cover	20 min	2 min
C/body	20 min	2 min
C/end	20 min	2 min

period to be simulated in a sequence arranged from the highest priority to lowest priority product by family. ProModel executes these orders in the order of arrangement. Because raw material and its operational characteristics are not the subject of this study, it was determined that the batch arrival process employed was of no significance to the outcome of the study.

Setup time between orders was incorporated through the use of subroutines. Each time a product entered the initial work center in a given cell, a subroutine was executed to identify if the current part was identical to the previous part. If the incoming part was different, then a setup cycle was executed to simulate the effects of this activity on the capacity of the operation. Setup times were normally distributed random variables with mean and standard deviation as indicated in Table 3.11.

Production Planning Tool

The planning tool was constructed utilizing a collection of interconnected spreadsheets. The tool performed the following tasks:

- Determination of the coming months production schedule
- Tracking of on-hand inventories
- Calculation of income statements by accounting method

Calculation of the Coming Month Production Schedule

The formula used for the calculation of the coming month's production quantity by part was

$$= safety\ stock\ target + forecast!_{ij} - inventory!_{ij},$$

where
  forecast!$_{ij}$ references the quantity contained in the appropriate cell on the forecast sheet for the part of interest.
  inventory!$_{ij}$ references the on-hand inventory for that part, (this will be elaborated on momentarily).

The safety stock level was established at twice the monthly forecast for high volume products and four times the monthly forecast for low volume products.

Tracking of On-Hand Inventories

On-hand inventory quantities are maintained in a sheet dedicated to that function. On-hand levels by part are calculated at the conclusion of each month simultaneous to the creation of the next month's production schedule. The logic used to arrive at current on-hand levels by part is:

$$= IF(cell_{ij} + production!cell_{ij} - sales!cell_{ij} \geq 0, cell_{ij} + production!cell_{ij} - sales!cell_{ij}, 0),$$

where
  cell$_{ij}$ references the previous month's ending inventory level.
  production!cell$_{ij}$ references the cell containing the quantity produced from one iteration of the simulation model for the part in question.
  sales!cell$_{ij}$ references the cell containing the quantity sold in the current time period for the part in question based on the randomly determined sales volume quantities discussed earlier.

The equation is formulated using an IF statement to provide an adjustment in the event of a stock shortage. If the quantity sold in the current period exceeds the quantity produced plus the starting balance, then a negative inventory situation is experienced. The IF statement evaluates whether or not there will be a balance of inventory at the end of the period. If not, then the inventory level is set to zero. No backlog is created and the quantity oversold is reduced from the quantity sold for calculation of the income statement. Thus, negative inventory is viewed as a lost sale and a missed opportunity.

Calculation of Income Statements by Accounting Method

The production planning tool maintains income statements for five accounting methods: full absorption, direct, TPC, ABC, and a fifth method that is in the early stages of development referred to here as the order-activity method. The subject of analysis in this research was both the gross profit and net profit values and their behavior under differing accounting methods and differing levels of aggressiveness for implementation of a lean program. This study is limited to the measure of differences in gross and net profits as would be influenced by a lean manufacturing program. A lean program would not directly influence many of the typical selling and administrative cost components. As a result, many of these costs are not modeled in the income statements, instead they are viewed as constants and left out so as not to mask the magnitude of the changes of interest. The components of interest are those that are incurred due to inventory. This would include factory indirect labor costs necessary to physically manage the inventories as well as administrative costs to account for this material. Also included would be traditional carrying costs that would include the cost for the physical plant space and the cost of having capital tied up in inventory instead of invested in interest granting investments. The basic calculations for the income statements are

Cost of goods manufactured +(–) changes in inventory =
Cost of goods sold

Sales – Cost of goods sold = gross profit

Gross profit – selling and administrative costs = net profit

Costs of goods manufactured include direct materials, direct labor, and factory overhead costs that are based on an engineered standard. Reductions in factory overhead are factored into the model to simulate a reduction in this expense that is the result of declining inventory levels. Carrying cost changes resulting from inventory reduction are captured in the selling and administrative component of the income statement.

Model Execution — Data Generation

The dataset for this study was generated using an iterative process in one-month steps. The initial conditions were chosen to have on-hand inventory levels equal to the previously stated safety stock levels. The first month's income statement was calculated based on the results of the application of the randomly generated sales values. The second month's production schedule was automatically generated as a result of the previously described logic. This schedule was written to an Excel .WK1 format file. The file was then accessed by the ProModel simulation software upon model execution. The schedule information was read into the arrivals table of the model. Once the loading of the arrivals information was complete, the model ran to termination, processing the arrivals file in sequence. Model execution terminates when either all products in the production schedule are completed or a run time of 163 hours is reached. The time of 163 hours was established by using 160 hours as 4 weeks' production hours plus 3 hours to charge the production lines, simulating the ending point of the previous month, i.e., WIP. The resulting production output from the simulation run was exported to an Excel file and inserted into the planning tool in a sheet designated for this data. This triggers the updating of the current month's income statement, adjustment of on-hand inventory, and calculation of the coming month's production schedule. The process is repeated until 12 months have been completed.

The procedure just described is repeated for each of three scenarios:

1. No change in inventory target (safety stock targets are level)
2. Moderate change in inventory targets (50 percent reduction in safety stock targets by the completion of the 12th month)
3. Aggressive change in inventory targets (50 percent reduction in safety stock target by the completion for the 6th month then fixed at the new level)

The resulting series of income statements allow a comparison of the effect on gross profit and net profit resulting from the reduction in on-hand finished goods inventories.

Technical Issues with the Simulation Model

Each iteration of the ProModel simulation model is terminating, meaning that the model runs until all scheduled products have been produced or until a maximum time is reached. The model terminates upon the occurrence of either.

Queue capacities for the initial staging prior to processing, the simulated paint operation, which occurs near the middle of the production sequence, and the first operation following the paint process, which emulates another curing process, were set to levels that would prevent bottlenecks. All other operations had a queue capacity of one, forcing a one-piece-flow scenario characteristic of JIT or lean manufacturing environments.

A steady state condition was achieved by allowing an additional three hours of run time beyond the normal month capacity of run hours. This allowed the system to return to a state that would be present at the close of a month in a normal manufacturing environment, i.e., production lines full of product. In a sense, this served as a warm-up period without the loss of production counts during the warm up.

Replication was used as the method to capture the variance of dependent variable means. The required number of replications was estimated using the formula adapted from Law and Kelton (2000):

$$n \geq \left(\frac{t_{n-1,1-\alpha/2} * S_{(n)}}{E} \right)^2.$$

where

n = number of replications

$t_{n-1,1-\alpha/2}$ = Student's t value with $n - 1$ degrees of freedom

$S_{(n)}$ = sample standard deviation of the dependent variable

E = half width of the confidence interval for sample means

The dependent variable chosen to measure variability for this model was the average time in the system for a unit of product A1, B1, and C1 to complete. These were the highest volume parts in each family based on the Pareto factors used. The model was run with ten replications, ensuring a different seed in the random number stream for each replication. Descriptive statistics were generated from the ten data points to obtain an estimate of the standard deviation, S. The half width of the confidence interval, E, was set at 0.05 percent of the sample mean. Using $\alpha = .05$, the equation identified a value for $n = 34.917$. Therefore, to obtain the desired level of statistical confidence,

35 replications were required for each month of the 12-month simulation periods or 420 simulation runs to produce the dataset for one inventory policy. A total of 1260 replications were required for the creation of a complete dataset for 3 inventory policies under a given sales stochasticity level. The 3 sales stochasticity levels resulted in 3780 total simulation runs.

References

Cochran, D. S., Oropeza, G., Tapia, C., and Kim, Y. (2002). The manufacturing system design decomposition in the automotive electronics industry, *Transactions of NAMRI/SME*, 30, 645–652.

Cooper, R. and Kaplan, R. S. (April 1988). How cost accounting distorts product costs, *Management Accounting*, 69(10), 20–27.

Drury, C. and Tayles, M. (1997). Evidence on the financial accounting mentality debate: a research note, *British Accounting Review*, 29, 263–276.

Goldratt, E. M. and Cox, J. (1982). *The Goal*, 2nd rev. ed., McGraw Hill, New York, NY.

Govindarajan, V. and Anthony, R. N. (1983). How to use cost data in pricing decisions, *Management Accounting*, 70, July, 30–37.

Hendricks, J. A. (1988). Applying cost accounting to factory automation, *Management Accounting*, 70(6), 24–30.

Hillier, F. S. and Lieberman, G. J. (2001). *Introduction to Operations Research*, 7th ed., McGraw Hill, New York, NY.

Horngren, C. T. (1995). Management accounting: this century and beyond, *Management Accounting Research*, 6, 281–286.

Johnson, H. T. and Kaplan, R. S. (1987). *Relevance Lost: The Rise and Fall of Management Accounting*, Harvard Business School Press, Boston, MA.

Kaplan, R. S. (1994). Management accounting (1984–1994): development of new practice and theory, *Management Accounting Research*, 5, 247–260.

Kensinger, K. (2004). Allocation schemes in cost accounting, personal interviews, Spring.

Krajewski, L. J. King, B. E., Ritzman, L. P., and Wong, D. S. (1987). Kanban, MRP, and shaping the manufacturing environment, *Management Science*, 33(1), 39–57.

Law, A. M. and Kelton, W. D. (2000). *Simulation Modeling and Analysis*, 3rd ed., McGraw Hill, New York, NY.

Lea, B.-R. (1998). The Impact of Management Accounting Alternatives in Different Manufacturing Environments, Ph.D. dissertation, Clemson University, Clemson, SC, UMI Co., Ann Arbor, MI.

Ramasesh, R. (1990). Dynamic job scheduling: a survey of simulation research, *Omega*, 18(1), 43–57.

Wantuck, K. A. (1989). *Just in Time for America: A Common Sense Production Strategy*, KWA Media, Southfield, MI.

Chapter 4

Analytical Findings from Lean Manufacturing Factory Operation

In this chapter, the results of the data analysis are discussed and detailed analysis is presented. Analysis is based on the data collected using the modeling tools described in Chapter 3, Experimental Design section. Microsoft Excel was used for the development and operation of a pseudoproduction planning and control system as well as for financial reporting. ProModel simulation software was used for the development and operation of a model manufacturing environment. Microsoft VBA was used to act as a data bridge between the Excel and ProModel packages. The data was analyzed using MINITAB® release 14. ANOVA was employed for testing of the research hypotheses presented in Chapter 3 and the Tukey all pairwise comparison method was employed to determine which factor levels had the greatest effect on the measurements of interest.

Raw Data and Descriptive Statistics

A sample of the raw data can be seen in Table 4.1 and a complete dataset for all inventory reduction policies at one sales stochasticity setting is included in the Appendices.

Table 4.1   Raw Data, Gross Profit for the Full-Absorption Costing Method with No Inventory Reduction Target

Dollars	January	February	March	April	May	June	...
Series (Year)							
1	62,512.78	218,387.4	96,471.45	88,444.78	167,306.9	131,101.6	...
2	74,384.54	190,270.8	135,024.7	94,349.53	75,907.17	230,553.4	...
3	99,957.47	119,442.3	163,868.3	143,971.1	75,954.97	161,201.6	...
4	135,156.5	123,652.3	90,084.61	92,479.76	119,973.8	189,381.9	...
5	141,845	104,079.5	138,371.5	74,051.91	146,695.6	138,990.1	...
·	·	·	·	·	·	·	
·	·	·	·	·	·	·	
·	·	·	·	·	·	·	
32	179,780.1	23,882.56	150,233.8	117,051.6	106,857	142,742.2	...
33	123,784.6	117,235.9	89,611.7	144,673.4	118,892.3	140,019	...
34	109,134.5	165,989.9	120,891.7	62,630.77	139,415.5	135,817.4	...
35	49,308.64	224,477.7	66,843.12	182,333.1	62,393.64	138,495.4	...
Mean	124,301.1	122,459.7	112,477.2	114,539.8	131,181.5	128,321.3	...
Standard deviation	35,488.46	59,431.07	53,192.13	55,940.68	46,566.71	56,581.41	...

Data was collected for gross profit and net profit in dollars and as a percent of sales. This was done for all management accounting methods, sales volatility levels, and inventory reduction policy combinations for 35 replications. Inventory value was also recorded for the 35 replications. Means for all data tables were calculated and used for creating plots of the data, allowing a visual review prior to detailed testing.

Tests of Hypotheses

Results of all ANOVA tests are summarized in Table 4.2 and Table 4.3 and are discussed below.

Table 4.2 ANOVA Results Summary for Gross Profit

Month	Source	Approximate F	P Value
January	Policy	239.31	0.000
	Method	1243.96	0.000
	Policy × Method	2.23	0.024
February	Policy	58.34	0.000
	Method	342.20	0.000
	Policy × Method	0.45	0.891
March	Policy	85.95	0.000
	Method	470.66	0.000
	Policy × Method	0.82	0.584
April	Policy	79.40	0.000
	Method	421.86	0.000
	Policy × Method	0.76	0.636
May	Policy	100.89	0.000
	Method	547.44	0.000
	Policy × Method	0.84	0.570
June	Policy	87.45	0.000
	Method	396.47	0.000
	Policy × Method	0.87	0.543
July	Policy	21.97	0.000
	Method	339.40	0.000
	Policy × Method	0.23	0.984
August	Policy	19.66	0.000
	Method	348.46	0.000
	Policy × Method	0.17	0.995
September	Policy	30.96	0.000
	Method	553.72	0.000
	Policy × Method	0.26	0.977

(continued)

Table 4.2 (continued)   ANOVA Results Summary for Gross Profit

Month	Source	Approximate F	P Value
October	Policy	35.71	0.000
	Method	456.38	0.000
	Policy × Method	0.34	0.951
November	Policy	25.36	0.000
	Method	352.65	0.000
	Policy × Method	0.27	0.976
December	Policy	30.95	0.000
	Method	442.75	0.000
	Policy × Method	0.30	0.966

Hypothesis 1

H_1: Within a given management accounting method, does rate of inventory reduction have an effect on reported gross profit?

$H_{1,0}$: $Policy_i = 0$ for gross profit.

The main effect for factor policy was significant for this performance measure. The one-way ANOVA test indicated that at least one of the three inventory reduction policies had a significant effect on the dependent measure indicating that the means were indeed different at a significance level of $\alpha = 0.05$. As a result, hypothesis $H_{1,0}$ was rejected.

Hypothesis 2

H_2: Within a given management accounting method, does rate of inventory reduction have an effect on reported net profit?

$H_{2,0}$: $Policy_i = 0$ for net profit.

The main effect for the factor policy was significant for this performance measure. The one-way ANOVA test indicated that at least one of the three inventory reduction policies had a significant effect on

Table 4.3   ANOVA Results Summary for Net Profit

Month	Source	Approximate F	P Value
January	Policy	226.46	0.000
	Method	5.56	0.000
	Policy × Method	2.21	0.025
February	Policy	53.43	0.000
	Method	1.96	0.099
	Policy × Method	0.45	0.890
March	Policy	75.21	0.000
	Method	3.33	0.010
	Policy × Method	0.82	0.589
April	Policy	66.73	0.000
	Method	2.90	0.022
	Policy × Method	0.76	0.642
May	Policy	80.60	0.000
	Method	2.27	0.061
	Policy × Method	0.83	0.575
June	Policy	67.48	0.000
	Method	1.16	0.326
	Policy × Method	0.86	0.549
July	Policy	21.13	0.000
	Method	1.10	0.356
	Policy × Method	0.23	0.985
August	Policy	18.83	0.000
	Method	0.54	0.705
	Policy × Method	0.16	0.996
September	Policy	29.37	0.000
	Method	1.36	0.245
	Policy × Method	0.25	0.981

(continued)

Table 4.3 (continued) ANOVA Results Summary for Net Profit

Month	Source	Approximate F	P Value
October	Policy	32.65	0.000
	Method	0.07	0.991
	Policy × Method	0.33	0.955
November	Policy	21.59	0.000
	Method	1.14	0.335
	Policy × Method	0.27	0.977
December	Policy	24.77	0.000
	Method	0.37	0.832
	Policy × Method	0.29	0.970

the dependent measure, indicating that the means were indeed different at a significance level of $\alpha = 0.05$. As a result, hypothesis $H_{2,0}$ was rejected; $H_{2,1}$: rate of inventory reduction has a significant effect on the level of reported gross and net profit, was accepted.

Hypothesis 3

H_3: Within a given inventory reduction policy, does the management accounting method have an effect on reported gross profit?

$H_{3,0}$: $Acct_j = 0$ for gross profit.

The main effect for the factor management accounting method was significant for this performance measure. One-way ANOVA testing indicated that at least one of the five management accounting methods had a significant effect on the mean value for gross profit at the $\alpha = 0.05$ level. Therefore, hypothesis $H_{3,0}$ was rejected.

Hypothesis 4

H_4: Within a given inventory reduction policy, does the management accounting method have an effect on reported net profit?

$H_{4,0}$: $Acct_j = 0$ for net profit.

The main effect for the factor management accounting method was not always significant for this performance measure. One-way ANOVA testing of monthly net profit indicated that the management accounting method had a significant effect on the mean value for net profit at the $\alpha = 0.05$ level in only 2 of the 11 months evaluated. Therefore, hypothesis $H_{4,0}$ was accepted, there is no evidence that the mean values for net profit are different as a result of the management accounting method used.

Hypothesis 5

H_5: Do various combinations of inventory reduction policy and management accounting method have an effect on reported gross profit?

$H_{5,0}$: Policy$_i$ × Acct$_j$ = 0 for gross profit.

Hypothesis 5 is concerned with the interaction between the rate of reduction of inventory and the management accounting method used for reporting of gross profit. Two-way ANOVA testing identified that the interaction between the inventory policy and management accounting method was not significant at the $\alpha = 0.05$ level. The test indicates that the effect on gross profit from rate of inventory reduction at each setting was not different under the various management accounting methods. Therefore, $H_{5,0}$ was accepted, there is no evidence that the mean values for gross profit are different as a result of the interaction between the inventory reduction policy and the management accounting method. With no interaction effects to consider, the results could be evaluated at the main effect level for the performance measure of gross profit.

Hypothesis 6

H_6: Do various combinations of inventory reduction policy and management accounting method have an effect on reported net profit?

$H_{6,0}$: Policy$_i$ × Acct$_j$ = 0 for net profit.

Hypothesis 6 is concerned with the interaction between the rate of reduction of inventory and the management accounting method used for reporting of net profit. Two-way ANOVA testing identified that the interaction between inventory policy and management accounting method was not significant at the $\alpha = 0.05$ level. The test indicates that the effect on net profit from the rate of inventory reduction at each setting was not different under the various management accounting methods. Therefore, $H_{6,0}$ was accepted. With no interaction effects to consider, the results could be evaluated at the main effect level for the performance measure of net profit.

Hypothesis 7

H_7: Does inventory reduction policy have an effect on the customer service level, measured by stock-outs, under the production and market environment modeled in this study?

$H_{7,0}$: Policy$_i = 0$.

The main effect for the factor policy was significant for this performance measure. The one-way ANOVA test indicated that at least one of the three inventory reduction policies had a significant effect on the dependent measure indicating that the means were indeed different at a significance level of $\alpha = 0.05$. As a result, hypothesis $H_{7,0}$ was rejected.

Hypothesis 8

H_8: Does volatility in the sales demand have an effect on reported gross and net profit under the production and market environment modeled in this study?

$H_{8,0}$: Sales$_i = 0$.

The main effect for the factor sales was not significant for this measure. The one-way ANOVA test indicated that sales volatility level was not significant at the $\alpha = 0.05$ level. Therefore, $H_{8,0}$ was accepted.

Hypothesis 9

H_9: Does volatility in the sales demand have an effect on the customer service level, measured by stock-outs, under the production and market environment modeled in this study?

$H_{9,0}$: Sales$_i = 0$.

The main effect for the factor sales was significant for this measure. One-way ANOVA testing indicated that at least one level of sales volatility produced results with mean values that were significantly different from the other levels. Therefore, $H_{9,0}$ was accepted.

In summary, the testing has shown that the rate of inventory reduction and the management accounting alternatives do have a significant effect on the level of reported gross profit although the interaction of these factors does not have a significant effect. For net profit, the results were different. Inventory reduction policy was still significant in all of the tested periods but management accounting method was significant in only 18 percent of the cases tested. Again the interaction of the two effects was not significant at the $\alpha = 0.05$ level under the operating conditions characterized by this model.

Results by Performance Measure and Period

The results presented in this section are limited to the operational environment detailed in Chapter 3 and cannot be generalized for other operational environments. However, inferences can be made from these results into other operational environments, including process manufacturing or service, as the methods of reporting gross and net profit are uniform across these operations. Lean strategies can be applied across these types of operations as well, resulting in a lowering of inventories, leading to the same effects at varying levels of magnitude.

The Tukey pairwise evaluation method was used to evaluate the mean value data in an effort to identify the factor level means that were, in fact, different, thus causing a significant effect on the two performance measures. In addition, it was of interest to identify which factor had the greatest effect.

Gross Profit

Values for gross profit for this study were calculated for the five management accounting methods at the completion of each month of simulated operation. Sales demand was a random factor that acted as a block. Every combination of inventory reduction policy and management accounting alternative was evaluated on each block.

ANOVA Results

Summary results for ANOVA testing on the effects of inventory reduction policy and management accounting method on the level of reported gross profit can be seen in Table 4.2.

Monthly gross profit as a percentage of sales was used as the dependent variable. The results imply that both inventory reduction policy and management accounting method have a significant effect on the level of reported gross profit at the $\alpha = 0.05$ level. The results also indicate that no interaction effect exists between inventory reduction policy and management accounting method at the gross profit level.

Evaluation of Gross Profit Mean Values

The results of the Tukey all pairwise tests on the mean values of gross profit indicate that each level of inventory reduction policy was significantly different from all other levels with policy 1, no inventory reduction, producing the highest mean value for reported gross profit for the first 5 months of the 11-month period evaluated. Policy 3, 50 percent reduction in finished goods inventory over the first six months and no further reduction for the balance of the year, produced the lowest values for reported gross profit. Starting with month 7 and continuing through month 12, the mean values for policy 1 and policy 3 were not significantly different. Both policies produced higher values for reported gross profit than policy 2.

Results of the management accounting method indicate that there is no significant difference in mean reported gross profit values for method 1, method 3, or method 5, which were full-absorption costing, ABC, and the order-activity method of product costing. Both method 2 and method 4 were significantly different from all other methods, with method 4 producing the highest reported values for gross profit, followed by method 2. Method 4 was TPC and method 2 was direct costing. These results were consistent across all periods evaluated in this study.

Plots of the mean values indicate that inventory reduction policy 1, or no reduction in finished goods inventory level, resulted in the highest mean value for gross profit for the months during which policy 2 and policy 3 were causing inventory levels to be reduced. In July, or mid way through the test period, when policy 3 ceased to reduce inventory, the mean values for policy 1 and 3 became equal.

Plots for the management accounting method indicated that the mean monthly value for gross profit reported by TPC was repeatedly the highest followed by direct costing. The mean values for the remaining three methods were not significantly different. Samples of the plots are included in Figure 4.1 and Figure 4.2.

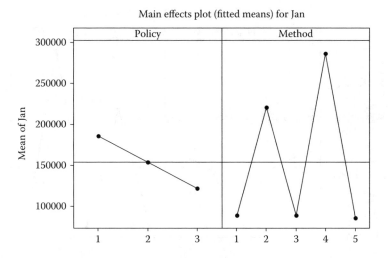

Figure 4.1 Sample plot of gross profit means, typical for months 1 to 6 for policy 1 — no inventory reduction, policy 2 — 50 percent reduction in finished goods inventory over 12 reporting periods, policy 3 — 50 percent reduction in finished goods inventory over 6 reporting periods and no further reduction. Method 1 — full absorption, method 2 — direct, method 3 — ABC, method 4 — TPC, and method 5 — order-activity.

Plots of the mean values for the complete 12-month series for gross profit by inventory reduction policy are shown on Figure 4.3. This graph allows the differences in reported gross profit to be more easily identified. Figure 4.3 displays the results using the full-absorption method of costing. The numeric results are different depending on the management accounting method, due to the way that components of cost are recognized differently between methods. Trend lines in Figure 4.3 are typical for all management accounting methods. As can be seen, the inventory reduction policy has a very noticeable impact on the three curves. This chart identifies the magnitude of the decrease in reported gross profit that results from the reduction in on-hand finished goods inventory. Inventory reduction policy 1, or no inventory reduction, reports the highest gross profit for periods 1 through 6. The reported gross profit for policy 1 is nearly 28 percent higher than policy 2 and 58 percent higher than policy 3 in the early months of the series. This separation in plots brings focus to the principle issue between management accounting practices and the impact of their support of lean manufacturing programs. In months 7 through 12, the curves for policy 1 and policy 3 coincide. As discussed earlier, policy 3 caused a rapid

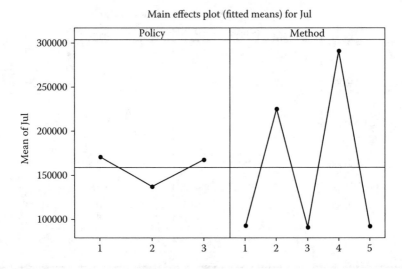

Figure 4.2 Sample plot of gross profit means, typical for months 7 to 12 for policy 1 — no inventory reduction, policy 2 — 50 percent reduction in finished goods inventory over 12 reporting periods, policy 3 — 50 percent reduction in finished goods inventory over 6 reporting periods and no further reduction. Method 1 — full absorption, method 2 — direct, method 3 — ABC, method 4 — TPC, and method 5 — order-activity.

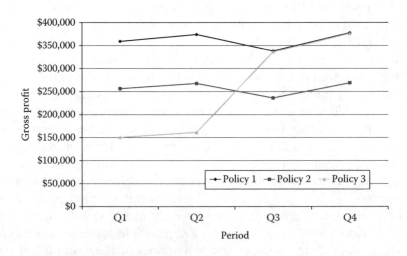

Figure 4.3 Trends of reported gross profit by inventory reduction policy, typical for all management accounting methods.

reduction in the target level for safety stock for the first half of the modeled period. In the second half of the modeled period, the target level is held constant at the new lower level, 50 percent of the initial target level. The graph shows that when inventory level ceases to be reduced, the reporting of gross profit returns to the level that would be experienced with no lean program. Differences in reported net income would reflect changes in other cost areas, such as inventory carrying costs, and will be discussed in the next section. The plot of mean values for policy 2 indicate that as long as inventory levels continue to be driven down, reported gross profit will continue to be lower. Policy 2 reduces the target level for safety stock, in a linear fashion, to 50 percent of the initial target over the course of the entire studied period. Figure 4.3 supports the previously discussed results indicating that inventory reduction policy had a significant effect on the level of reported gross income with all mean values being significantly different in periods 1 to 6, and only policy 2 being significantly different in periods 7 to 12.

In Figure 4.4 to Figure 4.6, the mean values from the 35-replication dataset for inventory policy can be seen plotted with the mean inventory level in dollars. Trend lines are added for reported gross profit to more clearly display the changes in this measure over time. Figure 4.4 shows the data for inventory reduction policy 1. This figure can be thought of as the baseline for the 35-replication dataset. The trend line shows

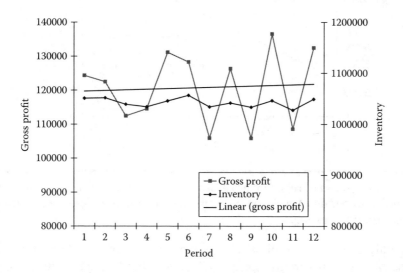

Figure 4.4 Trend of reported gross profit under no inventory reduction using full-absorption costing.

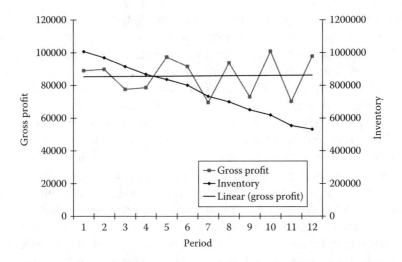

Figure 4.5 Trend of reported gross profit under moderate, linear, inventory reduction using full-absorption costing.

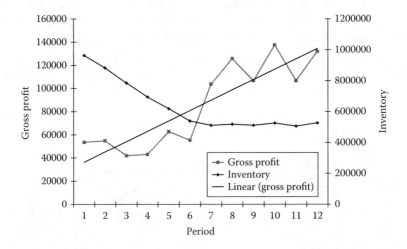

Figure 4.6 Trend of reported gross profit under aggressive, linear, inventory reduction in periods 1 to 6 and no further reduction in periods 7 to 12 using full-absorption costing.

a slightly increasing trend over time. If a second series of 35 replications was collected, this trend line could become flat or slightly decreasing. Sample data collected while developing the model exhibited this condition and can be considered a function of the stochastic nature of the model. Figure 4.5 and Figure 4.6 use the same baseline data, allowing direct comparisons to be made between the figures. Inventory reduction policy 1 and policy 2 exhibit an essentially flat reported gross profit for the studies period, implying that if the rate of inventory reduction is a constant then the reported level of gross profit will also be constant. Therefore, if the rate of reduction is linear over time, regardless of the slope, the trend of the impact or reduction in reported gross profit would be parallel to other reduction slopes including zero or no reduction. The greater the slope of reduction, the lower the reported gross profit. The noticeable change in the slope of the trend line in Figure 4.6 is explained by the effect that ceasing further reduction has on the reported level of gross profit. This graph has essentially two significant periods. In months 1 to 6, a trend line would again be parallel to Figure 4.4 and Figure 4.5. In addition, a trend line of periods 7 to 12 would be parallel to the other figures. This is due to the fact that in each period the rate of reduction is linear, downward in the first period and flat in the second. In the second period it can be seen that the values for reported gross profit for policy 3 are equal to those reported under policy 1, which is expected as no reduction is taking place during this period for either method.

Figure 4.7 displays the differences in reported gross income as a result of management accounting method. The curves included in this figure are the result of inventory reduction policy 3, aggressive reduction periods 1 to 6 and no further reduction periods 7 to 12. As can

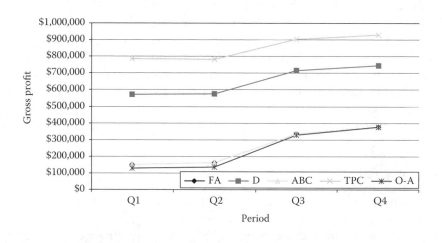

Figure 4.7 Trends of reported gross profit by management accounting method, inventory reduction for policy 3 by quarter.

be seen from the plots, the five curves are essentially parallel. This figure displays the magnitude of the differences between the recognition of cost components between the various management accounting alternatives. ANOVA tests on the mean values for all methods indicated that management accounting method did have a significant impact on the mean value for reported gross profit. Tukey tests on the confidence intervals indicated that method 2 and method 4 were significantly different from the other three methods. The remaining methods were not statistically different from each other. Method 4, TPC, reported the highest levels for gross profit followed by direct costing.

Net Profit

Values for net profit for this study were calculated under the same operational conditions and in the same manner as for gross profit as stated above. Sales demand was a random factor that acted as a block. Every combination of inventory reduction policy and management accounting alternative was evaluated on each block. Many customary factors contained in the calculation of net profit were not distinguished individually in the profit and loss statements used to create the dataset. The focus of this study was to investigate the impact on reported profit levels resulting from the adoption of lean strategies. In that light, only those measures that would be unique to a given management accounting method were separated in the profit and loss statements. For instance, cost items such as administrative salaries, depreciation, advertising, etc. were viewed as constants for all methods and as a result were not included in this study. Inventory carrying cost was considered significant in this study and thus became the sole, additional factor included in the preparation of the income statements. The location in the income statement of the recognition of several other items of cost changed between gross and net profit categories depending on unique characteristics of the management accounting method being modeled.

ANOVA Results

Summary results for ANOVA testing on the effects of inventory reduction policy and management accounting method on the level of reported net profit can be seen in Table 4.3. Monthly net profit as a percentage of sales was used as the dependent variable. The results imply that the inventory reduction policy has a significant effect on the level of reported net profit at the $\alpha = 0.05$ level for all periods tested. The management accounting method was only significant in April and June. The results also indicate that no interaction effect exists between inventory reduction policy and management accounting method at the net profit level.

Evaluation of Net Profit Mean Values

The results of the Tukey all pairwise tests on the means of net profit indicate the following: Each level of inventory reduction policy was significantly different from all other levels with policy 1, no inventory reduction, producing the highest mean value for reported net profit for the first 6 months of the 12-month period evaluated. Policy 3, 50 percent reduction in finished goods inventory over the first 6 months and no further reduction for the balance of the year, produced the lowest values for reported net profit during the same period. Starting with month 7 and continuing through month 12, the mean values for policy 1 and policy 3 were not significantly different. Both policies produced higher values for reported net profit than policy 2 during the later period.

Results for the management accounting method indicate that in 10 out of the 12 months simulated, there was no significant difference in mean value of reported net profit from any of the 5 methods. In January, the confidence interval lower limit for method 4 exceeds zero by 3.260 percent when compared to method 1. If the confidence interval had contained zero, the mean values would be identified as not significantly different from method 1. March had a P value of 0.01 but all confidence intervals using the Tukey method contained zero, indicating no difference.

Plots of the mean values indicate that inventory reduction policy 1, or no reduction in finished goods inventory level, resulted in the highest mean value for net profit for the months during which policy 2 and policy 3 were causing inventory levels to be reduced. In July, or mid way through the test period, when policy 3 ceased to reduce inventory, the mean values for policy 3 exceeded all other policies.

Plots for management accounting method indicate that the mean monthly value for net profit reported by TPC was repeatedly the highest followed by direct costing. The mean values for the remaining three methods were not significantly different. Samples of the plots are included in Figure 4.8 and Figure 4.9.

Plots of the mean values for the complete 12-month series for net profit by inventory reduction policy are shown on Figure 4.10. This graph allows the differences in reported net profit to be more easily

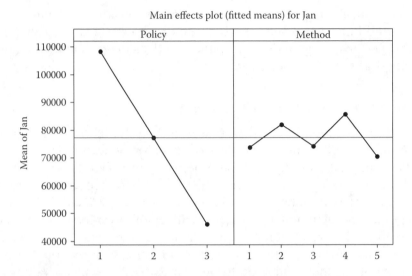

Figure 4.8 Sample plot of net profit means, typical for months 1 to 6 for policy 1 — no inventory reduction, policy 2 — 50 percent reduction in finished goods inventory over 12 reporting periods, policy 3 — 50 percent reduction in finished goods inventory over 6 reporting periods and no further reduction. Method 1 — full absorption, method 2 — direct, method 3 — ABC, method 4 — TPC, and method 5 — order-activity.

identified. Figure 4.10 displays the results using the full-absorption method of costing. The numeric results will be different depending on the management accounting method, due to differences in the way components of cost are recognized. However, the trend lines in Figure 4.10 are typical for all management accounting methods. The trend lines indicate that inventory reduction policy has a noticeable impact on reported net profit. This chart identifies the magnitude of the decrease in reported net profit that results from the reduction in on-hand finished goods inventory. Inventory reduction policy 1, or no inventory reduction, reports the highest net profit for periods 1 through 6. The reported net profit for policy 1 is roughly 32 percent higher than policy 2 and 64 percent higher than policy 3 in the early months of the series. It was previously identified that during months 7 through 12, the curves for policy 1 and policy 3 coincided for gross profit. When looking at the same information in regard to net profit, however, the curve for policy 3 is at a higher level of reported profit. This can be explained as the impact from the benefit gained at the net profit level for a reduction in inventory carrying costs. As stated in Chapter 2, the inventory carrying costs for this study were set at 1.5 percent per

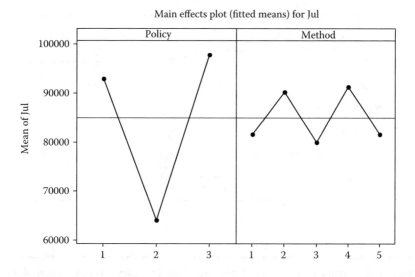

Figure 4.9   Sample plot of net profit means, typical for months 7 to 12 for policy 1 — no inventory reduction, policy 2 — 50 percent reduction in finished goods inventory over 12 reporting periods, policy 3 — 50 percent reduction in finished goods inventory over 6 reporting periods and no further reduction. Method 1 — full absorption, method 2 — direct, method 3 — ABC, method 4 — TPC, and method 5 — order-activity.

month of the inventory cost. It is, however, important to recall that the Tukey tests of mean confidence intervals did not find a significant difference between inventory reduction policy 1 and policy 3 for periods 7 to 12. The graph shows that when inventory level ceases to be reduced, the reporting of net profit returns to the level that would be experienced with no lean program with the addition of the benefit gained from a savings in inventory carrying costs.

The plot of mean values for policy 2 indicates that as long as inventory levels continue to be driven down, reported net profit will continue to be lower. Policy 2 reduces the target level for safety stock, in a linear fashion, by 50 percent of the initial level over the course of the entire studied period. Figure 4.10 supports the previously discussed results that indicated that inventory reduction policy had a significant effect on reported net income with all mean values being significantly different in periods 1 to 6, and only policy 2 being significantly different in periods 7 to 12.

In Figure 4.11 to Figure 4.13 the mean values from the 35-replication dataset for inventory policy can be seen plotted with the mean inventory level, shown in dollars. Trend lines are added for reported net

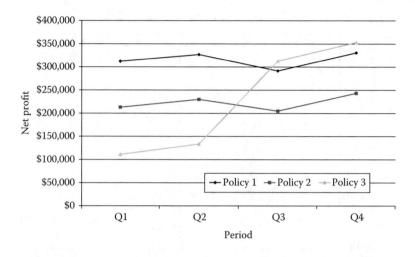

Figure 4.10 Trends of reported net profit by inventory reduction policy, typical for all management accounting methods.

profit to more clearly display the changes in this measure over time. Figure 4.11 shows the data for inventory reduction policy 1. This figure can be thought of as the baseline for the 35-replication dataset. The trend line shows a slightly increasing trend over time. If a second series of 35 replications was collected, this trend line could become flat or slightly decreasing. Sample data collected while developing the model exhibited this condition and can be considered a function of the stochastic nature of the model. Figure 4.12 and Figure 4.13 use the same baseline data allowing direct comparisons to be made between the figures. Inventory reduction policy 1 and policy 2 exhibit an essentially flat reported net profit for the studied period, implying that if the rate of inventory reduction is a constant, then the reported level of net profit will also be constant. Therefore, if the rate of reduction is linear over time, regardless of the slope, the trend of the reduction in reported net profit would be parallel to other reduction slopes including zero or no reduction. The greater the slope of reduction, the lower the reported gross profit. The noticeable difference in the slope of the trend line in Figure 4.13 is explained by the effect that ceasing further reduction has on the reported level of net profit. This graph has essentially two significant periods. In months 1 to 6, a trend line would again be parallel to Figure 4.11 and Figure 4.12. In addition, a trend line of periods 7 to 12 would be parallel to the other figures. This is due to the fact that in each period, the rate of reduction is linear, downward in the first period and flat in the second.

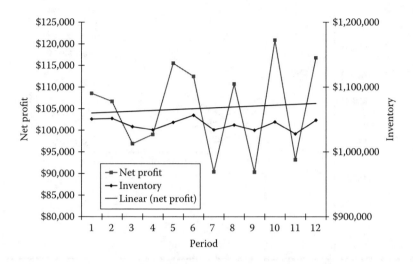

Figure 4.11   Trend of reported net profit under no linear inventory reduction throughout the modeled period using full-absorption costing.

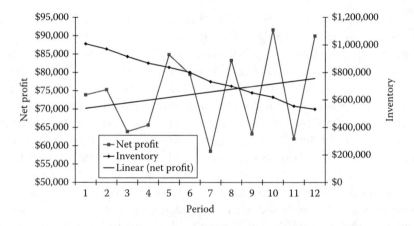

Figure 4.12   Trend of reported net profit under moderate, linear inventory reduction throughout the modeled period using full-absorption costing.

In the second period, it can be seen that the values for reported net profit for policy 3 are roughly equal to those reported under policy 1 in Figure 4.11.

Figure 4.14 displays the differences in reported net profit as a result of management accounting method. The curves included in this figure are the result of inventory reduction policy 3, aggressive reduction periods 1 to 6 (quarters 1 and 2) and no further reduction periods 7

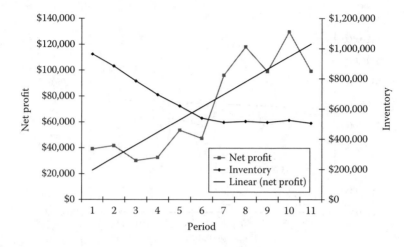

Figure 4.13 Trend of reported net profit under aggressive, linear inventory reduction in periods 1 to 6 and no further reduction in periods 7 to 12 using full-absorption costing.

to 12 (quarters 3 and 4). As can be seen from the plots, the five curves are essentially parallel but stratified in periods 1 to 6 (quarters 1 and 2) when inventory is being rapidly reduced. The curves then converge in periods 7 to 12 (periods 3 and 4) when inventory is no longer being reduced. What Figure 4.14 shows is what occurs between the various systems under a period of change and under a stable environment. In a stable environment, all methods report essentially the same results at the net profit level. At the net profit level, all the various cost components have been recognized by all systems meaning that items that are identified as fixed costs in one system and variable in another are included in the calculation of net profit. Therefore, by design all methods should report the same results under a stable environment. However, in an unstable environment, the reported results are vastly different. Methods that include more of the operational cost components in product cost (variable) for inventory valuation purposes show a greater reduction in reported net profit when the product is removed from inventory. Full-absorption, activity-based, and the order-activity costing methods fit this category. Direct includes fewer of the operational cost components in the calculation of product cost and throughput includes fewer yet. This figure displays the magnitude of the differences in the recognition of cost components between the various management accounting alternatives. However, ANOVA tests on the mean values for all methods indicated that management accounting method

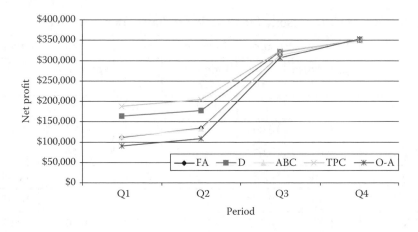

Figure 4.14   Trends of reported net profit by management accounting method, inventory reduction for policy 3 by quarter.

did not have a significant impact on reported net profit in 9 of the 11 months tested. Under net profit, all of the various operational components of cost are accounted for. This has the effect of bringing the reported values from the various methods back together. The variation induced by the stochastic nature of this study led to an inability to determine differences in mean values for net profit between methods.

Sensitivity to Sales Variability

ANOVA testing was used to evaluate the effect on net profit resulting from the level of variability in the actual sales as compared to the forecast. Three settings were used to create the dataset. The settings were 10, 25, and 40 percent of the forecasted value. These factors were used as the value for the standard deviation when using random numbers to create a normally distributed random number for sales with a mean equal to the forecast value. The ANOVA results are shown in Table 4.4. The p values indicate that a difference in the mean values of net profit between settings was not identified.

Service Level

Service level for this study is concerned with the ability to meet customer demand in each of the monthly periods modeled. If inventory was not sufficient to satisfy the demand in a given month, the sale

Table 4.4 ANOVA Results for Variation in Sales from Forecast

Month	10 Percent Variation		25 Percent Variation		40 Percent Variation	
	Approximate F	p	Approximate F	p	Approximate F	P
January	4.17	0.018	4.17	0.018	4.17	0.018
February	6.74	0.002	6.21	0.003	5.93	0.004
March	2.63	0.077	3.10	0.49	3.29	0.041
April	1.40	0.250	1.53	0.221	1.43	0.243
May	1.13	0.328	0.45	0.640	0.42	0.655
June	0.77	0.467	0.59	0.558	0.50	0.607
July	0.98	.0380	0.99	0.375	1.24	0.294
August	1.11	0.333	1.01	0.369	1.03	0.362
September	0.72	0.490	0.64	0.532	0.66	0.519
October	0.94	0.394	0.73	0.483	0.60	0.548
November	0.56	0.573	0.98	0.377	0.95	0.389
December	1.87	0.159	1.72	0.184	1.42	0.247

was considered to be lost. Therefore, unsatisfied demand was not carried forward to be satisfied by a future month's production output. If demand in a given month exceeded available inventory levels, a stock-out situation occurred. The total number of stock-out conditions, under the three inventory reduction policies, was captured in the dataset generated for this study.

This information was analyzed using one-way ANOVA in an effort to determine the effect of inventory reduction policy on service level. It is important to recall that the sales demand in this study displayed a significant level of volatility, as explained in Chapter 2. Therefore, as safety stock target levels decreased, the danger of a stock-out situation occurring increased. The results of the ANOVA test are shown below in Table 4.5. The test indicates that inventory reduction policy is indeed significant in terms of the impact on the occurrence of stock-out situations. A Tukey test on the mean values for inventory reduction policy indicates that there is no significant difference in the means for policy 1 and policy 2. Policy 3, however, was significantly different from the other two and was the highest value of the three. Highest in this case meant more stock-outs. Therefore, reduction of the safety stock target level to 50 percent of the initial target over a period of

Table 4.5   ANOVA Results, Stock-Outs Attributable to Reduction Policy

Source	DF	SS	MS	F	P
Policy	2	86.82	43.41	19.59	0.000
Error	87	192.83	2.22		
Total	89	279.66			

Note: DF = degrees of freedom; SS = sum of squares; MS = mean square.

Table 4.6   ANOVA Results, Stock-Outs Attributable to Sales Variation

Source	DF	SS	MS	F	P
Variation	2	3902.60	1951.30	64.71	0.000
Error	87	2623.50	30.20		
Total	89	6526.10			

Note: DF = degrees of freedom; SS = sum of squares; MS = mean square.

6 months, and then holding the target level through the balance of the year, resulted in more stock-outs than no reduction in target level or a 50 percent reduction in target level over a 12-month period.

Results of ANOVA testing in regard to stock-outs resulting from variations in actual sales as compared to the forecast are shown in Table 4.6. The ANOVA table indicates that volatility in sales is indeed significant in terms of the impact on the occurrence of stock-out situations. Tukey tests on the mean values for sales variability indicate that there is no significant difference in the means for policy 1 and policy 2. Policy 3, however, was significantly different from the other two and was the highest value of the three. Highest in this case meant more stock-outs. Therefore, using a standard deviation of 40 percent of the forecast value to calculate a random sales number resulted in more stock-outs than a standard deviation of 10 percent and 25 percent of the forecast value.

Sensitivity Analysis

Monte Carlo simulation software (Crystal Ball® software) was used to perform a sensitivity analysis on a series of composite income statements assembled using mean values from the 35-replication dataset. The purpose of the analysis was to determine what level of operational savings, in various areas of the income statement, would be required to offset the reported reductions in profit resulting from the decrease in inventory. The variables identified for cost reduction were inventory carrying costs, indirect labor, and direct labor. These are three areas where operational improvements are often recognized through the successful implementation of lean strategies. Three income statements were assembled for testing, all using data from the 25 percent sales volatility dataset. The three income statements represented a 12-month cycle for an operation under each of the 3 inventory reduction policies. The dependent variable tracked for comparison was the annual net profit. In the sensitivity analysis, varying values for improvement were applied to the three variables on the income statements, on a trial-and-error basis, to identify what level of savings would be required to end a year at a similar profit level, under each reduction program. Figure 4.15 to Figure 4.17 display the distributions created by Monte Carlo simulation when the following settings were used:

Direct labor reduction: 0 to 3%
Carrying cost interest rate: 3 to 5%
Overhead cost reduction: 10 to 20%

The distribution depicted in Figure 4.15 is for policy 1 and represents the spread that would result from the variation in carrying cost interest rate. This distribution centers on an annual net profit of approximately

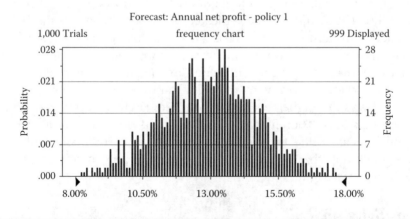

Figure 4.15 Distribution of annual net profit from Monte Carlo simulation, inventory reduction policy 1.

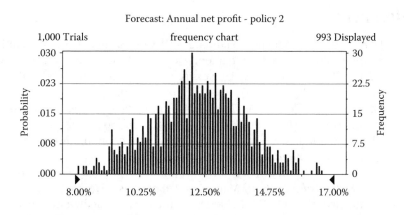

Figure 4.16   Distribution of annual net profit from Monte Carlo simulation, inventory reduction policy 2.

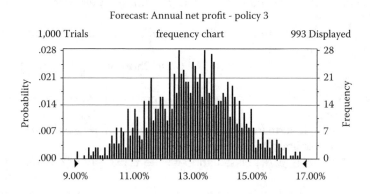

Figure 4.17   Distribution of annual net profit from Monte Carlo simulation, inventory reduction policy 3.

13 percent. The second and third policy distributions, Figure 4.16 and Figure 4.17, represent the benefit from labor, indirect cost, and savings from lower carrying costs. Policy 2 (Figure 4.16) centers on approximately 12.5 percent annual net profit and policy 3 (Figure 4.17) centers on approximately 13 percent. Therefore, at the above settings, the annual net profits are nearly equal. Stated another way, at a carrying cost rate of 3 to 5% on the cost of finished goods inventory, a savings of 0 to 3% in direct labor and of 10 to 20% in indirect costs (including indirect labor) would need to be realized, throughout the year, to offset the reported negative impact from a reduction in inventory of 50 percent over the course of the year.

References

Boyd, L. H. (1999). Production Planning and Control and Cost Accounting Systems: Effects on Management Decision Making and Firm Performance, Ph.D. dissertation, University of Georgia, Athens, GA, UMI Co., Ann Arbor, MI.

Chandler, A. (1977). *The Visible Hand: The Management Revolution in American Business,* Harvard University Press, Cambridge, MA.

Cooper, R. and Kaplan, R. S. (April 1988). How cost accounting distorts product costs, *Management Accounting,* 69(10), 20–27.

Cunningham, J. and Fiume, O. (2003). *Real Numbers: Management Accounting in a Lean Organization,* Managing Times Press, Durham, NC.

Drury, C. and Tayles, M. (1997). Evidence on the financial accounting mentality debate: a research note, *British Accounting Review,* 29, 263–276.

Elnicki, R. A. (1971). The genesis of management accounting, *Management Accounting,* 52(10), 15–17.

Fullerton, R. R. and McWatters, C. S. (2001). The production performance benefits from JIT implementation, *Journal of Operations Management,* 19, 81–96.

Garrison, R. H. and Noreen, E. W. (1994). *Managerial Accounting,* Irwin, Inc., Burr Ridge, IL.

Goldratt, E. M. and Cox, J. (1982). *The Goal,* 2nd rev. ed., McGraw Hill, New York, NY.

Hartley, R. V. (1983). *Cost and Managerial Accounting,* Allyn and Bacon, Inc., Newton, MA.

Hillier, F. S. and Lieberman, G. J. (2001). *Introduction to Operations Research,* 7th ed., McGraw Hill, New York, NY.

Hoffer, C. W. (1994). MAN class handout, The University of Georgia, Athens, GA, Winter.

Horngren, C. T. (1995). Management accounting: this century and beyond, *Management Accounting Research,* 6, 281–286.

Johnson, H. T. and Kaplan, R. S. (1987). *Relevance Lost: The Rise and Fall of Management Accounting,* Harvard Business School Press, Boston, MA.

Kaplan, R. S. (1994). Management accounting (1984–1994): development of new practice and theory, *Management Accounting Research,* 5, 247–260.

Kensinger, K. (2004). Allocation schemes in cost accounting, personal interviews, Spring.

Krajewski, L. J., King, B. E., Ritzman, L. P., and Wong, D. S. (1987). Kanban, MRP, and shaping the manufacturing environment, *Management Science,* 33(1), 39–57.

Law, A. M. and Kelton, W. D. (2000). *Simulation Modeling and Analysis,* 3rd ed., McGraw Hill, New York, NY.

Lea, B.-R. (1998). The Impact of Management Accounting Alternatives in Different Manufacturing Environments, Ph.D. dissertation, Clemson University, Clemson, SC, UMI Co., Ann Arbor, MI.

Lere, J. C. (2001). Your product-costing system seems to be broken: now what? *Industrial Marketing Management*, 30, 587–598.

Little, T. M. (1981). Interpretation and presentation of result, *HortScience*, 19, 637–640.

Martin-Vega, L. A. (2001). *Maynard's Industrial Engineering Handbook*, 5th ed., McGraw Hill, New York, NY.

Nachtmann, H. and Needy, K. (2003). Methods for handling uncertainty in activity based costing systems, *The Engineering Economist*, 48(3), 259–282.

Pine, B. J. (1993). *Mass Customization: The New Frontier in Business Competition,* Harvard Business School Press, Boston, MA.

Ramasesh, R. (1990). Dynamic job scheduling: a survey of simulation research, *Omega*, 18(1), 43–57.

Schonberger, R. J. (1982a). *Japanese Manufacturing Techniques: Nine Hidden Lessons in Simplicity,* The Free Press, New York, NY.

Schonberger, R. J. (1982b). Some observations on the advantages and implementation issues of just-in-time production systems, *Journal of Operations Management*, 3(1), 1–11.

Scott, D. R. (1931). *The Cultural Significance of Accounts,* Henry Holt, New York, NY.

Shah, R. and Ward, P. T. (2003). Lean manufacturing: context, practice bundles, and performance, *Journal of Operations Management*, 21, 129–149.

Soloman, J. M. (2003). *Who's Counting?* WCM Associates, Fort Wayne, IN.

Sugimori, Y., Kusunoki, F., Cho, F., and Uchikawa, S. (1977). Toyota production and Kanban system: materialization of just-in-time and respect for human systems, *International Journal of Production Research*, 15, 553–564.

Wantuck, K. A. (1989). *Just in Time for America: A Common Sense Production Strategy,* KWA Media, Southfield, MI.

Womak, J. and Jones, D. (2003). *Lean Thinking: Banish Waste and Create Wealth in Your Corporation,* The Free Press, New York, NY.

Chapter 5

Conclusions and Implications of Lean Manufacturing Factory Operation

The purpose of this study was to investigate and compare the impact of a lean manufacturing program upon various internal and external operational performance measures, as reported by a number of differing management accounting methods. Previous chapters introduced the focus of the research, provided a review of the existing literature surrounding the issues researched, described the experimental design and research tools employed, and reviewed the results in terms of the research questions at the center of this study. This chapter will provide a summary of the research findings. In addition, limitations of the models and evaluation methods will be discussed as well as directions for future research.

Summary of Research Findings

The findings in this study demonstrate the significance of the impact on two of the key external performance measures used by manufacturing firms throughout the United States and the United Kingdom. In addition, the impact on the internal measure of shipping performance is also quantified and evaluated. A summary of the results of the testing of the research questions presented in Chapter 2 of this document is shown in Table 5.1. The findings contained within this document pertain to an operation with the following characteristics:

- A repetitive manufacturing environment that follows a build-to-stock model.
- Multiple manufacturing cells dedicated to families of products.
- Manufacturing routings that contain 15 to 20 processing steps.
- Processing times that are normally distributed with a standard deviation of 10 to 20 percent of the mean processing time, $N[\mu, (.1 \text{ to } .2) \mu]$.
- Setups required between orders of different products within a family.
- Significant differences in sales volume within families of products, such as differences following a Pareto distribution (20 percent of products accounting for 80 percent of sales volume).
- Volatility in sales demand from month to month (forecast error) normally distributed with a mean equal to the sales forecast and a standard deviation equal to 10 to 40 percent of the forecast, N (forecast, 10 to 40 percent of forecast), resulting in a demand that ranged from 0 percent of forecast to 220 percent of forecast 95 percent of the time and exceeding the upper end of this range 2.5 percent of the time.
- Standard overhead rates based on labor hours and ranging from 150 to 250 percent.

As can be seen from the above list of characteristics, the results of this study would allow inferences to be made for a broad segment of operations throughout the manufacturing community.

The concern at the forefront of this study is that traditional financial reporting practices do not support the adaptation of those lean manufacturing practices that lead to a lowering of on-hand inventories. Elimination of all waste is the central focus behind lean manufacturing. In this light, excess inventories are considered a primary measure of waste. Therefore, any lean manufacturing program will lead to a lowering of inventory levels. The reduction in inventory leads to a shift in the location of recognition of the inventory costs, reporting period by reporting period. This shift is from the balance sheet, where the

Table 5.1   Results of Hypotheses Tests

Hypothesis	Result
H_1: Within a given management accounting method, does rate of inventory reduction have an effect on reported gross profit?	$H_{1,0}$ was rejected.
H_2: Within a given management accounting method, does rate of inventory reduction have an effect on reported net profit?	$H_{2,0}$ was rejected.
H_3: Within a given inventory reduction policy, does the management accounting method have an effect on reported gross profit?	$H_{3,0}$ was rejected.
H_4: Within a given inventory reduction policy, does the management accounting method have an effect on reported net profit?	$H_{4,0}$ was accepted.
H_5: For a given inventory reduction policy, does the management accounting method used have an effect on reported gross profit?	$H_{5,0}$ was accepted.
H_6: For a given inventory reduction policy, does the management accounting method used have an effect on reported net profit?	$H_{6,0}$ was accepted.
H_7: Does inventory reduction policy have an effect on the customer service level, measured by stock-outs, under the production and market environment modeled in this study?	$H_{7,0}$ was rejected.
H_8: Does volatility in the sales demand have an effect on reported gross and net profit under the production and market environment modeled in this study?	$H_{8,0}$ was accepted.
H_9: Does volatility in the sales demand have an effect on the customer service level, measured by stock-outs, under the production and market environment modeled in this study?	$H_{9,0}$ was accepted.

inventory is categorized as an asset, to the income statement. This shift results in a negative effect on the reported gross and net profits.

The research has shown that the magnitude of the impact on these external measures is influenced by the aggressiveness of the lean program. Under a moderate rate of inventory reduction, the drop in the performance measure of gross profit was nearly 30 percent. Under an aggressive rate of reduction, the performance measure for gross profit decreased nearly 60 percent. Results of this sort would lead to great concern in the viewpoint of a stakeholder.

This reduction in reported gross and net profit continued as long as inventory continued to be lowered. A linear reduction program, where inventory was reduced at a steady rate over a series of months resulted in a uniform lowering of the gross and net profit. When inventory reduction ceased, the gross profit figure immediately returned to a level equal to the baseline condition of "no reduction." The net profit rose to a level that exceeded the baseline condition due to the benefits of reduced carrying costs. However, this improvement was not substantiated by ANOVA testing. The improvement was evident when the mean values were graphed but the increase was not found to be significantly different using pairwise comparisons on the means. This indicates that the benefit gained from a reduction in carrying costs, when carrying costs are calculated at 1.5 percent per month of the inventory value, were not distinguishable. The stochasticity built into the model, both in the sales level and in the production capacity of the manufacturing model, likely lead to a high level of variation in the individual measures for gross and net profit. This would lead to an inability to identify a significant difference between the mean values for the baseline and the reduced inventory steady state conditions for net profit.

The key issue that must be kept in the forefront when evaluating the results discussed here is that the decreases in reported gross and net profit are, in a sense, a report on past poor performance. The fact that the reductions in reported gross and net profit coincide with the operational improvements brought by a lean program are unfortunate. The source of the problem, which ultimately led to the decline in the financial reports, is overproduction in past periods. Overproduction in traditional management accounting systems is recognized as an asset and is tracked on the balance sheet where it does not directly impact the income statement in the period in which it was produced. In a sense, overproduction is viewed as a positive by management accounting systems. Operations managers realize that they can increase machine utilization, a typical internal performance measure in manufacturing, by producing in excess of demand if necessary. When this occurs, the income statement for the period does not suffer, as the overproduction is moved to the balance sheet for tracking purposes. Included in the costs of the overproduction could be direct labor, direct materials, as well as factory overhead, depending on the management accounting method in use. Recognition of these stored costs is avoided in the current period and, therefore, does not negatively impact the income statement at that time. When this occurs, carrying costs on the over-production begin to accrue immediately. In addition, the risks of obsolescence or damage now exist. To later liquidate this inventory without negatively impacting the income statement, offsetting costs in other areas must be identified and eliminated. The costs that fit this category would need to be period costs that can be eliminated short term to provide the balancing transaction. Such costs are difficult to identify. Some authors argue that all costs are fixed in the short term, meaning that it is difficult to eliminate costs on an immediate basis. As a result, it is inevitable that reported operational performance would be negatively impacted by a lean program, particularly in the early months. The negative impact will continue until the benefits of reduced inventory carrying costs, indirect labor, scrap, and obsolescence costs reach a level sufficient to offset the negative impacts of the management accounting methods or until the inventory reduction subsides.

Also of interest in this study was the incidence of stock outages that occurred that could be identified as attributable to the lean effort. ANOVA testing identified that a difference did exist between the mean number of stock-outs between the three-inventory reduction policies modeled. Tukey tests on the means identified that the only mean that was different was that of the aggressive reduction program. The substantial variability in the sales demand created a risky environment as inventory levels were lowered. Safety stocks levels were initially two times the forecast for the high volume products. This target was reduced to 50 percent of the initial in both inventory reduction policies. As stated earlier, the actual sales demand in any one month period could range from 0 percent of the forecast to 220 percent of the forecast, when the stochasticity factor was set at the highest level with the standard deviation equal to 40 percent for the forecast value. Lower safety stocks offered less protection in the event that the latter occurred. In the extreme case of sales stochasticity, with the standard deviation of the normal distribution equal to 40 percent of the forecast values, the incidence of stock-outs was nearly ten times the quantity for inventory reduction policy 3 than the number of stock-outs under the mid value for stochasticity, 25 percent of the forecast value.

Comparison to Previous Studies

Previous research has chosen to focus on the area of evaluating which combination of manufacturing environment and management accounting system results in superior firm performance (Lea, 1998; Boyd, 1999). Net profit and total net profit are used as the metric for evaluation. Total net profit is defined as the accumulation of period net profit over some given time horizon. The current research is not concerned with the evaluation of manufacturing methods in an effort to determine the best method. It is an extremely difficult problem to identify the best manufacturing environment in terms of short- or long-term profit. MRP or batch may be superior to JIT in ship building, for instance, but TPC or TOC may be superior to JIT and MRP in industries with very high capital equipment costs. Lean strategies, however, can be defended in nearly any manufacturing environment. It is true that lean strategies would be most closely aligned with a JIT method of manufacturing, but aspects of lean could be applied to any manufacturing environment. If the strategies implemented had the effect of reducing on-hand inventories, then the impact on the income statement as previously discussed would be present. The research discussed in this document assumes that the benefits to a firm, which will come as the result of the adaptation of lean strategies, are evident and that lean has been accepted as the improvement strategy of choice. Additionally, this study accepts the fact that management accounting methods, required for the external reporting of operation performance, cannot be changed in the near future. It is believed that this view positions this study to be much better aligned with real-world applications.

Implications for Practice

The issue of greatest significance that was quantified by this research has to do with the ability of the financial reporting system to effectively erase the operational improvements brought by a lean manufacturing program during the initial stages. This issue is identified in the literature (Womack and Jones, 2003) but no previous study has explored the significance of this issue. This study has identified that the negative impact resulting from the shift of assets from the balance sheet to the income statement is essentially impossible to offset in the short term with operational savings brought by the lean program. It has been further identified that it is very likely that the financial reports will continue to report poorer firm performance until the decrease in inventory level ceases. This is due to the significant influence that the transfer of assets from the balance sheet to the income statement has on reported gross and net profit. This means that the problems in the design of the

financial systems will cause a perceived decrease in financial performance of the firm for many months and possibly years while a firm
works toward bringing down inventory levels. If this issue is not well
understood by the leadership of the firm and the other significant
stakeholders, issues will arise with the lean program. These issues
could easily result in resistance to the continuation of the program as
stated by Cunningham and Fiume (2003), "Managers who use standard
cost-based financial statements say I don't know what you're doing,
but whatever it is, stop it. Your killing profits." Armed with an understanding of the inevitable impact on the financial reports, managers
of firms initiating lean manufacturing programs would be in a better
position to be successful. This could be accomplished by preselling
projects with the understanding that the reported gross and net profits
will go down fictitiously throughout the initial months following the
initiation of the program. Using a model following the design of the
Excel model used for this study, a manager could emulate the impact
on the financial statements allowing them to predict, for a future range
of months or quarters, what the actual impact would be. The more
complete the model, the better the prediction, understanding that many
uncontrollable variables would need to be included in the model. The
knowledge of the fact that gross and net profit will decrease during
the initial stages of the lean program, specifically while inventories are
being reduced, will help to prevent the program from stalling. Having
the ability to accurately quantify the magnitude of the decrease through
a range of months or quarters would result in an increase in the
confidence level in the implementation team. The model in this study
identified that a decrease in net profit of nearly one-third would be
realized under a lean manufacturing program that would have the effect
of reducing on-hand inventories by 50 percent over the course of one
year and a reduction of two-thirds would be experienced if the inventory
levels were reduced at twice that rate. It was also identified that in the
second case, the reductions would continue for two quarters followed
by an immediate return to previous reported levels of profit plus the
gains from a lower inventory carrying cost. In an actual operation,
additional benefits would be identified prior to the initiation of the
project that could be quantified and added to the projections for preselling purposes. These abilities would significantly reduce the risks of
a lean program becoming stalled due to pressures from stakeholders
who use gross and net profit as a measure of financial health. Additionally, having the ability to predict the impact on key financial measures
would provide an additional tracking tool to the project manager.

Another important conclusion of this research is that the management accounting system can have a significant impact on the scale of the reported decreases in gross and net profit. The management accounting systems that include fewer cost categories in the attached costs of a product are more favorable to lean programs. These systems include direct costing and TPC, TPC being the least detrimental to a lean program. Unfortunately, neither of these systems is approved by the SEC and the IRS for external reporting. The systems most common throughout the manufacturing community, full absorption and ABC (Drury and Tayles, 1997), report the largest reductions in gross and net profit. However, reductions in gross and net profit will be reported regardless of the management accounting system used if the lean program leads to a reduction in on-hand inventories. For this reason, it is very important that additional metrics be established that will reflect operational improvements in the period in which they occur. Cash flow is a traditional measure that should be given a greater level of influence during a lean program, as it is a measure that will track the positive aspect of liquidating inventories. Additional metrics should be established that would track improvements in direct and indirect labor on a monthly basis. These improvements will be masked in any of the known management accounting systems except TPC. The reason for this is that the inventory being liquidated includes stored costs for direct labor and indirect labor. Until the reduction ceases, these stored costs will continue to confound the current financial reports.

An additional interesting discovery of this research has to do with the similarities in reported gross and net profit between the order-activity costing method and the most commonly used method of full-absorption costing (Drury and Tayles, 1997). The two methods followed similar trend lines for gross and net profit under all inventory reduction policies. This implies that the order-activity method emulates the performance of the method approved for external reporting by the SEC and IRS, meaning that the order-activity method is absorbing manufacturing costs proportionally to full absorption. However, the overhead rates that the order-activity method uses are significantly different from either full-absorption costing or ABC. The reason for the difference, as explained in Chapter 3, is that the order-activity method applies overhead costs using sales transactions as the allocation base as opposed to direct labor or some other traditional approach. The result of this allocation scheme shifts a greater proportion of the overhead costs to the low volume products. This results in a moderate decrease in product cost to high volume products while substantially increasing product costs of the low volume items. This shift would have a monumental impact on product mix decisions for production planners, sales managers, and other product line decision makers. Traditional allocation schemes are commonly attacked in the literature (Johnson and Kaplan, 1987; Drury and Tayles, 1997). The issue cited is that the allocation schemes do not allow an appropriate proportion of indirect costs to be allocated to the appropriate product. ABC attempts to correct this problem through a more elaborate system of allocation. Unfortunately, ABC has proven to be difficult and costly to maintain. The order-activity method has the benefit of being no more difficult to maintain than a full-absorption system using direct labor as the allocation base, while moving closer to the product costing accuracies offered by ABC. The order-activity method has the potential of providing product costs that are more accurate than ABC in situations where cost allocation is accomplished through product families versus individual products. The significance here is that better product cost information will lead to better decisions relating to product mix and financial management.

Limitations

This research is the first study of the longer-term dynamics of the impact on reported financial performance of a firm that results from the implementation of lean manufacturing strategies. Several interesting discoveries are presented and quantified but the reader must be cautioned that the results are unique to the operational characteristics modeled. However, as was stated previously, the modeled environment had many factors and attributes that would be common in a broad cross section of manufacturing. Therefore, the findings contained within this study have applications beyond the restrictions of the modeled environment and can be safely generalized to other operational situations.

The limitations of this study are primarily in the area of model operational mechanics and robustness. Further integration of the tools developed for the creation of the dataset would allow different scenarios to be run more easily. For instance, the tools provide for the entry of several operational factors, such as a rate for inventory carrying cost or rate of inventory reduction, that provide for flexibility in matching operational characteristics of other model firms. However, once changed, a new dataset must be run. The current interface between software packages requires a substantial manual effort. Automating the interface would allow new datasets to be generated for a large variety of operational scenarios, further expanding the body of knowledge in this area.

This study is limited to the manufacturing parameters described earlier in this chapter under the heading of Summary of Research Findings. More specifically, the simulation model contained three manufacturing cells, each supporting a specific product family. The numbers of operations were 18 for product family 1, 23 for product family 2, and 18 for product family 3. Product families consisted of ten products per family. The sales demand level within a family was distributed in a Pareto fashion with 50 percent of the family volume coming from one product, 36 percent from a second, 4 percent from the third and the remaining 10 percent distributed across the other seven products in a descending manner. This distribution is common in firms with multiple items within a family of products (Kensinger, 2003). The allocation base was direct labor and a 200 percent rate was used to determine manufacturing overhead for full-absorption costing. Family rates were used for ABC and were 150, 200, and 250 percent for families A, B, and C, respectively. Inventory carrying costs were set at 1.5 percent per month calculated on the ending inventory value each month for the full-absorption cost method. No other operational benefits were modeled and impact quantified. Reduction of indirect labor, reduction in scrap costs due to obsolescence, improvements in on-time shipping performance are all parameters that could be added to the model, enhancing the model's ability to more closely emulate a real-world application.

Many additional scenarios of model parameters can be envisioned that, if studied, would lead to a better understanding of the impact of this problem within a specific manufacturing operation. In addition, the study does not account for downtimes attributable to machine failure or material shortages, quality related problems, absenteeism, etc. Additionally, many items have been left out of the calculation for gross and net profit that would be present in a standard income statement. To be able to directly apply the calculated results from the modeling tools, these items would need to be added to the model. Their impact was viewed as uniform across management accounting methods in regard to this study and was therefore not included.

Suggestions for Future Research

As the scope of this study provides only a limited understanding of the issues discussed, the following recommendations for expansion of this research is presented.

Expansion of Time Horizon

In an application, it may be difficult to invoke the reductions in on-hand inventory at the rates modeled in this study. It would also be presumptuous to assume that all manufacturing operations would be able to work within the same time window of 12 months for the implementation of a lean program. Extending the model's time horizon would allow much more flexibility in matching the simulated environment with the real-world environment. An additional benefit from the expansion of the time horizon would be that results of gross and net profit could be evaluated for a series of years instead of months. This information could be used to communicate the long-term projected benefits of a lean program after the stakeholders have been informed of the short-term impacts that are expected.

Expansion of the Number of Inventory Reduction Policies Modeled per Dataset

It would be interesting to see the results of more than three inventory reduction policies per replication of the model. The current model included no inventory reduction, 50 percent reduction in safety stock target level over the course of 12 months, and 50 percent reduction in safety stock target level over 6 months and then level for the balance of the year. Once the parameters are chosen for inventory carrying cost, sales volume distribution within a family, and time horizon for the study, more could be learned by generating data from a broader set of inventory reduction scenarios. Reduction rates other than linear over a series of months would be more likely in practice and of significant interest from a research standpoint.

Customer Service Level Measures

The measure of customer service level for this study was limited to counting stock-out situations. In the event of a stock-out, the sale that caused it was lost. An expansion of the model could include measures for fill rate, days late, and lost sales based on model parameters.

Reduction in Reporting Cycle

Reducing the model execution cycle from a monthly schedule to a weekly or daily schedule would substantially enhance the tool's ability to model a real-world operation. This improvement would not be practical without an automated interface between software packages. This enhancement would be particularly enabling to the modeling of a JIT operation.

Expansion of Income Statements

Expanding the income statements to include all cost categories of the operation to be modeled would be necessary to be able to directly apply the results from the simulation to projections for the operation. This expansion would move the model from being a generic tool with a broad application to one with a limited application, but with substantially better accuracy in regard to the application of the results. Thought should be given to the creation of a user interface within the VBA application that would allow users to customize the tool for their application by selecting operational parameters, filling in data windows, and importing data files from actual operational performance for model setup purposes.

Use of Distributions Other Than Normal

In this study, all programmed model variability utilized a normal distribution. The argument for the use of this distribution is as follows:

- Sales variability from forecast: It was the developers opinion that there is typically an equal likelihood of missing the sales forecast on the high side as on the low side. In addition, there is a greater likelihood of the forecast missing the actual sales figure slightly than missing it substantially. For these reasons normal was chosen.
- Processing time variability: The manufacturing system modeled in this study was based on an operation that incorporated a significant level of manual operation, i.e., little automation. It was the developers' opinion that, with manual operations, there is an equal likelihood of an operation finishing before the standard time as after. In addition, the likelihood of finishing near the standard time is higher than significantly early or late. Therefore, the normal distribution was chosen as the most appropriate.

The use of distributions other than normal could result in significantly different results. A strong case could be made for the application of other distributions if the design assumptions were changed. For instance, if a highly automated process was being modeled, the negative exponential or Weibull distribution may be more appropriate choices with the likelihood of more operations ending above the mean than below. This expansion of the model would provide a more robust understanding of the impact on the financial measures resulting from a lean program.

Further Development of the Order-Activity Product Costing Method

The order-activity method for allocating overhead costs offers significant advantages over systems in use today. The order-activity method provides allocation factors that follow the logic of ABC to a certain degree without the significant costs of maintenance common with ABC systems. The fact that the order-activity method includes all the components of costs, including direct labor, direct material, and factory overhead, make this method a candidate for becoming an approved system for external reporting purposes. The results of this study provide an indication of the profound difference in calculated product costs resulting from the application of these concepts. Future research activity should focus in the area of identifying differences in firm financial performance resulting from the application of the order-activity method in product mix decisions. An additional aspect of future work in this area should focus in the area of verification of the accuracy of the order-activity method in identifying actual product costs when compared to established methods. This work is further developed in Chapter 6. A final recommendation focuses on development work in the area of commercialization of this approach of cost allocation. Commercialization efforts would focus on the integration of logic into existing MRP or enterprise resource planning costing modules. Once integrated into the costing logic, maintenance of the system would be less labor intensive then either ABC or labor- or asset-based systems.

References

Boyd, L. H. (1999). Production Planning and Control and Cost Accounting Systems: Effects on Management Decision Making and Firm Performance, Ph.D. dissertation, University of Georgia, Athens, GA, UMI Co., Ann Arbor, MI.

Cunningham, J. and Fiume, O. (2003). *Real Numbers: Management Accounting in a Lean Organization,* Managing Times Press, Durham, NC.

Drury, C. and Tayles, M. (1997). Evidence on the financial accounting mentality debate: a research note, *British Accounting Review*, 29, 263–276.

Johnson, H. T. and Kaplan, R. S. (1987). *Relevance Lost: The Rise and Fall of Management Accounting*, Harvard Business School Press, Boston, MA.

Krajewski, L. J., King, B. E., Ritzman, L. P., and Wong, D. S. (1987). Kanban, MRP, and shaping the manufacturing environment, *Management Science*, 33(1), 39–57.

Lea, B.-R. (1998). The Impact of Management Accounting Alternatives in Different Manufacturing Environments, Ph.D. dissertation, Clemson University, Clemson, SC, UMI Co., Ann Arbor, MI.

Womack, J. and Jones, D. (2003). *Lean Thinking: Banish Waste and Create Wealth in Your Corporation,* The Free Press, New York, NY.

Chapter 6

Impact of the Pareto Distribution on Product Cost Calculations

A basic description of an overhead allocation system based on operational activity levels, measured by the number of sales orders, was presented in Chapter 3. Further studies of the concepts introduced there have been documented in this chapter. The order-activity costing method is a concept under development designed to address the shortcomings of previous cost allocation schemes. This concept is predicated on the premise that operational activity level is distributed in a manner that follows a Pareto distribution when looking at the various end items of production. The Pareto distribution can be applied to a multitude of situations to explain behavior. Simply stated it means that 80 percent of the effect of some event is caused by 20 percent of the input to that event. One example of this in sales terms would be that 80 percent of sales dollars are the result of 20 percent of the product line. Surprisingly, this rule holds true in most cases studied over the past 15 years (Kensinger, 2005). Research has identified that the phenomenon can be better explained by a Pareto distribution where 80 percent of sales dollars come from 20 percent of the product line. Another 15 percent of the sales dollars come from 30 percent of the product line. The remaining 5 percent of the sales dollars come from 50 percent of the product line. These percentages often hold true when looking at all products offered by a firm or when looking within a product grouping or family within a firm.

The Pareto distribution of production volumes introduces a concern in the accuracy of the costing system with regard to cross-subsidizing (Koogler and Stell, 1991). A product becomes cross-subsidized when a portion of the overhead costs associated with the production of that product are shifted onto another product by the product costing system. Within the context of the Pareto distribution of production volumes, this shift occurs when a portion of the overhead costs from the lower volume products are borne by the higher volume products. The mechanics of this shift will be explained in the following text.

In a traditional full-absorption costing system, the significance of the Pareto distribution in terms of the allocation of overhead costs is completely lost. When these cost accounting practices were developed, direct labor in the United States constituted about 60 percent of the total product cost. Today direct labor in the United States accounts for 4 to 10 percent of the total product cost (Cunningham and Fiume, 2003; Boothroyd Dewhurst, 2005). In 68 to 73 percent of all cases studied, direct labor hour content was used for the determination of overhead distribution (Drury and Tayles, 1997). Under the full-absorption method, all overhead costs, including costs such as engineering, quality, purchasing, maintenance, and production supervision, are proportioned based on the amount of direct labor hours required to produce the product. Arguably, none of these overhead components fluctuate in proportion to direct labor hours. However, they are impacted by the number of orders that run through the manufacturing plant for the various products. Let us take a closer look at the case of the high volume product, the 20 percent category in the 80/20 distribution. This group of products would have a tendency to run through the plant on production orders of larger quantities. Therefore, if the costs mentioned above are more closely related to the quantity of orders and not direct labor hours, then the distribution of the costs should be based upon the order activity per unit instead of the direct labor content. Otherwise, the higher volume products will be cross-subsidizing the lower volume products. Applying this concept to a family of products whose annual volume follows a Pareto distribution would have the effect of lowering the calculated product cost for the higher volume products while profoundly increasing the calculated product costs for the 50 percent of the products that account for 5 percent of the sales dollars.

Although ABC can lead to a more accurate assignment of overhead costs to cost objects, such as products, than traditional systems (Cooper and Kaplan, 1988), ABC still fails to address the significance of the Pareto distribution of product volumes (Homburg, 2005). This is the result of aggregation errors that come as a result of pooling costs in a method that minimizes system complexity (Datar and Gupta, 1994). An example of this would be engineering costs that are the result of the engineering department's support of a family of products. For simplicity, the engineering department provides a percentage of total departmental effort used to support the product family. However, the family may contain dozens of products, which follow the Pareto distribution in terms of production volumes. Within the ABC system, all units would be viewed as equal and would equally share in the distribution of the engineering costs. However, as in the earlier example of full-absorption costing, the higher volume products would not be consuming the engineering resource in a similar amount per unit to the low volume products. Therefore, in the ABC system, the higher volume products still cross-subsidize the lower volume products.

The rest of this chapter is organized as follows. It describes the problem including the research questions that form the basis for this study. Next, various cost accounting methods, particularly the proposed order-activity method is described; and also, the integrated computer simulation research model used in this study is presented. The following section presents the results derived from the integrated computer simulation model. The discussion section analyzes various hypotheses associated with the research questions. The chapter wraps up with the section that summarizes conclusions and also presents practical and research implications from this research.

Definition of Problem

A fundamental problem with current allocation systems is that the traditionally accepted base has little or no relationship to the actual cost (Boyd and Cox, 2002). Table 6.1 contains a list of typically allocated costs, indicating the relationship to traditional bases as well as the proposed order-activity base. As can be seen from the table, the disconnect between current thinking in the area of product costing and reality presents a difficult challenge to the accounting function in regard to the calculation of reasonably accurate product costs using traditional methods. Based on the relationships identified in Table 6.1,

Table 6.1 Allocated (Indirect) Production Costs and Base Relationship

Allocated Cost	Consumed as a Function of	
	Direct Labor/Direct Materials/Machine Time/Plant Space	Production or Sales Order Activity
Order entry		X
Production scheduling		X
Purchasing		X
Shipping/receiving		X
Production supervision		X
Setup		X
Maintenance	X	X
Quality assurance/ quality control		X
Production engineering		X
Human resources	X	
Accounts receivable/ accounts payable		X
Warehousing		X
Transportation		X
Customer service		X
Production management	X	X
Rent		
Utilities		
Taxes		
Depreciation		

it could be argued that order-activity would be a significant improvement as an allocation base with respect to the indirect production costs listed. The impact of this thinking can be better understood through the evaluation of Figure 6.1. This chart identifies the annual consumption of direct labor by product number manufactured on the left hand

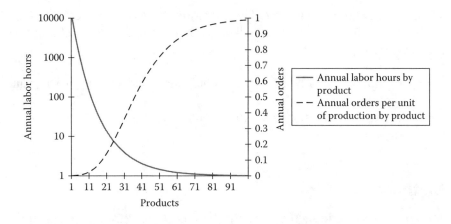

Figure 6.1 Relationship of annual direct labor consumption versus orders per product produced.

y axis and the corresponding orders per product displayed on the right hand y axis. Products are shown on the x axis. The relationship represented in this chart is common in manufacturing according to observations over the past two decades (Kensinger, 2005). This data indicates that the products with lower annual volumes are consuming more of the allocated resources per product annually, based on the relationship represented in Figure 6.1, than the higher volume products. On the extreme ends of the chart, the differences are profoundly different.

This research explores the problems identified with traditional costing methods through an evaluation of an alternative costing method. The research questions of interest are as follows.

Research Questions

Is the magnitude of difference in the calculated product cost noteworthy when using full-absorption versus order-activity costing?

H_o: Product cost values do not differ substantially.
H_a: Product cost values differ substantially.

Does the use of order-activity costing significantly impact the reported financial results of a firm?

H_o: Values for net profit do not differ significantly.
H_a: Values for net profit differ significantly.

Would the differences in calculated product cost or reported financial results under an order-activity costing environment cause a change to a firm's strategic direction?

H_o: Changes in financial factors would have no effect on strategic direction.

H_a: Changes in financial factors would have an effect on strategic direction.

Methods

The proposed order-activity method of cost accounting is currently being researched as an alternative method to others previously discussed. The proposed order-activity method uses a new approach to address the issue of an appropriate allocation base. As mentioned earlier, the traditional approach of full-absorption costing uses direct labor, direct materials, machine time, or plant square footage, among other bases to apportion overhead costs. The full absorption method of costing has been under attack in the literature for many years (Johnson and Kaplan, 1987; Cooper and Kaplan, 1988; Kaplan, 1994; Garrison and Noreen, 1994; Drury and Tayles, 1997; Lere, 2001; Nachtmann and Needy, 2003; Cunningham and Fiume, 2003; Soloman, 2003). ABC attempts to improve on this method by identifying cost drivers by product family for the equitable distribution of costs. The ABC method is an improvement over full absorption but still has two primary drawbacks:

1. The system is costly to maintain as the drivers and apportionment are determined through interviews and will change over time, requiring continued follow-up interviews to make adjustments (Haldane, 1998).
2. For purposes of efficiency, products are grouped into families and overhead costs factors are then applied by family. Not all products within a family will necessarily consume activities in the same apportionment as others in the family.

The proposed order-activity method addresses the issue of cost allocation based on unit production volumes. The types of costs that are being distributed through allocations have among them engineering, purchasing, accounting, maintenance, shipping and receiving, and others, many of which are influenced by transactions. This is to say that many of the allocated costs are equal for an order of 1 or 1000 products. When direct labor is used as the base, the total direct labor for the order is used to apportion the allocated component of the total product cost, i.e., direct labor, direct materials, and overhead. When the order is for 1 versus 1000, then the allocated amount is 1/1000th of the amount determined for an order for 1000, although the support from engineering, purchasing, accounting, shipping, and receiving will often be the same for either case. In this situation, the high volume product is penalized disproportionately, carrying a greater amount of the overhead costs than justified, thereby cross-subsidizing the lower volume products. The proposed order-activity method attempts to correct this by setting allocations based on transactions. One measure for transactions is the number of production orders. This is a simple number to retrieve from a production order entry system, eliminating the high maintenance costs of ABC. The factoring for allocation is based on the following equations:

$$transaction\_per\_product = $$

$$\frac{\displaystyle\sum_{month=1}^{12} production\_orders\_by\_product}{\displaystyle\sum_{month=1}^{12} units\_produced\_by\_product} \qquad (6.1)$$

$$order\_activity\_cost = \frac{annual\_budgeted\_fixed\_costs}{\displaystyle\sum_{all\_products} annual\_sales\_orders} \qquad (6.2)$$

$$product\_cost = direct\_labor + direct\_material + $$
$$(transaction\_per\_product * order\_activity\_cost) \qquad (6.3)$$

A research model was constructed using ProModel simulation software, Microsoft Excel, and Microsoft Visual Basic to evaluate the impact of the proposed order-activity method as compared to the more traditional methods of full-absorption costing and ABC. The metrics used for evaluation were calculated product cost and reported net profit. Three product families were identified, namely A, B, and C. Three families provided a contrast in the application of cost drivers under the ABC scenario. The product families are composed of ten unique products per family. Ten products allowed a relatively simple application of the Pareto principle for production volume distribution within the given family. The annual production volumes for the ten products within each family followed a Pareto distribution with product 1 (e.g., A1) having the greatest annual volume. The burden rate used for full-absorption calculations was 200 percent of direct labor for all products. The burden rate used for ABC was 250 percent for product family A, 200 percent for product family B, and 100 percent for product family C. To establish a burden rate under the proposed order-activity method, the following procedure was used:

1. An annual number of production orders, by product, was identified with the more popular family constituting more production orders by product than the less popular families. The order of popularity was family A followed by C and finally B.
2. The number of units per order by product was calculated using forecasted annual volumes for each product within the family. The reciprocal of this number was a fraction identifying the number of orders per product (Equation 6.1).
3. A cost per order was established by calculating the annual overhead pool using the forecast and the overhead values by product for the full-absorption method of costing and dividing this value by the total annual production orders (Equation 6.2).
4. Finally, an order cost per product was established by multiplying the orders per product value and the cost per order. This value was added to the direct labor and direct material costs to establish a product cost (Equation 6.3).

Results

The simulation model was executed for 12 iterations, simulating monthly cycles of a year's production. This 12-month cycle was replicated 35 times to create the dataset for evaluation. Replication was used as the method to capture the variance of dependent variable means. The required number of replications was estimated using the formula adapted from Law and Kelton (2000):

$$n \geq \left(\frac{t_{n-1,1-\alpha/2} * S_{(n)}}{E} \right)^2$$

where

n = number of replications

$t_{n-1,1-\alpha/2}$ = Student's t value with $n-1$ degrees of freedom

$S_{(n)}$ = sample standard deviation of the dependent variable

E = desired level of precision, 90 percent confidence interval for this study

The dependent variable chosen to measure variability for this model was the average time in the system for a unit of product A1, B1, and C1 to complete. These were the highest volume parts in each family based on the Pareto factors used. The model was run with ten replications, ensuring a different seed in the random number stream for each replication. Descriptive statistics were generated from the ten data points to obtain an estimate of the standard deviation, S. The half length of the confidence interval, E, was set at 0.05 percent of the sample mean. Using α = .05, the equation identified a value for n = 34.917. Therefore, to obtain the desired level of statistical confidence, 35 replications were required for each month of the 12-month simulation periods or 420 simulation runs to produce the dataset. It is important to remember that the production unit volumes used to create the various income statements in this evaluation were identical for the three cost allocation methods. Figure 6.2 shows the calculated monthly reported average net profit under each method at the cost of goods manufactured level between methods. Accruals and variance adjustments were not included in the financial statements, as they would

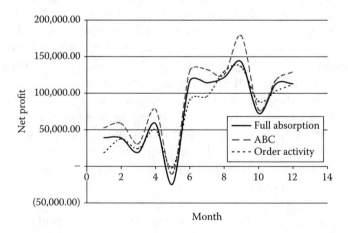

Figure 6.2   Reported net profit comparison of methods excluding variance correction.

have subdued the differences between systems that the study targeted to understand.

The gap between the full-absorption plot and the ABC line indicates the mismatch that can occur due to the selection of burden rate by family. Although at the aggregate level of reporting, i.e., the income statement, the net profit under the proposed order-activity method tracks closely to what is experienced under the full-absorption method, the impact at the unit cost level of this approach is significant, as can be seen in Table 6.2.

Discussion

Review of the three research questions:

1. Is the magnitude of difference in calculated product cost note-worthy when using full-absorption versus order-activity costing?
   H_o: Values do not differ substantially.
   H_a: Values differ substantially.

Table 6.2 summarized the impact to calculated product cost at the unit level. As can be seen in the table, the unit level cost resulting from order-activity costing for products in the high volume portion of the Pareto curve are moderately reduced as compared to the results of full absorption at a 200 percent burden rate. Moving down the curve to the lower volume products produces significantly different unit level product costs than either full-absorption costing or ABC. The reason for the difference, as explained earlier, is that the proposed order-activity method applies overhead costs using production order transactions as the allocation base as opposed to direct labor or some other traditional approach. The result of this allocation scheme shifts a greater propor-tion of the overhead costs to the low volume products where they belong, as has been argued. This results in a moderate decrease in product cost to high volume products while substantially increasing product costs of the low volume products. Therefore, we reject H_o and accept that the values produced under the order-activity costing approach are noteworthy.

1. Does the use of order-activity costing significantly impact the reported financial results of a firm?
   H_o: Values for net profit do not differ significantly.
   H_a: Values for net profit differ significantly.

Table 6.2   Calculated Product Costs Comparisons for Family A Using Full-Absorption, ABC, and Proposed Order-Activity Methods

Component of Cost	Full Absorption Product	Full Absorption Dollar Value	ABC Product	ABC Dollar Value	Proposed Order Activity Product	Proposed Order Activity Dollar Value
Direct labor	A1	3.7167	A1	3.7167	A1	3.7167
Direct materials		25.0000		25.0000		25.0000
Overhead		7.4333		9.2917		2.5400
Total		36.1500		38.0083		31.2566
Direct labor	A2	3.7167	A2	3.7167	A2	3.7167
Direct materials		25.0000		25.0000		25.0000
Overhead		7.4333		9.2917		3.4414
Total		36.1500		38.0083		32.1581
Direct labor	A3	3.3000	A3	3.3000	A3	3.3000
Direct materials		15.0000		15.0000		15.0000
Overhead		6.6000		8.2500		34.9770
Total		24.9000		26.5500		53.2770
Direct labor	A4	3.3000	A4	3.3000	A4	3.3000
Direct materials		15.0000		15.0000		15.0000
Overhead		6.6000		8.2500		45.0070
Total		24.9000		26.5500		63.3070
Direct labor	A5	3.3000	A5	3.3000	A5	3.3000
Direct materials		15.0000		15.0000		15.0000
Overhead		6.6000		8.2500		66.0425
Total		24.9000		26.5500		84.3425
Direct labor	A6	3.7167	A6	3.7167	A6	3.7167
Direct materials		25.0000		25.0000		25.0000
Overhead		7.4333		9.2917		84.1364
Total		36.1500		38.0083		112.8530

(continued)

Table 6.2 (continued)   Calculated Product Costs Comparisons for Family A Using Full-Absorption, ABC, and Proposed Order-Activity Methods

Component of Cost	Full Absorption		ABC		Proposed Order Activity	
	Product	Dollar Value	Product	Dollar Value	Product	Dollar Value
Direct labor	A7	3.7167	A7	3.7167	A7	3.7167
Direct materials		25.0000		25.0000		25.0000
Overhead		7.4333		9.2917		99.9234
Total		36.1500		38.0083		128.6400
Direct labor	A8	4.8500	A8	4.8500	A8	4.8500
Direct materials		35.0000		35.0000		35.0000
Overhead		9.7000		12.1250		132.5602
Total		49.5500		51.9750		172.4102
Direct labor	A9	4.8500	A9	4.8500	A9	4.8500
Direct materials		35.0000		35.0000		35.0000
Overhead		9.7000		12.1250		172.2044
Total		49.5500		51.9750		212.0544
Direct labor	A10	4.8500	A10	4.8500	A10	4.8500
Direct materials		35.0000		35.0000		35.0000
Overhead		9.7000		12.1250		238.6770
Total		49.5500		51.9750		278.5270

An interesting discovery of this research has to do with the similarities in the reported net profit between the proposed order-activity costing method and the most commonly used method of full-absorption costing (Drury and Tayles, 1997). The two methods followed similar trend lines for net profit as seen in Figure 6.2. This implies that the proposed order-activity method, as well as the ABC method, emulate the performance of the method approved for external reporting by the SEC and IRS, meaning that the proposed order-activity method is absorbing manufacturing costs proportionally to full absorption. Therefore, we accept H_o and agree that the values for net profit do not differ substantially between methods.

1. Would the differences in calculated product cost or reported financial results under an order-activity costing environment cause a change to a firm's strategic direction?

   H_o: Changes in financial factors would have no effect on strategic direction.

   H_a: Changes in financial factors would have an effect on strategic direction.

The shift in costs at the product level would have a monumental impact on product mix decisions for production planners, sales managers, and other product line decision makers. As an example, we will refer to the product values in Table 6.2. Product A1, being a high volume product, could be expected to have significant pricing pressures in the market as a result of being an attractive product for other manufacturers to offer, due to volume. Conversely, A10, being a low volume product and possibly a "special or custom" product in the market, could command a higher selling price due to lower competition. Under these circumstances, using full-absorption costing A1 may appear to be a break even or even a loss leader product but A10 would appear to be a high margin product. However, under the proposed order-activity method, it can be seen that A10 would need to support a selling price greater than 500 percent of the perceived costs under full absorption to be profitable if the proposed order-activity costing method produces more accurate cost figures. Under this scenario, the sales function would promote the sale of a product with potentially disastrous negative sales margins while deemphasizing product that actually delivers a positive margin. Therefore, we reject H_o and conclude that the resulting changes in product cost would have an impact on strategic decision making within a firm.

The above analysis on the research question 1 through question 3 is summarized in Table 6.3.

Conclusions and Implications of This Research

Traditional allocation schemes are commonly attacked in the literature (Johnson and Kaplan, 1987; Cooper and Kaplan, 1988; Kaplan, 1994; Garrison and Noreen, 1994; Drury and Tayles, 1997; Tayles and Walley, 1997; Lere, 2001; Nachtmann and Needy, 2003; Cunningham and Fiume, 2003; Soloman, 2003). The issue most commonly cited is that the allocation schemes do not allow an appropriate proportion of indirect costs to be allocated to the appropriate product due to the

Table 6.3   Research Questions Summary

	Research Question	Hypothesis	Conclusion
1	Is the magnitude of difference in calculated product cost noteworthy when using full-absorption versus order-activity costing?	H_o: Values do not differ substantially. H_a: Values differ significantly.	H_o: Reject. H_a: Accept.
2	Does the use of order activity costing significantly impact the reported financial results of a firm?	H_o: Values for net profit do not differ significantly. H_a: Values for net profit differ significantly.	H_o: Accept. H_a: Reject.
3	Would the differences in calculated product cost or reported financial results under an order-activity costing environment cause a change to a firm's strategic direction?	H_o: Changes in financial factors would have no effect on strategic direction. H_a: Changes in financial factors would have an effect on strategic direction.	H_o: Reject. H_a: Accept.

allocation base being used. ABC attempts to correct this problem through a more elaborate system of allocation. Unfortunately, ABC has proven to be difficult and costly to maintain.

In contrast, the proposed order-activity method has the benefit of being no more difficult to maintain than a full-absorption system using direct labor as the allocation base, while improving on the product costing accuracies offered by ABC. The significance here is that better product cost information will lead to better decisions relating to product mix and financial management.

The proposed order-activity method for allocating overhead costs offers significant advantages over systems in use today. The proposed order-activity method provides allocation factors that follow the logic of ABC costing, in terms of attaching costs by activity level, without the significant costs of maintenance common with ABC systems. Additionally, the proposed order-activity method improves on accuracies achieved by ABC by offering the ability to apply the allocation base to individual products instead of families of products. The fact that the proposed order-activity method includes all the components of costs, including direct labor, direct material, and factory overhead, make this method a candidate for becoming an approved system for external reporting purposes.

Implications of this research with regard to operational decisions influenced by product costs are profound. The impact on product cost calculations at the unit level shown in Table 6.2 would undoubtedly lead managers to alternative conclusions with respect to product pricing, markets to enter and exit, products to emphasize through sales efforts, and those to deemphasize as well as finished goods inventory decisions. Bottom-line results would track more closely with operational decisions when those decisions are predicated on accurate information.

The focus of this study was in an area that did not allow the potential of the proposed order-activity method to be fully quantified or understood. Future research activity should focus in the area of identifying differences in firm financial performance resulting from the application of the proposed order-activity method in product mix decisions. An additional aspect of future work on this topic should focus in the area of verification of the accuracy of the proposed order-activity method in identifying actual product costs when compared to established methods.

Costing system changes required to implement the proposed order-activity product costing approach are also unknown at this time. This work should be conducted jointly with a costing system provider such as SAP, Oracle, JD Edwards, Made-to-Manage, etc. Field-testing of this theory should include a period of dual system operation, allowing a comparison of the results obtained at the net profit levels over some period. Comparison of the averages over time also appears to be of interest as financial results appear to be equal or nearly equal when viewed on a multi-period basis, i.e., year-to-date after several periods.

References

Boothroyd Dewhurst, Inc. (2005). DFMA Overview, http://www.dfma.com/.

Boyd, L. H. and Cox, J. F. (2002). Optimal decision making using cost accounting information, *International Journal of Production Research*, 40(8), 1879–1898.

Cooper, R. and Kaplan, R. S. (1988). How cost accounting distorts product costs, *Management Accounting*, 69(10): 20–27.

Cunningham, J. and Fiume, O. (2003). *Real Numbers: Management Accounting in a Lean Organization*, Managing Times Press, Durham, NC.

Datar, S. and Gupta, M. (1994). Aggregation, specification and measurement errors in product costing, *The Accounting Review*, 69(4), 567–591.

Drury, C. and Tayles, M. (1997). Evidence on the financial accounting mentality debate: a research note, *British Accounting Review*, 29, 263–276.

Garrison, R. H. and Noreen, E. W. (1994). *Managerial Accounting*, Irwin, Inc., Burr Ridge, IL.

Haldane, G. (1998). Fixed overheads, *Accountancy*, 121(1257), 60–62.

Homburg, C. (2005). Using relative profits as an alternative to activity-based costing, *International Journal of Production Economics*, 95, 387–397.

Johnson, H. T. and Kaplan, R. S. (1987). *Relevance Lost: The Rise and Fall of Management Accounting*, Harvard Business School Press, Boston, MA.

Kaplan, R. S. (1994). Management accounting (1984–1994): development of new practice and theory, *Management Accounting Research*, 5, 247–260.

Kensinger, K. (2005). Allocation schemes in cost accounting, personal interviews.

Koogler, P. and Stell, R. (1991). Cross subsidies in overhead application, *Journal of Accounting Education*, 9, 149–159.

Law, A. M. and Kelton, W. D. (2000). *Simulation Modeling and Analysis*, 3rd ed., McGraw Hill, New York, NY.

Lere, J. C. (2001). Your product-costing system seems to be broken: now what? *Industrial Marketing Management*, 30, 587–598.

Microsoft Excel 2002, Microsoft Corporation, One Microsoft Way, Redmond, WA 98052-6399.

Microsoft Visual Basic for Applications 2002, Microsoft Corporation, One Microsoft Way, Redmond, WA 98052-6399.

Nachtmann, H. and Needy, K. (2003). Methods for handling uncertainty in activity based costing systems, *The Engineering Economist*, 48(3), 259–282.

ProModel Simulation Software, version 6.1, ProModel Corporation, 556 East Technology Ave., Orem, UT 84097.

Soloman, J. M. (2003). *Who's Counting?* WCM Associates, Fort Wayne, IN.

Tayles, M. and Walley, P. (1997). Integrating manufacturing and management accounting strategy: case study insights, *International Journal of Production Economics*, 53, 43–55.

Appendix 1

Simulation Data

Inventory Reduction Policy 1 — No-Reduction; Maintain Finished Goods Inventory Levels throughout the 12-Month Evaluation Period

Finished goods inventory trends
Inventory reduction policy: no reduction

Percent Series (yr)	Jan	Feb	Mar	Apr	May	Jun	Jul	Aug	Sep	Oct	Nov	Dec	sum	mean	std. dev.
1	8.34%	37.95%	16.10%	13.21%	29.39%	24.70%	16.90%	21.90%	6.93%	19.12%	19.81%	26.28%	240.63%	20.05%	8.81%
2	10.27%	33.30%	23.13%	15.82%	10.78%	40.30%	16.88%	17.83%	15.02%	12.70%	26.81%	6.10%	228.93%	19.08%	10.08%
3	14.71%	15.99%	25.20%	23.26%	11.64%	25.10%	14.39%	48.86%	8.64%	20.82%	6.45%	26.42%	241.49%	20.12%	11.27%
4	24.58%	20.99%	14.27%	14.70%	16.75%	29.89%	13.97%	18.93%	13.10%	34.50%	7.22%	40.73%	249.65%	20.80%	9.87%
5	24.30%	17.62%	23.01%	12.10%	24.35%	26.07%	-4.88%	27.47%	17.96%	35.67%	14.32%	12.49%	230.48%	19.21%	10.26%
6	25.11%	22.20%	13.11%	20.85%	20.51%	31.43%	7.38%	29.75%	6.61%	14.74%	38.82%	9.56%	240.08%	20.01%	10.16%
7	9.70%	42.82%	1.11%	23.88%	19.73%	44.01%	14.33%	3.78%	29.98%	33.98%	0.61%	28.65%	252.59%	21.05%	15.38%
8	27.18%	14.37%	30.47%	-1.57%	36.31%	15.54%	25.07%	7.78%	25.03%	19.79%	16.11%	43.37%	259.45%	21.62%	12.34%
9	22.73%	24.27%	26.00%	5.25%	25.58%	16.83%	29.41%	17.96%	9.95%	13.46%	33.12%	15.90%	240.45%	20.04%	8.23%
10	32.39%	7.09%	33.16%	12.81%	15.08%	23.35%	11.12%	32.78%	24.86%	7.15%	14.55%	36.14%	250.48%	20.87%	10.84%
11	17.95%	21.38%	17.43%	24.93%	14.11%	22.88%	17.69%	18.32%	21.86%	28.55%	28.45%	8.90%	242.44%	20.20%	5.71%
12	23.10%	15.52%	13.64%	24.25%	26.60%	9.00%	26.30%	30.49%	11.94%	23.71%	15.47%	16.21%	236.22%	19.69%	6.84%
13	28.37%	14.24%	20.32%	27.50%	17.46%	14.88%	33.27%	12.91%	3.36%	45.79%	6.97%	22.81%	247.90%	20.66%	11.81%
14	15.17%	27.15%	12.39%	34.37%	16.07%	22.72%	11.12%	26.26%	23.93%	24.53%	13.42%	13.92%	241.06%	20.09%	7.36%
15	22.41%	20.96%	10.15%	31.04%	28.23%	1.99%	19.27%	34.29%	6.58%	18.81%	27.44%	30.30%	251.45%	20.95%	10.25%
16	33.33%	25.52%	2.97%	23.93%	28.92%	3.76%	33.11%	10.29%	24.66%	27.64%	21.37%	6.78%	237.10%	19.76%	10.74%
17	24.95%	6.29%	24.56%	35.98%	8.16%	14.87%	29.82%	7.94%	0.83%	17.71%	9.34%	21.35%	236.00%	19.67%	10.50%
18	14.22%	2.25%	47.09%	5.51%	23.54%	43.25%	-0.93%	63.69%	30.37%	23.80%	11.33%	34.22%	276.46%	23.04%	20.71%
19	8.54%	28.16%	11.81%	31.78%	14.48%	32.37%	4.28%	19.38%	22.73%	23.80%	11.20%	18.80%	240.66%	20.06%	9.23%
20	21.51%	39.87%	10.50%	36.07%	6.70%	38.71%	12.27%	14.41%	25.25%	8.98%	29.94%	34.83%	263.54%	21.96%	13.12%
21	32.31%	23.94%	7.53%	10.00%	46.31%	18.06%	19.86%	13.40%	26.31%	14.15%	29.93%	12.72%	242.66%	20.22%	10.56%
22	25.00%	1.91%	32.94%	12.87%	15.19%	27.17%	34.18%	8.43%	32.62%	13.89%	19.08%	23.19%	247.46%	20.62%	10.40%
23	33.48%	11.09%	20.63%	14.63%	16.74%	31.48%	10.38%	16.76%	13.94%	37.57%	10.54%	10.97%	238.42%	19.87%	9.62%
24	20.28%	12.18%	3.68%	30.19%	30.99%	19.52%	21.29%	21.19%	21.08%	11.83%	35.56%	17.11%	249.11%	20.76%	9.95%
25	21.70%	19.43%	24.85%	6.90%	32.81%	27.87%	14.14%	22.87%	17.21%	38.25%	0.25%	35.14%	255.50%	21.29%	11.02%
26	22.46%	29.51%	10.31%	20.06%	26.13%	-1.55%	2.43%	25.54%	20.09%	31.72%	16.93%	19.78%	249.19%	20.77%	8.39%
27	22.88%	14.99%	22.03%	18.20%	30.46%	30.75%	52.38%	5.12%	8.66%	45.66%	5.23%	15.02%	250.09%	20.84%	15.88%
28	17.57%	9.12%	20.30%	26.54%	22.14%	8.20%	5.39%	28.24%	9.87%	28.15%	17.10%	29.72%	248.97%	20.75%	8.85%
29	15.32%	23.00%	15.01%	23.93%	22.21%	9.32%	28.76%	34.98%	18.31%	27.61%	12.44%	12.73%	236.31%	19.69%	8.37%
30	10.71%	24.32%	35.35%	0.90%	33.70%	23.74%	16.42%	39.95%	18.27%	30.64%	24.38%	23.48%	249.85%	20.82%	11.73%
31	36.69%	34.41%	19.75%	19.50%	36.78%	26.62%	8.75%	21.32%	15.43%	26.81%	2.80%	34.71%	254.79%	21.23%	11.36%
32	19.89%	3.77%	26.23%	23.12%	18.02%	21.64%	12.54%	16.48%	10.85%	26.16%	20.52%	30.38%	249.21%	20.77%	9.22%
33	16.41%	19.36%	14.52%	9.94%	19.86%	22.46%	25.14%	15.23%	16.52%	15.96%	35.67%	16.47%	235.31%	19.61%	6.74%
34	7.02%	29.34%	21.16%	30.96%	22.03%	22.83%	24.44%	10.71%	24.83%	12.38%	13.05%	32.56%	235.29%	19.61%	7.12%
35		41.20%	9.76%	19.12%	10.03%			14.58%			21.78%	24.75%	244.56%	20.38%	10.02%
mean	21.11%	21.01%	18.87%	19.12%	22.22%	22.50%	17.79%	21.71%	17.43%	23.47%	17.66%	22.64%			
std. dev	7.86%	10.96%	9.89%	10.15%	9.03%	10.99%	11.46%	12.54%	8.25%	10.29%	10.34%	10.14%			

Finished goods inventory trends
Inventory reduction policy: no reduction

Dollars Series (yr)	Jan	Feb	Mar	Apr	May	Jun	Jul	Aug	Sep	Oct	Nov	Dec	sum	mean	std. dev.
1	62,513	218,387	96,471	88,445	167,307	131,102	102,565	128,154	48,699	128,242	139,761	162,960	1,474,606	122,884	47,246
2	74,385	190,271	135,025	94,350	75,907	230,553	93,657	98,366	90,304	84,377	165,590	47,618	1,380,403	115,034	54,275
3	99,957	119,442	163,868	143,971	75,955	161,202	109,404	227,112	52,185	122,365	47,196	157,640	1,480,298	123,358	51,619
4	135,157	123,652	90,085	92,480	119,974	189,382	87,163	122,438	93,230	195,684	50,374	230,808	1,530,425	127,535	52,814
5	141,845	104,080	138,372	74,052	146,696	138,990	-38,416	173,873	109,498	212,522	100,247	85,340	1,387,098	115,591	61,997
6	141,995	119,898	84,585	124,241	116,382	169,343	45,998	166,356	41,975	106,347	222,102	59,618	1,398,839	116,570	53,964
7	64,068	241,841	7,665	167,943	126,891	228,893	73,804	26,026	171,674	169,159	4,169	170,476	1,452,608	121,051	83,557
8	158,189	82,871	171,526	-11,286	209,094	99,542	153,404	50,553	159,354	125,497	111,320	220,203	1,530,267	127,522	66,084
9	136,188	137,526	128,314	33,208	151,769	101,459	166,787	99,268	64,384	92,578	198,509	103,343	1,413,331	117,778	45,096
10	163,582	45,984	187,181	68,022	96,398	140,261	75,731	195,308	138,792	43,498	98,758	194,953	1,448,468	120,706	56,777
11	116,891	135,814	106,723	144,272	95,982	143,558	113,221	111,609	142,159	158,080	144,458	53,806	1,466,571	122,214	28,818
12	131,892	99,907	86,564	148,150	152,495	59,527	167,361	170,001	73,509	140,745	129,509	102,453	1,429,194	119,099	37,356
13	160,632	84,004	125,536	141,579	102,664	84,769	172,617	67,811	22,942	228,906	43,154	136,853	1,371,469	114,289	58,431
14	96,983	156,885	79,423	189,052	96,816	126,812	70,605	163,829	124,872	126,781	75,284	81,813	1,389,154	115,763	38,802
15	131,638	118,112	66,101	176,548	141,785	13,116	133,561	197,237	44,634	125,782	159,150	176,240	1,483,904	123,659	56,034
16	159,002	131,061	18,564	147,066	157,739	27,023	194,599	68,528	149,778	159,409	117,123	45,971	1,375,863	114,655	59,187
17	182,124	40,888	145,670	180,951	47,592	95,150	163,102	47,064	152,762	104,350	66,140	137,147	1,362,940	113,578	53,554
18	135,662	17,433	264,583	37,246	139,105	206,298	-6,581	280,361	4,886	118,923	74,803	183,804	1,456,523	121,377	98,817
19	95,985	165,342	80,441	185,449	94,595	167,213	28,411	129,931	179,235	143,158	75,348	126,402	1,471,509	122,626	48,467
20	62,236	213,886	74,335	190,678	44,173	200,953	71,730	92,190	135,088	65,958	189,402	184,223	1,524,853	127,071	64,757
21	133,085	137,654	51,939	74,045	257,084	103,391	117,315	87,701	151,592	85,424	162,970	78,990	1,441,191	120,099	54,828
22	172,733	12,489	189,600	87,895	110,394	158,697	181,343	54,551	155,315	86,728	14,026	136,964	1,460,736	121,728	54,349
23	148,815	72,966	135,807	101,554	117,338	179,763	72,208	119,199	195,754	195,611	61,204	74,522	1,474,741	122,895	48,968
24	168,665	67,206	26,655	178,187	170,711	104,657	124,057	116,967	84,044	80,075	208,678	96,335	1,426,238	118,853	53,413
25	124,096	117,423	146,791	46,729	185,868	120,599	89,077	147,261	129,640	174,900	1,564	199,645	1,483,593	123,633	56,783
26	134,017	150,281	59,588	123,140	142,751	135,210	16,592	154,310	104,683	182,258	93,081	110,877	1,406,787	117,232	44,943
27	131,199	90,580	133,635	120,518	160,861	-11,610	264,677	34,965	133,377	238,185	29,182	94,960	1,420,530	118,378	80,521
28	133,289	64,571	136,474	167,327	129,517	168,470	36,449	172,568	58,003	170,942	111,055	170,235	1,518,901	126,575	49,053
29	110,655	135,327	89,910	140,751	127,037	60,969	183,627	189,465	61,631	154,589	79,128	78,297	1,411,387	117,616	44,733
30	106,983	156,647	173,706	5,928	195,842	61,679	119,228	227,483	100,460	57,388	155,924	137,389	1,498,657	124,888	63,047
31	74,070	202,073	113,985	39,716	207,069	137,200	92,689	124,957	110,595	165,265	19,296	189,058	1,475,972	122,998	60,988
32	179,780	23,883	150,234	117,052	106,857	142,742	55,770	102,220	94,803	169,016	136,158	173,327	1,451,840	120,987	47,670
33	123,785	117,236	89,612	144,673	118,892	140,019	86,883	108,173	71,374	170,408	205,382	102,535	1,478,973	123,248	37,619
34	109,134	165,990	120,892	62,631	139,416	135,817	143,267	70,902	105,053	111,047	97,032	183,453	1,444,634	120,386	35,624
35	49,309	224,478	66,843	182,333	62,394	138,495	144,729	94,804	147,938	85,410	146,756	149,326	1,492,816	124,401	52,959
mean	124,301	122,460	112,477	114,540	131,181	128,321	105,904	126,330	105,835	136,560	108,597	132,502			
std. dev	35,488	59,431	53,192	55,941	46,567	56,581	62,274	59,486	47,389	48,749	59,289	51,810			

Finished goods inventory trends
Inventory reduction policy: no reduction

Percent	Jan	Feb	Mar	Apr	May	Jun	Jul	Aug	Sep	Oct	Nov	Dec	sum	mean	std. dev.
Series (yr)															
1	6.46%	35.20%	13.47%	10.96%	26.57%	21.55%	14.29%	19.16%	4.84%	16.90%	17.74%	23.79%	210.92%	17.58%	8.56%
2	8.28%	30.50%	20.37%	13.14%	8.70%	37.48%	13.91%	14.84%	12.38%	10.42%	24.29%	4.34%	198.66%	16.56%	9.83%
3	12.51%	14.12%	23.01%	20.89%	9.38%	22.74%	12.59%	45.31%	6.01%	18.09%	4.49%	23.88%	213.03%	17.75%	10.92%
4	21.58%	18.27%	11.81%	12.23%	14.73%	27.48%	11.51%	16.56%	11.06%	31.68%	5.11%	37.86%	219.87%	18.32%	9.65%
5	21.54%	14.91%	20.38%	9.56%	21.71%	22.94%	-6.61%	25.28%	15.68%	33.32%	12.39%	10.51%	201.61%	16.80%	10.03%
6	22.23%	19.12%	10.73%	18.17%	17.64%	28.35%	4.90%	26.82%	4.17%	12.74%	36.02%	7.10%	207.98%	17.33%	9.94%
7	7.40%	39.94%	-1.04%	17.79%	17.35%	40.77%	11.05%	1.62%	27.20%	30.55%	-1.57%	25.97%	221.03%	18.42%	15.05%
8	24.41%	11.61%	27.56%	-3.60%	33.51%	13.14%	22.49%	5.43%	22.64%	11.39%	13.98%	40.02%	228.57%	19.05%	12.03%
9	20.08%	21.39%	22.55%	2.80%	22.89%	14.20%	26.53%	14.98%	7.58%	11.31%	30.48%	13.55%	208.32%	17.36%	8.04%
10	29.01%	4.73%	30.29%	9.66%	12.67%	20.71%	8.95%	30.12%	21.92%	4.55%	12.35%	33.08%	218.04%	18.17%	10.61%
11	15.60%	18.98%	14.89%	22.14%	11.92%	20.42%	15.28%	15.78%	19.52%	25.58%	25.10%	6.28%	211.47%	17.62%	5.51%
12	20.25%	13.13%	11.22%	21.67%	23.77%	6.71%	23.87%	27.54%	9.39%	21.02%	12.97%	13.75%	205.28%	17.11%	6.68%
13	25.49%	11.53%	17.78%	24.21%	14.73%	12.02%	30.02%	9.71%	1.18%	42.42%	4.44%	20.16%	213.69%	17.81%	11.53%
14	12.76%	24.35%	9.99%	31.38%	13.43%	19.79%	8.68%	23.76%	20.70%	21.26%	10.50%	11.19%	207.79%	17.32%	7.20%
15	19.67%	18.12%	7.83%	28.23%	24.85%	-0.31%	17.13%	31.49%	4.37%	16.60%	24.69%	27.54%	220.22%	18.35%	9.99%
16	25.26%	22.22%	0.47%	21.37%	25.89%	1.75%	30.44%	8.02%	22.06%	24.83%	18.35%	4.57%	205.23%	17.10%	10.46%
17	30.30%	3.94%	21.87%	32.58%	5.40%	12.46%	26.80%	5.28%	23.85%	14.99%	7.28%	18.99%	203.72%	16.98%	10.23%
18	21.90%	0.47%	44.33%	3.35%	20.91%	39.62%	-2.99%	59.75%	-1.87%	17.91%	9.03%	31.12%	243.53%	20.29%	20.17%
19	12.00%	25.45%	9.62%	29.06%	12.18%	29.19%	2.00%	17.13%	27.65%	21.16%	8.97%	16.59%	211.01%	17.58%	8.97%
20	6.57%	36.84%	8.44%	32.95%	4.40%	35.46%	9.52%	12.00%	20.05%	7.04%	27.52%	31.66%	232.43%	19.37%	12.71%
21	18.98%	21.12%	5.38%	8.15%	43.48%	15.22%	17.15%	11.07%	22.60%	11.52%	26.89%	10.20%	211.75%	17.65%	10.33%
22	29.19%	-0.42%	30.12%	10.69%	13.30%	24.54%	31.02%	6.06%	23.64%	11.39%	16.41%	20.48%	216.42%	18.03%	10.12%
23	22.31%	8.78%	18.34%	12.55%	14.71%	28.74%	8.26%	14.76%	30.03%	34.34%	7.76%	8.77%	209.34%	17.45%	9.36%
24	30.10%	9.19%	1.72%	27.56%	28.08%	14.98%	18.54%	18.21%	11.31%	9.62%	32.83%	14.20%	216.34%	18.03%	9.73%
25	17.70%	16.81%	22.16%	4.76%	30.04%	17.01%	11.71%	20.48%	18.52%	34.39%	-2.25%	32.27%	223.60%	18.63%	10.72%
26	19.16%	26.17%	7.51%	17.52%	23.10%	24.31%	0.24%	22.94%	14.61%	28.89%	13.94%	16.88%	215.28%	17.94%	8.16%
27	19.71%	12.37%	19.46%	15.91%	27.31%	-3.42%	49.10%	2.94%	17.81%	42.44%	2.29%	12.57%	218.47%	18.21%	15.53%
28	20.11%	7.08%	18.12%	24.18%	19.47%	27.73%	3.17%	25.69%	6.41%	25.55%	14.74%	26.90%	219.17%	18.26%	8.62%
29	15.10%	20.27%	12.36%	21.20%	19.37%	6.29%	26.41%	31.91%	7.37%	24.69%	10.01%	10.18%	205.16%	17.10%	8.16%
30	13.21%	22.00%	31.92%	-1.42%	30.93%	7.03%	14.44%	37.23%	15.39%	6.23%	22.00%	20.74%	219.69%	18.31%	11.47%
31	8.57%	31.70%	16.94%	3.64%	33.93%	20.94%	13.08%	18.57%	15.65%	27.55%	0.65%	31.67%	222.91%	18.58%	11.08%
32	33.18%	1.32%	23.40%	16.87%	15.33%	23.51%	6.39%	14.02%	12.98%	24.38%	18.25%	27.53%	217.15%	18.10%	8.96%
33	17.38%	16.74%	11.97%	20.63%	17.25%	19.27%	10.44%	13.29%	8.78%	24.03%	33.00%	13.99%	206.77%	17.23%	6.62%
34	14.13%	26.54%	18.32%	7.50%	19.58%	19.88%	22.29%	8.42%	14.14%	13.84%	11.17%	29.80%	205.60%	17.13%	6.90%
35	4.93%	38.20%	7.59%	28.24%	7.51%	20.27%	21.76%	12.22%	22.17%	10.23%	19.61%	22.12%	214.87%	17.91%	9.78%
mean	18.49%	18.36%	16.31%	16.59%	19.60%	19.79%	15.27%	19.10%	14.91%	20.82%	15.18%	20.01%			
std dev	7.46%	10.74%	9.66%	9.91%	8.82%	10.66%	11.19%	12.24%	8.12%	9.95%	10.19%	9.88%			

Finished goods inventory trends
Inventory reduction policy: no reduction

Dollars Series (yr)	Jan	Feb	Mar	Apr	May	Jun	Jul	Aug	Sep	Oct	Nov	Dec	sum	mean	std. dev.
1	48,408	202,599	80,719	73,358	151,250	114,366	86,753	112,116	34,024	113,326	125,113	147,526	1,289,558	107,463	46,881
2	59,962	174,279	118,956	78,393	61,237	214,422	77,207	81,885	74,415	69,244	150,055	33,882	1,193,938	99,495	53,821
3	85,008	105,472	149,624	129,325	61,216	146,060	95,696	210,617	36,329	106,314	32,864	142,456	1,300,982	108,415	51,356
4	118,637	107,606	74,547	76,913	105,471	174,115	71,786	107,097	78,674	179,717	35,634	214,535	1,344,731	112,061	52,467
5	125,748	88,056	122,534	58,517	130,826	122,276	-52,064	160,020	95,636	198,483	86,751	71,786	1,208,570	100,714	61,710
6	125,672	103,268	69,228	108,290	100,078	152,773	30,508	149,959	26,490	91,902	206,041	44,247	1,208,456	100,705	53,608
7	48,894	225,553	-7,149	153,301	111,568	212,027	56,879	11,171	155,761	152,058	-10,721	154,504	1,263,847	105,321	83,034
8	142,067	66,929	155,175	-25,773	192,945	84,121	137,634	35,245	144,141	110,265	96,582	203,188	1,342,518	111,877	65,538
9	120,271	121,227	111,285	17,689	135,781	85,581	150,485	82,797	49,042	77,816	182,654	88,038	1,222,665	101,889	44,841
10	146,537	30,649	170,990	51,295	80,960	124,421	60,971	179,443	122,398	77,693	83,784	178,464	1,257,604	104,800	56,451
11	101,602	120,569	91,186	128,108	81,036	128,116	97,795	96,146	126,933	141,609	127,445	37,949	1,278,495	106,541	28,620
12	115,631	84,524	71,185	132,379	136,271	44,363	151,885	153,584	57,821	124,755	80,963	86,932	1,240,292	103,358	37,083
13	144,320	67,984	109,860	124,643	86,615	68,494	155,733	51,010	8,037	212,037	27,473	120,939	1,177,145	98,095	58,025
14	81,545	140,715	64,011	172,603	80,932	110,443	55,114	148,204	108,028	109,880	58,911	65,766	1,196,152	99,679	38,609
15	115,581	102,095	51,023	160,523	124,824	-2,070	118,766	181,167	29,667	111,022	143,227	160,180	1,296,004	108,000	55,656
16	142,680	114,118	2,956	131,333	141,188	12,554	178,929	53,406	133,979	143,218	100,591	30,997	1,185,949	98,829	58,723
17	165,573	25,589	129,750	131,873	31,478	79,723	146,562	31,264	136,714	88,320	51,533	121,957	1,172,337	97,695	53,131
18	119,087	3,629	249,107	22,630	123,560	188,995	-21,185	263,000	-11,019	102,695	59,618	167,148	1,267,274	105,606	98,025
19	80,979	149,449	65,503	169,613	79,577	150,777	13,287	114,862	163,219	127,261	60,310	111,500	1,286,337	107,195	48,057
20	47,880	197,640	59,731	64,204	28,981	184,072	55,643	76,760	119,112	51,667	174,126	167,464	1,337,279	111,440	64,084
21	117,393	121,455	37,112	60,285	241,375	87,161	101,305	72,445	135,682	69,550	146,396	63,339	1,253,498	104,458	54,495
22	156,041	-2,756	173,405	72,982	96,606	143,340	164,596	39,204	139,585	71,115	98,095	120,942	1,273,157	106,096	53,914
23	132,846	57,747	120,692	87,087	103,103	164,080	57,454	104,945	180,203	178,824	45,061	59,565	1,291,606	107,634	48,626
24	151,607	50,716	12,438	162,690	154,671	88,783	108,048	100,485	68,171	65,086	192,652	79,988	1,235,337	102,945	53,071
25	108,337	101,558	130,935	32,275	170,142	105,121	73,778	131,881	113,917	157,278	-14,057	183,369	1,294,533	107,878	56,371
26	118,320	133,289	43,416	107,526	126,197	117,928	1,668	138,600	88,878	166,042	76,638	94,608	1,213,109	101,092	44,635
27	115,104	74,730	118,019	105,357	144,213	-25,704	248,107	20,060	118,264	221,405	12,768	79,444	1,231,767	102,647	79,956
28	117,179	50,130	121,867	152,495	113,928	151,928	21,470	156,979	42,930	155,180	95,744	154,122	1,333,953	111,163	48,686
29	95,106	119,279	73,987	124,707	110,817	46,784	168,629	172,861	46,009	138,198	63,660	62,617	1,222,655	101,888	44,415
30	92,256	141,676	156,831	-9,292	179,733	46,512	104,836	211,973	84,430	42,647	140,662	121,363	1,313,625	109,469	62,753
31	59,263	186,117	97,791	24,785	191,035	121,029	76,615	108,873	94,747	148,628	4,477	172,493	1,285,855	107,155	60,491
32	162,547	8,392	133,993	101,253	90,862	126,066	40,713	86,993	79,711	153,687	121,123	157,075	1,262,416	105,201	47,272
33	108,141	101,388	73,910	129,083	103,274	124,674	72,310	94,374	57,767	156,530	190,001	87,079	1,298,531	108,211	37,477
34	93,996	150,126	104,649	47,231	123,901	120,210	127,005	55,742	89,943	96,295	83,078	167,873	1,260,049	105,004	35,330
35	34,635	208,137	51,952	166,314	46,748	122,960	128,878	79,501	132,077	70,575	132,141	133,474	1,307,392	108,949	52,550
mean	108,539	106,684	96,892	99,028	115,497	112,472	90,394	110,705	90,335	120,866	93,183	116,766			
std. dev	34,754	59,107	52,908	55,568	46,298	56,064	61,824	59,184	47,183	48,348	59,119	51,345			

Finished goods inventory trends
Inventory reduction policy: no reduction

Percent Series (yr)	Jan	Feb	Mar	Apr	May	Jun	Jul	Aug	Sep	Oct	Nov	Dec	sum	mean	std. dev.
1	31.22%	55.05%	36.71%	35.08%	45.92%	45.57%	37.82%	41.41%	30.22%	39.26%	39.36%	44.58%	482.19%	40.18%	6.93%
2	32.15%	51.23%	42.36%	36.89%	33.03%	55.39%	36.63%	38.94%	35.71%	35.22%	45.47%	29.73%	472.76%	39.40%	7.82%
3	36.19%	37.13%	44.73%	41.95%	32.63%	45.50%	35.62%	62.39%	31.97%	40.41%	29.28%	44.99%	482.79%	40.23%	8.83%
4	42.54%	41.22%	35.62%	37.27%	37.11%	47.68%	35.03%	39.76%	33.83%	50.64%	30.70%	55.97%	487.37%	40.61%	7.48%
5	43.31%	38.81%	42.58%	33.55%	42.39%	46.63%	20.50%	46.38%	40.07%	52.03%	35.51%	34.46%	476.22%	39.68%	8.12%
6	43.90%	42.07%	34.71%	40.42%	40.98%	50.11%	30.11%	47.84%	29.77%	35.74%	55.21%	32.51%	483.37%	40.28%	8.09%
7	32.26%	58.30%	25.21%	43.06%	39.61%	58.98%	35.28%	27.89%	47.61%	50.61%	25.07%	46.86%	490.73%	40.89%	12.00%
8	46.93%	34.77%	49.57%	23.34%	52.26%	36.66%	43.95%	30.91%	44.24%	40.41%	36.46%	58.47%	497.97%	41.50%	9.77%
9	42.35%	43.54%	45.56%	27.86%	44.36%	36.94%	47.79%	38.79%	33.16%	34.70%	50.23%	36.96%	482.24%	40.19%	6.57%
10	49.44%	30.45%	50.59%	33.76%	36.45%	43.16%	32.72%	50.54%	44.23%	31.03%	36.04%	52.13%	490.54%	40.88%	8.37%
11	39.17%	41.25%	38.01%	43.80%	35.57%	41.35%	38.74%	38.99%	41.09%	46.86%	47.54%	30.64%	483.00%	40.25%	4.64%
12	43.23%	36.56%	34.77%	43.20%	44.78%	31.82%	44.27%	49.71%	32.99%	43.09%	36.82%	37.79%	479.02%	39.92%	5.52%
13	46.88%	35.13%	40.63%	45.91%	37.91%	36.00%	49.95%	36.47%	27.28%	60.34%	29.88%	42.28%	488.65%	40.72%	9.12%
14	35.59%	45.56%	34.82%	51.06%	37.91%	42.53%	32.34%	45.77%	42.51%	44.18%	34.46%	35.02%	481.76%	40.15%	5.89%
15	41.86%	41.57%	32.84%	48.72%	45.89%	26.24%	38.83%	51.28%	29.96%	39.63%	46.03%	47.04%	489.89%	40.82%	7.77%
16	46.70%	44.57%	26.92%	42.44%	47.78%	28.14%	49.10%	33.10%	43.26%	46.23%	41.11%	29.70%	479.05%	39.92%	8.15%
17	50.26%	30.22%	42.96%	52.10%	31.23%	36.46%	48.04%	30.67%	45.26%	38.18%	31.76%	41.56%	478.70%	39.89%	7.97%
18	43.85%	27.29%	60.88%	29.16%	42.84%	56.91%	24.92%	74.42%	25.32%	41.02%	33.61%	51.62%	511.85%	42.65%	15.80%
19	35.95%	46.25%	34.34%	49.56%	35.96%	49.82%	27.78%	40.00%	47.01%	43.55%	33.25%	39.32%	482.78%	40.23%	7.06%
20	30.51%	56.38%	33.09%	52.09%	29.62%	54.87%	34.02%	36.44%	41.90%	31.35%	47.52%	51.52%	499.31%	41.61%	10.30%
21	40.94%	43.81%	31.40%	31.96%	59.20%	38.94%	39.64%	35.48%	44.11%	34.65%	47.76%	35.34%	483.23%	40.27%	7.81%
22	50.19%	25.98%	50.24%	35.77%	35.84%	45.22%	51.58%	31.86%	44.56%	35.92%	38.79%	42.01%	487.95%	40.66%	8.01%
23	44.39%	32.21%	41.63%	34.71%	37.40%	49.04%	32.47%	37.70%	50.02%	53.95%	31.63%	34.48%	479.63%	39.97%	7.73%
24	50.34%	33.88%	27.77%	47.90%	49.03%	38.70%	41.57%	40.09%	35.67%	34.36%	51.84%	38.29%	489.43%	40.79%	7.56%
25	40.62%	40.47%	45.34%	29.56%	50.20%	40.42%	34.69%	42.24%	41.10%	52.77%	25.00%	52.29%	494.69%	41.22%	8.52%
26	41.09%	48.77%	32.06%	39.77%	45.03%	46.59%	26.94%	44.30%	37.83%	50.31%	36.99%	40.47%	490.15%	40.85%	6.81%
27	42.28%	36.26%	41.17%	39.02%	47.78%	24.04%	64.93%	28.66%	39.55%	61.03%	27.95%	37.24%	489.90%	40.82%	12.34%
28	43.42%	31.73%	40.42%	44.81%	41.49%	48.17%	28.72%	46.22%	32.37%	45.56%	38.18%	48.28%	489.36%	40.78%	6.69%
29	38.83%	41.70%	36.43%	44.14%	40.77%	31.39%	46.20%	51.91%	32.53%	44.84%	34.81%	35.34%	478.87%	39.91%	6.16%
30	36.87%	43.69%	53.45%	25.31%	50.05%	31.60%	38.07%	54.99%	39.33%	30.89%	44.01%	42.32%	490.56%	40.88%	9.12%
31	33.04%	51.81%	40.08%	28.28%	52.83%	43.67%	36.32%	41.57%	38.46%	48.04%	27.33%	51.84%	493.27%	41.11%	8.91%
32	52.63%	27.83%	45.19%	40.22%	38.76%	44.23%	32.33%	37.60%	35.87%	45.67%	40.02%	48.90%	489.24%	40.77%	7.01%
33	40.09%	39.38%	36.12%	43.39%	39.54%	41.92%	35.05%	35.81%	32.09%	45.31%	50.80%	37.68%	477.19%	39.77%	5.09%
34	38.33%	46.36%	42.25%	31.05%	42.96%	41.54%	33.34%	34.39%	36.23%	36.52%	34.53%	49.86%	477.37%	39.78%	5.52%
35	29.75%	57.01%	31.91%	48.06%	32.77%	42.05%	43.30%	34.95%	44.49%	34.95%	40.62%	43.85%	483.70%	40.31%	7.85%
mean	41.06%	41.09%	39.50%	39.29%	41.65%	42.24%	38.25%	41.70%	38.05%	42.84%	38.16%	42.32%			
std. dev	6.13%	8.66%	7.81%	7.94%	6.84%	8.44%	8.78%	9.67%	6.30%	7.94%	8.00%	7.76%			

Finished goods inventory trends
Inventory reduction policy: no reduction

Dollars Series (yr)	Jan	Feb	Mar	Apr	May	Jun	Jul	Aug	Sep	Oct	Nov	Dec	sum	mean	std. dev.
1	233,979	316,844	219,941	234,862	261,420	241,867	229,565	242,364	212,268	263,317	277,631	276,377	3,010,436	250,870	29,513
2	232,800	292,661	247,336	220,064	232,544	316,928	203,267	214,854	214,733	234,053	280,814	231,992	2,922,045	243,504	35,017
3	245,824	277,436	290,906	259,680	212,860	292,215	270,833	289,980	193,194	237,474	214,213	268,409	3,053,024	254,419	33,710
4	233,882	242,824	224,862	234,421	265,757	302,046	218,511	257,191	240,734	287,249	214,215	317,116	3,038,807	253,234	33,465
5	252,887	229,199	256,044	205,325	255,392	248,538	161,356	293,552	244,344	309,946	248,662	235,456	2,940,702	245,059	37,905
6	248,220	227,164	224,010	240,934	232,552	269,976	187,609	267,478	189,165	257,841	315,843	202,686	2,863,477	238,623	36,887
7	213,161	329,243	173,364	302,888	254,713	306,727	181,696	191,883	272,613	251,922	171,645	278,802	2,928,659	244,055	56,125
8	273,069	200,522	279,035	167,319	300,933	234,749	268,884	200,785	281,682	256,306	252,001	296,914	3,012,198	251,017	42,105
9	253,725	246,712	224,873	176,240	263,187	222,705	271,055	214,450	214,619	238,682	301,082	240,174	2,867,503	238,959	32,116
10	249,724	197,342	285,613	179,243	232,955	259,245	222,952	301,149	246,979	188,772	244,556	281,218	2,889,749	240,812	38,754
11	255,130	262,073	232,776	253,432	241,869	259,493	247,939	237,566	267,219	259,458	241,395	185,168	2,943,519	245,293	21,727
12	246,874	235,375	220,622	263,919	256,758	210,352	281,738	277,184	203,077	255,724	229,832	238,929	2,920,383	243,365	25,009
13	265,426	207,241	251,053	236,396	222,930	205,056	259,117	191,495	186,026	301,610	184,904	253,636	2,764,888	230,407	36,819
14	227,473	263,291	223,180	280,865	228,375	237,378	205,342	285,506	221,828	228,405	193,309	205,819	2,800,771	233,398	29,164
15	245,960	234,262	213,870	277,089	230,484	173,212	269,156	294,973	203,338	265,043	266,971	273,570	2,947,928	245,661	35,664
16	263,763	228,875	168,254	260,850	260,596	202,432	288,570	220,302	262,742	266,655	225,319	201,450	2,849,808	237,484	35,300
17	274,680	196,503	254,855	260,058	182,130	233,344	262,717	181,724	259,433	224,995	224,827	266,889	2,824,154	235,346	35,580
18	238,403	211,497	342,118	196,921	253,124	271,507	176,320	327,573	149,560	235,279	221,931	277,299	2,901,531	241,794	57,103
19	242,588	271,541	233,821	289,245	234,836	257,350	184,566	268,111	277,462	261,946	223,665	264,326	3,009,457	250,788	28,608
20	222,442	302,438	234,243	275,402	195,331	284,818	198,865	233,101	248,991	230,248	300,673	272,508	2,999,059	249,922	36,890
21	253,306	251,922	216,627	236,561	328,589	222,970	234,197	232,290	264,803	209,127	260,014	219,460	2,929,866	244,156	32,040
22	268,333	169,968	289,189	244,221	260,413	264,158	273,667	206,203	263,050	224,340	231,827	248,073	2,943,442	245,287	33,020
23	264,297	211,843	273,965	240,889	262,175	279,992	225,992	268,133	300,187	280,923	183,612	234,156	3,026,163	252,180	33,503
24	253,553	186,927	201,239	282,560	270,053	229,365	242,206	221,281	215,046	232,490	304,244	215,619	2,854,713	237,893	34,436
25	248,586	244,542	267,856	200,332	284,365	249,770	218,531	271,969	252,800	241,319	155,868	297,131	2,933,067	244,422	38,451
26	253,790	248,372	185,312	244,108	245,996	226,021	183,765	267,662	230,050	289,108	203,404	226,835	2,804,424	233,702	31,585
27	246,919	219,161	249,673	258,398	252,320	180,483	328,130	195,849	262,585	318,336	155,817	235,420	2,903,091	241,924	50,483
28	252,995	224,697	271,807	282,560	242,726	263,909	194,368	282,402	216,690	276,668	247,966	276,569	3,033,359	252,780	28,626
29	244,516	245,343	218,148	259,626	233,174	233,497	294,978	281,190	203,119	251,016	221,399	217,374	2,903,379	241,948	26,991
30	257,400	281,373	262,629	165,924	290,855	209,115	276,452	313,107	215,788	211,318	281,427	247,601	3,012,992	251,083	42,572
31	228,471	304,202	231,320	192,397	297,420	252,334	212,742	243,660	232,849	259,157	188,536	282,328	2,925,417	243,785	37,524
32	257,843	176,351	258,782	241,420	229,794	237,179	205,927	233,213	220,321	287,880	265,607	279,032	2,893,350	241,112	31,461
33	249,477	238,454	223,004	271,546	236,745	271,199	242,814	254,290	211,116	295,231	292,503	234,498	3,020,878	251,740	26,268
34	254,909	262,300	241,387	195,541	271,816	251,209	246,985	227,609	230,431	254,191	256,719	280,935	2,974,033	247,836	22,462
35	209,038	310,579	218,490	282,995	203,847	255,046	256,478	227,279	265,040	241,099	273,692	264,568	3,008,151	250,679	31,932
mean	247,527	244,259	240,291	240,468	249,401	247,320	235,065	249,067	233,539	255,061	238,746	252,238			
std. dev	15,327	40,515	35,192	37,516	29,993	33,397	39,771	37,980	32,599	29,467	42,841	31,436			

Finished goods inventory trends
Inventory reduction policy: no reduction

Percent Series (yr)	Jan	Feb	Mar	Apr	May	Jun	Jul	Aug	Sep	Oct	Nov	Dec	sum	mean	std. dev.
1	12.30%	30.12%	12.77%	13.75%	20.67%	18.36%	14.18%	16.85%	9.95%	18.00%	19.18%	21.49%	207.61%	17.30%	5.40%
2	12.73%	26.34%	18.00%	13.06%	13.02%	30.52%	10.92%	13.08%	12.08%	13.95%	22.52%	11.80%	198.02%	16.50%	6.47%
3	14.83%	17.84%	22.53%	18.56%	10.42%	22.88%	16.70%	30.84%	7.81%	15.54%	9.53%	20.63%	208.12%	17.34%	6.48%
4	16.55%	17.04%	13.14%	14.70%	17.44%	25.32%	12.30%	17.85%	14.02%	25.55%	10.48%	30.79%	215.19%	17.93%	6.16%
5	18.75%	14.54%	18.77%	10.21%	18.63%	19.61%	2.59%	24.08%	16.92%	28.30%	15.40%	13.85%	201.67%	16.81%	6.50%
6	19.52%	16.48%	13.50%	17.36%	16.69%	24.48%	8.12%	23.17%	8.21%	16.89%	31.16%	10.55%	206.14%	17.18%	6.82%
7	11.34%	33.62%	5.16%	23.48%	18.09%	32.07%	8.10%	7.84%	23.34%	22.45%	4.92%	23.49%	213.90%	17.83%	10.14%
8	22.70%	10.36%	24.48%	3.90%	27.77%	14.75%	20.96%	9.33%	22.24%	18.32%	16.26%	30.53%	221.62%	18.47%	7.90%
9	19.48%	19.29%	17.58%	6.27%	21.26%	14.22%	23.57%	13.91%	12.08%	14.95%	27.39%	15.97%	205.98%	17.16%	5.58%
10	22.15%	9.44%	26.33%	7.86%	15.13%	20.41%	12.83%	27.61%	19.66%	8.57%	16.03%	26.68%	212.68%	17.72%	7.17%
11	17.85%	19.40%	15.30%	19.65%	15.20%	19.20%	17.02%	16.17%	19.75%	21.57%	19.85%	7.57%	208.55%	17.38%	3.68%
12	18.74%	14.97%	12.87%	20.39%	20.39%	10.83%	22.42%	24.60%	10.36%	19.57%	14.52%	15.79%	205.43%	17.12%	4.58%
13	23.44%	12.69%	19.26%	20.02%	15.39%	12.71%	24.26%	11.11%	8.03%	33.68%	8.54%	20.23%	209.35%	17.45%	7.51%
14	14.73%	22.37%	14.02%	26.64%	15.71%	18.48%	11.34%	24.37%	16.69%	18.11%	10.53%	12.23%	205.22%	17.10%	5.15%
15	18.20%	16.91%	11.64%	24.28%	18.03%	5.31%	18.96%	27.11%	9.64%	19.04%	22.08%	23.13%	214.33%	17.86%	6.32%
16	22.25%	17.56%	4.94%	20.07%	22.42%	9.20%	25.71%	12.53%	20.61%	22.31%	15.88%	9.54%	203.04%	16.92%	6.51%
17	25.17%	9.32%	19.95%	24.73%	7.79%	15.21%	22.96%	7.65%	21.42%	15.00%	12.66%	20.41%	202.27%	16.86%	6.46%
18	18.51%	9.87%	36.56%	9.05%	19.70%	27.88%	5.73%	42.94%	2.11%	17.06%	12.96%	25.96%	228.34%	19.03%	12.41%
19	14.79%	21.78%	13.38%	24.96%	14.10%	21.91%	6.27%	18.69%	22.65%	19.67%	12.02%	18.10%	208.34%	17.36%	5.38%
20	11.50%	30.19%	13.48%	25.48%	8.48%	27.68%	10.02%	14.61%	18.31%	12.49%	25.47%	24.86%	222.56%	18.55%	7.73%
21	18.43%	19.50%	11.34%	13.41%	34.10%	14.52%	16.01%	14.28%	20.87%	11.55%	22.02%	12.92%	208.95%	17.41%	6.36%
22	23.89%	4.71%	25.89%	15.43%	16.89%	21.38%	25.06%	10.34%	22.65%	13.58%	15.39%	18.31%	211.76%	17.65%	6.29%
23	20.17%	10.40%	19.85%	14.15%	17.07%	23.83%	11.93%	17.67%	26.06%	26.10%	6.76%	13.40%	207.38%	17.28%	6.21%
24	23.22%	9.23%	9.31%	25.02%	24.42%	15.85%	18.31%	15.45%	13.21%	14.48%	28.74%	14.16%	211.41%	17.62%	6.36%
25	18.12%	17.67%	22.02%	9.44%	25.90%	18.19%	12.91%	20.92%	18.72%	22.26%	2.94%	27.97%	217.06%	18.09%	6.95%
26	19.58%	22.43%	9.00%	18.14%	20.56%	18.88%	7.58%	22.31%	15.97%	27.10%	12.70%	16.67%	210.92%	17.58%	5.66%
27	18.47%	13.29%	18.32%	18.16%	21.34%	5.78%	37.32%	8.48%	18.75%	34.24%	2.95%	15.34%	212.43%	17.70%	10.20%
28	18.90%	11.79%	19.39%	22.35%	17.15%	22.01%	7.77%	22.92%	11.18%	22.08%	16.30%	23.33%	215.17%	17.93%	5.23%
29	16.77%	18.00%	13.17%	20.44%	16.36%	12.90%	24.53%	26.07%	10.27%	19.87%	12.98%	12.73%	204.09%	17.01%	4.97%
30	16.61%	21.69%	24.23%	3.67%	25.48%	10.16%	18.64%	30.02%	13.32%	10.22%	21.81%	17.93%	213.79%	17.82%	7.50%
31	13.31%	28.37%	16.20%	8.20%	28.37%	19.82%	12.81%	18.07%	15.75%	22.41%	7.55%	26.46%	217.31%	18.11%	7.21%
32	24.47%	6.34%	21.27%	17.47%	15.70%	18.61%	11.01%	15.68%	13.76%	24.09%	19.57%	24.90%	212.86%	17.74%	5.67%
33	17.01%	15.62%	12.84%	20.45%	15.55%	19.76%	14.47%	15.84%	10.56%	23.54%	25.90%	14.63%	206.17%	17.18%	4.44%
34	17.02%	21.19%	17.25%	8.51%	20.50%	18.03%	18.28%	12.98%	13.96%	16.22%	15.63%	24.64%	204.21%	17.02%	4.17%
35	9.69%	30.83%	11.29%	23.89%	9.95%	18.67%	19.30%	13.18%	20.63%	14.49%	19.71%	20.29%	211.92%	17.66%	6.25%
mean	18.03%	17.75%	16.72%	16.66%	18.45%	18.55%	15.74%	18.53%	15.42%	19.52%	15.95%	19.07%			
std. dev	3.96%	7.28%	6.41%	6.65%	5.66%	6.31%	7.27%	7.69%	5.51%	6.03%	7.17%	6.17%			

Finished goods inventory trends
Inventory reduction policy: no reduction

Dollars Series (yr)	Jan	Feb	Mar	Apr	May	Jun	Jul	Aug	Sep	Oct	Nov	Dec	sum	mean	std. dev.
1	92,176	173,357	76,491	92,077	117,666	97,434	86,055	98,629	69,895	120,702	135,285	133,245	1,293,012	107,751	29,445
2	92,181	150,472	105,070	77,911	91,677	174,600	60,621	72,176	72,647	92,723	139,082	92,060	1,221,222	101,768	34,949
3	100,739	133,329	146,525	114,898	67,985	146,938	126,989	143,349	47,202	91,286	69,746	123,088	1,312,073	109,339	33,843
4	90,986	100,401	82,948	92,477	124,878	160,403	76,758	115,473	99,801	144,905	73,098	174,466	1,336,593	111,383	33,312
5	109,494	85,879	112,909	62,493	112,225	104,528	20,411	152,402	103,185	168,610	107,869	94,606	1,234,610	102,884	37,926
6	110,374	89,012	87,131	103,460	94,725	131,883	50,596	129,557	52,158	121,873	178,259	65,793	1,214,821	101,235	36,691
7	74,920	189,889	35,483	165,180	116,323	166,794	41,705	53,961	133,633	111,754	33,689	139,762	1,263,096	105,258	55,825
8	132,088	59,720	137,824	27,972	159,924	94,468	128,254	60,617	141,610	116,214	112,403	155,038	1,326,131	110,511	41,662
9	116,728	109,334	86,764	39,642	126,120	85,747	133,675	76,900	78,198	102,841	164,148	103,789	1,223,884	101,990	32,056
10	111,870	61,198	148,613	41,707	96,707	122,597	87,383	164,476	109,775	52,158	108,773	143,920	1,249,177	104,098	38,653
11	116,283	123,269	93,680	113,710	103,364	120,493	108,955	98,545	128,435	119,429	100,824	45,753	1,272,741	106,062	21,819
12	107,012	96,390	81,643	124,547	116,933	71,586	142,661	137,165	63,787	116,134	90,607	99,808	1,248,274	104,023	24,795
13	132,734	74,840	118,996	103,079	90,500	72,400	125,851	58,313	54,740	168,361	52,842	121,341	1,173,996	97,833	36,529
14	94,161	129,248	89,895	146,543	94,618	103,136	71,977	152,007	87,110	93,631	59,063	71,899	1,193,288	99,441	29,163
15	106,935	95,277	75,823	138,095	90,555	35,058	131,393	155,935	65,403	127,314	128,081	134,542	1,284,412	107,034	35,494
16	125,680	90,171	30,885	123,357	122,283	66,202	151,140	83,420	125,182	128,703	87,027	64,716	1,198,768	99,897	35,005
17	137,533	60,607	118,339	124,384	45,420	97,321	125,581	45,327	122,789	88,369	89,624	131,103	1,186,396	98,866	33,351
18	100,636	76,503	205,450	61,114	116,388	133,013	40,524	189,030	12,464	97,860	85,555	139,452	1,257,988	104,832	56,535
19	99,835	127,901	91,136	145,662	92,070	113,167	41,694	125,295	133,699	118,302	80,880	121,677	1,291,317	107,610	28,331
20	83,855	161,961	95,407	134,697	55,908	143,707	58,546	93,441	108,784	91,727	161,165	131,519	1,320,718	110,060	36,440
21	114,037	112,146	78,224	99,225	189,303	83,164	94,611	93,458	125,317	69,676	119,863	80,232	1,259,253	104,938	31,913
22	127,709	30,791	149,061	55,376	122,692	124,868	132,986	66,924	123,388	84,795	91,964	108,119	1,268,673	105,723	32,787
23	120,094	68,391	130,617	98,188	119,197	136,075	83,004	125,647	156,403	135,902	39,237	90,965	1,304,230	108,686	33,465
24	116,971	50,912	67,498	147,668	134,489	93,967	106,673	85,274	79,649	97,977	168,693	79,747	1,229,519	102,460	34,362
25	110,917	106,767	130,090	63,969	146,729	112,382	81,322	134,679	115,167	101,786	18,337	158,945	1,281,092	106,758	38,240
26	120,953	114,238	52,000	111,353	112,300	91,597	51,700	134,811	97,103	155,750	69,821	93,425	1,205,051	100,421	31,493
27	107,853	80,340	111,087	120,268	112,702	43,419	188,589	57,974	124,502	178,586	16,433	96,934	1,238,687	103,224	50,094
28	110,097	83,470	130,413	140,942	100,351	120,580	52,602	140,027	74,830	134,119	105,869	133,669	1,326,968	110,581	28,398
29	105,597	105,925	78,855	120,213	93,586	95,944	156,612	141,217	64,128	101,257	82,562	78,326	1,234,222	102,852	26,923
30	115,998	139,727	119,080	24,030	148,071	67,273	135,386	170,922	73,083	69,902	139,490	104,901	1,307,863	108,989	42,510
31	92,011	166,593	93,473	55,812	159,733	114,509	75,015	105,923	95,347	120,866	52,063	144,110	1,275,455	106,288	37,121
32	119,891	40,142	121,822	104,903	93,081	99,785	70,152	97,268	84,512	151,832	129,854	142,061	1,255,304	104,609	31,272
33	105,826	94,599	79,295	127,948	93,119	127,847	100,233	112,483	69,501	153,345	149,114	91,035	1,304,345	108,695	26,307
34	113,210	119,876	98,584	53,581	129,741	109,041	104,164	85,889	88,761	112,879	116,204	138,795	1,270,722	105,894	22,466
35	68,078	167,951	77,312	140,690	61,915	113,225	114,341	85,689	122,892	99,977	132,791	122,429	1,307,289	108,941	31,602
mean	108,156	104,875	101,098	101,348	110,108	107,861	95,947	109,834	94,431	115,758	99,723	112,893			
std. dev	15,627	39,345	34,565	37,412	29,876	31,837	39,627	37,355	31,974	29,352	42,349	30,535			

Finished goods inventory trends
Inventory reduction policy: no reduction

Percent	Jan	Feb	Mar	Apr	May	Jun	Jul	Aug	Sep	Oct	Nov	Dec	sum	mean	std. dev.
Series (yr)															
1	8.41%	38.62%	15.53%	13.26%	27.95%	27.71%	16.08%	21.35%	7.13%	18.91%	19.12%	25.59%	239.67%	19.97%	8.97%
2	9.75%	34.08%	23.05%	15.96%	10.87%	39.34%	15.88%	19.37%	14.45%	13.65%	26.90%	6.43%	229.74%	19.14%	9.99%
3	14.97%	16.14%	25.42%	22.11%	11.24%	26.81%	13.76%	48.62%	9.47%	20.17%	5.68%	26.50%	240.91%	20.08%	11.34%
4	23.50%	21.60%	14.39%	16.38%	15.59%	29.83%	13.54%	19.74%	12.34%	33.57%	8.64%	40.24%	249.35%	20.78%	9.49%
5	23.90%	18.08%	22.52%	12.17%	23.19%	29.06%	-5.88%	27.10%	19.56%	35.08%	13.74%	13.26%	231.79%	19.32%	10.47%
6	24.85%	22.93%	12.46%	20.97%	20.74%	31.93%	6.88%	29.86%	6.83%	14.18%	38.83%	10.29%	240.74%	20.06%	10.26%
7	10.06%	42.99%	0.54%	23.65%	19.68%	44.34%	13.52%	4.17%	29.75%	34.05%	0.82%	28.84%	252.42%	21.03%	15.46%
8	28.46%	12.33%	31.80%	-1.79%	35.82%	15.39%	24.88%	8.43%	24.90%	20.39%	15.20%	43.48%	259.29%	21.61%	12.58%
9	22.63%	24.04%	27.14%	4.59%	25.21%	16.17%	30.49%	18.01%	10.72%	13.12%	32.83%	15.65%	240.61%	20.05%	8.44%
10	31.88%	7.28%	33.60%	11.97%	15.12%	23.75%	10.55%	33.64%	24.92%	8.25%	14.25%	34.84%	250.05%	20.84%	10.76%
11	18.58%	20.93%	17.20%	25.01%	14.00%	21.72%	18.24%	19.04%	21.30%	29.07%	29.32%	7.56%	241.96%	20.16%	6.06%
12	23.96%	14.72%	13.53%	24.38%	26.18%	9.62%	25.25%	32.03%	10.74%	23.87%	15.96%	16.29%	236.54%	19.71%	7.09%
13	28.57%	13.08%	21.12%	27.07%	17.10%	15.02%	32.82%	15.79%	2.92%	45.19%	6.60%	22.84%	248.13%	20.68%	11.66%
14	14.28%	27.81%	13.16%	33.99%	16.60%	22.80%	9.70%	26.96%	23.87%	24.76%	12.68%	14.01%	240.61%	20.05%	7.61%
15	21.73%	21.78%	10.42%	30.61%	27.63%	2.56%	18.59%	34.35%	7.01%	19.42%	27.70%	28.85%	250.66%	20.89%	9.90%
16	28.72%	25.10%	3.01%	22.81%	30.27%	4.21%	31.58%	11.54%	23.89%	28.09%	21.38%	6.44%	237.05%	19.75%	10.55%
17	32.75%	7.17%	23.42%	35.32%	9.01%	15.32%	29.47%	7.81%	26.82%	17.76%	9.56%	21.76%	236.16%	19.68%	10.08%
18	25.19%	3.02%	45.69%	5.54%	23.73%	42.11%	0.65%	63.44%	0.20%	20.69%	11.45%	34.23%	275.95%	23.00%	20.25%
19	14.27%	27.77%	12.77%	31.79%	14.18%	32.03%	3.97%	20.11%	28.67%	24.57%	11.42%	18.74%	240.28%	20.02%	9.00%
20	7.94%	41.03%	10.42%	35.48%	6.76%	38.70%	12.16%	15.20%	22.01%	8.95%	29.83%	34.65%	263.14%	21.93%	13.22%
21	20.83%	24.88%	8.53%	9.51%	44.38%	19.10%	19.49%	14.06%	25.41%	12.96%	30.40%	13.81%	243.36%	20.28%	10.09%
22	32.53%	1.84%	32.70%	13.99%	13.92%	26.98%	34.66%	9.31%	25.28%	14.42%	18.37%	22.54%	246.54%	20.55%	10.29%
23	25.45%	9.59%	22.41%	13.27%	16.57%	32.07%	10.43%	17.40%	32.47%	37.86%	9.19%	12.57%	239.29%	19.94%	9.96%
24	32.91%	11.80%	4.29%	29.79%	31.52%	17.85%	21.56%	19.95%	14.78%	12.17%	34.83%	17.61%	249.06%	20.75%	9.65%
25	20.79%	20.30%	25.14%	5.53%	33.42%	19.40%	13.08%	22.70%	21.81%	36.37%	1.01%	35.72%	255.27%	21.27%	11.00%
26	21.16%	31.29%	8.77%	20.33%	26.55%	27.86%	2.63%	25.64%	16.85%	32.54%	15.18%	20.91%	249.71%	20.81%	8.93%
27	22.47%	14.88%	21.51%	18.47%	30.10%	-0.36%	51.67%	4.91%	20.17%	46.09%	4.31%	16.41%	250.62%	20.88%	15.71%
28	24.35%	8.26%	20.89%	25.43%	21.71%	30.78%	4.92%	28.11%	10.53%	26.80%	17.27%	30.16%	249.21%	20.77%	8.73%
29	18.27%	21.84%	15.50%	25.40%	20.06%	8.91%	27.81%	35.19%	10.12%	26.28%	13.09%	14.40%	236.85%	19.74%	7.90%
30	15.71%	23.86%	37.24%	0.17%	32.37%	9.27%	17.87%	38.66%	18.89%	7.80%	24.75%	23.01%	249.58%	20.80%	11.75%
31	10.79%	34.93%	19.32%	4.99%	36.79%	24.58%	15.25%	21.78%	17.73%	30.01%	3.68%	34.93%	254.79%	21.23%	11.44%
32	35.95%	4.57%	25.88%	19.98%	18.43%	24.20%	10.14%	16.53%	15.07%	27.84%	19.45%	31.47%	249.51%	20.79%	8.88%
33	20.03%	19.18%	15.17%	24.02%	18.58%	21.93%	12.78%	13.95%	10.30%	26.66%	34.27%	17.68%	234.55%	19.55%	6.60%
34	17.59%	27.45%	22.90%	7.86%	24.03%	21.33%	24.13%	12.50%	14.90%	16.08%	13.04%	33.16%	234.98%	19.58%	7.19%
35	7.00%	41.54%	9.55%	30.30%	10.45%	22.59%	24.68%	13.97%	25.54%	13.41%	20.10%	25.40%	244.53%	20.38%	10.03%
mean	21.15%	21.05%	19.06%	18.87%	21.99%	22.71%	17.52%	22.03%	17.35%	23.46%	17.45%	22.87%			
std. dev	7.81%	11.17%	9.95%	10.24%	8.86%	10.81%	11.36%	12.32%	8.12%	10.13%	10.23%	9.94%			

Finished goods inventory trends
Inventory reduction policy: no reduction

Dollars (yr)	Jan	Feb	Mar	Apr	May	Jun	Jul	Aug	Sep	Oct	Nov	Dec	sum	mean	std. dev.
Series															
1	63,064	222,270	93,055	88,772	159,140	147,066	97,605	124,981	50,102	126,817	134,841	158,687	1,466,402	122,200	47,467
2	70,618	194,728	134,567	95,195	76,550	225,114	88,101	106,857	86,902	90,693	166,158	50,175	1,385,658	115,472	53,676
3	101,722	120,628	165,301	136,867	73,321	172,195	104,656	225,998	57,258	118,505	41,556	158,077	1,476,085	123,007	52,639
4	129,218	127,234	90,869	103,017	111,611	188,960	84,460	127,687	87,833	190,418	60,258	227,991	1,529,557	127,463	50,433
5	139,549	106,741	135,439	74,483	139,732	154,885	-46,325	171,522	119,280	209,003	96,251	90,617	1,391,177	115,931	63,205
6	140,494	123,801	80,392	124,998	117,658	172,030	42,893	166,964	43,376	102,296	222,134	64,188	1,401,225	116,769	54,354
7	66,505	242,776	3,744	166,381	126,566	230,628	69,632	28,661	170,309	169,526	5,584	171,585	1,451,896	120,991	83,930
8	165,612	71,113	179,004	-12,818	206,246	98,582	152,203	54,771	158,563	129,326	105,037	220,754	1,528,393	127,366	67,474
9	135,570	136,225	133,952	29,057	149,593	97,489	172,908	99,581	69,402	90,253	196,774	101,728	1,412,531	117,711	45,905
10	161,004	47,196	189,664	63,549	96,656	142,683	71,866	200,424	139,166	50,199	96,668	187,945	1,447,021	120,585	56,619
11	121,001	133,009	105,347	144,689	95,183	136,291	116,749	116,004	138,498	160,942	148,870	45,707	1,462,290	121,858	30,499
12	136,860	94,802	85,863	148,983	150,123	63,585	160,699	178,623	66,110	141,648	99,636	102,954	1,429,886	119,157	38,349
13	161,771	77,175	130,529	139,386	150,563	85,545	160,258	82,897	19,904	225,891	40,853	137,031	1,371,804	114,317	57,943
14	91,270	160,708	84,331	186,951	99,984	127,241	61,586	168,197	124,543	128,006	71,161	82,314	1,386,292	115,524	40,537
15	127,689	122,758	67,842	174,076	138,803	16,899	128,887	197,582	47,601	129,871	160,637	167,812	1,480,456	123,371	53,879
16	162,236	128,908	18,826	140,178	165,107	30,275	185,635	76,803	145,116	162,002	117,175	43,699	1,375,961	114,663	57,721
17	178,972	46,626	138,916	177,655	52,512	98,069	161,177	46,292	153,724	104,630	67,646	139,754	1,365,973	113,831	51,128
18	136,959	23,429	256,748	37,395	140,219	200,905	4,567	279,263	1,197	118,668	75,601	183,846	1,458,797	121,566	95,782
19	96,283	163,031	86,963	185,529	92,587	165,445	26,364	134,811	169,206	147,764	76,831	125,990	1,470,804	122,567	47,305
20	57,907	220,124	73,793	187,604	44,566	200,896	71,083	97,234	130,795	65,731	188,733	183,264	1,521,729	126,811	65,340
21	128,875	143,080	58,860	70,366	246,330	109,393	115,130	92,051	152,564	78,189	165,489	85,794	1,446,120	120,510	51,992
22	173,905	12,043	188,235	95,546	101,111	157,610	183,899	60,240	149,220	90,060	109,812	133,125	1,454,805	121,234	53,299
23	151,536	63,066	147,487	92,128	116,154	183,110	72,587	123,770	194,867	197,133	53,357	85,370	1,480,565	123,380	51,422
24	165,784	65,126	31,117	175,828	153,594	125,831	125,598	110,085	89,077	82,366	204,386	99,153	1,427,945	118,995	51,560
25	127,213	122,658	148,550	37,497	189,323	119,870	82,410	146,140	134,160	166,323	6,296	202,948	1,483,387	123,616	57,668
26	130,672	159,369	50,682	124,777	145,064	135,152	17,914	154,874	102,502	186,984	83,488	117,216	1,408,695	117,391	47,711
27	131,211	89,940	130,467	122,332	158,945	-2,669	261,125	33,524	133,893	240,402	24,004	103,725	1,426,900	118,908	79,349
28	141,864	58,502	140,493	160,383	127,007	168,638	33,269	171,773	70,471	162,772	112,142	172,778	1,520,090	126,674	48,170
29	115,045	128,485	92,804	149,381	114,714	66,290	177,583	190,632	63,218	147,118	83,239	88,539	1,417,047	118,087	41,750
30	109,656	153,646	182,970	1,092	188,128	61,366	129,754	220,140	103,628	53,358	158,229	134,648	1,496,614	124,718	63,004
31	74,631	205,125	111,518	33,916	207,130	142,028	89,359	127,669	107,330	161,906	25,409	190,215	1,476,235	123,020	61,457
32	176,134	28,948	148,228	119,929	109,254	129,759	64,599	102,534	92,578	175,515	129,075	179,575	1,456,129	121,344	45,991
33	124,669	116,109	93,643	150,292	111,256	141,873	88,546	99,043	67,783	173,688	197,326	110,044	1,474,271	122,856	37,200
34	117,012	155,307	130,861	49,494	152,034	128,994	137,529	82,723	94,729	111,921	96,944	186,829	1,444,377	120,365	36,740
35	49,166	226,328	65,409	178,428	64,978	137,017	146,154	90,846	152,171	92,496	135,456	153,243	1,491,692	124,308	52,640
mean	124,619	122,600	113,613	112,952	129,764	129,687	104,299	128,320	105,345	136,641	107,344	133,923			
std dev	35,619	60,400	53,367	56,765	45,515	55,235	61,816	58,048	46,537	48,091	58,395	50,539			

Finished goods inventory trends
Inventory reduction policy: no reduction

Percent	Jan	Feb	Mar	Apr	May	Jun	Jul	Aug	Sep	Oct	Nov	Dec	sum	mean	std. dev.
Series (yr)															
1	6.53%	35.88%	12.90%	11.01%	25.13%	24.56%	13.47%	18.61%	5.04%	16.68%	17.04%	23.10%	209.97%	17.50%	8.71%
2	7.76%	31.28%	20.30%	13.28%	8.79%	36.53%	12.91%	16.38%	11.81%	11.37%	24.39%	4.67%	199.47%	16.62%	9.74%
3	12.77%	14.27%	23.23%	19.74%	8.98%	24.46%	11.96%	45.07%	6.85%	17.44%	3.72%	23.95%	212.45%	17.70%	10.98%
4	20.50%	18.88%	11.93%	13.90%	13.56%	27.42%	11.07%	17.37%	10.30%	30.76%	6.52%	37.37%	219.57%	18.30%	9.27%
5	21.14%	15.36%	19.89%	9.63%	20.56%	25.92%	-7.62%	24.91%	17.29%	32.73%	11.82%	11.28%	202.91%	16.91%	10.23%
6	21.96%	19.85%	10.08%	18.30%	17.86%	28.85%	4.40%	26.93%	4.39%	12.18%	36.02%	7.83%	208.64%	17.39%	10.03%
7	7.77%	40.10%	-1.61%	21.57%	17.30%	41.10%	10.24%	2.01%	26.97%	30.62%	-1.36%	26.16%	220.86%	18.40%	15.13%
8	25.69%	9.57%	28.89%	-3.81%	33.01%	12.99%	22.30%	6.07%	22.51%	17.99%	13.07%	40.12%	228.41%	19.03%	12.27%
9	19.97%	21.16%	23.69%	2.14%	22.52%	13.54%	27.61%	15.03%	8.35%	10.98%	30.19%	13.30%	208.48%	17.37%	8.24%
10	28.50%	4.92%	30.73%	8.82%	12.71%	21.12%	8.38%	30.98%	21.99%	5.65%	12.04%	31.78%	217.61%	18.13%	10.53%
11	16.23%	18.54%	14.66%	22.21%	11.80%	19.26%	15.83%	16.50%	18.96%	26.09%	25.97%	4.94%	210.99%	17.58%	5.86%
12	21.12%	12.33%	11.11%	21.80%	23.35%	7.32%	22.82%	29.09%	8.19%	21.17%	13.46%	13.83%	205.60%	17.13%	6.93%
13	25.69%	10.37%	18.59%	23.78%	14.37%	12.16%	29.56%	12.59%	0.73%	41.82%	4.07%	20.19%	213.92%	17.83%	11.38%
14	11.86%	25.01%	10.75%	31.00%	13.96%	19.86%	7.26%	24.46%	20.64%	21.49%	9.77%	11.28%	207.35%	17.28%	7.45%
15	19.00%	18.94%	8.10%	27.79%	24.26%	0.26%	16.46%	31.55%	4.81%	17.21%	24.95%	26.09%	219.43%	18.29%	9.64%
16	25.83%	21.80%	0.51%	20.25%	27.24%	2.20%	28.92%	9.27%	21.29%	25.28%	18.36%	4.24%	205.19%	17.10%	10.27%
17	29.72%	4.82%	20.73%	31.93%	6.24%	12.91%	26.45%	5.15%	24.02%	15.04%	7.49%	19.40%	203.89%	16.99%	9.81%
18	22.14%	1.24%	42.94%	3.37%	21.10%	38.49%	-1.42%	59.50%	-2.49%	17.86%	9.15%	31.13%	243.01%	20.25%	19.71%
19	12.04%	25.06%	10.58%	29.08%	11.88%	28.85%	1.69%	17.86%	25.96%	21.92%	9.19%	16.53%	210.63%	17.55%	8.74%
20	5.97%	38.01%	8.36%	32.37%	4.45%	35.45%	9.41%	12.79%	19.32%	7.00%	27.42%	31.48%	232.03%	19.34%	12.81%
21	18.29%	22.06%	6.38%	7.65%	41.55%	16.27%	16.78%	11.73%	22.76%	10.33%	27.35%	11.29%	212.45%	17.70%	9.86%
22	29.41%	-0.49%	29.89%	11.81%	12.02%	24.35%	31.50%	6.94%	22.61%	11.92%	15.71%	19.83%	215.49%	17.96%	10.00%
23	22.77%	7.27%	20.11%	11.19%	14.54%	29.32%	8.31%	15.40%	29.88%	34.64%	6.41%	10.37%	210.21%	17.52%	9.71%
24	29.53%	8.81%	2.33%	27.16%	28.61%	15.18%	18.81%	16.96%	12.14%	9.96%	32.10%	14.70%	216.29%	18.02%	9.43%
25	18.21%	17.67%	22.46%	3.40%	30.65%	16.89%	10.65%	20.31%	19.25%	32.52%	-1.50%	32.85%	223.37%	18.61%	10.71%
26	18.62%	27.95%	5.97%	17.78%	23.52%	24.30%	0.44%	23.03%	14.25%	29.72%	12.19%	18.01%	215.80%	17.98%	8.70%
27	19.71%	12.26%	18.94%	16.18%	26.94%	-2.23%	48.39%	2.72%	17.89%	42.87%	1.36%	13.95%	218.99%	18.25%	15.37%
28	21.58%	6.22%	18.72%	23.08%	19.04%	27.76%	2.70%	25.56%	8.28%	24.21%	14.91%	27.35%	219.41%	18.28%	8.50%
29	15.80%	19.11%	12.84%	22.67%	17.22%	7.00%	25.46%	32.13%	7.62%	23.35%	10.65%	11.85%	205.70%	17.14%	7.69%
30	13.60%	21.53%	33.80%	-2.15%	29.60%	6.98%	15.89%	35.94%	15.97%	5.65%	22.36%	20.27%	219.42%	18.29%	11.48%
31	8.65%	32.22%	16.52%	2.79%	33.94%	21.78%	12.51%	19.04%	15.11%	26.93%	1.54%	31.89%	222.91%	18.58%	11.16%
32	32.43%	2.12%	23.05%	17.35%	15.73%	21.09%	7.78%	14.07%	12.62%	25.41%	17.18%	28.62%	217.45%	18.12%	8.62%
33	17.52%	16.56%	12.63%	21.52%	15.97%	19.56%	10.68%	12.00%	8.23%	24.53%	31.60%	15.20%	206.00%	17.17%	6.48%
34	15.32%	24.65%	20.06%	5.41%	21.57%	18.75%	21.28%	10.21%	12.52%	13.96%	11.16%	30.40%	205.29%	17.11%	6.98%
35	4.91%	38.54%	7.38%	27.58%	7.93%	20.03%	22.00%	11.62%	22.88%	11.26%	17.93%	22.77%	214.83%	17.90%	9.78%
mean	18.53%	18.40%	16.50%	16.33%	19.37%	20.01%	15.00%	19.42%	14.83%	20.81%	14.98%	20.23%			
std. dev	7.42%	10.96%	9.72%	10.00%	8.64%	10.47%	11.09%	12.01%	7.99%	9.79%	10.08%	9.68%			

Finished goods inventory trends
Inventory reduction policy: no reduction

Dollars Series (yr)	Jan	Feb	Mar	Apr	May	Jun	Jul	Aug	Sep	Oct	Nov	Dec	sum	mean	std. dev.
1	48,959	206,482	77,303	73,685	143,083	130,330	81,793	108,944	35,427	111,901	120,193	143,253	1,281,354	106,779	47,076
2	56,196	178,736	118,499	79,239	61,880	208,982	71,651	90,376	71,013	75,559	150,623	36,440	1,199,193	99,933	53,222
3	86,773	106,657	151,057	122,221	58,582	157,053	90,948	209,503	41,402	102,453	27,225	142,893	1,296,769	108,064	52,361
4	112,698	111,187	75,331	87,450	97,109	173,693	69,084	112,346	73,276	174,451	45,518	211,718	1,343,862	111,989	50,074
5	123,452	90,717	119,601	58,948	123,862	138,172	-59,972	157,669	105,418	194,964	82,756	77,064	1,212,650	101,054	62,890
6	124,172	107,172	65,035	109,047	101,355	155,460	27,402	150,566	27,892	87,851	206,073	48,818	1,210,842	100,903	53,981
7	51,332	226,488	-11,070	151,740	111,243	213,761	52,707	13,807	154,396	152,425	-9,306	155,613	1,263,136	105,261	83,411
8	149,491	55,171	162,653	-27,306	190,097	83,161	136,433	39,464	143,351	114,093	90,298	203,739	1,340,644	111,720	66,926
9	119,652	119,925	116,923	13,539	133,604	81,610	156,607	83,110	54,061	75,491	180,920	86,423	1,221,866	101,822	45,633
10	143,960	31,860	173,473	46,822	81,217	126,843	57,105	184,560	122,772	34,394	81,694	171,456	1,256,157	104,680	56,300
11	105,712	117,764	89,810	128,525	80,237	101,324	57,832	100,541	123,273	144,472	131,858	29,850	1,274,214	106,184	30,285
12	120,599	79,418	70,485	133,212	133,899	48,420	145,223	162,204	50,422	125,658	84,012	87,433	1,240,985	103,415	38,062
13	145,460	61,154	114,853	122,450	84,514	69,270	153,373	66,096	4,999	209,023	25,172	121,116	1,177,480	98,123	57,522
14	75,832	144,538	68,919	170,503	84,100	110,872	46,095	152,572	107,699	111,105	54,788	66,267	1,193,290	99,441	40,346
15	111,633	106,741	52,763	158,050	121,842	1,713	114,092	181,512	32,634	115,110	144,714	151,751	1,292,556	107,713	53,506
16	145,914	311,965	3,218	124,446	148,555	15,806	169,965	61,682	129,316	145,811	100,644	28,726	1,186,047	98,837	57,246
17	162,421	31,327	122,996	160,577	36,398	82,643	144,637	30,492	137,676	88,600	53,039	124,564	1,175,370	97,948	50,712
18	120,384	9,625	241,272	22,779	124,674	183,601	-10,037	261,911	-14,708	102,441	60,416	167,190	1,269,548	105,796	94,996
19	81,277	147,139	72,025	169,692	77,569	149,009	11,240	119,742	153,190	131,867	61,793	111,089	1,285,632	107,136	46,906
20	43,551	203,878	59,188	171,129	29,374	184,015	54,995	81,804	114,819	51,439	173,456	106,506	1,334,155	111,180	64,668
21	113,282	126,881	44,032	56,606	230,620	93,163	99,120	76,795	136,654	62,314	148,915	70,143	1,258,427	104,869	51,631
22	157,214	-3,201	172,040	80,632	87,322	142,253	167,151	44,893	133,490	74,447	93,880	117,103	1,267,226	105,602	52,837
23	135,566	47,847	132,373	77,661	101,919	167,426	57,832	109,517	179,316	180,345	37,214	70,413	1,297,430	108,119	51,100
24	148,727	48,635	16,900	160,332	157,555	89,957	109,589	93,603	73,204	67,377	188,359	82,805	1,237,043	103,087	51,235
25	111,454	106,793	132,694	23,044	173,597	104,392	67,111	130,759	118,437	148,700	-9,325	186,672	1,294,327	107,861	57,260
26	114,976	142,376	34,511	109,162	128,509	117,870	2,990	139,164	86,697	170,769	67,046	100,948	1,215,017	101,251	47,408
27	115,115	74,090	114,851	107,172	142,298	-16,763	244,554	18,620	118,780	223,622	7,590	88,209	1,238,137	103,178	78,801
28	125,753	44,062	125,886	145,551	111,418	152,096	18,290	156,184	55,398	147,010	96,832	156,664	1,335,143	111,262	47,781
29	99,495	112,437	76,880	133,337	98,494	52,105	162,584	174,029	47,596	130,727	67,771	72,859	1,228,315	102,360	41,443
30	94,929	138,674	166,095	-14,128	172,018	46,199	115,362	204,629	87,598	38,617	142,966	118,622	1,311,582	109,298	62,709
31	59,824	189,170	95,324	18,984	191,097	125,857	73,285	111,585	91,482	145,269	10,590	173,651	1,286,118	107,177	60,968
32	158,901	13,457	131,987	104,130	93,259	113,083	49,542	87,308	77,487	160,186	114,041	163,323	1,266,705	105,559	45,615
33	109,025	100,261	77,942	134,701	95,637	126,528	73,973	85,244	54,175	159,810	181,945	94,588	1,293,829	107,819	37,023
34	101,873	139,443	114,618	34,095	136,520	113,385	121,268	67,563	79,619	97,169	82,990	171,249	1,259,792	104,983	36,463
35	34,492	209,987	50,517	162,409	49,333	121,482	130,303	75,543	136,310	77,661	120,841	137,391	1,306,268	108,856	52,211
mean	108,857	106,824	98,028	97,441	114,080	113,837	88,789	112,695	89,845	120,947	91,930	118,187			
std. dev	34,897	60,073	53,083	56,386	45,226	54,717	61,369	57,728	46,336	47,701	58,222	50,079			

Finished goods inventory trends
Inventory reduction policy: no reduction

Percent	Jan	Feb	Mar	Apr	May	Jun	Jul	Aug	Sep	Oct	Nov	Dec	sum	mean	std. dev.
Series (yr)															
1	42.65%	63.61%	47.02%	46.02%	54.19%	56.01%	48.28%	51.16%	41.87%	49.33%	49.13%	53.72%	602.97%	50.25%	6.05%
2	43.09%	60.19%	51.98%	47.43%	44.15%	62.94%	46.51%	49.50%	46.06%	46.48%	54.79%	41.55%	594.67%	49.56%	6.71%
3	46.92%	47.70%	54.50%	51.30%	43.13%	55.71%	46.23%	69.15%	43.63%	50.21%	40.69%	54.27%	603.44%	50.29%	7.64%
4	51.52%	51.34%	46.30%	48.56%	47.29%	56.57%	55.55%	50.17%	44.19%	58.71%	42.44%	63.58%	606.23%	50.52%	6.31%
5	52.82%	49.41%	52.36%	44.28%	51.41%	56.90%	33.18%	55.84%	51.13%	60.21%	46.11%	45.45%	599.09%	49.92%	7.10%
6	53.29%	52.00%	45.51%	50.21%	59.45%	59.45%	41.47%	56.88%	41.36%	46.24%	63.40%	43.98%	605.02%	50.42%	7.06%
7	43.54%	66.03%	37.26%	52.65%	49.55%	66.46%	45.76%	39.94%	56.43%	58.92%	37.30%	66.03%	609.81%	50.82%	10.30%
8	56.80%	44.98%	55.34%	35.80%	60.23%	47.22%	53.38%	42.47%	53.85%	50.73%	46.64%	47.49%	617.23%	51.44%	8.50%
9	52.16%	53.17%	59.31%	39.16%	53.75%	56.99%	56.99%	49.21%	44.77%	45.32%	58.79%	60.12%	603.14%	50.26%	5.76%
10	57.97%	42.12%	48.30%	44.23%	47.14%	53.06%	43.53%	59.43%	53.92%	42.97%	46.79%	41.51%	610.58%	50.88%	7.15%
11	49.78%	51.19%	45.33%	53.23%	46.29%	50.59%	49.26%	49.32%	50.71%	56.02%	57.08%	52.01%	603.28%	50.27%	4.13%
12	53.30%	47.08%	50.79%	52.67%	53.87%	53.26%	53.26%	59.26%	43.52%	52.77%	47.50%	55.40%	600.42%	50.03%	4.90%
13	56.13%	45.58%	46.03%	55.12%	48.13%	46.56%	58.28%	48.25%	39.23%	67.61%	41.34%	41.16%	609.03%	50.75%	7.80%
14	45.80%	54.77%	44.19%	59.41%	48.83%	52.43%	42.95%	55.52%	51.80%	54.01%	44.97%	51.66%	602.11%	50.18%	5.19%
15	51.59%	51.88%	38.90%	57.56%	54.72%	38.37%	48.61%	59.77%	41.66%	50.04%	55.33%	60.33%	609.11%	50.76%	6.55%
16	55.97%	54.09%	52.17%	51.70%	57.21%	40.43%	57.09%	44.50%	52.56%	55.53%	50.98%	49.58%	600.02%	50.00%	6.88%
17	58.73%	42.18%	67.78%	60.16%	42.77%	47.26%	57.14%	79.78%	37.57%	48.42%	42.97%	59.87%	629.55%	52.46%	13.35%
18	53.30%	39.81%	55.60%	40.98%	52.49%	63.75%	37.84%	42.03%	55.33%	51.17%	44.75%	46.65%	603.84%	50.32%	5.99%
19	46.81%	55.29%	44.38%	58.46%	46.70%	58.55%	39.53%	50.30%	51.49%	53.42%	44.28%	51.41%	617.19%	51.43%	8.89%
20	41.50%	64.63%	33.34%	60.10%	41.09%	62.95%	44.90%	47.45%	53.53%	42.54%	56.32%	46.24%	603.51%	50.29%	6.46%
21	50.66%	53.75%	58.89%	42.94%	65.64%	49.38%	49.53%	46.52%	53.58%	44.90%	56.67%	60.87%	608.19%	50.68%	6.84%
22	59.13%	38.01%	52.12%	47.22%	46.16%	54.25%	40.28%	43.58%	53.68%	46.94%	48.65%	50.82%	600.26%	50.02%	6.82%
23	54.09%	42.76%	39.82%	44.75%	47.73%	57.84%	43.52%	48.17%	58.72%	62.14%	42.17%	57.56%	609.59%	50.80%	6.37%
24	58.76%	44.73%	55.58%	56.75%	58.05%	49.22%	51.71%	49.54%	46.54%	45.62%	59.98%	46.65%	614.28%	51.19%	7.31%
25	50.79%	50.99%	42.94%	40.89%	58.89%	50.87%	44.97%	51.92%	51.11%	60.03%	37.37%	51.74%	610.63%	50.89%	6.05%
26	50.79%	58.40%	50.73%	49.62%	54.48%	55.95%	39.19%	53.69%	48.13%	59.61%	47.02%	60.40%	609.80%	50.82%	10.58%
27	52.18%	46.90%	50.48%	49.42%	56.43%	36.83%	71.21%	40.44%	49.28%	68.71%	39.30%	58.17%	609.56%	50.80%	5.63%
28	53.70%	43.03%	47.14%	53.95%	51.16%	56.88%	40.39%	55.20%	44.22%	54.26%	48.72%	48.28%	600.15%	50.01%	5.10%
29	49.45%	51.04%	62.50%	54.24%	50.04%	42.99%	54.92%	60.38%	43.86%	53.45%	45.99%	53.40%	610.92%	50.91%	7.84%
30	47.64%	53.37%	50.25%	37.51%	58.22%	42.73%	48.90%	62.50%	49.84%	42.14%	53.83%	52.17%	612.50%	51.04%	7.69%
31	44.20%	60.51%	54.66%	39.50%	60.85%	53.63%	56.57%	51.70%	48.56%	56.74%	39.60%	40.40%	609.25%	50.77%	5.92%
32	60.59%	39.86%	46.93%	50.57%	49.13%	53.03%	44.11%	48.16%	46.09%	55.10%	49.78%	58.17%	598.15%	49.85%	4.33%
33	50.19%	49.39%	52.79%	53.53%	49.38%	52.06%	46.31%	46.10%	42.70%	54.92%	58.37%	48.28%	598.45%	49.87%	4.83%
34	49.29%	54.87%	42.99%	41.60%	53.42%	51.08%	52.44%	46.23%	54.32%	46.81%	45.27%	53.40%	603.27%	50.27%	6.78%
35	41.12%	64.91%	49.81%	56.60%	51.37%	52.11%	48.47%	51.69%	48.35%	52.52%	48.41%	52.17%	603.27%	50.27%	6.59%
mean	51.04%	51.13%	49.81%	49.38%	51.37%	52.11%	48.47%	51.69%	48.35%	52.52%	48.41%	52.17%		50.27%	
std. dev	5.29%	7.53%	6.79%	6.85%	5.77%	7.19%	7.46%	8.25%	5.35%	6.78%	6.84%	6.59%			

Finished goods inventory trends
Inventory reduction policy: no reduction

Dollars Series (yr)	Jan	Feb	Mar	Apr	May	Jun	Jul	Aug	Sep	Oct	Nov	Dec	sum	mean	std. dev.
1	319,712	366,072	281,675	308,071	308,477	297,250	293,065	299,470	294,053	330,854	346,566	333,086	3,778,351	314,863	25,014
2	312,008	343,856	303,491	282,921	310,862	360,116	258,071	273,097	276,947	308,891	338,426	324,179	3,692,866	307,739	30,952
3	318,757	356,432	354,425	317,535	281,312	357,722	351,547	321,414	263,699	295,029	297,722	323,793	3,839,387	319,949	31,248
4	283,244	302,410	292,251	305,391	338,649	358,378	284,186	324,567	314,486	333,031	296,135	360,270	3,792,998	316,083	26,926
5	308,409	291,759	314,880	270,961	309,740	303,312	261,242	353,392	311,767	358,658	322,870	310,514	3,717,504	309,792	28,162
6	301,332	280,797	293,723	299,280	290,637	320,292	258,415	318,039	262,761	333,588	362,714	274,220	3,595,797	299,650	30,265
7	287,707	372,945	256,214	370,361	318,625	345,644	235,643	274,811	323,082	293,304	255,384	332,965	3,666,684	305,557	45,558
8	330,509	259,348	332,790	256,622	346,852	302,353	326,624	275,900	342,846	321,710	322,342	335,269	3,753,164	312,764	31,803
9	312,493	301,305	273,153	247,756	318,897	283,327	323,190	272,041	289,736	311,734	352,368	308,589	3,594,589	299,549	27,992
10	292,794	273,021	334,829	234,854	301,233	318,737	296,563	354,070	301,072	261,409	317,455	324,350	3,610,389	300,866	32,896
11	324,250	325,202	295,802	308,013	314,812	317,461	315,297	300,545	329,749	310,147	289,863	250,850	3,681,993	306,833	21,341
12	304,365	303,108	287,651	321,804	308,889	285,764	338,926	330,775	267,860	313,214	296,454	307,167	3,665,978	305,498	19,793
13	317,823	268,859	313,811	283,804	283,062	265,199	302,366	253,336	267,567	337,962	255,779	312,027	3,461,597	288,466	27,664
14	292,718	316,494	295,058	326,772	294,155	292,661	272,710	346,345	270,306	279,217	252,321	267,822	3,506,579	292,215	26,870
15	303,121	292,336	287,755	327,360	274,834	253,266	336,954	343,841	282,689	334,673	320,882	322,235	3,679,940	306,662	28,560
16	316,143	277,781	243,099	317,742	312,024	290,136	335,556	296,189	319,224	320,278	279,418	279,190	3,586,781	298,898	26,025
17	320,958	274,310	309,447	302,612	249,399	302,441	312,524	249,053	312,769	285,318	304,170	331,760	3,554,761	296,230	26,540
18	289,773	308,529	380,885	276,759	310,133	304,112	267,770	351,179	221,897	293,457	295,495	324,046	3,624,035	302,003	40,148
19	315,890	324,640	310,511	341,144	304,957	302,418	262,643	337,201	326,575	321,340	297,823	333,288	3,778,431	314,869	21,520
20	302,544	346,713	314,196	317,764	270,910	326,751	262,432	303,557	305,942	312,393	356,308	316,651	3,736,162	311,347	26,600
21	313,417	309,055	298,972	317,819	364,341	282,760	292,638	304,584	321,408	270,979	308,536	289,695	3,674,204	306,184	23,575
22	316,133	248,707	338,984	322,385	335,422	316,888	319,828	282,029	316,917	293,147	290,728	303,628	3,684,795	307,066	25,228
23	322,038	281,281	343,044	310,557	334,593	330,248	302,883	342,601	352,404	323,578	244,817	313,973	3,802,016	316,835	29,965
24	295,997	246,788	288,531	334,940	319,724	291,720	301,280	273,438	280,547	308,697	352,027	275,261	3,568,950	297,413	28,695
25	310,830	308,102	328,388	277,134	333,613	314,356	283,258	334,323	314,380	274,528	233,019	345,874	3,657,804	304,817	32,297
26	313,677	297,417	248,175	304,592	297,619	271,426	267,352	324,338	292,734	342,532	258,566	284,814	3,503,243	291,937	27,651
27	304,778	283,451	307,691	327,339	298,050	276,530	359,856	276,292	327,189	358,411	219,135	305,650	3,644,371	303,698	38,566
28	312,848	304,761	339,474	340,177	299,331	311,628	273,328	327,320	296,034	329,530	316,422	329,736	3,790,588	315,882	20,482
29	311,446	300,350	282,266	319,063	286,243	319,761	350,654	327,052	273,863	299,230	292,534	286,913	3,649,374	304,115	22,144
30	332,608	343,736	307,091	245,923	338,362	282,833	355,065	355,920	273,453	288,283	344,179	302,707	3,770,159	314,180	36,011
31	305,671	355,267	289,988	268,738	342,596	309,901	272,769	303,012	293,977	306,103	273,156	328,963	3,650,139	304,178	27,387
32	296,874	252,585	313,056	303,605	291,263	284,398	281,006	298,709	283,081	347,312	330,332	331,884	3,614,105	301,175	26,230
33	312,324	299,064	289,700	334,982	295,671	336,790	320,779	327,349	280,987	357,811	336,064	300,480	3,791,998	316,000	23,291
34	327,796	310,456	301,634	261,596	338,017	308,904	298,845	305,963	293,120	325,763	336,562	329,914	3,738,970	311,581	21,792
35	288,902	353,629	294,314	333,326	274,574	313,322	312,353	293,516	323,590	318,943	337,160	322,189	3,765,819	313,818	22,680
mean	309,140	305,159	304,199	303,431	308,511	306,823	299,646	310,436	297,392	314,316	303,821	312,113			
std. dev	12,571	33,918	28,722	31,240	25,026	25,772	32,475	30,281	27,085	25,063	37,633	24,047			

Finished goods inventory trends
Inventory reduction policy: no reduction

Percent	Jan	Feb	Mar	Apr	May	Jun	Jul	Aug	Sep	Oct	Nov	Dec	sum	mean	std. dev.
Series (yr)															
1	10.50%	29.59%	14.09%	13.48%	22.05%	21.63%	14.77%	17.95%	9.49%	17.08%	17.30%	21.41%	209.34%	17.45%	5.62%
2	11.31%	26.58%	18.79%	14.57%	11.94%	29.77%	14.27%	16.43%	13.65%	13.77%	21.70%	9.32%	202.09%	16.84%	6.27%
3	14.33%	15.39%	21.48%	19.00%	11.78%	22.24%	13.95%	35.10%	10.31%	17.26%	8.93%	21.79%	211.56%	17.63%	7.09%
4	19.19%	18.35%	13.72%	15.24%	14.94%	23.74%	13.36%	17.40%	12.66%	26.27%	10.38%	30.30%	215.54%	17.96%	6.01%
5	19.79%	16.08%	19.07%	11.93%	19.32%	22.60%	1.58%	22.80%	17.52%	26.75%	13.95%	13.46%	204.85%	17.07%	6.49%
6	20.17%	18.52%	12.79%	17.63%	18.02%	24.76%	8.62%	23.28%	8.81%	14.27%	29.63%	10.96%	207.47%	17.29%	6.54%
7	11.18%	31.99%	5.16%	20.25%	17.33%	32.34%	12.52%	7.62%	23.58%	25.17%	5.21%	23.14%	215.50%	17.96%	9.67%
8	22.57%	12.36%	24.70%	3.63%	27.42%	14.60%	20.50%	10.11%	20.89%	17.59%	14.49%	32.11%	220.97%	18.41%	7.92%
9	19.03%	19.76%	20.86%	7.04%	21.01%	14.88%	23.65%	15.79%	11.60%	13.11%	25.71%	14.75%	207.19%	17.27%	5.36%
10	24.40%	9.41%	25.59%	11.51%	14.51%	19.80%	11.48%	25.96%	20.09%	9.60%	14.10%	26.75%	213.20%	17.77%	6.75%
11	16.61%	18.14%	15.58%	20.25%	13.78%	18.66%	16.69%	16.63%	18.31%	22.81%	22.54%	9.09%	209.11%	17.43%	3.74%
12	19.68%	14.22%	13.19%	20.10%	21.08%	10.83%	21.02%	25.05%	11.06%	19.87%	14.73%	15.49%	206.32%	17.19%	4.53%
13	22.55%	12.88%	17.83%	21.57%	15.14%	13.89%	24.92%	13.72%	6.58%	33.19%	8.54%	19.08%	209.89%	17.49%	7.38%
14	13.83%	22.05%	13.22%	25.87%	15.17%	18.69%	10.79%	22.17%	18.68%	20.02%	12.13%	13.18%	205.80%	17.15%	4.77%
15	18.65%	18.25%	11.28%	24.04%	21.24%	6.11%	16.86%	26.65%	9.39%	17.36%	22.05%	22.54%	214.42%	17.87%	6.19%
16	22.33%	20.12%	6.40%	19.38%	23.44%	7.65%	24.69%	12.05%	20.06%	22.27%	17.69%	9.02%	205.10%	17.09%	6.54%
17	25.16%	9.20%	19.56%	26.60%	9.84%	14.41%	23.44%	9.35%	21.42%	15.53%	10.87%	18.95%	204.35%	17.03%	6.37%
18	20.05%	7.28%	34.14%	8.37%	19.68%	30.29%	5.08%	44.25%	4.39%	17.74%	12.03%	26.25%	229.54%	19.13%	12.63%
19	14.15%	22.29%	12.78%	24.83%	13.75%	24.77%	7.18%	17.71%	22.88%	20.24%	11.88%	17.06%	209.52%	17.46%	5.66%
20	9.98%	30.78%	11.65%	26.75%	8.87%	29.19%	11.96%	14.41%	18.57%	10.64%	23.74%	26.43%	222.98%	18.58%	8.30%
21	18.05%	20.18%	10.26%	11.17%	33.02%	16.39%	16.82%	13.81%	20.56%	12.96%	23.67%	13.44%	210.34%	17.53%	6.33%
22	25.06%	5.65%	25.54%	13.77%	14.06%	21.84%	26.43%	10.35%	20.66%	13.91%	16.18%	18.98%	212.41%	17.70%	6.49%
23	20.70%	10.95%	19.05%	13.30%	16.00%	24.96%	11.67%	16.07%	25.66%	28.06%	9.94%	13.19%	209.56%	17.46%	6.19%
24	25.06%	11.83%	7.69%	23.90%	24.37%	15.72%	18.01%	16.68%	13.74%	12.88%	26.71%	15.48%	212.07%	17.67%	6.04%
25	17.69%	17.47%	21.08%	8.38%	25.52%	17.25%	12.85%	19.41%	15.42%	26.87%	5.17%	27.19%	217.17%	18.10%	6.85%
26	18.12%	23.91%	10.06%	17.12%	21.19%	21.68%	6.48%	20.81%	17.26%	25.36%	13.95%	17.32%	211.41%	17.62%	5.55%
27	18.93%	14.03%	16.70%	16.70%	23.22%	4.68%	37.25%	8.00%	17.26%	34.05%	6.71%	15.09%	214.14%	17.85%	9.94%
28	19.81%	10.41%	17.89%	21.38%	18.53%	23.62%	8.23%	22.53%	11.42%	21.70%	15.99%	23.75%	215.24%	17.94%	5.35%
29	16.33%	18.41%	14.42%	20.49%	17.24%	10.70%	22.63%	26.85%	11.02%	20.96%	13.25%	13.57%	205.86%	17.15%	4.93%
30	14.92%	20.38%	27.42%	4.78%	25.21%	10.62%	16.30%	29.36%	16.27%	9.85%	20.87%	18.96%	214.96%	17.91%	7.36%
31	11.89%	26.86%	16.83%	7.84%	27.89%	20.09%	13.91%	18.53%	15.85%	23.44%	7.12%	26.66%	216.90%	18.08%	7.18%
32	26.89%	7.18%	21.39%	17.11%	15.87%	20.19%	11.13%	15.37%	14.07%	22.09%	17.45%	24.40%	213.14%	17.76%	5.60%
33	17.34%	16.77%	14.26%	19.97%	16.59%	18.80%	13.31%	14.26%	11.59%	22.17%	26.17%	15.91%	207.14%	17.26%	4.06%
34	16.04%	22.01%	18.76%	9.69%	20.04%	18.23%	19.72%	12.91%	14.11%	15.18%	13.68%	25.67%	206.05%	17.17%	4.42%
35	9.31%	31.09%	10.70%	23.94%	11.62%	19.02%	19.99%	13.36%	21.26%	13.37%	17.97%	20.76%	212.40%	17.70%	6.33%
mean	18.05%	18.01%	16.73%	16.62%	18.59%	18.99%	15.77%	18.65%	15.63%	19.53%	15.78%	19.18%			
std. dev	4.69%	7.08%	6.27%	6.46%	5.52%	6.71%	7.11%	7.73%	5.18%	6.25%	6.50%	6.24%			

Finished goods inventory trends
Inventory reduction policy: no reduction

Dollars Series (yr)	Jan	Feb	Mar	Apr	May	Jun	Jul	Aug	Sep	Oct	Nov	Dec	sum	mean	std. dev.
1	78,735	170,298	84,417	90,267	125,519	114,820	89,668	105,053	66,630	114,593	122,002	132,737	1,294,739	107,895	28,395
2	81,866	151,832	109,714	86,913	84,082	170,344	79,159	90,636	82,057	91,487	134,017	72,758	1,234,864	102,905	31,905
3	97,378	115,020	139,676	117,630	76,813	142,840	106,045	163,135	62,329	101,423	65,314	130,016	1,317,619	109,802	31,458
4	105,511	108,075	86,589	95,818	106,997	150,417	83,357	112,535	90,112	149,008	72,446	171,661	1,332,525	111,044	30,523
5	115,522	94,986	114,679	73,009	116,405	120,476	12,410	144,301	106,831	159,369	97,694	91,949	1,247,630	103,969	36,909
6	114,073	99,978	82,523	105,103	102,250	133,394	53,736	130,150	55,982	102,958	169,518	68,339	1,218,004	101,500	33,647
7	73,858	180,680	35,490	142,410	111,456	168,215	64,473	52,433	135,033	125,314	35,687	137,672	1,262,720	105,227	50,952
8	131,353	71,285	139,036	26,020	157,913	93,519	125,413	65,663	132,995	111,575	100,130	163,035	1,317,937	109,828	40,522
9	113,979	111,991	102,970	44,556	124,638	134,122	95,870	87,283	75,052	90,204	154,109	89,720	1,224,494	102,041	28,721
10	123,216	61,002	144,475	61,110	92,707	118,957	78,182	154,670	112,182	58,435	95,696	144,332	1,244,964	103,747	34,535
11	108,193	115,279	95,431	117,156	93,712	117,101	106,835	101,335	119,085	126,311	114,484	54,943	1,269,864	105,822	18,795
12	112,405	91,534	83,688	122,824	120,893	71,600	133,806	139,702	68,067	117,907	91,923	97,917	1,252,265	104,355	23,659
13	127,681	75,985	110,178	111,075	89,054	79,098	129,263	72,042	44,871	165,895	52,836	114,443	1,172,422	97,702	35,052
14	88,372	127,430	84,760	142,275	91,370	104,323	68,536	138,316	97,488	103,515	68,033	77,438	1,191,856	99,321	25,231
15	109,589	102,816	73,460	136,711	106,679	40,355	116,872	153,339	63,694	116,134	127,873	131,095	1,278,616	106,551	32,601
16	126,152	103,323	39,986	119,116	127,870	55,014	145,141	80,179	121,812	128,464	96,941	61,180	1,205,177	100,431	33,970
17	137,508	59,848	116,006	133,817	57,405	92,245	128,180	55,433	122,785	91,533	76,967	121,700	1,193,426	99,452	31,134
18	108,984	56,400	191,863	56,496	116,264	144,494	35,964	194,769	25,933	101,715	79,473	140,992	1,253,346	104,445	56,402
19	95,483	130,888	87,014	144,921	89,783	47,729	127,915	118,692	135,060	121,767	79,893	114,662	1,293,807	107,817	28,148
20	72,799	165,127	82,495	141,427	58,482	151,542	69,885	92,192	110,327	78,168	150,194	139,799	1,312,437	109,370	38,121
21	111,691	116,050	70,780	82,671	183,288	93,875	99,344	90,388	123,462	78,225	128,859	83,497	1,262,131	105,178	30,783
22	133,966	36,957	147,003	93,995	102,136	127,579	140,209	66,962	121,977	86,883	96,688	112,076	1,266,431	105,536	32,038
23	123,222	72,048	125,405	92,323	112,140	142,489	81,189	114,307	153,997	146,131	57,712	89,579	1,310,541	109,212	30,835
24	126,206	65,301	55,710	141,055	134,241	93,183	104,933	92,060	82,807	87,162	156,776	87,175	1,226,610	102,217	31,092
25	108,284	105,544	124,538	56,806	144,539	106,592	80,957	124,985	112,472	122,886	32,263	154,505	1,274,371	106,198	34,849
26	111,889	121,779	58,125	105,096	115,746	105,163	44,218	125,731	93,812	145,707	76,710	97,047	1,201,023	100,085	28,797
27	110,569	84,790	110,533	110,588	122,639	35,150	188,212	54,662	114,575	177,636	37,399	95,394	1,242,147	103,512	47,819
28	115,422	73,718	120,278	134,795	108,397	79,575	105,526	137,654	76,427	131,765	103,857	136,061	1,323,475	110,290	27,764
29	102,860	108,341	86,328	120,498	98,635	70,311	153,742	145,463	68,802	117,317	84,273	83,436	1,240,006	103,334	24,882
30	104,200	131,287	134,738	31,331	146,499	116,115	72,563	167,212	89,265	67,365	133,448	110,959	1,304,982	108,748	38,515
31	82,191	157,731	97,125	53,326	157,046	108,286	89,301	108,604	95,926	126,459	49,084	145,176	1,270,255	105,855	36,565
32	131,739	122,492	122,492	102,711	94,109	121,633	92,211	95,345	86,398	139,247	115,791	139,234	1,251,748	104,312	28,211
33	107,875	101,574	88,013	124,956	99,308	110,239	103,604	101,262	76,232	144,442	150,697	99,050	1,307,252	108,938	22,390
34	106,663	124,508	107,210	61,058	126,841	115,375	107,252	85,405	89,728	105,671	101,697	144,651	1,276,059	106,338	21,442
35	65,424	169,396	73,259	141,005	72,274	118,368	118,399	86,857	123,680	92,247	121,099	125,230	1,307,238	108,937	31,362
mean	107,567	105,951	100,742	100,596	110,518	109,754	95,478	109,964	95,454	114,998	98,045	113,303			
std dev	18,414	36,975	32,418	34,658	27,363	32,426	37,047	35,133	29,076	28,009	36,670	30,133			

Finished goods inventory trends
Inventory reduction policy: no reduction

Percent Series (yr)	Jan	Feb	Mar	Apr	May	Jun	Jul	Aug	Sep	Oct	Nov	Dec	sum	mean	std. dev.
1	10.32%	29.06%	20.20%	16.72%	23.96%	27.40%	16.67%	22.03%	10.02%	19.27%	18.72%	18.19%	232.56%	19.38%	5.82%
2	12.35%	21.88%	31.67%	17.38%	11.97%	34.23%	16.78%	19.47%	14.68%	14.47%	24.99%	10.34%	230.20%	19.18%	7.70%
3	15.02%	18.31%	17.27%	28.80%	12.65%	17.54%	21.63%	33.01%	19.95%	18.68%	7.79%	12.71%	223.36%	18.61%	6.91%
4	25.10%	21.60%	13.13%	17.60%	14.42%	29.25%	16.02%	17.07%	14.24%	21.76%	19.86%	34.51%	244.57%	20.38%	6.52%
5	22.59%	18.22%	22.09%	10.40%	24.84%	30.49%	-2.70%	15.72%	6.01%	34.73%	34.32%	10.91%	227.62%	18.97%	11.52%
6	26.34%	20.71%	11.84%	21.52%	20.79%	29.88%	5.64%	32.83%	8.67%	14.38%	30.27%	14.23%	237.11%	19.76%	8.93%
7	11.32%	39.70%	4.24%	22.69%	18.95%	41.27%	13.91%	7.78%	24.55%	34.73%	3.45%	28.72%	251.31%	20.94%	13.27%
8	27.38%	12.80%	29.21%	2.30%	32.78%	16.59%	25.85%	8.69%	20.92%	18.91%	19.79%	40.80%	256.01%	21.33%	10.68%
9	22.11%	24.80%	20.69%	10.58%	24.24%	15.98%	29.10%	17.42%	13.12%	14.35%	29.54%	16.80%	238.72%	19.89%	6.18%
10	28.75%	10.77%	28.17%	15.73%	16.52%	22.12%	10.46%	31.63%	25.98%	11.57%	14.55%	31.02%	247.27%	20.61%	8.22%
11	17.71%	21.36%	19.43%	23.46%	13.42%	22.87%	17.11%	18.44%	20.94%	30.10%	27.73%	8.00%	240.56%	20.05%	5.94%
12	23.71%	16.10%	11.68%	24.86%	23.27%	12.39%	25.99%	29.27%	12.32%	24.40%	15.64%	17.85%	237.46%	19.79%	6.13%
13	26.49%	15.48%	18.65%	29.35%	17.11%	16.59%	31.39%	12.70%	5.01%	42.79%	9.31%	22.62%	247.48%	20.62%	10.51%
14	15.57%	25.99%	15.14%	28.11%	19.11%	22.98%	11.97%	24.88%	23.51%	25.05%	11.45%	16.36%	240.13%	20.01%	5.77%
15	21.82%	18.57%	11.31%	27.75%	27.78%	8.57%	19.16%	25.38%	14.85%	15.82%	26.99%	28.18%	246.18%	20.51%	6.87%
16	26.52%	25.81%	5.43%	22.70%	28.18%	15.59%	32.46%	11.76%	23.37%	27.15%	19.45%	10.05%	238.14%	19.84%	9.36%
17	31.29%	8.77%	22.69%	34.00%	9.68%	15.59%	29.15%	6.48%	27.07%	17.40%	12.62%	19.06%	233.80%	19.48%	9.33%
18	23.88%	6.34%	39.24%	7.54%	20.99%	43.21%	3.62%	57.30%	2.12%	21.52%	13.23%	32.38%	271.36%	22.61%	17.49%
19	15.02%	22.88%	16.19%	31.63%	14.36%	30.91%	4.21%	21.94%	27.12%	24.17%	13.13%	17.15%	238.72%	19.89%	8.04%
20	10.00%	26.77%	19.02%	34.01%	9.68%	33.63%	13.59%	15.47%	23.08%	10.02%	22.69%	39.35%	257.30%	21.44%	10.28%
21	20.81%	20.73%	13.06%	11.96%	31.73%	28.14%	17.13%	16.21%	24.92%	15.32%	26.97%	13.60%	240.58%	20.05%	6.58%
22	29.56%	5.03%	31.12%	14.28%	15.76%	21.73%	38.58%	8.96%	25.15%	15.45%	19.06%	21.10%	245.79%	20.48%	9.57%
23	25.05%	10.74%	18.91%	17.07%	9.01%	21.67%	27.85%	9.74%	30.20%	43.17%	14.26%	12.17%	239.85%	19.99%	10.21%
24	31.04%	12.93%	4.50%	20.23%	35.40%	21.90%	21.15%	20.67%	14.55%	15.49%	31.26%	19.41%	248.54%	20.71%	8.66%
25	20.45%	20.39%	26.05%	4.84%	29.19%	22.64%	14.93%	21.40%	21.49%	36.73%	2.83%	30.78%	251.73%	20.98%	9.85%
26	22.95%	27.56%	10.94%	17.60%	27.82%	25.98%	5.01%	24.84%	16.97%	32.22%	16.41%	18.58%	246.89%	20.57%	7.79%
27	21.93%	16.30%	17.42%	22.21%	26.82%	4.56%	38.33%	12.87%	19.71%	38.82%	9.18%	18.28%	246.43%	20.54%	10.32%
28	22.53%	10.80%	18.52%	25.63%	23.54%	29.60%	6.19%	23.84%	14.69%	25.12%	18.10%	26.50%	245.05%	20.42%	6.96%
29	18.18%	21.11%	17.06%	22.86%	20.74%	10.82%	25.27%	35.13%	12.51%	23.93%	13.26%	14.00%	234.87%	19.57%	6.83%
30	16.06%	23.57%	34.35%	2.73%	30.72%	10.86%	17.37%	35.82%	19.76%	9.25%	25.04%	23.14%	248.65%	20.72%	10.15%
31	12.21%	31.33%	21.21%	6.69%	23.72%	34.34%	14.84%	23.65%	17.64%	27.47%	6.45%	33.01%	252.56%	21.05%	9.67%
32	34.02%	5.37%	25.73%	17.70%	20.46%	26.13%	8.21%	16.89%	10.45%	28.14%	25.78%	29.16%	248.05%	20.67%	9.07%
33	19.85%	19.66%	14.57%	23.17%	21.68%	20.17%	14.36%	13.77%	-0.36%	18.44%	29.18%	34.26%	228.75%	19.06%	8.57%
34	18.90%	25.21%	21.96%	10.92%	22.07%	20.64%	24.33%	13.79%	13.50%	18.85%	6.97%	19.39%	216.72%	18.06%	5.62%
35	9.69%	28.96%	19.06%	26.93%	12.21%	21.80%	21.49%	17.52%	21.71%	17.11%	18.89%	24.29%	239.66%	19.97%	5.55%
mean	21.04%	19.59%	19.19%	19.20%	21.02%	22.79%	18.21%	20.70%	17.15%	23.05%	18.26%	21.91%			
std. dev	6.55%	7.85%	8.11%	8.65%	7.07%	9.28%	9.97%	10.21%	7.49%	9.10%	8.45%	8.83%			

Finished goods inventory trends
Inventory reduction policy: no reduction

Dollars / Series (yr)	Jan	Feb	Mar	Apr	May	Jun	Jul	Aug	Sep	Oct	Nov	Dec	sum	mean	std. dev.
1	77,355	167,240	121,021	111,950	136,399	145,424	101,207	128,952	70,397	129,264	132,019	112,784	1,434,012	119,501	27,310
2	89,379	125,024	184,915	103,656	84,283	195,863	93,092	107,405	88,265	96,189	154,327	80,645	1,403,043	116,920	39,937
3	102,036	136,804	112,335	178,250	82,485	112,662	164,506	153,432	120,538	109,756	56,976	75,843	1,405,623	117,135	36,363
4	137,974	127,266	82,888	110,709	103,265	185,295	99,969	110,403	101,357	123,434	138,557	195,559	1,516,676	126,390	34,111
5	131,885	107,621	132,857	63,637	149,648	162,521	-21,226	99,479	36,675	206,871	240,356	74,508	1,384,833	115,403	72,288
6	148,958	111,854	76,414	128,262	117,969	161,010	35,122	183,551	55,103	103,753	173,157	88,714	1,383,867	115,322	46,534
7	74,786	224,222	29,144	159,578	121,886	214,644	71,623	53,537	140,588	172,904	23,592	170,847	1,457,351	121,446	69,755
8	159,330	73,808	164,429	16,484	188,741	106,260	158,132	56,440	133,203	119,954	136,737	207,172	1,520,690	126,724	55,832
9	132,467	140,540	102,129	66,941	143,803	96,352	165,021	96,296	84,906	98,671	177,039	109,181	1,413,346	117,779	33,608
10	145,225	69,807	159,047	83,521	105,575	132,863	71,245	188,454	145,055	70,388	98,742	167,361	1,437,284	119,774	41,812
11	115,328	135,719	119,004	135,750	91,237	143,503	109,516	112,369	136,193	166,653	140,793	48,326	1,454,392	121,199	30,236
12	135,399	103,663	74,092	151,882	133,448	81,878	165,390	163,211	75,815	144,801	97,606	112,836	1,440,019	120,002	33,453
13	149,984	91,290	115,247	151,132	100,632	94,492	162,847	66,672	34,160	213,899	57,591	135,687	1,373,633	114,469	50,794
14	99,541	150,164	97,067	154,590	115,125	128,273	76,015	155,173	122,683	129,511	64,253	96,144	1,388,539	115,712	29,952
15	128,187	104,629	73,662	157,811	139,524	56,546	132,782	146,030	100,765	105,803	156,564	163,920	1,466,222	122,185	34,257
16	149,804	132,536	33,936	139,502	153,686	37,871	190,785	78,284	141,924	156,602	106,569	68,194	1,389,693	115,808	50,396
17	171,011	57,024	134,595	170,996	56,450	99,761	159,415	38,402	155,160	102,526	89,322	122,420	1,357,089	113,091	46,668
18	129,819	49,125	220,504	50,948	124,012	206,112	25,608	252,214	12,524	123,401	87,336	173,940	1,455,545	121,295	79,389
19	101,358	134,336	110,234	184,611	93,807	159,675	27,955	147,069	160,075	145,391	88,288	115,306	1,468,105	122,342	42,105
20	72,885	143,627	134,628	179,786	63,820	174,542	79,423	98,973	137,170	73,560	143,571	208,154	1,510,138	125,845	47,820
21	128,750	119,202	90,096	88,522	176,144	161,098	101,201	106,143	149,615	92,450	146,820	84,480	1,444,522	120,377	31,571
22	158,057	32,942	179,151	97,470	114,501	126,938	204,682	57,990	148,494	96,497	113,928	124,598	1,455,248	121,271	48,177
23	149,144	70,659	124,453	118,497	63,162	123,700	193,829	69,275	181,218	224,802	82,788	82,652	1,484,179	123,682	53,870
24	156,370	71,342	32,643	119,409	194,997	129,780	123,206	114,081	87,700	104,840	183,473	109,321	1,427,163	118,930	45,216
25	125,174	123,202	153,926	32,796	165,364	139,893	94,073	137,821	132,207	167,977	17,633	174,895	1,464,962	122,080	50,567
26	141,724	140,344	63,253	108,057	152,007	126,056	34,200	150,063	103,203	185,177	90,207	104,132	1,398,423	116,535	41,670
27	128,057	98,494	105,674	147,082	141,652	34,274	193,674	87,933	130,843	202,523	51,199	115,577	1,436,982	119,748	49,927
28	131,246	76,471	124,517	161,611	137,709	162,157	41,898	145,698	98,324	152,547	117,579	151,820	1,501,576	125,131	36,750
29	114,482	124,232	102,157	134,443	118,633	80,480	161,346	190,304	78,106	133,985	84,367	86,110	1,408,644	117,387	34,481
30	112,106	151,828	168,769	17,906	178,518	71,848	126,116	203,958	108,411	63,261	160,131	135,379	1,498,232	124,853	53,618
31	84,420	183,930	122,418	45,487	133,525	198,409	86,923	138,611	106,814	148,212	44,518	179,794	1,473,060	122,755	51,198
32	166,694	34,012	147,358	106,283	131,315	140,145	52,306	104,784	64,173	177,408	171,060	166,389	1,451,927	120,994	49,444
33	123,495	119,039	89,975	144,974	129,806	130,461	99,503	97,756	-2,344	120,158	167,983	213,253	1,434,059	119,505	51,010
34	125,693	142,630	125,460	68,797	139,626	124,808	139,762	91,230	85,850	131,158	51,821	109,270	1,336,106	111,342	30,117
35	68,075	157,764	130,467	158,605	75,978	132,250	127,270	113,968	129,323	118,031	127,275	146,531	1,485,536	123,795	27,919
mean	124,749	115,211	130,467	115,712	124,250	130,796	109,955	121,313	104,414	134,639	113,548	128,907			
std. dev	27,886	41,993	43,050	47,285	35,037	44,719	56,309	47,519	43,030	41,207	50,950	44,430			

Finished goods inventory trends
Inventory reduction policy: no reduction

Percent Series (yr)	Jan	Feb	Mar	Apr	May	Jun	Jul	Aug	Sep	Oct	Nov	Dec	sum	mean	std. dev.
1	8.44%	26.31%	17.57%	14.47%	21.14%	24.25%	14.07%	19.29%	7.93%	17.05%	16.64%	15.70%	202.86%	16.90%	5.51%
2	10.35%	19.08%	28.92%	14.70%	9.89%	31.41%	13.81%	16.48%	12.04%	12.20%	22.47%	8.58%	199.93%	16.66%	7.46%
3	12.82%	16.44%	15.08%	26.43%	10.39%	15.19%	19.83%	29.46%	17.32%	15.95%	5.83%	10.17%	194.90%	16.24%	6.65%
4	22.09%	18.88%	10.67%	15.13%	12.40%	26.84%	13.56%	14.70%	12.20%	18.95%	17.74%	31.64%	214.79%	17.90%	6.33%
5	19.83%	15.51%	19.46%	7.86%	22.20%	27.35%	-4.43%	13.53%	3.74%	32.37%	32.40%	8.92%	198.75%	16.56%	11.35%
6	23.46%	17.64%	9.46%	18.84%	17.92%	26.81%	3.15%	29.90%	6.24%	12.38%	27.46%	11.76%	205.01%	17.08%	8.69%
7	9.02%	36.82%	2.08%	20.61%	16.57%	38.03%	10.62%	5.62%	21.78%	31.30%	1.27%	26.03%	219.74%	18.31%	12.93%
8	24.61%	10.03%	26.30%	0.28%	29.97%	14.19%	23.27%	6.33%	18.53%	16.51%	17.65%	37.45%	225.13%	18.76%	10.38%
9	19.45%	21.93%	17.24%	8.13%	21.54%	13.35%	26.22%	14.44%	10.75%	12.20%	26.89%	14.45%	206.59%	17.22%	6.03%
10	25.38%	8.40%	25.31%	12.58%	14.10%	19.48%	8.29%	28.97%	23.04%	8.97%	12.35%	27.97%	214.83%	17.90%	7.97%
11	15.36%	18.96%	16.89%	20.67%	11.22%	20.41%	14.70%	15.90%	18.60%	27.13%	24.38%	5.37%	209.59%	17.47%	5.75%
12	20.86%	13.71%	9.25%	22.28%	20.45%	10.09%	23.56%	26.32%	9.77%	21.70%	13.13%	15.39%	206.52%	17.21%	5.99%
13	23.61%	12.76%	16.11%	26.06%	14.38%	13.73%	28.14%	9.50%	2.82%	39.42%	6.77%	19.97%	213.27%	17.77%	10.23%
14	13.16%	23.19%	12.74%	25.12%	16.47%	20.05%	9.53%	22.37%	20.28%	21.78%	8.53%	13.63%	206.86%	17.24%	5.62%
15	19.09%	15.72%	9.00%	24.93%	24.40%	6.27%	17.02%	22.59%	12.64%	13.61%	24.25%	25.42%	214.94%	17.91%	6.59%
16	23.63%	22.51%	2.93%	20.14%	25.14%	3.25%	29.79%	9.49%	20.77%	24.34%	16.43%	7.85%	206.28%	17.19%	9.09%
17	28.26%	6.42%	20.01%	30.60%	6.92%	13.18%	26.12%	3.81%	24.27%	14.68%	10.56%	16.70%	201.52%	16.79%	9.07%
18	20.83%	4.56%	36.49%	5.38%	18.36%	39.58%	1.56%	53.36%	-0.57%	18.69%	10.93%	29.28%	238.42%	19.87%	16.94%
19	12.80%	20.17%	13.99%	28.92%	12.06%	27.73%	1.93%	19.69%	24.41%	21.53%	10.89%	14.94%	209.07%	17.42%	7.79%
20	8.03%	23.75%	16.95%	30.89%	7.37%	30.77%	10.84%	13.06%	20.40%	8.07%	20.28%	36.18%	226.18%	18.85%	9.88%
21	18.27%	17.91%	10.91%	10.10%	28.90%	25.30%	14.42%	13.88%	22.27%	12.69%	23.92%	11.08%	209.67%	17.47%	6.33%
22	26.44%	2.70%	28.31%	12.09%	13.86%	19.10%	35.42%	6.59%	22.49%	12.95%	16.40%	18.38%	214.74%	17.90%	9.28%
23	22.37%	8.43%	16.61%	14.99%	6.98%	18.92%	25.73%	7.74%	27.61%	39.95%	11.48%	9.97%	210.77%	17.56%	9.94%
24	27.66%	9.94%	2.54%	17.61%	32.49%	19.22%	18.40%	17.68%	11.92%	13.28%	28.53%	16.51%	215.77%	17.98%	8.43%
25	17.88%	17.76%	23.37%	2.71%	26.42%	20.13%	12.51%	19.02%	18.94%	32.88%	0.32%	27.92%	219.84%	18.32%	9.54%
26	20.40%	24.22%	8.15%	15.06%	24.79%	22.42%	2.83%	22.24%	14.37%	29.40%	13.41%	15.68%	212.98%	17.75%	7.59%
27	19.17%	13.67%	14.85%	19.92%	23.67%	2.69%	35.05%	10.69%	17.43%	35.61%	6.24%	15.83%	214.81%	17.90%	9.99%
28	19.76%	8.76%	16.35%	23.28%	20.87%	26.58%	3.98%	21.29%	12.44%	22.52%	15.75%	13.69%	215.26%	17.94%	6.72%
29	15.71%	18.39%	14.40%	20.13%	17.90%	8.91%	22.92%	32.07%	10.01%	21.01%	10.83%	11.45%	203.72%	16.98%	6.62%
30	13.95%	21.25%	30.91%	0.41%	27.95%	8.56%	15.39%	33.09%	16.84%	7.09%	22.66%	20.40%	218.49%	18.21%	9.88%
31	10.07%	28.61%	18.41%	4.49%	20.87%	31.54%	12.10%	20.90%	15.03%	24.39%	4.31%	29.97%	220.67%	18.39%	9.40%
32	30.50%	2.92%	22.89%	15.07%	17.76%	23.02%	5.85%	14.44%	7.99%	25.71%	23.51%	26.31%	216.00%	18.00%	8.85%
33	17.33%	17.04%	12.03%	20.68%	19.07%	17.79%	12.26%	11.82%	-2.42%	16.31%	26.50%	31.78%	200.20%	16.68%	8.41%
34	16.62%	22.41%	19.11%	8.48%	19.61%	18.06%	21.67%	11.49%	11.12%	16.73%	5.09%	16.63%	187.03%	15.59%	5.39%
35	7.60%	25.96%	16.88%	24.21%	9.70%	19.24%	18.81%	15.17%	19.05%	14.96%	16.72%	21.66%	209.96%	17.50%	5.33%
mean	18.42%	16.94%	16.63%	16.66%	18.39%	20.09%	15.68%	18.08%	14.63%	20.41%	15.79%	19.28%			
std. dev	6.16%	7.64%	7.91%	8.42%	6.83%	8.93%	9.74%	9.91%	7.34%	8.75%	8.35%	8.57%			

Finished goods inventory trends
Inventory reduction policy: no reduction

Dollars / Series (yr)	Jan	Feb	Mar	Apr	May	Jun	Jul	Aug	Sep	Oct	Nov	Dec	sum	mean	std. dev.
1	63,250	151,451	105,268	96,863	120,343	128,689	85,395	112,915	55,722	114,348	117,371	97,350	1,248,964	104,080	26,846
2	74,957	109,032	168,846	87,700	69,613	179,731	76,642	90,924	72,375	81,055	138,792	66,909	1,216,578	101,381	39,551
3	87,087	122,834	98,090	163,604	67,746	97,521	150,798	136,937	104,682	93,704	42,645	60,659	1,226,307	102,192	36,394
4	121,455	111,219	67,351	95,142	88,763	170,027	84,593	95,062	86,800	107,467	123,817	179,286	1,330,981	110,915	33,873
5	115,788	91,597	117,019	48,102	133,779	145,807	-34,874	85,626	22,812	192,833	226,861	60,955	1,206,305	100,525	72,067
6	132,635	95,225	61,058	112,310	101,665	144,441	19,631	167,153	39,618	89,308	157,096	73,344	1,193,484	99,457	46,151
7	59,613	207,935	14,330	144,937	106,562	197,777	54,699	38,683	124,676	155,803	8,703	154,875	1,268,591	105,716	69,238
8	143,208	57,866	148,078	1,997	172,592	90,839	142,361	41,132	117,991	104,722	121,998	190,157	1,332,941	111,078	55,315
9	116,550	124,241	85,100	51,422	127,815	80,474	148,720	79,825	69,565	83,910	161,184	93,876	1,222,680	101,890	33,442
10	128,180	54,472	142,856	66,794	90,136	117,024	56,485	172,590	128,660	54,583	83,768	150,872	1,246,420	103,868	41,464
11	100,039	120,474	103,467	119,586	76,291	128,062	94,091	96,906	120,967	150,183	123,780	32,470	1,266,315	105,526	30,040
12	119,138	88,279	58,713	136,111	117,223	66,714	149,914	146,793	60,126	128,811	81,981	97,315	1,251,118	104,260	33,210
13	133,673	75,269	99,571	134,196	84,583	78,216	145,962	49,871	19,255	197,030	41,910	119,773	1,179,309	98,276	50,378
14	84,103	133,993	81,656	138,142	99,241	111,905	60,524	139,547	105,838	112,610	47,880	80,097	1,195,537	99,628	29,800
15	112,131	88,612	58,583	141,785	122,563	41,360	117,987	129,960	85,798	91,043	140,641	147,860	1,278,322	106,527	33,872
16	133,481	115,593	18,328	123,769	137,135	23,402	175,115	63,163	126,125	140,411	90,037	53,221	1,199,779	99,982	49,953
17	154,460	41,724	118,675	153,917	40,336	84,340	142,875	22,602	139,113	86,496	74,715	107,230	1,166,485	97,207	46,281
18	113,243	35,322	205,028	36,333	108,467	188,808	11,004	234,862	-3,381	107,174	72,151	157,284	1,266,295	105,525	78,590
19	86,352	118,443	95,296	168,774	78,788	143,240	12,830	132,000	144,060	129,495	73,250	100,404	1,282,933	106,911	41,751
20	58,529	127,381	120,023	163,311	48,628	157,661	63,335	83,543	121,194	59,269	128,294	191,395	1,322,564	110,214	47,163
21	113,058	103,003	75,269	74,762	160,434	144,869	85,192	90,887	133,706	76,576	130,246	68,828	1,256,829	104,736	31,186
22	141,366	17,698	162,956	82,557	100,713	111,581	187,934	42,644	132,764	80,884	97,997	108,576	1,267,669	105,639	47,715
23	133,175	55,441	109,338	104,029	48,927	179,074	107,198	55,021	165,667	208,014	66,646	67,695	1,301,044	108,420	53,447
24	139,312	54,852	18,426	103,913	178,958	113,906	78,774	97,599	71,827	89,851	167,447	92,974	1,236,262	103,022	44,848
25	109,415	107,337	138,070	18,342	149,638	124,415	19,276	122,441	116,484	150,354	2,013	158,619	1,275,902	106,325	50,126
26	126,027	123,351	47,082	92,443	135,452	108,773	177,103	134,353	87,398	168,961	73,765	87,863	1,204,745	100,395	41,406
27	111,962	82,643	90,058	131,921	125,004	20,179	26,919	73,028	115,730	185,743	34,784	100,061	1,248,218	104,018	49,442
28	115,135	62,030	109,910	146,779	122,120	145,615	146,348	130,109	83,251	136,785	102,268	135,706	1,316,628	109,719	36,375
29	98,932	108,183	86,233	118,399	102,413	56,681	111,725	173,700	62,484	117,595	68,899	70,430	1,219,911	101,659	34,170
30	97,379	136,857	151,894	2,686	162,408	182,238	70,850	188,448	92,381	48,520	144,868	119,354	1,313,200	109,433	53,333
31	69,613	167,975	106,224	30,555	117,492	123,469	37,250	122,527	90,966	131,575	29,699	163,230	1,282,943	106,912	50,701
32	149,461	18,522	131,117	90,484	105,320	115,116	84,930	89,558	49,082	162,078	156,025	150,137	1,262,502	105,209	49,122
33	107,851	103,191	74,273	129,384	114,187	109,200	123,501	83,957	-15,952	106,280	152,602	197,797	1,253,617	104,468	50,531
34	110,555	126,766	109,217	53,398	124,112	116,715	111,419	76,070	70,741	116,406	37,866	93,690	1,151,521	95,960	29,704
35	53,401	141,423	115,575	142,586	60,333	114,946	44,445	98,665	113,462	103,195	112,660	130,679	1,300,112	108,343	27,611
mean	108,986	99,435	99,799	100,201	108,565	118,366	90,599	105,689	88,914	118,945	99,569	113,171			
std. dev	27,179	41,722	42,784	46,953	34,680	44,143	55,998	47,138	42,659	40,763	50,979	43,954			

Finished goods inventory trends
Inventory reduction policy: no reduction

Month	Jan	Feb	Mar	Apr	May	Jun	Jul	Aug	Sep	Oct	Nov	Dec	mean	std.dev.
Series (yr)														
1	940318	1052565	1050142	1005804	1070450	1115690	1054151	1069183	978343	994416	976534	1028922	1028043	49899
2	961481	1066133	1071253	1063779	978010	1075446	1096633	1098740	1059291	1008889	1035666	915704	1035919	57805
3	996611	931350	949623	976416	982582	1009435	913871	1099652	1057067	1070116	955409	1012271	996200	56967
4	1101301	1069778	1035831	1037790	966838	1017804	1025107	1022739	970433	1064473	982661	1084872	1031636	43622
5	1073121	1068252	1055865	1035659	1057965	1114253	909857	923537	924168	935911	899703	903557	991821	81575
6	1088184	1108606	1023772	1063425	1086902	1104660	1032696	1093190	1032327	963016	1070741	1024683	1057684	43187
7	1011575	1085836	987607	976083	1021572	1124418	1128275	990302	1060830	1140073	992624	1064830	1048669	60208
8	1074771	1062807	1090067	965828	1076601	1028058	1051361	1020521	1014135	1015501	982577	1134373	1043050	47758
9	1061169	1086616	1135272	1034574	1065885	1058542	1086739	1098063	1022773	984119	1056986	1020312	1059254	40389
10	1136322	1022372	1079423	1115139	1029238	1055943	984020	1057647	1092970	1053666	998255	1099266	1060355	46593
11	1019288	1016352	1035798	1077603	996402	1029435	1028364	1030874	1015041	1098025	1134143	1057100	1044869	39899
12	1084067	1025580	1025224	1051412	1081603	1010981	1031752	1094571	1045899	1066008	1041649	1034685	1049453	26607
13	1087435	1068052	1045071	1129073	1069932	1085025	1125662	1120073	993670	1124570	1045424	1060956	1079578	41164
14	1029208	1078011	1027418	1096545	1058945	1091235	1032743	1041693	1122957	1126745	1091515	1069798	1072234	34949
15	1070430	1067803	1005251	1068397	1130740	1012417	986328	1071315	997771	984018	1061515	1070696	1043890	45437
16	1088172	1129540	1040546	1048827	1103455	964598	1044658	1008122	1053292	1079397	1102100	998224	1055078	48400
17	1103401	1019964	1061340	1138549	1074245	1028421	1102656	1053338	1069829	1068661	973804	1012665	1058906	45277
18	1105043	920210	1031767	974381	1036333	1153564	973644	1156766	1060351	1081836	1012334	1110384	1051384	73996
19	1000385	1059490	995856	1055755	1001243	1095692	1008296	1004600	1067681	1059784	1002539	993448	1028731	35945
20	957057	1083074	973654	1098289	1012794	1125373	1072516	1028671	1065062	952752	1018463	1117237	1042078	60578
21	1046162	1079965	988487	917330	1047321	1081971	1067321	1017035	1060624	1058322	1104928	1043409	1042740	49840
22	1112745	1016280	1079681	994214	919222	1023788	1116530	1023075	1048644	1040885	1062077	1068125	1042105	53784
23	1064619	1014581	1007620	964512	948997	1045561	983651	950241	1036740	1119167	1076178	997140	1017417	52956
24	1137172	1099360	947798	1033104	1069294	1058263	1067228	1098810	1058194	999260	1068423	1089847	1060563	49650
25	1050609	1057678	1057069	963561	1048411	1031877	1019933	1025358	1048236	1174837	1041369	1085059	1050333	48909
26	1046428	1132845	1078097	1040949	1103648	1152140	994961	1047322	1053694	1081056	1096170	1084568	1075990	42952
27	1073052	1056710	1041064	1010695	1109829	939631	1104713	993661	1007541	1118675	1094304	1034355	1048686	54636
28	1074056	962683	973819	988786	1039233	1102806	998607	1039263	1004867	1050800	1020701	1074237	1027488	43502
29	1036635	1069905	1061577	1069579	1081331	945640	999882	1106692	1041471	1092698	1031187	1045331	1048513	43654
30	981815	998113	1124948	1014667	1073970	1011171	959440	1034023	1068682	982746	1017511	1068375	1027955	47844
31	987081	1063689	1079591	995426	1068871	1078055	1071572	1072277	1056538	1109129	987923	1104291	1056204	42622
32	1148868	1032705	1082732	1053228	1066347	1111714	1003800	1015113	1006071	1021948	1002293	1083472	1052358	47319
33	1042925	1056524	1046766	1039360	1041254	1022979	971541	919943	907158	925226	1025418	1030388	1002457	55539
34	1009240	1057609	1082844	1026637	1034305	1040516	1084093	1010658	1007310	983466	930291	1038678	1025471	42509
35	978241	1089409	992752	1067931	1043061	1035672	1056728	1020200	1057411	989035	974328	1056818	1030132	38489
mean	1050828	1051727	1039018	1034094	1045624	1056651	1033981	1041643	1033345	1046264	1027650	1049088		
std. dev	53711	47251	45121	51010	46994	53530	55719	52648	43533	62405	52807	49553		

Appendix 2

Simulation Data

Inventory Reduction Policy 2 — Moderate-Reduction; 50 Percent Reduction in On-Hand Finished Goods Inventory Levels over a 12-Month Period

Gross profit using the full absorption costing method
Inventory reduction policy: 50% reduction over 12 reporting periods

Percent	Jan	Feb	Mar	Apr	May	Jun	Jul	Aug	Sep	Oct	Nov	Dec	sum	mean	std. dev.
Series (yr)															
1	3.62%	34.04%	9.52%	6.61%	24.90%	16.20%	11.05%	15.83%	1.94%	13.82%	14.80%	23.06%	171.76%	15.61%	9.01%
2	5.39%	30.12%	14.58%	9.44%	5.77%	34.12%	10.48%	11.40%	9.18%	7.35%	22.59%	0.35%	155.38%	14.13%	10.49%
3	9.51%	11.25%	21.60%	15.60%	6.27%	22.32%	8.28%	43.35%	1.10%	14.78%	1.61%	25.96%	171.27%	15.57%	12.40%
4	18.15%	14.99%	8.69%	9.05%	11.82%	24.32%	-9.39%	13.44%	8.17%	31.97%	-0.88%	35.01%	164.85%	14.99%	10.99%
5	18.24%	11.64%	17.78%	7.83%	16.29%	19.45%	2.43%	30.60%	17.05%	26.66%	-0.16%	8.97%	146.72%	13.34%	11.43%
6	18.86%	15.66%	7.65%	14.88%	14.29%	25.76%	7.44%	21.72%	1.08%	9.82%	34.68%	3.57%	151.53%	13.78%	10.47%
7	4.35%	37.19%	-4.53%	19.01%	14.03%	37.22%	19.27%	-1.37%	25.60%	25.17%	-4.80%	22.69%	177.65%	16.15%	15.37%
8	21.11%	8.24%	24.21%	-6.54%	30.85%	9.42%	23.15%	2.32%	21.02%	15.40%	8.61%	36.20%	169.01%	15.36%	12.57%
9	16.83%	18.03%	20.67%	-1.79%	19.63%	10.97%	7.00%	11.54%	4.53%	8.30%	27.22%	10.44%	152.67%	13.88%	8.66%
10	25.39%	1.64%	28.51%	4.42%	9.56%	18.08%	12.14%	26.00%	17.45%	1.31%	9.34%	29.55%	152.87%	13.90%	10.59%
11	12.52%	15.81%	11.67%	18.79%	8.92%	17.25%	20.72%	14.05%	15.81%	21.20%	21.48%	3.03%	160.14%	14.56%	5.47%
12	16.91%	10.02%	9.27%	17.20%	20.44%	3.66%	26.43%	24.12%	6.58%	17.38%	9.80%	10.59%	149.79%	13.62%	6.62%
13	22.13%	8.25%	14.74%	20.44%	11.45%	8.68%	5.53%	6.16%	-1.78%	38.69%	1.25%	16.89%	151.20%	13.75%	11.64%
14	9.64%	21.03%	6.89%	28.58%	9.60%	16.39%	14.15%	20.58%	17.21%	17.66%	7.11%	7.88%	158.44%	14.40%	7.48%
15	16.39%	16.35%	5.44%	25.33%	19.38%	-4.56%	27.07%	29.68%	0.09%	14.90%	22.32%	22.29%	165.36%	15.03%	10.71%
16	21.89%	18.63%	-2.67%	18.14%	22.56%	-1.25%	23.33%	4.97%	18.88%	21.48%	14.91%	1.54%	144.29%	13.12%	10.50%
17	26.86%	0.85%	18.62%	28.91%	2.10%	9.35%	-6.76%	3.62%	21.00%	9.55%	4.34%	16.79%	138.46%	12.59%	9.60%
18	18.45%	-2.31%	42.49%	-0.60%	19.15%	34.31%	-1.07%	55.63%	-5.10%	14.53%	5.97%	27.69%	185.00%	16.82%	21.03%
19	8.99%	23.73%	5.27%	25.69%	9.08%	25.53%	6.20%	14.09%	24.42%	17.90%	5.94%	13.52%	164.09%	14.92%	9.33%
20	3.69%	37.13%	2.60%	29.34%	1.34%	31.91%	13.85%	8.86%	16.83%	4.15%	26.79%	25.18%	190.34%	17.30%	13.20%
21	15.80%	17.79%	2.42%	5.20%	42.97%	8.96%	26.28%	7.98%	19.40%	8.27%	23.43%	7.00%	157.27%	14.30%	11.51%
22	25.70%	-3.50%	26.82%	7.67%	10.33%	22.20%	-0.15%	2.95%	20.36%	8.20%	13.16%	17.18%	151.65%	13.79%	9.74%
23	19.06%	5.72%	16.25%	8.59%	14.80%	28.12%	14.80%	14.73%	25.48%	29.19%	3.56%	5.75%	152.02%	13.82%	10.21%
24	26.47%	5.77%	0.15%	28.46%	22.85%	8.71%	8.54%	13.78%	8.12%	6.59%	30.03%	10.28%	149.54%	13.59%	9.66%
25	14.50%	13.58%	18.88%	2.54%	28.28%	11.26%	-2.77%	17.36%	15.37%	30.48%	-5.42%	29.06%	169.93%	15.45%	11.23%
26	15.98%	22.56%	4.21%	15.69%	18.07%	20.59%	48.41%	19.67%	11.44%	25.54%	10.49%	14.83%	160.31%	14.57%	8.33%
27	16.41%	9.14%	17.84%	11.34%	25.19%	-7.25%	0.14%	-2.34%	15.05%	39.25%	-1.78%	9.41%	164.27%	14.93%	17.24%
28	16.81%	4.12%	15.65%	20.28%	16.13%	24.30%	23.20%	24.37%	1.65%	22.78%	11.20%	24.90%	165.52%	15.05%	9.46%
29	11.96%	16.99%	9.13%	17.88%	16.04%	3.45%	11.53%	28.43%	4.25%	21.27%	6.88%	7.33%	154.83%	14.08%	8.36%
30	10.26%	18.83%	28.33%	-4.63%	27.86%	3.77%	9.76%	33.72%	11.92%	3.20%	18.85%	17.41%	170.79%	15.53%	11.83%
31	5.60%	29.60%	12.42%	0.61%	34.32%	13.91%	4.82%	15.27%	12.47%	24.05%	-2.33%	28.20%	178.27%	16.21%	11.73%
32	29.48%	-1.81%	20.08%	14.68%	10.95%	20.03%	7.42%	12.39%	10.45%	19.62%	13.01%	24.15%	148.38%	13.49%	7.52%
33	14.21%	13.52%	8.81%	17.44%	13.96%	16.18%	18.91%	11.55%	13.92%	24.28%	23.68%	4.02%	154.77%	14.07%	6.26%
34	11.10%	23.09%	14.99%	4.30%	16.45%	16.62%	18.55%	5.35%	11.91%	10.20%	10.24%	30.37%	162.42%	14.77%	7.64%
35	1.99%	37.42%	2.46%	24.92%	4.35%	18.59%	11.95%	7.55%	20.05%	6.28%	16.53%	19.10%	175.80%	15.98%	10.31%
mean	15.26%	15.57%	13.18%	13.29%	16.57%	16.24%	11.38%	16.27%	12.08%	17.46%	11.56%	16.86%			
std. dev	7.25%	11.29%	9.96%	10.08%	9.25%	10.84%	11.38%	12.43%	8.26%	9.81%	10.50%	10.16%			

Gross profit using the full absorption costing method
Inventory reduction policy: 50% reduction over 12 reporting periods

Dollars Series (yr)	Jan	Feb	Mar	Apr	May	Jun	Jul	Aug	Sep	Oct	Nov	Dec	sum	mean	std. dev.
1	27,166	195,883	57,030	44,237	141,779	85,979	67,053	92,678	13,607	92,730	104,370	142,964	1,038,310	94,392	51,251
2	39,038	172,062	85,126	56,303	40,589	195,221	58,145	62,891	55,213	48,865	139,547	2,765	916,727	83,339	59,695
3	64,611	84,083	140,501	96,699	41,006	143,334	56,427	202,610	6,649	86,853	11,804	154,856	1,024,822	93,166	62,331
4	99,810	88,293	54,847	56,923	84,656	154,049	51,650	86,963	58,139	181,325	-6,171	198,372	1,009,046	91,731	61,854
5	106,498	68,720	106,946	47,909	98,152	163,658	-73,928	193,316	103,627	160,434	-1,104	62,348	870,079	79,098	72,949
6	106,648	84,538	49,347	88,685	81,064	138,797	15,114	121,465	6,883	70,835	198,391	22,265	877,385	79,762	57,622
7	28,721	210,054	-31,145	133,724	90,236	193,561	38,291	-9,450	146,397	125,317	-32,847	134,972	999,110	90,828	87,077
8	122,842	47,512	136,288	-46,842	177,676	60,310	117,892	15,077	133,861	97,662	59,518	183,833	982,787	89,344	70,246
9	100,842	102,167	102,048	-11,321	116,451	66,127	131,274	63,792	29,292	57,066	163,117	67,838	887,851	80,714	48,865
10	128,235	10,625	160,935	23,474	61,081	108,614	47,707	154,901	97,457	7,986	63,366	159,448	895,595	81,418	58,690
11	81,544	100,455	71,485	108,716	60,665	108,225	77,709	85,591	102,805	117,372	109,066	18,301	960,389	87,308	29,160
12	96,546	64,548	58,843	105,076	117,177	24,195	131,849	134,527	40,474	103,176	61,196	66,948	908,010	82,546	37,450
13	125,285	48,645	91,056	105,265	67,346	49,436	137,105	32,336	-12,149	193,394	7,763	101,349	821,546	74,686	59,232
14	61,636	121,526	44,185	157,178	57,816	91,479	35,093	128,354	89,781	91,269	39,892	46,308	902,880	82,080	41,062
15	96,291	92,140	35,445	144,044	97,430	-30,119	98,048	170,714	590	129,662	129,470	99,638	967,062	87,915	61,754
16	123,656	95,702	-16,674	111,510	123,071	-8,959	158,988	33,052	114,687	123,896	81,731	10,466	827,470	75,225	60,427
17	146,777	5,529	110,432	145,395	12,274	59,817	127,590	21,454	120,386	56,257	30,748	107,836	797,719	72,520	51,201
18	100,316	-17,926	238,753	-4,038	113,116	163,694	-47,830	244,885	-30,131	83,336	39,411	148,733	932,002	84,727	105,712
19	60,639	139,305	35,881	149,893	59,278	131,880	-7,101	94,455	144,143	107,645	39,956	90,897	986,232	89,657	51,807
20	26,889	199,194	18,430	155,122	8,855	165,620	36,218	56,714	99,997	30,446	169,531	133,197	1,073,326	97,575	69,854
21	97,739	102,295	16,701	38,489	238,565	51,288	81,803	52,225	116,500	49,912	127,578	43,485	918,842	83,531	62,182
22	137,386	-22,870	154,362	52,339	75,077	130,250	139,438	19,075	120,223	51,216	78,634	101,460	899,204	81,746	54,357
23	113,468	37,607	106,961	59,606	103,732	160,738	-1,037	104,788	152,881	151,979	20,648	39,018	936,920	85,175	57,100
24	133,319	31,847	1,088	168,022	126,502	51,677	86,461	76,079	48,953	44,563	176,209	57,908	869,309	79,028	55,919
25	88,750	82,064	111,553	17,220	160,182	69,586	54,000	111,786	94,549	139,388	-33,828	165,115	971,615	88,329	60,284
26	98,670	114,922	24,350	96,313	98,705	99,878	-18,920	118,834	69,591	146,745	57,689	83,086	891,192	81,017	46,562
27	95,853	55,221	108,227	75,131	133,047	-54,447	244,648	-15,994	99,909	204,766	-9,926	59,455	900,040	81,822	91,150
28	97,943	29,211	105,242	128,033	95,373	133,137	937	148,934	11,071	138,353	72,740	142,628	1,005,659	91,424	55,029
29	75,309	99,968	54,672	105,194	91,720	25,636	148,115	153,990	26,540	119,076	43,736	45,066	913,713	83,065	46,582
30	71,636	121,288	139,225	-30,386	161,932	24,939	83,716	192,008	65,424	21,875	120,533	101,885	1,002,439	91,131	66,371
31	38,723	173,780	71,681	4,160	193,250	80,369	57,176	89,481	75,503	129,753	-16,096	153,553	1,012,611	92,056	66,025
32	144,434	-11,477	114,996	88,108	64,926	107,410	30,734	77,125	64,903	123,679	86,354	137,823	884,581	80,416	43,116
33	88,438	81,877	54,374	109,117	83,575	104,686	51,371	82,000	91,568	158,909	136,482	24,996	978,954	88,996	38,262
34	73,788	130,631	85,654	27,074	104,098	100,485	107,754	35,427	75,715	70,971	76,105	171,116	985,029	89,548	40,704
35	13,962	203,893	16,831	146,777	27,076	112,735	109,864	49,109	119,448	43,297	111,364	115,218	1,055,612	95,965	56,428
mean	88,955	89,809	77,591	78,661	97,356	91,522	69,525	93,748	72,985	100,857	70,199	97,862			
std. dev	35,488	63,119	55,870	57,688	49,939	59,368	64,079	62,695	48,936	49,689	62,076	54,822			

Gross profit using the full absorption costing method
Inventory reduction policy: 50% reduction over 12 reporting periods

Percent	Jan	Feb	Mar	Apr	May	Jun	Jul	Aug	Sep	Oct	Nov	Dec	sum	mean	std. dev.
Series (yr)															
1	1.83%	31.45%	7.19%	4.75%	22.63%	13.79%	9.20%	13.98%	0.69%	12.56%	13.74%	21.80%	151.77%	13.80%	8.80%
2	3.49%	27.50%	12.16%	7.20%	4.15%	31.97%	8.34%	9.36%	7.52%	6.06%	21.22%	-0.40%	135.08%	12.28%	10.19%
3	7.41%	9.54%	19.63%	13.57%	4.44%	20.53%	6.19%	40.82%	-0.55%	13.16%	0.64%	24.65%	152.61%	13.87%	12.12%
4	15.27%	12.49%	6.54%	6.99%	10.25%	22.49%	6.51%	11.88%	6.95%	30.25%	-1.96%	33.52%	145.91%	13.26%	10.94%
5	15.60%	9.14%	15.47%	5.69%	14.20%	17.05%	-10.54%	29.10%	15.49%	25.12%	-1.18%	8.00%	127.54%	11.59%	11.24%
6	16.09%	12.82%	5.57%	12.64%	11.99%	23.40%	0.65%	19.73%	-0.43%	8.72%	33.10%	2.34%	130.54%	11.87%	10.32%
7	2.15%	34.53%	-6.40%	17.30%	12.15%	34.73%	5.04%	-2.77%	23.82%	23.05%	-5.92%	21.32%	156.84%	14.26%	15.07%
8	18.45%	5.66%	21.65%	-8.19%	28.61%	7.62%	17.44%	0.77%	19.54%	13.99%	7.51%	34.40%	149.01%	13.55%	12.44%
9	14.28%	15.38%	17.59%	-3.83%	17.48%	8.99%	21.08%	9.51%	3.07%	7.09%	25.76%	9.29%	131.42%	11.95%	8.50%
10	22.14%	-0.52%	25.96%	1.76%	7.65%	16.09%	5.48%	24.20%	15.57%	-0.21%	8.19%	27.93%	132.11%	12.01%	10.55%
11	10.27%	13.58%	9.42%	16.45%	7.20%	15.39%	10.45%	12.35%	14.36%	19.41%	19.55%	1.71%	139.86%	12.71%	5.33%
12	14.17%	7.84%	7.14%	15.05%	18.18%	1.96%	19.01%	22.12%	4.98%	15.79%	8.45%	9.38%	129.89%	11.81%	6.51%
13	19.36%	5.75%	12.51%	17.66%	9.28%	6.51%	24.06%	3.96%	-3.10%	36.58%	-0.12%	15.55%	128.65%	11.70%	11.44%
14	7.33%	18.46%	4.79%	26.05%	7.50%	14.15%	3.81%	18.91%	15.11%	15.65%	5.48%	6.49%	136.40%	12.40%	7.25%
15	13.77%	13.72%	3.40%	22.93%	16.64%	-6.27%	12.67%	27.77%	-1.25%	13.65%	20.78%	20.87%	144.90%	13.17%	10.58%
16	19.12%	15.59%	-4.85%	16.01%	20.13%	-2.71%	25.15%	3.48%	17.25%	19.81%	13.21%	0.49%	123.56%	11.23%	10.28%
17	23.95%	-1.30%	16.25%	26.03%	-0.10%	7.55%	21.14%	1.81%	19.20%	7.94%	3.30%	15.62%	117.44%	10.68%	9.40%
18	15.52%	-3.93%	40.02%	-2.43%	17.02%	31.49%	-8.18%	52.83%	-6.82%	12.84%	4.76%	26.05%	163.67%	14.88%	20.59%
19	6.86%	21.22%	3.36%	23.39%	7.24%	23.02%	-2.65%	12.62%	22.71%	16.34%	4.78%	12.45%	144.48%	13.13%	9.06%
20	1.81%	34.29%	0.82%	26.68%	-0.46%	29.41%	4.23%	7.27%	15.13%	3.09%	25.48%	23.50%	169.44%	15.40%	12.86%
21	13.37%	15.20%	0.56%	3.66%	40.61%	6.81%	11.91%	6.45%	17.74%	6.72%	21.71%	5.75%	137.12%	12.47%	11.31%
22	22.70%	-5.62%	24.34%	5.87%	8.85%	20.18%	23.99%	1.39%	18.67%	6.75%	11.70%	15.80%	131.90%	11.99%	9.59%
23	16.49%	3.60%	14.24%	6.85%	13.18%	25.96%	-1.61%	13.42%	23.81%	27.21%	2.02%	4.70%	133.38%	12.13%	10.04%
24	23.21%	3.02%	-1.56%	26.19%	20.48%	6.68%	12.83%	11.75%	6.46%	5.34%	28.51%	8.78%	128.47%	11.68%	9.61%
25	12.03%	11.17%	16.50%	0.73%	25.99%	9.36%	6.81%	15.79%	13.77%	28.06%	-6.77%	27.58%	148.97%	13.54%	11.05%
26	13.54%	19.48%	1.75%	13.55%	15.64%	17.84%	-4.29%	17.91%	9.81%	23.85%	8.80%	13.30%	137.65%	12.51%	8.16%
27	13.77%	6.73%	15.57%	9.45%	22.64%	-8.61%	45.95%	-3.75%	13.65%	37.28%	-3.43%	8.20%	143.68%	13.06%	16.94%
28	14.16%	2.25%	13.71%	18.26%	13.97%	22.00%	-1.40%	22.65%	0.28%	21.26%	9.95%	23.44%	146.36%	13.31%	9.34%
29	9.59%	14.48%	6.80%	15.60%	13.77%	2.07%	21.53%	26.33%	2.69%	19.51%	5.58%	6.05%	134.41%	12.22%	8.14%
30	8.24%	16.68%	25.23%	-6.56%	25.65%	2.07%	10.18%	31.87%	9.99%	1.98%	17.56%	16.01%	150.66%	13.70%	11.59%
31	3.55%	27.08%	9.95%	-1.20%	32.00%	11.79%	7.80%	13.42%	10.83%	22.18%	-3.44%	26.60%	157.01%	14.27%	11.51%
32	26.09%	-4.05%	17.59%	12.47%	8.81%	17.65%	3.16%	10.74%	8.91%	18.19%	11.81%	22.68%	127.95%	11.63%	7.56%
33	11.80%	11.12%	6.58%	15.36%	11.87%	14.42%	5.94%	10.26%	12.54%	22.96%	22.12%	2.77%	135.94%	12.36%	6.27%
34	8.92%	20.48%	12.49%	2.25%	14.52%	14.65%	16.86%	3.85%	10.41%	9.02%	9.30%	28.89%	142.71%	12.97%	7.51%
35	-0.01%	34.62%	0.57%	22.64%	2.36%	16.65%	16.62%	6.00%	18.36%	5.08%	15.40%	17.77%	156.08%	14.19%	10.04%
mean	12.75%	13.13%	10.93%	11.17%	14.47%	14.19%	10.15%	14.51%	10.49%	15.89%	10.22%	15.52%			
std. dev	6.87%	11.09%	9.76%	9.88%	9.08%	10.57%	11.16%	12.21%	8.18%	9.58%	10.39%	10.00%			

Gross profit using the full absorption costing method
Inventory reduction policy: 50% reduction over 12 reporting periods

Dollars Series (yr)	Jan	Feb	Mar	Apr	May	Jun	Jul	Aug	Sep	Oct	Nov	Dec	sum	mean	std. dev.
1	13,715	180,998	43,077	31,769	128,847	73,171	55,825	81,840	4,822	84,222	96,924	135,159	916,654	83,332	50,781
2	25,269	157,122	70,979	42,966	29,191	182,907	46,279	51,652	45,213	40,280	131,074	-3,117	794,545	72,231	58,441
3	50,315	71,255	127,633	84,095	29,017	131,858	47,101	190,790	-3,318	77,349	4,675	147,043	907,499	82,500	61,690
4	83,944	73,555	41,268	43,976	73,421	142,475	40,617	76,864	49,472	171,589	-13,709	189,914	889,441	80,858	62,066
5	91,055	54,005	93,010	34,795	85,554	90,871	-82,992	183,866	94,126	151,159	-8,319	55,626	751,701	68,336	72,493
6	90,979	69,218	35,949	75,353	68,032	126,083	4,067	110,310	-2,712	62,938	189,357	14,609	753,202	68,473	57,389
7	14,201	195,021	-44,043	121,682	78,119	180,622	25,951	-19,062	136,225	114,740	-40,534	126,861	875,582	79,598	86,202
8	107,374	32,666	121,896	-58,724	164,740	48,816	106,706	5,012	124,395	88,719	51,908	174,679	860,812	78,256	70,354
9	85,577	87,176	86,844	-24,221	103,734	54,176	119,557	52,563	19,840	48,760	154,404	60,395	763,229	69,384	48,769
10	111,844	-3,402	146,567	9,367	48,913	96,647	37,363	144,185	86,952	-1,271	55,594	150,682	771,598	70,145	58,935
11	66,908	86,298	57,694	95,171	48,990	96,575	66,867	75,228	93,391	107,449	99,256	10,306	837,226	76,111	28,624
12	80,938	50,473	45,311	91,924	104,224	12,957	120,957	123,351	30,645	93,734	52,773	59,290	785,639	71,422	37,204
13	109,627	33,933	77,327	90,948	54,569	37,088	124,804	20,777	-21,165	182,847	-717	93,296	693,708	63,064	58,822
14	46,852	106,664	30,732	143,294	45,203	78,990	24,186	117,971	78,826	80,915	30,721	38,123	775,625	70,511	40,134
15	80,888	77,291	22,116	130,382	83,622	-41,378	87,837	159,752	-8,487	91,284	120,523	121,403	844,346	76,759	61,856
16	107,986	80,067	-30,323	98,397	109,781	-19,501	147,702	23,173	104,759	114,254	72,401	3,355	704,064	64,006	60,012
17	130,879	-8,462	66,401	130,936	-568	48,318	115,634	10,748	110,039	46,775	23,343	100,301	673,466	61,224	50,990
18	84,393	-30,421	224,858	-16,416	100,539	150,232	-57,851	232,565	-40,257	73,657	31,428	139,932	808,266	73,479	104,924
19	46,286	124,581	22,902	136,475	47,285	118,908	-17,642	84,629	134,017	98,297	32,120	83,721	865,292	78,663	51,104
20	13,187	183,947	5,784	141,073	-3,066	152,667	24,714	46,527	89,910	22,703	161,224	124,301	949,783	86,344	69,209
21	82,699	87,404	3,833	27,114	225,473	38,986	70,377	42,212	106,480	40,585	118,206	35,696	796,367	72,397	61,693
22	121,348	-36,806	140,126	40,045	64,324	118,399	127,274	8,971	110,193	42,151	69,905	93,300	777,882	70,717	54,342
23	98,152	23,697	93,709	47,572	92,416	148,416	-11,208	95,461	142,866	141,663	11,707	31,922	818,220	74,384	56,732
24	116,914	16,665	-11,315	154,619	113,351	39,613	74,955	64,839	38,969	36,122	167,341	39,422	744,582	67,689	56,055
25	73,644	67,507	97,482	4,926	147,227	57,820	43,052	101,648	84,715	128,313	-42,247	156,686	847,129	77,012	60,022
26	83,627	99,238	10,137	83,187	85,421	86,523	-29,261	108,218	59,676	137,078	48,382	74,563	763,162	69,378	46,397
27	80,410	40,679	94,423	62,590	119,559	-64,614	232,222	-25,656	90,661	194,478	-19,138	51,802	777,005	70,637	90,415
28	82,485	15,922	92,180	115,289	82,635	120,523	-9,458	138,409	1,887	129,085	64,631	134,258	885,361	80,487	55,001
29	60,413	85,228	40,708	91,770	78,755	15,379	137,503	142,616	16,807	109,234	35,471	37,214	790,684	71,880	45,881
30	57,562	107,424	123,973	-43,003	149,073	13,699	73,908	181,498	54,857	13,528	112,293	93,656	880,906	80,082	66,031
31	24,570	159,027	57,446	-8,152	180,166	68,125	45,687	78,639	65,545	119,664	-23,713	144,847	887,281	80,662	65,282
32	127,854	-25,659	100,714	74,830	52,202	94,661	20,103	66,823	55,338	114,682	78,402	129,432	761,530	69,230	43,988
33	73,447	67,338	40,631	96,146	71,041	93,269	41,162	72,843	82,486	150,260	127,489	162,819	859,882	78,171	38,587
34	59,303	115,859	71,370	14,149	91,855	88,594	96,077	25,509	66,201	62,749	69,118	107,207	864,298	78,573	40,721
35	-58	188,639	3,898	133,351	14,701	100,983	98,444	39,048	109,377	35,010	103,760	89,883	934,418	84,947	55,753
mean	73,845	75,261	63,866	65,648	84,810	79,510	58,529	83,252	63,222	91,571	61,887	89,883			
std. dev	34,754	62,734	55,526	57,292	49,627	58,826	63,574	62,372	48,749	49,180	61,805	54,381			

Gross profit using the full absorption costing method
Inventory reduction policy: 50% reduction over 12 reporting periods

Percent Series (yr)	Jan	Feb	Mar	Apr	May	Jun	Jul	Aug	Sep	Oct	Nov	Dec	sum	mean	std. dev.
1	27.64%	52.13%	31.60%	30.13%	42.42%	39.22%	33.38%	36.81%	26.43%	35.24%	35.55%	42.18%	405.11%	36.83%	7.04%
2	28.45%	48.86%	35.80%	32.08%	29.22%	50.71%	31.78%	34.06%	31.28%	31.17%	42.19%	25.43%	392.58%	35.69%	8.12%
3	32.24%	33.54%	42.08%	36.08%	28.57%	43.47%	30.27%	58.35%	26.18%	35.83%	25.61%	44.55%	404.52%	36.77%	9.79%
4	37.66%	36.67%	31.39%	32.98%	33.37%	43.45%	30.71%	35.60%	30.09%	48.80%	24.48%	51.64%	399.17%	36.29%	8.35%
5	38.72%	34.27%	38.58%	30.24%	36.38%	41.60%	17.07%	48.92%	39.17%	45.16%	24.67%	31.88%	387.94%	35.27%	9.13%
6	39.16%	37.10%	30.57%	35.90%	36.26%	45.76%	26.32%	41.83%	25.58%	32.01%	52.15%	27.80%	391.28%	35.57%	8.39%
7	28.20%	53.99%	20.96%	39.38%	35.27%	53.82%	30.05%	23.98%	44.23%	43.97%	20.98%	42.33%	408.97%	37.18%	12.00%
8	42.32%	30.12%	44.82%	19.58%	48.11%	32.02%	39.54%	26.76%	41.13%	37.03%	30.89%	53.05%	403.05%	36.64%	9.91%
9	37.88%	38.80%	41.44%	22.58%	39.84%	32.49%	43.04%	33.92%	29.05%	30.78%	45.75%	32.81%	390.53%	35.50%	6.90%
10	44.13%	26.31%	46.99%	27.48%	32.26%	39.13%	29.56%	45.53%	38.56%	26.60%	32.08%	47.13%	391.63%	35.60%	8.22%
11	35.05%	37.03%	33.64%	39.14%	31.63%	37.08%	34.53%	35.69%	36.51%	41.34%	42.25%	26.18%	395.01%	35.91%	4.51%
12	38.53%	32.39%	31.40%	37.90%	40.11%	27.76%	40.04%	44.88%	28.90%	38.30%	32.52%	33.53%	387.74%	35.25%	5.34%
13	42.14%	30.59%	36.39%	40.57%	33.35%	31.29%	44.75%	31.34%	23.37%	54.95%	25.54%	37.79%	389.94%	35.45%	8.98%
14	31.39%	40.92%	30.64%	46.64%	33.02%	37.72%	28.10%	41.45%	37.41%	38.97%	29.67%	30.44%	395.00%	35.91%	5.93%
15	37.30%	38.02%	29.23%	44.36%	39.24%	21.34%	34.94%	47.84%	24.98%	36.61%	42.10%	41.03%	399.69%	36.34%	8.18%
16	41.95%	39.34%	22.64%	38.06%	42.95%	24.35%	44.51%	29.05%	38.88%	41.56%	36.21%	25.73%	383.29%	34.84%	7.93%
17	45.36%	26.09%	38.46%	46.74%	26.64%	32.27%	43.11%	27.30%	40.97%	32.08%	27.97%	38.14%	379.77%	34.52%	7.30%
18	38.92%	23.83%	57.31%	24.56%	39.44%	50.19%	20.54%	68.31%	20.82%	36.32%	29.54%	46.67%	417.53%	37.96%	16.04%
19	31.97%	42.81%	29.43%	34.94%	31.86%	44.63%	23.72%	35.98%	42.50%	39.07%	29.26%	35.31%	399.52%	36.32%	7.13%
20	26.83%	54.31%	27.09%	46.99%	25.56%	49.70%	29.41%	32.23%	37.42%	27.68%	45.24%	44.08%	419.72%	38.16%	10.30%
21	36.61%	39.14%	27.53%	28.32%	56.71%	31.98%	35.08%	31.37%	39.67%	30.19%	42.83%	31.00%	393.82%	35.80%	8.52%
22	45.18%	21.88%	45.59%	31.82%	32.15%	41.54%	45.53%	27.71%	40.05%	31.61%	34.30%	37.44%	389.62%	35.42%	7.42%
23	39.89%	28.13%	38.34%	30.08%	35.94%	46.59%	24.39%	36.18%	44.68%	47.44%	26.37%	30.52%	388.66%	35.33%	8.21%
24	45.01%	29.02%	25.03%	46.59%	42.72%	32.05%	36.68%	34.53%	31.26%	30.37%	47.62%	33.14%	389.00%	35.36%	7.33%
25	36.23%	36.03%	40.81%	36.22%	46.68%	34.27%	30.46%	38.06%	36.77%	46.88%	20.69%	47.67%	404.54%	36.78%	8.68%
26	36.75%	43.50%	27.44%	36.39%	38.99%	41.06%	22.99%	39.85%	33.45%	45.62%	32.11%	36.65%	398.04%	36.19%	6.80%
27	37.69%	31.82%	37.90%	33.90%	43.72%	19.75%	61.90%	23.02%	35.71%	56.22%	22.60%	32.98%	399.52%	36.32%	13.36%
28	38.82%	27.94%	36.86%	40.11%	36.97%	43.27%	24.74%	43.23%	27.10%	41.46%	33.73%	44.56%	399.97%	36.36%	7.08%
29	34.57%	37.14%	31.96%	39.55%	36.08%	27.79%	41.98%	46.94%	28.26%	40.03%	30.59%	31.22%	391.54%	35.59%	6.16%
30	33.02%	39.52%	48.11%	21.11%	45.61%	27.40%	34.36%	50.26%	34.48%	26.95%	39.81%	37.71%	405.34%	36.85%	9.20%
31	29.16%	48.10%	34.57%	24.32%	51.01%	36.16%	31.72%	36.98%	34.07%	43.05%	23.44%	46.90%	410.30%	37.30%	9.17%
32	47.15%	23.60%	40.52%	36.52%	33.44%	39.23%	29.30%	34.38%	32.13%	40.38%	34.36%	44.18%	388.02%	35.27%	5.80%
33	35.78%	34.95%	31.79%	39.08%	35.07%	37.78%	31.16%	32.98%	34.43%	44.04%	41.72%	28.18%	391.18%	35.56%	4.73%
34	34.30%	41.62%	37.57%	26.77%	38.72%	37.11%	38.61%	30.33%	32.70%	32.19%	32.45%	48.15%	396.21%	36.02%	5.94%
35	25.94%	54.23%	26.30%	33.48%	28.46%	37.36%	33.80%	29.69%	40.91%	30.28%	36.63%	39.57%	407.13%	37.01%	8.08%
mean	36.63%	36.96%	35.17%	34.87%	37.36%	37.51%	33.80%	37.58%	33.97%	38.29%	33.54%	37.93%			
std. dev	5.68%	8.93%	7.85%	7.88%	6.98%	8.31%	8.72%	9.60%	6.28%	7.58%	8.14%	7.77%			

Gross profit using the full absorption costing method
Inventory reduction policy: 50% reduction over 12 reporting periods

Dollars — Series (yr)	Jan	Feb	Mar	Apr	May	Jun	Jul	Aug	Sep	Oct	Nov	Dec	sum	mean	std. dev.
1	207,160	300,042	189,340	201,730	241,518	208,163	202,624	215,452	185,641	236,376	250,781	261,539	2,493,206	226,655	34,987
2	205,981	279,131	209,049	191,345	205,748	290,117	176,326	187,942	188,106	207,113	260,610	198,411	2,393,898	217,627	39,660
3	219,005	250,609	273,654	223,608	186,865	279,126	230,171	272,753	158,205	210,534	187,362	265,811	2,538,698	230,791	41,352
4	207,063	215,998	198,123	207,452	238,961	275,235	191,570	230,279	214,107	276,829	170,843	292,594	2,511,991	228,363	38,933
5	226,069	202,373	232,015	185,044	219,197	221,727	134,415	309,095	238,041	271,692	173,947	221,642	2,409,190	219,017	46,962
6	221,401	200,338	197,271	213,965	205,756	246,560	163,981	233,858	162,538	230,900	298,343	173,368	2,326,878	211,534	40,153
7	186,342	304,928	144,114	276,996	226,842	279,916	154,756	164,971	252,926	218,875	143,654	251,867	2,419,844	219,986	59,221
8	246,250	173,696	252,296	140,350	277,053	205,022	241,943	173,873	261,874	234,844	213,460	269,370	2,443,782	222,162	44,746
9	226,906	219,886	204,545	142,860	236,391	195,894	244,115	187,538	187,992	211,741	274,231	213,239	2,318,431	210,766	34,375
10	222,905	170,516	265,271	145,878	206,159	235,033	201,377	271,294	215,331	161,832	217,706	254,283	2,344,678	213,153	41,783
11	228,311	235,247	206,036	226,464	215,073	232,683	220,998	217,487	237,411	228,865	214,544	158,234	2,393,041	217,549	21,959
12	220,055	208,548	199,248	231,585	229,962	183,541	254,797	250,272	177,895	227,338	202,981	211,994	2,378,162	216,197	25,046
13	238,607	180,415	224,846	208,894	196,134	178,245	232,176	164,583	159,399	274,669	158,053	226,701	2,204,115	200,374	36,814
14	200,654	236,465	196,440	256,534	198,942	210,567	178,401	258,594	195,201	201,464	166,458	178,884	2,277,951	207,086	30,975
15	219,141	214,244	190,338	252,288	197,236	175,164	242,215	275,226	169,546	244,864	244,175	238,634	2,409,614	219,056	40,457
16	236,944	202,048	141,514	233,881	234,256	206,533	261,385	193,390	236,115	239,714	198,469	174,515	2,290,454	208,223	36,006
17	247,861	169,676	228,116	235,090	155,334	239,422	235,776	161,790	234,841	189,041	197,976	244,935	2,259,108	205,373	32,800
18	211,584	184,671	322,025	165,893	233,047	230,539	245,347	122,988	250,668	208,284	195,080	250,668	2,368,086	215,281	61,706
19	215,769	251,352	200,444	262,277	208,041	258,007	157,625	241,199	250,834	235,005	196,814	237,391	2,471,521	224,684	30,857
20	195,623	291,337	191,778	248,433	168,535	183,133	171,924	206,190	222,363	203,308	286,226	233,170	2,481,270	225,570	42,180
21	226,488	225,095	189,888	209,592	314,890	243,706	207,256	205,378	238,175	182,187	233,163	192,525	2,381,283	216,480	37,858
22	241,514	143,141	262,450	217,253	233,617	266,342	241,588	179,291	236,423	197,400	204,977	221,139	2,380,983	216,453	33,848
23	237,478	185,016	252,366	208,780	251,939	190,193	169,767	257,313	268,140	246,992	153,081	207,221	2,466,956	224,269	41,192
24	226,734	160,101	181,353	275,102	236,478	211,782	214,243	190,565	188,419	205,549	279,448	186,630	2,308,081	209,826	38,591
25	221,767	217,716	241,116	177,689	264,420	199,210	192,537	245,057	226,173	214,378	129,017	270,881	2,390,766	217,342	40,648
26	226,972	221,545	158,573	223,349	212,991	148,291	156,825	240,750	203,423	262,167	176,554	205,412	2,260,798	205,527	32,464
27	220,100	192,335	229,840	224,523	230,906	237,098	312,807	157,320	237,099	293,242	125,978	208,485	2,360,825	214,620	57,443
28	226,176	197,871	247,883	253,275	218,618	206,686	268,038	264,178	181,376	251,781	219,061	255,287	2,493,856	226,714	32,613
29	217,697	218,516	191,408	232,657	206,378	181,315	249,512	254,278	176,492	224,075	194,548	192,037	2,365,114	215,010	28,090
30	230,581	254,547	236,423	138,423	265,049	208,930	185,801	286,196	189,301	184,377	254,577	220,666	2,460,385	223,671	44,895
31	201,652	282,441	199,516	165,429	287,217	210,368	186,669	216,749	206,222	232,216	161,685	255,393	2,401,599	218,327	42,519
32	231,024	149,524	232,043	219,206	198,244	244,389	215,873	213,912	199,616	254,518	227,989	252,097	2,344,187	213,108	30,009
33	222,659	211,628	196,264	244,577	209,949	224,398	220,045	234,189	226,492	288,227	240,424	175,395	2,487,407	226,128	29,736
34	228,090	235,474	214,647	168,572	245,021	235,156	229,903	200,697	207,961	224,049	241,226	238,745	2,453,395	223,036	26,596
35	182,219	295,444	180,059	256,026	177,051	219,524	207,435	193,080	243,716	208,854	246,842	226,013	2,504,878	227,716	35,476
mean	220,708	219,483	213,723	213,286	223,823	219,524	207,435	224,440	208,582	228,094	209,722	226,013			
std. dev	15,327	43,328	37,128	38,810	32,980	36,081	40,557	41,290	33,850	30,908	44,679	34,070			

Gross profit using the full absorption costing method
Inventory reduction policy: 50% reduction over 12 reporting periods

Percent Series (yr)	Jan	Feb	Mar	Apr	May	Jun	Jul	Aug	Sep	Oct	Nov	Dec	sum	mean	std. dev.
1	8.81%	27.36%	7.96%	9.20%	17.72%	12.75%	10.49%	13.14%	7.00%	14.93%	16.39%	20.33%	157.27%	14.30%	6.01%
2	9.12%	24.15%	11.77%	8.69%	9.68%	26.50%	6.90%	9.15%	8.63%	10.88%	20.39%	8.50%	145.24%	13.20%	6.98%
3	10.96%	14.39%	20.07%	13.03%	6.82%	21.39%	11.91%	27.96%	2.98%	12.04%	6.83%	21.41%	158.84%	14.44%	7.57%
4	11.79%	12.71%	9.21%	10.83%	14.15%	21.67%	8.68%	14.50%	11.11%	24.81%	5.29%	27.84%	160.82%	14.62%	7.14%
5	14.20%	10.14%	15.02%	7.22%	13.09%	15.23%	-0.30%	27.21%	16.59%	22.38%	5.53%	12.54%	144.64%	13.15%	7.66%
6	14.89%	11.76%	9.66%	13.27%	12.55%	20.85%	5.04%	18.10%	4.95%	14.07%	29.33%	7.09%	146.65%	13.33%	7.28%
7	7.38%	29.54%	1.19%	20.17%	14.25%	27.67%	3.76%	4.70%	20.93%	17.12%	1.89%	20.29%	161.52%	14.68%	10.30%
8	18.20%	5.89%	20.08%	0.50%	24.18%	10.72%	17.31%	6.00%	20.03%	15.93%	11.72%	26.66%	159.03%	14.46%	8.23%
9	15.12%	14.79%	13.83%	1.40%	17.29%	10.43%	19.63%	9.99%	8.88%	11.97%	24.10%	13.04%	145.35%	13.21%	5.98%
10	16.97%	5.50%	23.05%	2.06%	11.45%	17.02%	10.31%	23.46%	15.05%	5.22%	13.13%	23.12%	149.37%	13.58%	7.58%
11	13.84%	15.35%	11.22%	15.44%	11.74%	15.53%	13.53%	13.71%	16.06%	17.23%	15.99%	4.41%	150.22%	13.66%	3.59%
12	14.16%	11.01%	9.79%	15.52%	16.29%	7.37%	18.90%	20.71%	7.22%	15.89%	11.37%	12.77%	146.84%	13.35%	4.48%
13	18.82%	8.36%	15.33%	15.19%	11.39%	8.69%	19.95%	6.98%	4.99%	29.56%	5.36%	17.05%	142.84%	12.99%	7.42%
14	10.64%	17.95%	10.16%	22.69%	11.36%	14.37%	7.82%	20.89%	12.72%	14.17%	7.03%	8.99%	148.14%	13.47%	5.21%
15	13.75%	13.56%	8.30%	20.34%	12.03%	1.00%	25.73%	24.56%	5.52%	16.98%	19.35%	18.47%	155.83%	14.17%	6.99%
16	17.62%	12.59%	0.98%	16.11%	18.19%	5.96%	21.86%	9.28%	17.20%	18.78%	12.30%	6.73%	139.97%	12.72%	6.43%
17	20.38%	5.40%	15.76%	19.89%	3.75%	11.63%	18.87%	5.14%	18.13%	10.01%	9.89%	18.19%	136.65%	12.42%	6.04%
18	13.70%	6.58%	33.27%	4.79%	16.80%	21.96%	2.00%	37.97%	-1.41%	13.50%	9.98%	22.47%	167.90%	15.26%	12.69%
19	10.92%	18.54%	8.77%	20.75%	10.46%	17.39%	2.91%	15.46%	19.14%	16.28%	9.10%	15.24%	154.05%	14.00%	5.48%
20	7.91%	28.31%	7.75%	20.83%	4.91%	23.28%	6.19%	11.22%	14.82%	9.71%	24.29%	18.91%	170.23%	15.48%	8.08%
21	14.20%	15.06%	7.75%	10.08%	32.10%	8.25%	12.23%	10.96%	17.42%	8.17%	18.41%	9.85%	150.28%	13.66%	7.14%
22	18.98%	0.80%	21.58%	11.86%	13.61%	18.39%	19.87%	6.98%	17.35%	10.30%	12.09%	15.07%	147.89%	13.44%	6.05%
23	15.78%	6.52%	16.85%	9.87%	16.03%	22.00%	4.50%	16.84%	21.64%	20.82%	2.74%	10.59%	148.39%	13.49%	6.99%
24	18.01%	4.58%	6.81%	24.06%	18.73%	9.86%	14.23%	10.82%	9.76%	11.45%	25.72%	10.39%	146.41%	13.31%	6.79%
25	13.84%	13.44%	17.79%	6.41%	22.86%	12.63%	9.44%	17.54%	15.34%	17.79%	-0.22%	24.73%	157.76%	14.34%	7.20%
26	15.35%	17.42%	4.71%	15.16%	15.11%	14.16%	4.30%	18.70%	12.56%	23.55%	9.11%	14.23%	149.03%	13.55%	5.76%
27	13.99%	9.07%	15.34%	13.44%	17.88%	2.02%	35.11%	3.61%	15.80%	30.67%	-1.11%	12.32%	154.15%	14.01%	11.18%
28	14.38%	8.14%	16.04%	17.99%	13.35%	17.80%	4.45%	20.74%	6.76%	19.03%	12.94%	20.94%	158.19%	14.38%	5.76%
29	12.61%	13.67%	9.03%	16.30%	12.25%	9.82%	21.00%	22.07%	6.95%	16.23%	9.89%	9.89%	147.08%	13.37%	4.99%
30	12.86%	17.70%	19.23%	-0.13%	21.60%	6.56%	15.57%	26.17%	9.48%	7.21%	18.71%	14.66%	156.75%	14.25%	7.70%
31	9.52%	24.87%	11.03%	4.62%	27.08%	12.98%	8.99%	14.37%	12.32%	18.63%	4.70%	22.96%	162.56%	14.78%	7.72%
32	19.09%	2.28%	16.91%	14.16%	10.90%	14.31%	8.66%	13.29%	11.13%	19.77%	14.94%	21.52%	147.87%	13.44%	5.29%
33	12.79%	11.40%	8.82%	16.55%	11.58%	16.22%	11.20%	13.66%	13.58%	23.15%	17.94%	6.35%	152.06%	13.68%	4.64%
34	13.09%	16.64%	12.92%	4.62%	16.79%	14.21%	14.35%	9.70%	11.30%	12.83%	14.48%	24.21%	152.06%	13.82%	4.85%
35	5.97%	28.25%	5.97%	19.75%	6.17%	16.01%	15.57%	8.72%	18.02%	10.77%	16.76%	17.31%	163.30%	14.85%	6.59%
mean	13.70%	13.82%	12.68%	12.65%	14.69%	14.48%	12.03%	15.27%	12.28%	16.05%	12.47%	15.97%			
std. dev	3.56%	7.62%	6.54%	6.73%	5.97%	6.38%	7.31%	7.81%	5.60%	5.91%	7.42%	6.34%			

Gross profit using the full absorption costing method
Inventory reduction policy: 50% reduction over 12 reporting periods

Dollars	Jan	Feb	Mar	Apr	May	Jun	Jul	Aug	Sep	Oct	Nov	Dec	sum	mean	std. dev.
Series (yr)															
1	66,011	157,459	47,689	61,564	100,888	67,657	63,698	76,917	49,157	100,171	115,637	126,036	966,871	87,897	35,084
2	66,016	137,994	68,706	51,812	68,153	151,607	38,264	50,506	51,909	72,331	125,940	66,333	883,554	80,323	39,127
3	74,452	107,523	130,529	80,747	44,619	137,392	90,587	130,675	17,981	70,772	49,976	127,740	988,542	89,867	40,716
4	64,820	74,883	58,168	68,128	101,350	137,285	54,160	93,804	79,063	140,716	36,928	157,760	1,002,244	91,113	39,332
5	82,876	59,909	90,331	44,181	78,851	81,192	-2,397	171,897	100,792	134,669	38,983	87,171	885,579	80,507	47,098
6	84,209	63,494	62,351	79,110	71,201	112,323	31,411	101,179	31,420	101,480	167,786	44,189	865,944	78,722	40,384
7	48,769	166,842	8,164	141,901	91,672	143,924	19,363	32,306	119,701	85,245	12,913	120,703	942,735	85,703	58,405
8	105,922	33,991	113,044	3,609	139,257	68,668	105,897	38,947	127,548	101,041	80,990	135,356	948,348	86,213	45,149
9	90,562	83,816	68,260	8,882	102,595	62,863	111,318	55,230	57,460	82,355	144,439	84,716	861,935	78,358	35,025
10	85,704	35,680	130,095	10,961	73,183	102,257	70,224	139,769	84,017	31,766	89,125	124,707	891,783	81,071	42,263
11	90,117	97,531	68,687	89,361	79,840	97,474	86,598	83,566	104,439	95,385	81,176	26,680	910,735	82,794	21,159
12	80,847	70,872	62,115	94,832	93,409	48,703	120,304	115,495	44,465	94,295	70,958	80,735	896,184	81,471	24,885
13	106,568	49,322	94,737	78,197	66,976	49,516	103,494	36,643	34,002	147,742	33,193	102,268	796,090	72,372	36,666
14	67,996	103,730	65,115	124,776	68,456	80,204	49,620	130,338	66,373	73,238	39,414	52,826	854,089	77,644	29,893
15	80,762	76,419	54,033	115,650	60,452	6,612	109,028	141,288	37,493	113,536	112,252	107,399	934,161	84,924	40,964
16	99,526	64,665	6,117	99,020	99,218	42,874	128,350	61,762	104,439	108,323	67,391	45,655	827,815	75,256	36,006
17	111,367	35,089	93,488	100,035	21,896	74,437	103,224	30,488	103,898	58,963	69,975	116,804	808,297	73,482	33,165
18	74,470	50,985	186,938	32,325	99,279	104,769	14,135	167,150	-8,329	77,413	65,906	120,677	911,247	82,841	60,862
19	73,669	108,881	59,718	121,111	68,301	89,819	19,337	103,625	112,961	97,909	61,231	102,467	945,360	85,942	30,468
20	57,689	151,859	54,901	110,153	32,384	120,823	36,189	71,771	88,046	71,334	153,687	100,042	991,191	90,108	41,799
21	87,868	86,624	53,440	74,638	178,218	47,250	72,250	71,784	104,576	49,280	100,211	61,155	899,426	81,766	37,285
22	101,483	5,212	124,220	80,966	98,871	107,861	105,431	45,194	102,399	64,341	72,254	88,985	895,735	81,430	33,772
23	93,916	42,860	110,869	68,500	112,378	125,774	31,350	119,740	129,879	108,429	15,894	71,880	937,552	85,232	40,896
24	90,702	25,291	49,322	142,072	103,698	58,502	83,109	59,697	58,808	77,480	150,592	58,516	867,448	78,859	38,948
25	84,709	81,207	105,093	43,442	129,512	78,064	59,636	112,967	94,387	81,351	-1,354	140,500	924,805	84,073	40,286
26	84,787	88,720	27,219	93,082	82,566	68,714	29,343	112,993	76,366	135,358	50,106	79,748	844,214	76,747	32,675
27	81,687	54,823	93,066	89,012	94,447	15,154	177,410	24,687	104,881	159,985	-6,205	77,861	885,121	80,466	56,831
28	83,786	57,649	107,889	113,598	78,948	97,551	30,100	126,721	45,260	115,581	84,020	119,984	977,302	88,846	32,581
29	79,432	80,408	54,075	95,864	70,045	73,060	134,057	119,535	43,391	90,864	62,914	60,816	885,029	80,457	27,699
30	89,825	114,001	94,488	-875	125,508	43,393	113,022	149,004	52,052	49,348	119,655	85,756	945,353	85,941	44,842
31	65,845	146,034	63,627	31,463	152,479	75,033	52,658	84,253	74,610	100,474	32,415	125,033	938,078	85,280	41,787
32	93,541	14,439	96,858	85,025	64,617	76,717	55,135	82,708	69,148	124,617	99,134	122,804	891,203	81,018	31,267
33	79,603	69,023	54,457	103,541	69,350	104,906	77,598	96,966	89,344	151,513	103,365	39,552	959,616	87,238	30,268
34	87,043	94,140	73,802	29,084	106,215	85,945	81,805	64,218	71,885	89,265	107,677	136,445	940,480	85,498	27,526
35	41,912	153,903	40,841	116,314	38,390	97,118	92,197	56,733	107,359	74,281	112,950	104,447	994,533	90,412	35,072
mean	81,957	81,294	76,356	76,631	87,635	83,870	72,797	90,302	75,177	95,167	77,768	94,393			
std. dev	15,618	42,085	36,506	38,824	32,714	34,381	40,557	40,412	33,111	30,544	44,310	33,117			

Gross profit using the full absorption costing method
Inventory reduction policy: 50% reduction over 12 reporting periods

Percent Series (yr)	Jan	Feb	Mar	Apr	May	Jun	Jul	Aug	Sep	Oct	Nov	Dec	sum	mean	std. dev.
1	3.72%	34.82%	8.89%	6.68%	23.50%	19.23%	10.25%	15.32%	2.16%	13.64%	14.12%	22.53%	171.13%	15.56%	9.13%
2	4.89%	31.09%	14.36%	9.61%	5.88%	33.19%	9.50%	12.96%	8.64%	8.33%	22.71%	0.70%	156.98%	14.27%	10.39%
3	9.79%	11.43%	21.94%	14.38%	5.89%	24.20%	6.69%	43.25%	1.88%	14.15%	0.86%	26.29%	170.97%	15.54%	12.62%
4	17.10%	15.62%	8.84%	10.75%	10.67%	24.27%	7.87%	14.28%	7.43%	31.27%	0.39%	34.56%	165.95%	15.09%	10.63%
5	17.87%	12.11%	17.32%	7.93%	15.16%	22.46%	-10.38%	30.60%	18.83%	25.85%	-0.92%	9.75%	148.70%	13.52%	11.81%
6	18.62%	16.41%	7.02%	15.03%	14.54%	26.29%	1.95%	21.86%	1.33%	9.28%	34.81%	4.23%	152.74%	13.89%	10.61%
7	4.74%	37.38%	-5.08%	18.82%	13.99%	37.58%	6.65%	-0.97%	25.39%	25.28%	-4.57%	22.90%	177.38%	16.13%	15.49%
8	22.41%	6.23%	25.56%	-6.73%	30.40%	9.28%	19.10%	2.99%	20.92%	16.03%	7.72%	36.34%	167.84%	15.26%	12.79%
9	16.75%	17.83%	21.85%	-2.42%	19.28%	10.33%	24.25%	11.62%	5.32%	7.98%	26.95%	10.21%	153.21%	13.93%	8.90%
10	24.91%	1.85%	28.97%	3.61%	9.62%	18.51%	6.46%	26.93%	17.49%	2.44%	9.05%	28.28%	153.22%	13.93%	10.57%
11	13.17%	15.39%	11.47%	18.89%	8.82%	16.11%	12.71%	14.79%	15.27%	21.75%	22.38%	1.71%	159.30%	14.48%	5.88%
12	17.80%	9.25%	9.19%	17.36%	20.05%	4.30%	19.69%	25.70%	5.40%	17.56%	10.32%	10.69%	149.50%	13.59%	6.83%
13	22.35%	7.11%	15.57%	20.05%	11.12%	8.84%	26.00%	9.06%	-2.20%	38.12%	0.91%	16.95%	151.52%	13.77%	11.46%
14	8.77%	21.72%	7.68%	28.22%	10.15%	16.49%	4.13%	21.30%	17.17%	17.92%	6.40%	7.99%	159.18%	14.47%	7.68%
15	15.74%	17.20%	5.73%	24.92%	18.82%	-3.97%	13.49%	29.84%	0.48%	15.53%	22.60%	20.87%	165.52%	15.05%	10.44%
16	22.49%	18.24%	-2.60%	17.05%	23.94%	-0.77%	25.57%	6.23%	18.14%	21.96%	14.95%	1.23%	143.94%	13.09%	10.24%
17	26.31%	1.76%	17.50%	28.28%	2.97%	9.83%	23.00%	3.51%	21.20%	9.62%	4.58%	17.27%	139.52%	12.68%	9.21%
18	18.72%	-1.52%	41.12%	-0.55%	19.36%	33.21%	-5.16%	55.42%	-5.70%	14.51%	6.11%	27.72%	184.52%	16.77%	20.55%
19	9.05%	23.36%	6.25%	25.73%	8.79%	25.22%	-1.36%	14.84%	22.75%	18.69%	6.18%	13.48%	163.93%	14.90%	9.09%
20	3.11%	38.55%	2.37%	28.79%	1.42%	31.92%	6.11%	9.68%	16.13%	4.14%	26.84%	24.88%	190.83%	17.35%	13.34%
21	15.14%	18.76%	3.45%	4.72%	41.22%	9.87%	13.50%	8.66%	19.59%	7.10%	23.92%	8.12%	158.92%	14.45%	11.03%
22	25.94%	-3.54%	26.60%	8.81%	9.07%	22.10%	26.73%	3.85%	19.36%	8.76%	12.48%	16.55%	150.77%	13.71%	9.55%
23	19.54%	4.23%	18.10%	7.21%	14.83%	28.87%	-0.38%	15.50%	25.34%	29.38%	2.23%	7.36%	152.68%	13.88%	10.66%
24	25.92%	5.42%	0.79%	28.24%	23.23%	8.93%	15.09%	12.56%	8.98%	6.95%	29.32%	10.81%	150.32%	13.67%	9.40%
25	15.03%	14.47%	19.20%	1.20%	28.91%	11.17%	7.51%	17.21%	16.13%	28.64%	-4.64%	29.67%	169.47%	15.41%	11.24%
26	15.46%	24.38%	2.70%	15.98%	18.52%	20.61%	-2.56%	19.79%	11.11%	26.39%	8.77%	15.98%	161.66%	14.70%	8.94%
27	16.44%	9.06%	17.35%	11.64%	24.86%	-6.04%	47.80%	-2.58%	15.15%	39.74%	-2.72%	10.82%	165.08%	15.01%	17.09%
28	18.31%	3.29%	16.27%	19.20%	15.73%	24.36%	-0.31%	24.29%	3.52%	21.46%	11.39%	25.37%	164.56%	14.96%	9.27%
29	12.68%	15.85%	9.64%	19.38%	13.91%	4.18%	22.27%	28.67%	4.53%	19.96%	7.55%	9.02%	154.95%	14.09%	7.89%
30	10.66%	18.39%	30.25%	-5.35%	26.56%	3.74%	13.00%	32.45%	12.52%	2.63%	19.23%	16.97%	170.40%	15.49%	11.85%
31	5.70%	30.14%	12.02%	-0.22%	34.54%	14.59%	9.22%	15.75%	11.96%	23.46%	-1.43%	25.37%	178.47%	16.22%	11.83%
32	28.76%	-0.99%	19.76%	15.18%	11.38%	17.63%	6.23%	12.47%	10.11%	20.73%	11.92%	25.27%	149.70%	13.61%	7.29%
33	14.38%	13.36%	9.48%	18.36%	12.71%	16.49%	7.68%	10.28%	13.77%	25.09%	21.97%	4.97%	154.16%	14.01%	6.08%
34	12.30%	21.23%	16.76%	2.24%	18.47%	15.51%	17.93%	7.16%	10.31%	10.35%	20.35%	31.21%	161.51%	14.68%	7.84%
35	1.99%	37.93%	2.16%	24.29%	4.79%	18.37%	18.81%	6.96%	20.84%	7.28%	14.87%	19.78%	176.08%	16.01%	10.38%
mean	15.33%	15.65%	13.39%	13.07%	16.37%	16.48%	11.69%	16.63%	12.04%	17.48%	11.36%	17.11%			
std. dev	7.21%	11.55%	10.04%	10.19%	9.08%	10.66%	11.30%	12.22%	8.14%	9.66%	10.45%	9.99%			

Gross profit using the full absorption costing method
Inventory reduction policy: 50% reduction over 12 reporting periods

Dollars Series (yr)	Jan	Feb	Mar	Apr	May	Jun	Jul	Aug	Sep	Oct	Nov	Dec	sum	mean	std. dev.
1	27,862	200,410	53,264	44,721	133,757	102,089	62,236	89,648	15,163	91,462	99,594	139,687	1,032,032	93,821	51,405
2	35,416	177,628	83,854	57,306	41,377	189,927	52,731	71,524	51,963	55,337	140,259	5,465	927,373	84,307	59,016
3	66,521	85,414	142,679	89,156	38,516	155,409	50,886	202,159	11,354	83,150	6,309	156,870	1,021,903	92,900	64,382
4	94,016	92,020	55,779	67,617	76,438	153,773	49,091	92,354	52,894	177,374	2,700	195,821	1,015,863	92,351	59,478
5	104,347	71,528	104,163	48,497	91,332	119,699	-81,694	193,309	114,424	155,504	-6,452	67,768	878,078	79,825	75,396
6	105,293	88,587	45,303	89,599	82,485	141,630	12,152	122,215	8,438	66,941	199,150	26,395	882,895	80,263	58,242
7	31,303	211,134	-34,917	132,385	89,990	195,441	34,262	-6,672	145,185	125,840	-31,287	136,223	997,585	90,690	87,645
8	130,411	35,899	143,915	-48,218	175,057	59,411	116,834	19,438	133,223	101,648	53,379	184,526	975,113	88,647	71,461
9	100,368	101,011	107,836	-15,315	114,420	62,302	137,538	64,247	34,463	54,898	161,527	66,366	889,294	80,845	49,886
10	125,803	11,983	163,566	19,158	61,483	111,182	43,985	160,466	97,678	14,843	61,421	152,583	898,349	81,668	58,770
11	85,800	97,795	70,258	109,290	60,010	101,105	81,380	90,129	99,297	120,390	113,623	10,345	953,621	86,693	31,165
12	101,658	59,589	58,292	106,066	114,950	28,398	125,330	143,290	33,228	104,236	64,389	67,592	905,359	82,305	38,244
13	126,569	41,961	96,198	103,229	65,390	50,358	134,889	47,564	-15,035	190,536	5,606	101,669	822,365	74,760	58,615
14	56,068	125,495	49,241	155,234	61,128	92,054	26,217	132,864	89,604	92,651	35,914	46,952	907,354	82,487	42,526
15	92,488	96,932	37,334	141,729	94,592	-26,190	93,518	171,649	3,262	103,882	131,101	121,376	969,186	88,108	60,040
16	127,035	93,695	-16,263	104,779	130,584	-5,561	150,167	41,470	110,177	126,646	81,928	8,337	825,959	75,087	58,580
17	143,770	11,413	103,827	142,256	17,339	62,883	125,808	20,824	121,500	56,694	32,399	110,889	805,831	73,257	48,941
18	101,758	-11,785	231,067	-3,732	114,374	158,447	-36,539	243,929	-33,667	83,238	40,353	148,917	934,603	84,964	102,483
19	61,081	137,140	42,552	150,129	57,414	130,258	-9,005	99,478	134,267	112,409	41,584	90,629	986,853	89,714	50,467
20	22,705	206,813	16,801	152,204	9,393	165,709	35,713	61,901	95,856	30,375	169,786	131,602	1,076,154	97,832	70,605
21	93,673	107,867	23,771	34,967	228,891	56,501	141,823	56,718	117,625	42,833	130,242	50,432	929,606	84,510	59,330
22	138,704	-23,170	153,146	60,146	65,938	129,622	24,906	110,218	114,281	54,705	12,946	97,763	893,724	81,248	52,961
23	116,334	27,852	119,103	50,024	103,980	165,055	-2,628	110,218	152,083	153,005	172,061	50,008	941,647	85,604	60,227
24	130,583	29,912	5,699	166,740	128,611	52,997	88,145	69,339	54,138	47,010	-28,951	60,868	875,520	79,593	54,242
25	92,011	87,445	113,461	8,146	163,782	69,003	47,476	110,806	99,221	130,968	48,241	168,560	969,916	88,174	61,181
26	95,471	124,156	15,593	98,106	101,161	99,966	-17,455	119,541	67,563	151,629	-15,141	89,568	898,069	81,643	49,688
27	96,009	54,727	105,208	77,103	131,277	-45,360	241,564	-17,617	100,578	207,321	73,972	68,363	908,022	82,547	90,005
28	106,662	23,289	109,409	121,251	93,003	133,451	-2,101	148,411	23,561	130,339	47,992	145,313	999,898	90,900	53,800
29	79,843	93,272	57,715	113,982	79,541	31,103	142,213	155,299	28,279	111,762	122,981	55,450	916,608	83,328	43,530
30	74,455	118,433	148,638	-35,065	154,362	24,773	94,385	184,806	68,745	18,002	-9,839	99,286	999,346	90,850	66,403
31	39,429	176,978	69,363	-1,484	194,473	84,325	83,989	92,336	72,391	126,550	79,108	154,853	1,013,937	92,176	66,616
32	140,933	-6,266	113,139	91,142	67,468	94,572	39,706	77,581	62,832	130,644	126,626	144,213	894,140	81,285	41,986
33	89,467	80,895	58,554	114,892	76,083	106,686	53,177	73,012	90,542	164,218	76,938	30,904	975,591	88,690	37,592
34	81,810	120,094	95,772	14,095	116,861	93,806	102,160	47,390	65,543	72,059	100,208	175,872	980,591	89,145	42,257
35	13,964	206,660	14,774	143,029	29,805	111,402	111,432	45,293	124,158	50,216	69,007	119,341	1,056,318	96,029	56,511
mean	89,418	90,195	78,803	77,233	96,150	93,035	67,976	95,995	72,709	101,123	69,007	99,452			
std. dev	35,619	64,347	56,201	58,587	48,991	58,118	63,692	61,402	48,107	49,074	61,553	53,769			

Gross profit using the full absorption costing method
Inventory reduction policy: 50% reduction over 12 reporting periods

Percent Series (yr)	Jan	Feb	Mar	Apr	May	Jun	Jul	Aug	Sep	Oct	Nov	Dec	sum	mean	std. dev.
1	1.92%	32.24%	6.56%	4.82%	21.22%	16.82%	8.40%	13.46%	0.91%	12.37%	13.06%	21.27%	151.14%	13.74%	8.89%
2	2.99%	28.48%	11.94%	7.37%	4.26%	31.04%	7.36%	10.93%	6.98%	7.04%	21.34%	-0.05%	136.67%	12.42%	10.09%
3	7.69%	9.71%	19.96%	12.35%	4.06%	22.41%	5.47%	40.72%	0.23%	12.53%	-0.11%	24.98%	152.32%	13.85%	12.35%
4	14.21%	13.12%	6.69%	8.69%	9.11%	22.45%	6.10%	12.72%	6.21%	29.55%	-0.69%	33.07%	147.01%	13.36%	10.58%
5	15.23%	9.62%	15.00%	5.78%	13.07%	20.06%	-11.53%	29.10%	17.27%	24.30%	-1.94%	8.78%	129.51%	11.77%	11.61%
6	15.85%	13.57%	4.94%	12.80%	12.24%	23.93%	0.18%	19.86%	-0.18%	8.18%	33.23%	3.01%	131.75%	11.98%	10.45%
7	2.54%	34.72%	-6.95%	17.11%	12.11%	35.09%	4.26%	-2.37%	23.61%	23.15%	-5.69%	21.53%	156.57%	14.23%	15.20%
8	19.75%	3.65%	23.01%	-8.38%	28.15%	7.48%	17.27%	1.44%	19.44%	14.62%	6.62%	34.54%	147.83%	13.44%	12.66%
9	14.21%	15.18%	18.77%	-4.46%	17.14%	8.35%	22.19%	9.59%	3.86%	6.77%	25.50%	9.07%	131.96%	12.00%	8.72%
10	21.66%	-0.32%	26.43%	0.95%	7.72%	16.52%	4.94%	25.13%	15.61%	0.92%	7.91%	26.66%	132.46%	12.04%	10.54%
11	10.93%	13.16%	9.22%	16.55%	7.11%	14.26%	11.02%	13.09%	13.82%	19.95%	20.44%	0.39%	139.01%	12.64%	5.74%
12	15.07%	7.07%	7.05%	15.21%	17.79%	2.60%	17.98%	23.69%	3.80%	15.97%	8.97%	9.48%	129.61%	11.78%	6.72%
13	19.59%	4.62%	13.35%	17.27%	8.95%	6.67%	23.63%	6.86%	-3.53%	36.01%	-0.46%	15.60%	128.96%	11.72%	11.26%
14	6.46%	19.15%	5.58%	25.70%	8.05%	14.25%	2.41%	19.63%	15.07%	15.92%	4.77%	6.60%	137.14%	12.47%	7.45%
15	13.12%	14.57%	3.69%	22.52%	16.07%	-5.67%	12.02%	27.93%	-0.86%	14.28%	21.06%	19.45%	145.06%	13.19%	10.30%
16	19.72%	15.20%	-4.79%	14.92%	21.51%	-2.24%	23.65%	4.75%	16.51%	20.28%	13.25%	0.18%	123.21%	11.20%	10.03%
17	23.40%	-0.40%	15.14%	25.41%	0.77%	8.03%	20.82%	1.71%	19.39%	8.01%	3.53%	16.09%	118.50%	10.77%	9.01%
18	15.79%	-3.13%	38.65%	-2.39%	17.23%	30.39%	-6.58%	52.62%	-7.41%	12.83%	4.90%	26.09%	163.19%	14.84%	20.11%
19	6.92%	20.85%	4.34%	23.43%	6.96%	22.71%	-2.94%	13.37%	21.03%	17.13%	5.02%	12.41%	144.31%	13.12%	8.81%
20	1.23%	35.71%	0.59%	26.13%	-0.38%	29.43%	4.14%	8.08%	14.43%	3.08%	25.52%	23.20%	169.93%	15.45%	13.00%
21	12.71%	16.17%	1.58%	3.19%	38.87%	7.72%	11.57%	7.13%	17.92%	5.55%	22.20%	6.87%	138.76%	12.61%	10.82%
22	22.94%	-5.67%	24.13%	7.01%	7.59%	20.08%	24.44%	2.29%	17.66%	7.31%	11.02%	15.17%	131.02%	11.91%	9.40%
23	16.97%	2.12%	16.08%	5.47%	13.22%	26.72%	-1.84%	14.19%	23.67%	27.40%	0.69%	6.32%	134.04%	12.19%	10.51%
24	22.67%	2.67%	-0.93%	25.97%	20.86%	6.90%	13.12%	10.53%	7.32%	5.70%	27.81%	9.30%	129.25%	11.75%	9.36%
25	12.57%	12.06%	16.82%	-0.61%	26.63%	9.26%	5.78%	15.63%	14.53%	26.22%	-5.99%	28.18%	148.51%	13.50%	11.07%
26	13.02%	21.30%	0.24%	13.84%	16.09%	17.85%	-4.07%	18.03%	9.48%	24.70%	7.08%	14.46%	139.00%	12.64%	8.76%
27	13.79%	6.65%	15.07%	9.75%	22.30%	-7.40%	45.34%	-3.99%	13.76%	37.77%	-4.37%	9.60%	144.49%	13.14%	16.79%
28	15.65%	1.41%	14.33%	17.18%	13.57%	22.05%	-1.85%	22.57%	2.15%	19.94%	10.14%	23.90%	145.40%	13.22%	9.17%
29	10.31%	13.35%	7.31%	17.10%	11.64%	2.80%	20.61%	26.57%	2.97%	18.21%	6.25%	7.74%	134.53%	12.23%	7.69%
30	8.65%	16.24%	27.15%	-7.27%	24.35%	2.04%	11.65%	30.61%	10.60%	1.41%	17.94%	15.56%	150.27%	13.66%	11.61%
31	3.66%	27.63%	9.55%	-2.03%	32.22%	12.47%	7.26%	13.90%	10.31%	21.59%	-2.53%	26.84%	157.21%	14.29%	11.62%
32	25.38%	-3.23%	17.26%	12.97%	9.23%	15.26%	4.56%	10.81%	8.57%	19.30%	10.72%	23.80%	129.27%	11.75%	7.35%
33	11.97%	10.96%	7.26%	16.29%	10.61%	14.73%	6.20%	8.99%	12.38%	23.77%	20.41%	3.72%	135.32%	12.30%	6.09%
34	10.12%	18.62%	14.26%	0.19%	16.53%	13.55%	15.88%	5.66%	8.81%	9.17%	9.41%	29.74%	141.81%	12.89%	7.73%
35	-0.01%	35.13%	0.27%	22.01%	2.80%	16.43%	16.89%	5.42%	19.15%	6.08%	13.74%	18.45%	156.37%	14.22%	10.11%
mean	12.82%	13.20%	11.13%	10.94%	14.28%	14.43%	9.89%	14.88%	10.44%	15.92%	10.02%	15.77%			
std. dev	6.84%	11.35%	9.84%	9.98%	8.91%	10.40%	11.08%	11.99%	8.05%	9.42%	10.34%	9.83%			

Gross profit using the full absorption costing method
Inventory reduction policy: 50% reduction over 12 reporting periods

Dollars Series (yr)	Jan	Feb	Mar	Apr	May	Jun	Jul	Aug	Sep	Oct	Nov	Dec	sum	mean	std. dev.
1	14,411	185,525	39,311	32,254	120,825	89,281	51,008	78,810	6,378	82,954	92,148	131,882	910,376	82,761	50,843
2	21,647	162,688	69,707	43,969	29,978	177,614	40,866	60,285	41,963	46,752	131,786	-417	805,191	73,199	57,779
3	52,225	72,586	129,811	76,552	26,528	143,932	41,560	190,339	1,388	73,646	-820	149,057	904,580	82,235	63,728
4	78,150	77,282	42,201	54,670	65,203	142,199	38,057	82,255	44,227	167,637	-4,838	187,364	896,259	81,478	59,657
5	88,903	56,813	90,227	35,383	78,734	106,912	-90,758	183,859	104,923	146,229	-13,667	61,045	759,701	69,064	74,919
6	89,623	73,267	31,905	76,267	69,453	128,915	1,104	111,060	-1,158	59,044	190,116	18,739	758,712	68,974	57,993
7	16,783	196,102	-47,814	120,343	77,873	182,502	21,922	-16,284	135,013	115,263	-38,975	128,113	874,058	79,460	86,796
8	114,942	21,054	129,523	-60,100	162,121	47,917	105,647	9,373	123,757	92,704	45,769	175,372	853,138	77,558	71,591
9	85,104	86,021	92,631	-28,214	101,703	50,351	125,821	53,018	25,011	46,591	152,814	58,923	764,671	69,516	49,760
10	109,411	-2,044	149,199	5,051	49,316	99,215	33,640	149,749	87,174	5,586	53,649	143,817	774,352	70,396	58,994
11	71,164	83,639	56,467	95,745	48,335	89,454	70,538	79,766	89,884	110,468	103,813	2,350	830,458	75,496	30,653
12	86,051	45,513	44,759	92,914	101,997	17,160	114,437	132,113	23,398	94,794	55,966	59,933	782,987	71,181	38,052
13	110,911	27,249	82,470	88,913	52,612	38,010	122,587	36,005	-24,050	179,989	-2,874	93,616	694,528	63,139	58,207
14	41,283	110,633	35,789	141,350	48,516	79,565	15,309	122,481	78,649	82,298	26,743	38,767	780,100	70,918	41,562
15	77,084	82,083	24,005	128,067	80,784	-37,449	83,307	160,687	-5,815	95,529	122,155	113,117	846,470	76,952	60,119
16	111,365	78,060	-29,913	91,666	117,294	-16,103	138,881	31,591	100,249	117,003	72,598	1,226	702,552	63,868	58,167
17	127,872	-2,578	89,796	127,797	4,497	51,384	113,851	10,118	111,154	47,212	24,994	103,354	681,578	61,962	48,771
18	85,835	-24,279	217,172	-16,109	101,797	144,984	-46,560	231,610	-43,793	73,559	32,370	140,117	810,867	73,715	101,707
19	46,729	122,417	29,573	136,711	45,422	117,286	-19,546	89,651	124,141	103,060	33,748	83,452	865,914	78,719	49,759
20	9,003	191,566	4,155	138,155	-2,527	152,756	24,209	51,713	85,769	22,632	161,478	122,705	952,612	86,601	69,933
21	78,634	92,976	10,902	23,592	215,799	44,198	68,335	46,704	107,605	33,507	20,870	42,642	807,131	73,376	58,821
22	122,666	-37,106	138,909	47,852	55,185	117,771	129,659	14,802	104,251	45,639	65,835	89,603	772,402	70,218	52,902
23	101,018	13,942	105,852	37,990	92,664	152,733	-12,799	100,891	142,068	142,688	4,005	42,913	822,947	74,813	59,944
24	114,178	14,730	-6,704	153,337	115,459	40,933	76,639	58,099	44,154	38,569	163,193	52,382	750,794	68,254	54,404
25	76,905	72,888	99,390	-4,149	150,827	57,237	36,527	100,668	89,387	119,893	-37,370	160,131	845,430	76,857	60,932
26	80,427	108,471	1,381	84,581	87,878	86,611	-27,796	108,925	57,647	141,961	38,934	81,046	770,039	70,004	49,503
27	80,567	40,185	91,404	64,562	117,788	-55,527	229,137	-27,280	91,330	197,033	-24,354	60,709	784,988	71,363	89,312
28	91,204	9,999	96,347	108,506	80,265	120,836	-12,496	137,887	14,377	121,071	65,864	136,943	879,600	79,964	53,842
29	64,947	78,532	43,750	100,557	66,577	20,846	131,602	143,925	18,547	101,920	39,726	47,598	793,578	72,143	42,915
30	60,381	104,568	133,386	-47,682	141,503	13,532	84,577	174,297	58,178	9,654	114,742	91,058	877,813	79,801	66,048
31	25,276	162,225	55,128	-13,796	181,389	72,081	42,500	81,494	62,433	116,461	-17,455	146,146	888,607	80,782	65,903
32	124,353	-20,448	98,857	77,864	54,744	81,823	29,076	67,280	53,267	121,646	71,156	135,823	771,088	70,099	42,908
33	74,476	66,356	44,812	101,921	63,549	95,269	42,968	63,855	81,460	155,570	117,633	23,126	856,518	77,865	37,887
34	67,325	105,322	41,488	1,169	104,618	81,915	90,482	37,472	56,029	63,838	69,951	167,575	859,860	78,169	42,374
35	-56	191,466	1,842	129,603	17,431	99,651	100,012	35,232	114,087	41,928	92,604	111,329	935,124	85,011	55,823
mean	74,308	75,647	65,078	64,220	83,604	81,023	56,980	85,499	62,945	91,838	60,694	91,473			
std. dev	34,897	63,961	55,858	58,190	48,665	57,579	63,189	61,069	47,920	48,577	61,283	53,334			

Gross profit using the full absorption costing method
Inventory reduction policy: 50% reduction over 12 reporting periods

Percent Series (yr)	Jan	Feb	Mar	Apr	May	Jun	Jul	Aug	Sep	Oct	Nov	Dec	sum	mean	std. dev.
1	39.65%	61.18%	42.65%	41.90%	51.18%	50.73%	44.54%	47.30%	38.68%	45.95%	45.93%	51.75%	521.78%	47.43%	6.13%
2	39.98%	58.23%	46.42%	43.40%	40.95%	59.00%	42.43%	45.39%	42.33%	43.07%	51.99%	37.97%	511.18%	46.47%	6.96%
3	43.60%	44.68%	52.32%	46.32%	39.72%	54.04%	41.69%	65.85%	38.72%	46.35%	37.60%	53.85%	521.14%	47.38%	8.50%
4	47.42%	47.51%	42.73%	44.95%	44.14%	53.01%	41.92%	46.68%	41.04%	57.22%	37.17%	59.95%	516.33%	46.94%	7.05%
5	48.96%	45.58%	48.98%	41.45%	46.42%	52.67%	30.31%	58.09%	50.23%	54.40%	37.09%	33.34%	508.55%	46.23%	8.01%
6	49.30%	47.82%	42.03%	46.41%	47.25%	55.76%	36.12%	51.88%	37.83%	43.10%	60.89%	39.92%	511.15%	46.47%	7.36%
7	40.12%	62.39%	33.70%	49.56%	45.89%	62.12%	41.36%	36.66%	53.54%	53.36%	33.88%	52.16%	524.62%	47.69%	10.32%
8	52.92%	41.06%	55.12%	32.64%	56.74%	43.32%	49.68%	38.99%	51.18%	47.84%	42.02%	61.47%	520.07%	47.28%	8.60%
9	48.40%	49.19%	51.82%	34.77%	49.95%	43.26%	52.99%	45.11%	41.31%	42.03%	55.02%	44.00%	509.45%	46.31%	6.04%
10	53.50%	38.64%	56.23%	39.00%	43.61%	49.65%	40.84%	55.30%	49.12%	39.24%	43.46%	55.92%	511.01%	46.46%	7.06%
11	46.32%	47.63%	44.63%	49.31%	42.98%	47.00%	45.72%	46.51%	46.86%	51.41%	52.63%	37.76%	512.45%	46.59%	4.05%
12	49.35%	43.57%	42.46%	48.26%	49.94%	39.82%	49.70%	45.26%	40.07%	48.76%	43.88%	45.00%	506.72%	46.07%	4.74%
13	52.15%	41.76%	47.22%	50.63%	44.30%	42.60%	53.92%	43.94%	35.95%	63.08%	37.69%	48.24%	509.31%	46.30%	7.67%
14	42.27%	50.87%	42.52%	55.67%	44.74%	48.39%	39.38%	51.89%	47.51%	49.63%	40.95%	41.72%	513.28%	46.66%	5.19%
15	47.76%	48.85%	41.12%	53.88%	49.16%	34.29%	53.34%	56.93%	37.43%	47.47%	51.99%	40.40%	516.86%	46.99%	6.94%
16	51.98%	49.70%	35.30%	48.01%	53.14%	37.15%	53.23%	41.10%	48.87%	51.60%	46.86%	37.82%	502.78%	45.71%	6.66%
17	54.60%	38.71%	48.37%	55.66%	38.91%	43.74%	53.00%	39.14%	50.95%	43.35%	39.78%	48.81%	500.42%	45.49%	6.15%
18	49.15%	36.90%	64.72%	37.14%	49.59%	58.13%	34.19%	74.64%	33.79%	47.21%	41.33%	56.15%	533.79%	48.53%	13.55%
19	43.47%	52.35%	41.52%	54.57%	43.25%	54.18%	36.12%	46.93%	51.54%	49.66%	40.92%	46.21%	517.24%	47.02%	6.05%
20	38.40%	62.90%	39.33%	55.81%	37.67%	58.60%	41.02%	43.91%	47.72%	39.45%	54.46%	53.53%	534.41%	48.58%	8.86%
21	47.02%	49.82%	40.08%	39.88%	63.59%	43.50%	45.70%	43.07%	49.80%	41.15%	52.52%	43.00%	512.10%	46.55%	7.05%
22	54.91%	34.56%	54.98%	43.90%	43.06%	51.21%	55.16%	40.08%	49.89%	43.31%	44.87%	57.58%	508.60%	46.24%	6.29%
23	50.31%	39.33%	49.39%	40.83%	46.51%	55.83%	36.67%	46.90%	54.29%	56.56%	37.78%	42.90%	506.97%	46.09%	7.24%
24	54.29%	40.64%	37.46%	55.66%	52.65%	43.72%	47.62%	44.90%	42.82%	42.27%	56.41%	44.57%	508.73%	46.25%	6.18%
25	47.10%	47.26%	51.78%	38.06%	55.88%	45.78%	41.42%	48.41%	47.47%	55.08%	33.75%	56.98%	521.84%	47.44%	7.45%
26	47.13%	53.97%	39.05%	46.73%	49.45%	51.30%	35.87%	49.94%	44.45%	55.66%	42.92%	47.56%	516.90%	46.99%	6.06%
27	48.32%	33.17%	47.92%	45.18%	52.98%	33.25%	68.65%	35.71%	46.04%	64.70%	34.78%	44.77%	517.15%	47.01%	11.44%
28	49.83%	39.85%	47.47%	50.03%	47.39%	52.76%	37.04%	52.66%	39.82%	50.80%	44.99%	54.39%	517.20%	47.02%	5.91%
29	45.87%	47.21%	43.38%	50.39%	46.10%	39.95%	51.37%	56.20%	40.27%	49.41%	42.44%	43.17%	509.89%	46.35%	5.11%
30	44.41%	49.87%	58.01%	33.99%	54.48%	39.21%	45.78%	58.53%	45.77%	38.83%	50.29%	47.87%	522.61%	47.51%	7.92%
31	40.94%	57.36%	55.65%	36.17%	59.36%	47.28%	42.70%	47.84%	44.86%	52.54%	36.32%	56.25%	526.32%	47.85%	7.91%
32	55.99%	36.30%	50.74%	47.43%	44.68%	48.83%	41.54%	45.37%	42.97%	50.76%	45.03%	54.20%	507.84%	46.17%	4.98%
33	46.57%	45.66%	43.28%	49.91%	45.62%	48.57%	43.03%	43.70%	44.69%	53.92%	50.74%	40.26%	509.39%	46.31%	4.03%
34	45.90%	50.89%	48.85%	38.00%	49.86%	47.35%	48.47%	42.81%	43.10%	43.19%	43.55%	57.04%	513.11%	46.65%	5.18%
35	37.91%	62.63%	38.22%	52.75%	40.51%	48.86%	48.95%	48.24%	51.34%	42.28%	46.68%	48.47%	522.79%	47.53%	6.99%
mean	47.31%	47.66%	46.16%	45.66%	47.76%	48.14%	44.73%	48.24%	44.92%	48.70%	44.53%	48.47%			
std. dev	4.92%	7.77%	6.82%	6.81%	5.88%	7.08%	7.41%	8.21%	5.33%	6.50%	6.99%	6.60%			

Gross profit using the full absorption costing method
Inventory reduction policy: 50% reduction over 12 reporting periods

Dollars Series (yr)	Jan	Feb	Mar	Apr	May	Jun	Jul	Aug	Sep	Oct	Nov	Dec	sum	mean	std. dev.
1	297,157	352,122	255,495	280,476	291,387	269,255	270,410	276,840	271,658	308,199	323,986	320,826	3,220,654	292,787	29,694
2	289,453	332,666	271,011	258,866	288,327	337,566	235,416	250,467	254,552	286,236	321,141	326,234	3,132,484	284,771	34,549
3	296,202	333,872	340,230	287,063	259,794	347,022	317,042	307,824	233,984	272,374	275,142	321,288	3,295,636	299,603	36,473
4	260,689	279,850	269,761	282,716	316,114	335,828	261,531	301,937	292,091	324,581	259,350	339,705	3,263,464	296,679	29,018
5	285,854	269,199	294,550	253,611	279,720	280,762	238,587	366,985	305,248	327,322	261,472	301,289	3,178,746	288,977	36,185
6	278,777	258,237	271,233	276,605	268,102	300,442	238,415	290,054	240,366	310,933	348,319	248,920	3,051,624	277,420	33,226
7	265,152	352,365	231,744	348,631	295,145	323,094	212,988	252,181	306,190	265,654	231,904	310,315	3,130,210	284,565	48,499
8	307,954	236,788	310,300	233,947	326,742	277,378	303,969	253,270	325,881	303,435	290,432	312,139	3,174,280	288,571	33,727
9	289,938	278,745	255,793	219,951	296,362	260,777	300,535	249,411	267,341	289,079	329,788	285,939	3,033,721	275,793	29,581
10	270,239	250,461	317,439	207,079	278,698	298,242	278,213	329,490	274,267	238,754	294,875	301,700	3,069,220	279,020	35,769
11	301,695	302,642	273,312	285,338	292,277	294,911	292,642	283,435	304,714	284,612	267,283	228,200	3,109,368	282,670	21,282
12	281,810	280,548	269,451	294,839	286,354	263,214	316,271	308,145	246,605	289,419	273,874	284,517	3,113,238	283,022	19,807
13	295,268	246,299	291,741	260,709	260,527	242,649	279,711	230,706	245,172	315,307	233,199	289,377	2,895,399	263,218	27,368
14	270,163	293,934	272,568	306,212	269,505	270,111	250,055	323,715	247,911	256,562	229,741	245,172	2,965,486	269,590	28,422
15	280,566	275,296	267,785	306,410	247,140	226,330	314,299	327,481	254,024	317,478	301,527	293,120	3,130,889	284,626	32,771
16	293,588	255,221	220,609	295,067	289,849	267,226	312,584	273,559	296,829	297,623	256,838	256,540	3,021,945	274,722	26,657
17	298,403	251,750	286,957	279,937	226,864	279,891	289,869	231,958	292,069	255,433	281,590	313,485	2,989,803	271,800	26,849
18	267,218	285,969	363,660	250,859	293,013	277,287	241,935	328,549	199,547	270,757	272,915	301,636	3,086,128	280,557	43,519
19	293,335	307,375	278,726	318,469	282,422	279,868	239,988	314,571	304,180	298,685	275,243	310,638	3,214,166	292,197	23,016
20	279,989	337,408	278,451	295,089	248,375	304,201	239,777	280,927	283,547	289,738	344,573	283,156	3,185,243	289,568	31,639
21	290,862	286,495	276,482	295,144	353,052	249,055	269,983	281,954	299,013	248,324	285,956	267,045	3,112,503	282,955	28,556
22	293,578	226,147	316,494	299,710	312,887	300,434	292,663	259,399	294,522	270,492	268,148	280,978	3,121,873	283,807	26,434
23	299,483	258,721	325,069	283,367	326,043	319,144	255,168	333,576	325,769	294,498	219,297	291,323	3,231,974	293,816	36,950
24	273,442	224,228	271,486	328,643	291,466	259,451	278,134	247,808	258,152	286,042	331,067	250,991	3,027,467	275,224	32,947
25	288,275	285,542	305,898	257,924	316,538	282,881	261,805	311,693	291,985	251,873	210,439	323,764	3,100,341	281,849	33,939
26	291,122	274,857	225,685	286,867	270,134	248,876	244,697	301,708	270,339	319,877	235,986	266,574	2,945,601	267,782	28,225
27	282,223	260,891	290,646	299,219	279,835	249,660	346,886	243,977	305,694	337,481	193,930	283,000	3,091,218	281,020	43,485
28	290,293	282,201	319,204	315,896	280,241	289,078	250,673	321,800	266,529	308,495	292,222	311,616	3,237,954	294,359	23,226
29	288,891	277,790	259,776	296,388	263,708	297,211	327,999	304,422	251,468	276,575	269,954	265,523	3,090,814	280,983	22,957
30	310,053	321,176	285,021	222,828	316,607	259,503	332,410	333,290	251,239	265,628	321,599	280,057	3,189,357	289,942	37,434
31	283,116	336,772	263,433	246,063	334,201	273,211	250,114	280,382	271,582	283,448	250,576	306,313	3,096,093	281,463	31,849
32	274,319	230,025	290,566	284,755	264,903	261,848	264,636	282,306	266,973	319,937	298,807	309,234	3,073,989	279,454	25,299
33	289,769	276,504	267,210	312,307	273,136	314,240	298,124	310,284	293,954	352,886	292,395	250,595	3,241,633	294,694	27,991
34	305,241	287,896	279,144	239,321	315,482	286,354	276,190	283,333	274,085	300,588	323,787	321,398	3,187,577	289,780	24,659
35	266,585	341,219	261,674	310,651	252,039	296,367	276,390	265,066	305,850	291,713	314,580	300,509	3,229,511	293,592	26,043
mean	286,585	284,320	281,789	280,599	287,057	283,525	276,390	289,786	276,381	291,713	279,484	290,089			
std. dev	12,571	36,107	30,170	32,213	27,553	28,234	32,567	33,465	28,107	26,624	38,912	26,445			

Gross profit using the full absorption costing method
Inventory reduction policy: 50% reduction over 12 reporting periods

Percent	Jan	Feb	Mar	Apr	May	Jun	Jul	Aug	Sep	Oct	Nov	Dec	sum	mean	std. dev.
Series (yr)															
1	7.58%	27.32%	10.02%	9.75%	19.60%	17.10%	11.79%	14.97%	7.14%	14.66%	15.12%	20.66%	168.13%	15.28%	5.77%
2	8.28%	24.80%	13.56%	10.98%	9.21%	26.50%	11.01%	13.28%	10.90%	11.34%	20.04%	6.75%	158.36%	14.40%	6.47%
3	11.11%	12.53%	19.51%	14.34%	8.77%	21.15%	9.98%	32.74%	6.37%	14.52%	6.82%	22.61%	169.34%	15.39%	8.01%
4	15.21%	14.74%	10.46%	12.05%	12.25%	20.77%	10.43%	14.71%	10.34%	25.88%	6.14%	28.05%	165.81%	15.07%	6.93%
5	16.04%	12.49%	16.00%	9.49%	14.88%	19.11%	-0.72%	25.75%	17.37%	21.71%	5.74%	12.15%	153.97%	14.00%	7.42%
6	16.30%	14.58%	9.61%	14.27%	14.63%	21.79%	6.13%	19.21%	6.21%	12.04%	28.34%	8.14%	154.94%	14.09%	6.89%
7	7.86%	28.57%	1.88%	17.53%	14.18%	28.76%	9.01%	5.09%	21.71%	20.93%	2.84%	20.65%	171.15%	15.56%	9.71%
8	18.81%	8.64%	21.05%	0.83%	24.49%	11.32%	17.54%	7.43%	19.13%	15.70%	10.90%	29.10%	166.13%	15.10%	8.24%
9	15.37%	16.01%	17.71%	3.06%	17.76%	11.79%	20.46%	12.64%	9.05%	10.76%	23.14%	12.48%	154.87%	14.08%	5.66%
10	20.06%	6.13%	22.83%	6.77%	11.49%	17.04%	9.43%	22.70%	16.34%	6.96%	11.84%	23.99%	155.52%	14.14%	6.81%
11	13.25%	14.76%	12.20%	16.78%	10.95%	15.67%	13.87%	14.66%	15.36%	19.39%	19.52%	6.64%	159.79%	14.53%	3.69%
12	15.85%	10.92%	10.61%	16.12%	17.73%	8.01%	18.19%	21.93%	8.56%	16.96%	12.26%	13.15%	154.43%	14.04%	4.45%
13	18.68%	9.28%	14.57%	17.60%	11.87%	10.62%	21.43%	10.41%	4.16%	29.92%	6.05%	16.61%	152.52%	13.87%	7.35%
14	10.40%	18.37%	10.02%	22.60%	11.62%	15.35%	7.95%	19.39%	15.52%	16.91%	9.39%	10.66%	157.76%	14.34%	4.73%
15	14.93%	15.43%	8.48%	20.77%	16.31%	2.63%	14.25%	24.70%	6.03%	15.75%	19.91%	18.88%	163.14%	14.83%	6.67%
16	18.46%	15.98%	3.11%	16.12%	19.98%	5.01%	21.59%	9.43%	17.34%	19.48%	14.88%	6.84%	149.76%	13.61%	6.43%
17	21.15%	5.94%	16.08%	22.62%	6.54%	11.50%	20.13%	7.33%	18.80%	11.57%	8.70%	17.30%	146.52%	13.32%	5.92%
18	16.02%	4.54%	31.36%	4.86%	17.28%	25.47%	2.08%	40.25%	1.59%	14.92%	9.71%	23.54%	175.59%	15.96%	12.92%
19	10.90%	19.55%	8.99%	21.36%	10.76%	21.07%	4.46%	15.11%	20.09%	17.57%	9.59%	14.84%	163.39%	14.85%	5.70%
20	6.98%	29.23%	6.88%	22.92%	5.95%	25.61%	8.86%	11.69%	15.79%	8.45%	22.99%	21.58%	179.95%	16.36%	8.39%
21	14.51%	16.49%	7.28%	8.43%	31.44%	11.19%	13.76%	11.15%	17.81%	10.29%	20.84%	11.06%	159.75%	14.52%	6.95%
22	20.96%	2.40%	21.97%	10.83%	11.37%	19.35%	22.17%	7.66%	17.83%	11.33%	13.61%	16.47%	155.00%	14.09%	6.15%
23	17.02%	7.72%	16.61%	9.73%	15.19%	23.56%	5.47%	15.50%	22.15%	23.72%	6.79%	11.01%	157.44%	14.31%	6.73%
24	20.71%	7.98%	5.59%	23.17%	19.48%	10.87%	14.68%	12.99%	11.00%	10.50%	24.36%	12.57%	153.18%	13.93%	6.03%
25	14.11%	13.95%	17.57%	5.87%	22.99%	12.76%	9.98%	16.71%	15.60%	23.35%	2.71%	24.68%	166.17%	15.11%	7.09%
26	14.57%	19.74%	6.50%	14.64%	16.76%	17.84%	3.83%	17.91%	12.71%	22.55%	11.14%	15.44%	159.07%	14.46%	5.60%
27	15.18%	10.51%	15.71%	12.85%	20.37%	1.63%	35.50%	4.04%	14.90%	31.29%	3.48%	12.75%	163.03%	14.82%	10.84%
28	16.05%	7.39%	15.10%	17.77%	15.20%	20.22%	5.56%	20.82%	7.89%	19.30%	13.37%	21.94%	164.57%	14.96%	5.80%
29	12.86%	14.80%	10.99%	17.08%	13.87%	8.19%	19.77%	23.64%	8.37%	18.08%	10.83%	11.36%	156.99%	14.27%	4.94%
30	11.79%	17.05%	23.26%	1.65%	22.02%	7.69%	13.81%	26.27%	13.19%	7.47%	18.44%	16.43%	167.28%	15.21%	7.45%
31	8.72%	23.92%	12.57%	4.89%	26.93%	14.42%	10.82%	15.56%	13.12%	20.46%	4.89%	23.94%	171.52%	15.59%	7.48%
32	22.42%	3.82%	17.80%	14.39%	11.98%	16.72%	9.26%	13.36%	11.78%	18.75%	13.77%	21.81%	153.45%	13.95%	4.91%
33	13.82%	13.27%	10.93%	16.76%	13.34%	15.92%	10.67%	12.51%	14.26%	22.00%	19.65%	9.13%	158.44%	14.40%	3.91%
34	12.74%	18.21%	15.17%	6.49%	17.00%	15.12%	16.55%	10.28%	12.00%	12.50%	12.90%	25.49%	161.70%	14.70%	4.90%
35	6.19%	29.01%	6.22%	20.53%	8.52%	16.85%	16.95%	9.79%	19.26%	10.36%	15.66%	18.46%	171.62%	15.60%	6.55%
mean	14.43%	14.74%	13.38%	13.31%	15.51%	16.85%	12.76%	16.05%	13.13%	16.78%	13.04%	16.78%			
std. dev	4.33%	7.32%	6.33%	6.44%	5.69%	6.68%	7.11%	7.77%	5.23%	6.07%	6.68%	6.36%			

Gross profit using the full absorption costing method
Inventory reduction policy: 50% reduction over 12 reporting periods

Dollars Series (yr)	Jan	Feb	Mar	Apr	May	Jun	Jul	Aug	Sep	Oct	Nov	Dec	sum	mean	std. dev.
1	56,833	157,251	60,036	65,292	111,554	90,752	71,597	87,623	50,124	98,347	106,624	128,106	1,027,306	93,391	31,784
2	59,964	141,693	79,156	65,478	64,818	151,612	61,088	73,248	65,552	75,380	123,794	52,666	954,484	86,771	34,886
3	75,476	93,601	126,858	88,858	57,397	135,805	75,922	153,029	38,504	85,316	49,936	134,882	1,040,108	94,555	38,431
4	83,609	86,824	66,058	75,763	87,729	131,560	65,045	95,147	73,606	146,789	42,863	158,912	1,030,294	93,663	36,721
5	93,620	73,735	96,251	58,080	89,657	101,853	-5,661	162,703	105,535	130,617	40,445	84,471	937,685	85,244	44,753
6	92,172	78,727	61,992	85,347	82,986	117,399	38,178	107,407	39,477	86,851	162,150	50,753	910,968	82,815	36,695
7	51,956	161,355	12,937	123,280	91,183	149,592	46,402	35,045	124,135	104,187	19,409	122,883	990,407	90,037	52,955
8	109,451	49,822	118,505	5,950	141,016	72,471	107,342	48,275	121,776	99,589	75,349	147,767	987,861	89,806	43,699
9	92,077	90,739	87,434	19,370	105,374	71,097	116,051	69,895	58,547	74,004	138,671	81,083	912,266	82,933	31,331
10	101,314	39,751	128,909	35,955	73,444	102,334	64,248	135,239	91,267	42,328	80,318	129,405	923,195	83,927	36,893
11	86,291	93,807	74,687	97,100	74,448	98,342	88,764	89,326	99,862	107,324	99,105	40,154	962,920	87,538	18,738
12	90,503	70,283	67,334	98,479	101,629	52,977	115,735	122,314	52,671	100,660	76,545	83,128	941,754	85,614	23,897
13	105,779	54,734	90,056	90,600	69,791	60,475	111,191	54,655	28,366	149,562	37,458	99,654	846,541	76,958	35,429
14	66,470	106,178	64,229	124,280	69,992	85,652	50,465	120,929	80,982	87,408	52,655	62,649	905,418	82,311	25,730
15	87,687	86,944	55,239	118,125	81,993	17,352	98,801	142,087	40,918	105,494	115,494	109,782	972,081	88,371	37,145
16	104,250	82,072	19,455	99,061	108,957	36,032	126,771	62,791	105,289	112,357	81,563	46,391	880,737	80,067	34,795
17	115,606	38,597	95,405	113,762	38,141	73,622	110,109	43,432	107,786	68,196	61,589	111,080	861,717	78,338	30,519
18	87,083	35,149	176,219	32,834	102,111	121,510	14,712	177,171	9,363	85,563	64,095	126,437	945,164	85,924	60,378
19	73,582	114,791	61,188	124,664	70,274	108,828	29,657	101,304	118,554	105,660	64,515	99,737	999,174	90,834	29,927
20	50,898	156,820	48,709	121,177	39,218	132,920	51,814	74,805	93,821	62,061	145,428	114,165	1,040,938	94,631	41,794
21	89,789	94,799	50,249	62,381	174,555	64,098	81,273	73,000	106,957	62,118	113,481	68,709	951,619	86,511	35,337
22	112,064	15,706	126,472	73,939	82,637	113,537	117,628	49,574	105,281	70,776	81,310	97,288	934,148	84,923	32,499
23	101,320	50,796	109,293	67,566	106,510	134,660	38,058	110,209	132,898	123,521	39,394	74,791	987,696	89,791	36,799
24	104,304	44,050	40,479	136,775	107,857	64,484	85,758	71,672	66,302	71,055	142,974	70,767	902,173	82,016	33,869
25	86,382	84,292	103,833	39,755	130,235	78,829	63,088	107,597	95,966	106,779	16,885	140,242	967,502	87,955	36,969
26	89,987	100,527	37,594	89,860	91,533	86,541	26,147	108,195	77,306	129,600	61,265	86,553	895,120	81,375	30,047
27	88,667	63,539	95,299	85,087	107,583	12,208	179,386	27,589	98,945	163,199	19,396	80,605	932,837	84,803	54,049
28	80,958	52,309	101,553	112,227	89,916	110,804	37,604	127,199	52,811	117,225	86,859	125,684	1,014,189	92,199	31,566
29		87,090	65,797	100,443	79,355	60,953	126,208	128,063	52,296	101,210	68,895	69,874	940,184	85,471	25,675
30	82,299	109,834	114,289	10,839	127,994	83,352	100,296	149,583	72,389	51,104	117,891	96,106	1,001,234	91,021	40,626
31	60,289	140,439	72,529	33,271	151,600	89,663	63,401	91,216	79,421	110,352	91,348	130,384	989,670	89,970	39,927
32	109,837	24,227	101,961	86,381	71,021	103,010	58,976	83,157	73,205	118,204	113,223	124,445	922,587	83,872	27,757
33	85,973	80,322	67,482	104,900	79,859	91,406	73,920	88,839	93,808	143,985	105,529	56,843	1,006,191	91,472	24,287
34	84,761	103,040	86,679	40,857	107,578	102,203	94,315	68,018	76,289	87,026	95,889	143,625	994,723	90,429	25,523
35	43,522	158,073	42,578	120,923	53,010	90,253	100,400	63,649	114,726	71,485	80,744	111,391	1,043,966	94,906	33,981
mean	85,666	86,340	80,193	80,239	92,084		76,705	94,399	80,135	98,719		98,898			
std. dev	18,414	39,373	34,083	35,702	29,610	34,336	37,975	37,594	30,121	28,834	38,455	32,210			

Gross profit using the full absorption costing method
Inventory reduction policy: 50% reduction over 12 reporting periods

Percent	Jan	Feb	Mar	Apr	May	Jun	Jul	Aug	Sep	Oct	Nov	Dec	sum	mean	std. dev.
Series (yr)															
1	5.07%	30.73%	9.00%	7.60%	20.04%	16.69%	10.15%	15.20%	4.51%	13.35%	13.09%	21.05%	161.43%	14.68%	7.36%
2	6.95%	25.58%	15.80%	9.66%	6.40%	27.38%	9.70%	12.27%	8.29%	8.54%	21.56%	2.94%	148.13%	13.47%	8.08%
3	9.20%	12.95%	18.60%	14.64%	6.58%	21.65%	7.71%	33.83%	6.17%	11.88%	2.34%	17.99%	154.35%	14.03%	8.87%
4	17.95%	14.85%	6.99%	11.28%	8.90%	23.02%	9.69%	10.89%	8.81%	28.22%	3.25%	30.08%	155.97%	14.18%	8.92%
5	15.91%	11.54%	17.26%	6.84%	13.82%	23.16%	-7.69%	18.69%	20.45%	29.75%	1.02%	7.01%	141.86%	12.90%	10.67%
6	19.52%	13.48%	5.94%	14.96%	13.96%	24.71%	1.02%	22.07%	2.69%	8.98%	31.23%	3.13%	142.17%	12.92%	9.85%
7	5.40%	34.18%	-2.60%	18.21%	11.58%	33.71%	6.27%	2.00%	19.64%	25.72%	-3.04%	22.07%	167.74%	15.25%	13.44%
8	20.69%	5.97%	22.39%	-3.20%	28.68%	8.06%	19.45%	2.60%	16.91%	16.51%	9.15%	32.56%	159.06%	14.46%	11.05%
9	15.65%	17.89%	16.57%	1.57%	17.68%	9.54%	22.24%	10.30%	7.24%	8.67%	23.03%	10.78%	145.51%	13.23%	6.71%
10	21.06%	4.70%	24.59%	4.91%	10.41%	17.03%	7.03%	25.46%	14.32%	5.13%	8.78%	23.74%	146.10%	13.28%	8.24%
11	11.73%	15.16%	13.17%	16.65%	7.66%	16.64%	11.00%	13.73%	15.68%	20.32%	20.00%	1.49%	151.51%	13.77%	5.48%
12	16.92%	10.00%	8.25%	15.73%	6.47%	6.49%	19.86%	22.20%	7.05%	16.84%	9.37%	11.65%	143.91%	13.08%	5.39%
13	19.67%	8.85%	12.84%	21.35%	10.51%	9.78%	23.91%	5.23%	-0.56%	35.00%	3.02%	16.12%	146.06%	13.28%	10.29%
14	9.54%	19.22%	9.21%	22.60%	11.21%	16.04%	5.86%	18.58%	16.24%	17.52%	4.52%	9.72%	150.72%	13.70%	5.90%
15	15.18%	13.46%	8.56%	22.12%	16.39%	-0.48%	13.50%	24.46%	4.15%	11.58%	24.10%	17.64%	155.48%	14.13%	7.99%
16	19.64%	18.15%	-0.71%	16.30%	21.35%	-0.42%	25.81%	5.83%	17.07%	20.35%	12.30%	4.26%	140.32%	12.76%	9.15%
17	24.21%	2.74%	16.26%	26.20%	3.01%	9.51%	22.03%	2.73%	22.50%	5.85%	7.11%	17.15%	135.08%	12.28%	8.81%
18	16.71%	1.25%	35.41%	0.81%	16.25%	34.02%	-4.35%	48.30%	-4.34%	14.64%	7.28%	25.33%	174.60%	15.87%	17.85%
19	9.21%	19.09%	7.96%	24.84%	8.33%	23.29%	-1.72%	16.00%	20.60%	17.60%	7.26%	11.26%	154.50%	14.05%	8.12%
20	4.71%	28.94%	6.50%	26.63%	3.81%	26.17%	6.96%	9.35%	16.70%	4.72%	25.41%	21.40%	176.60%	16.05%	9.97%
21	14.48%	13.84%	7.47%	6.60%	35.31%	10.93%	10.47%	10.14%	18.51%	8.77%	19.73%	7.23%	148.98%	13.54%	8.44%
22	22.23%	-1.03%	24.41%	8.46%	10.33%	19.66%	26.01%	2.80%	18.62%	9.11%	12.45%	14.38%	145.20%	13.20%	8.49%
23	18.46%	4.71%	17.07%	7.52%	11.65%	28.30%	2.76%	14.12%	21.66%	26.64%	5.41%	6.33%	146.18%	13.29%	9.05%
24	23.40%	5.86%	1.63%	27.28%	19.67%	10.33%	13.52%	11.03%	8.26%	9.75%	25.78%	11.32%	144.43%	13.13%	7.99%
25	14.09%	13.87%	19.55%	0.99%	24.68%	11.95%	8.76%	15.26%	15.26%	28.14%	-3.46%	24.36%	159.36%	14.49%	9.79%
26	16.66%	19.85%	4.32%	14.12%	17.41%	17.95%	-0.70%	18.32%	10.69%	25.41%	9.30%	14.56%	151.23%	13.75%	7.44%
27	15.22%	9.73%	13.86%	13.64%	22.58%	-2.95%	39.75%	0.22%	14.61%	33.77%	-1.12%	12.02%	156.11%	14.19%	13.62%
28	15.84%	5.23%	14.22%	17.95%	16.79%	22.46%	0.40%	22.77%	4.04%	19.86%	10.93%	22.54%	157.20%	14.29%	8.05%
29	12.07%	14.49%	10.72%	16.24%	13.98%	5.62%	19.21%	27.92%	6.45%	17.00%	7.17%	8.66%	147.46%	13.41%	6.67%
30	10.46%	17.44%	26.99%	-3.65%	24.65%	4.33%	11.96%	28.85%	12.77%	3.49%	18.89%	16.39%	162.09%	14.74%	10.29%
31	6.58%	27.24%	11.89%	0.89%	30.17%	14.51%	8.16%	16.90%	11.31%	20.19%	0.77%	25.79%	167.83%	15.26%	9.99%
32	26.12%	-0.82%	19.07%	13.72%	11.32%	18.88%	3.71%	14.44%	5.09%	23.67%	12.46%	22.30%	143.85%	13.08%	7.86%
33	13.51%	13.06%	8.27%	16.79%	15.06%	14.04%	8.64%	9.48%	10.22%	24.03%	22.71%	6.77%	149.09%	13.55%	5.77%
34	13.00%	18.19%	15.19%	4.62%	15.83%	14.12%	17.61%	7.76%	9.57%	12.21%	8.84%	22.09%	146.03%	13.28%	5.21%
35	4.07%	32.11%	5.02%	20.15%	5.84%	17.09%	17.27%	7.41%	20.15%	7.06%	12.99%	19.09%	164.16%	14.92%	8.25%
mean	14.60%	14.36%	12.90%	12.72%	15.09%	15.81%	11.31%	15.06%	11.75%	16.82%	11.25%	15.46%			
std. dev	5.91%	9.20%	8.08%	8.63%	7.54%	9.17%	9.89%	10.16%	6.83%	8.70%	8.97%	8.10%			

Gross profit using the full absorption costing method
Inventory reduction policy: 50% reduction over 12 reporting periods

Dollars Series (yr)	Jan	Feb	Mar	Apr	May	Jun	Jul	Aug	Sep	Oct	Nov	Dec	sum	mean	std. dev.
1	37,991	176,874	53,915	50,901	114,105	88,603	61,645	88,948	31,691	89,536	92,369	130,529	979,117	89,011	40,992
2	50,313	146,156	92,250	57,605	45,025	156,636	53,831	67,726	49,846	56,773	133,179	22,977	882,003	80,182	45,264
3	62,482	96,746	120,949	90,752	43,066	139,053	58,648	158,133	37,258	69,834	17,108	107,335	938,883	85,353	44,500
4	98,666	87,461	44,124	70,917	63,738	145,816	60,467	70,446	62,691	160,078	22,648	170,428	958,814	87,165	49,100
5	92,868	68,127	103,798	41,878	83,281	123,450	-60,523	118,103	124,286	179,005	7,212	48,703	837,320	76,120	65,676
6	110,358	72,793	38,319	89,167	79,202	133,130	6,384	123,379	17,107	64,783	178,639	19,525	822,429	74,766	54,102
7	35,660	193,014	-17,866	128,074	74,443	175,333	32,303	13,774	112,318	128,034	-20,809	131,289	949,907	86,355	74,928
8	120,380	34,404	126,022	-22,923	165,141	51,616	118,983	16,895	107,639	104,733	63,215	165,313	931,038	84,640	60,865
9	93,781	101,356	81,770	9,958	104,899	57,501	126,131	56,969	46,829	59,638	138,048	70,071	853,170	77,561	37,507
10	106,361	30,479	138,834	26,081	66,503	102,303	47,874	151,679	79,981	31,188	59,595	128,093	862,611	78,419	45,558
11	76,430	96,299	80,662	96,349	52,120	104,423	70,406	83,670	101,995	112,480	101,582	8,995	908,982	82,635	29,971
12	96,611	64,381	52,371	96,077	94,429	42,935	126,407	123,785	43,379	99,933	58,511	73,640	875,847	79,622	30,262
13	111,391	52,219	79,308	109,930	61,830	55,732	124,063	27,454	-3,818	174,955	18,716	96,678	797,067	72,461	51,711
14	60,952	111,063	59,008	124,312	67,513	89,515	37,238	115,923	84,727	90,573	25,346	57,137	862,356	78,396	32,172
15	89,210	75,850	55,728	125,789	82,385	-3,153	93,605	140,707	28,151	77,476	139,784	102,592	918,913	83,538	44,872
16	110,917	93,231	-4,410	100,160	116,466	-2,988	151,598	38,839	103,669	117,393	67,432	28,914	810,303	73,664	51,989
17	132,289	17,820	96,433	131,802	17,525	60,876	120,493	16,203	128,960	34,452	50,312	110,124	785,000	71,364	47,158
18	90,874	9,685	198,948	5,488	95,999	162,297	-30,770	212,623	-25,615	83,964	48,078	136,036	896,732	81,521	87,656
19	62,181	112,069	54,208	144,943	54,429	120,310	-11,415	107,250	121,559	105,840	48,839	75,687	933,718	84,883	45,179
20	34,350	155,234	46,028	140,788	25,094	135,854	40,691	59,841	99,262	34,690	160,779	113,199	1,011,461	91,951	52,034
21	89,609	79,563	51,496	48,869	196,038	62,561	61,861	66,365	111,111	52,921	107,415	84,884	883,086	80,281	44,442
22	118,838	-6,770	140,496	57,763	75,080	115,315	137,991	18,128	109,940	56,910	74,432	84,942	864,226	78,566	46,485
23	109,908	30,957	12,355	52,204	81,669	161,807	19,237	100,402	130,004	138,705	31,431	43,007	901,778	81,980	49,658
24	117,846	32,361	11,825	161,058	108,888	61,274	79,003	60,848	49,763	65,992	151,303	63,770	846,084	76,917	46,254
25	86,216	83,805	115,493	6,723	139,822	73,845	55,355	98,268	93,872	128,704	-21,605	138,439	912,720	82,975	52,352
26	102,925	101,086	24,964	86,693	95,110	87,085	-4,792	110,655	65,014	146,026	51,147	81,628	844,616	76,783	41,511
27	88,869	58,776	84,059	90,367	119,272	-22,136	200,852	1,495	97,030	176,150	-6,225	75,951	875,593	79,599	70,923
28	92,298	37,050	95,624	113,369	99,317	123,065	2,735	139,133	27,018	120,594	71,012	129,109	958,026	87,093	46,142
29	76,013	85,281	64,214	95,497	79,966	41,837	122,680	151,218	40,258	95,163	45,616	53,267	874,996	79,545	35,456
30	73,051	112,301	132,598	-23,949	143,258	28,626	86,873	164,279	70,080	23,847	120,809	95,896	954,618	86,783	57,507
31	45,482	159,939	68,601	6,086	169,867	83,844	47,788	99,076	68,496	108,938	5,306	140,452	958,394	87,127	55,786
32	127,989	-5,226	109,185	82,366	67,105	101,273	23,657	89,955	31,606	149,214	82,673	127,262	859,071	78,097	46,203
33	84,051	79,107	51,076	105,052	90,158	90,841	59,862	67,335	67,234	157,289	130,875	42,150	940,981	85,544	34,743
34	86,463	102,894	86,783	29,070	100,184	85,395	100,331	51,351	60,872	84,996	65,702	124,494	892,072	81,097	27,196
35	28,625	174,963	34,383	118,644	36,307	103,635	102,272	48,162	120,039	48,676	87,520	115,158	989,760	89,978	43,990
mean	85,779	83,467	76,673	75,653	88,835	89,643	66,393	87,401	71,264	97,985	68,800	90,219			
std. dev	27,976	51,103	44,624	49,064	40,119	48,716	55,781	50,414	39,990	44,356	52,601	42,855			

Gross profit using the full absorption costing method
Inventory reduction policy: 50% reduction over 12 reporting periods

Percent Series (yr)	Jan	Feb	Mar	Apr	May	Jun	Jul	Aug	Sep	Oct	Nov	Dec	sum	mean	std. dev.
1	3.27%	28.15%	6.67%	5.74%	17.77%	14.28%	8.31%	13.35%	3.26%	12.08%	12.04%	19.79%	141.43%	12.86%	7.15%
2	5.05%	22.97%	13.38%	7.42%	4.78%	25.22%	7.56%	10.24%	6.63%	7.25%	20.19%	2.19%	127.83%	11.62%	7.79%
3	7.09%	11.23%	16.62%	12.61%	4.75%	19.87%	6.49%	31.30%	4.52%	10.27%	1.36%	16.68%	135.69%	12.34%	8.56%
4	15.06%	12.35%	4.84%	9.22%	7.33%	21.19%	7.92%	9.33%	7.59%	26.51%	2.17%	28.59%	137.02%	12.46%	8.88%
5	13.26%	9.04%	14.94%	4.70%	11.73%	20.76%	-8.84%	17.20%	18.89%	28.21%	0.00%	6.04%	122.67%	11.15%	10.44%
6	16.75%	10.64%	3.86%	12.72%	11.66%	22.35%	-0.75%	20.07%	1.18%	7.89%	29.65%	1.90%	121.18%	11.02%	9.70%
7	3.20%	31.51%	-4.47%	16.50%	9.69%	31.22%	3.88%	0.60%	17.86%	23.59%	-4.16%	20.70%	146.93%	13.36%	13.15%
8	18.03%	3.39%	19.83%	-4.86%	26.43%	6.27%	17.62%	1.05%	15.42%	15.10%	8.05%	30.75%	139.05%	12.64%	10.94%
9	13.11%	15.24%	13.49%	-0.46%	15.54%	7.56%	20.17%	8.27%	5.78%	7.46%	21.58%	9.64%	124.26%	11.30%	6.57%
10	17.81%	2.54%	22.05%	2.26%	8.50%	15.04%	5.51%	23.66%	12.44%	3.60%	7.64%	22.12%	125.35%	11.40%	8.20%
11	9.49%	12.93%	10.92%	14.31%	5.95%	14.78%	9.31%	12.03%	14.24%	18.52%	18.07%	0.17%	131.23%	11.93%	5.32%
12	14.18%	7.81%	6.12%	13.57%	14.21%	4.79%	18.15%	20.19%	5.45%	15.25%	8.02%	10.44%	124.01%	11.27%	5.31%
13	16.91%	6.36%	10.61%	18.57%	8.34%	7.62%	21.54%	3.03%	-1.88%	32.89%	1.65%	14.77%	123.51%	11.23%	10.09%
14	7.22%	16.65%	7.11%	20.08%	9.11%	13.80%	4.15%	16.92%	14.14%	15.52%	2.88%	8.33%	128.68%	11.70%	5.66%
15	12.56%	10.82%	6.51%	19.72%	13.64%	-2.18%	12.03%	22.55%	2.81%	10.34%	22.56%	16.22%	135.02%	12.27%	7.89%
16	16.86%	15.11%	-2.89%	14.16%	18.92%	-1.88%	23.89%	4.35%	15.43%	18.68%	10.60%	3.21%	119.59%	10.87%	8.93%
17	21.30%	0.59%	13.89%	23.33%	0.80%	7.72%	19.85%	0.93%	20.69%	4.24%	6.06%	15.97%	114.07%	10.37%	8.65%
18	13.79%	-0.36%	32.93%	-1.02%	14.12%	31.20%	-5.77%	45.51%	-6.05%	12.95%	6.07%	23.69%	153.27%	13.93%	17.40%
19	7.09%	16.58%	6.05%	22.54%	6.50%	20.78%	-3.30%	14.53%	18.88%	16.04%	6.10%	10.19%	134.89%	12.26%	7.85%
20	2.83%	26.10%	4.72%	23.97%	2.00%	23.68%	4.99%	7.76%	15.01%	3.67%	24.10%	19.72%	155.70%	14.15%	9.65%
21	12.05%	11.25%	5.60%	5.07%	32.95%	8.78%	8.54%	8.61%	16.84%	7.22%	18.01%	5.97%	128.83%	11.71%	8.25%
22	19.23%	-3.16%	21.93%	6.66%	8.85%	17.64%	13.72%	1.24%	16.92%	7.66%	10.99%	13.00%	125.45%	11.40%	8.33%
23	15.89%	2.59%	15.06%	5.79%	10.04%	26.15%	1.30%	12.81%	19.99%	24.66%	3.87%	5.29%	127.54%	11.59%	8.88%
24	20.14%	3.11%	-0.08%	25.01%	17.29%	8.29%	11.56%	8.99%	6.60%	8.50%	24.27%	9.82%	123.36%	11.21%	7.97%
25	11.62%	11.46%	17.17%	-0.82%	22.40%	10.05%	7.03%	13.69%	13.66%	25.72%	-4.81%	22.88%	138.41%	12.58%	9.59%
26	14.23%	16.77%	1.86%	11.99%	14.98%	15.20%	-2.22%	16.56%	9.06%	23.73%	7.61%	13.04%	128.57%	11.69%	7.30%
27	12.57%	7.32%	11.58%	11.75%	20.03%	-4.30%	37.29%	-1.20%	13.22%	31.80%	-2.77%	10.80%	135.53%	12.32%	13.33%
28	13.19%	3.36%	12.28%	15.94%	14.64%	20.16%	-1.13%	21.05%	2.66%	18.33%	9.69%	21.08%	138.04%	12.55%	7.94%
29	9.70%	11.99%	8.39%	13.95%	11.71%	4.25%	17.55%	25.82%	4.89%	15.24%	5.87%	7.38%	127.04%	11.55%	6.45%
30	8.45%	15.28%	23.88%	-5.58%	22.44%	2.63%	10.61%	27.00%	10.84%	2.27%	17.60%	14.98%	141.96%	12.91%	10.06%
31	4.53%	24.73%	9.42%	-0.92%	27.85%	12.39%	6.20%	15.05%	9.67%	18.32%	-0.33%	24.19%	146.57%	13.32%	9.78%
32	22.74%	-3.06%	16.57%	11.51%	9.17%	16.51%	2.04%	12.80%	3.55%	22.24%	11.26%	20.83%	123.43%	11.22%	7.90%
33	11.10%	10.66%	6.05%	14.71%	12.96%	12.28%	7.17%	8.19%	8.84%	22.71%	21.15%	5.52%	130.25%	11.84%	5.78%
34	10.82%	15.58%	12.69%	2.56%	13.90%	12.16%	15.56%	6.26%	8.08%	11.03%	7.90%	20.62%	126.32%	11.48%	5.06%
35	2.08%	29.31%	3.13%	17.87%	3.85%	15.15%	15.34%	5.86%	18.46%	5.85%	11.86%	17.76%	144.44%	13.13%	7.98%
mean	12.09%	11.91%	10.59%	10.59%	13.00%	13.75%	9.52%	13.30%	10.16%	15.30%	9.91%	14.12%			
std. dev	5.53%	9.02%	7.89%	8.43%	7.37%	8.90%	9.68%	9.94%	6.75%	8.48%	8.87%	7.93%			

Gross profit using the full absorption costing method
Inventory reduction policy: 50% reduction over 12 reporting periods

Dollars Series (yr)	Jan	Feb	Mar	Apr	May	Jun	Jul	Aug	Sep	Oct	Nov	Dec	sum	mean	std. dev.
1	24,539	161,989	39,962	38,434	101,173	75,795	50,417	78,111	22,905	81,029	84,923	122,724	857,461	77,951	40,573
2	36,544	131,215	78,103	44,268	33,626	144,323	41,965	56,487	39,846	48,188	124,706	17,095	759,821	69,075	44,111
3	48,186	83,918	108,082	78,148	31,078	127,577	49,322	146,313	27,291	60,331	9,979	99,522	821,561	74,687	43,522
4	82,800	72,723	30,546	57,969	52,503	134,242	49,433	60,347	54,024	150,342	15,110	161,970	839,210	76,292	49,401
5	77,424	53,412	89,862	28,765	70,683	110,663	-69,587	108,653	114,785	169,729	-3	41,981	718,943	65,358	65,117
6	94,688	57,472	24,921	75,835	66,170	120,416	-4,664	112,224	7,512	56,886	169,605	11,869	698,246	63,477	53,894
7	21,140	177,981	-30,763	116,032	62,326	162,394	19,963	4,162	102,146	117,457	-28,496	123,178	826,380	75,125	74,089
8	104,912	19,558	111,630	-34,805	152,205	40,122	107,797	6,829	98,173	95,789	55,605	156,159	809,063	73,551	61,059
9	78,517	86,366	66,565	-2,941	92,182	45,550	114,414	45,740	37,377	51,331	129,335	62,628	728,547	66,232	37,527
10	89,969	16,452	124,466	1,974	54,336	90,336	37,529	140,963	69,476	21,931	51,823	119,327	738,614	67,147	45,755
11	61,794	82,142	66,871	82,804	40,446	92,773	59,565	73,307	92,581	102,558	91,772	1,000	785,819	71,438	29,352
12	81,003	50,306	38,839	82,925	81,477	31,697	115,514	112,608	33,549	90,491	50,088	65,981	753,476	68,498	30,246
13	95,733	37,506	65,579	95,613	49,052	43,384	111,762	15,895	-12,834	164,408	10,237	88,626	669,230	60,839	51,303
14	46,167	96,201	45,556	170,429	54,900	77,025	26,330	105,540	33,772	80,220	16,175	48,952	735,101	66,827	31,167
15	73,807	61,001	42,398	112,127	68,577	-14,412	83,393	129,746	19,074	69,124	130,837	94,333	796,197	72,382	45,077
16	95,248	77,596	-18,059	87,047	103,176	-13,529	140,312	28,959	93,741	107,750	58,102	21,802	686,897	62,445	51,608
17	116,391	3,829	82,401	117,343	4,683	49,377	108,537	5,497	118,613	24,970	42,907	102,588	660,746	60,068	47,131
18	74,951	-2,810	185,052	-6,889	83,422	148,835	-40,791	200,303	-35,741	74,284	40,095	127,236	772,996	70,272	86,872
19	47,829	97,346	41,229	131,525	42,437	107,338	-21,956	97,423	111,433	96,491	41,003	68,510	812,778	73,889	44,517
20	20,647	139,987	33,382	126,738	13,174	122,901	29,188	49,653	89,176	26,947	152,471	104,302	887,918	80,720	51,479
21	74,570	64,672	38,628	37,495	182,946	50,259	50,435	56,352	101,092	43,594	98,043	37,095	760,611	69,146	43,943
22	102,800	-20,706	126,260	45,469	64,327	103,463	125,827	8,024	99,910	47,845	65,703	76,781	742,904	67,537	46,354
23	94,592	17,047	99,104	40,170	70,354	149,485	9,066	91,075	119,989	128,388	22,490	35,912	783,078	71,189	49,323
24	101,441	17,179	-578	147,655	95,736	49,210	67,497	49,609	39,779	57,551	142,435	55,284	721,357	65,578	46,513
25	71,111	69,248	101,422	-5,572	126,867	62,079	44,406	88,130	84,038	117,629	-30,024	130,010	788,234	71,658	51,981
26	87,882	85,402	10,752	73,567	81,826	73,730	-15,132	100,039	55,098	136,359	41,841	73,106	716,586	65,144	41,512
27	73,427	44,234	70,255	77,826	105,784	-32,303	188,426	-8,168	87,782	165,863	-15,438	68,297	752,559	68,414	70,276
28	76,841	23,760	82,562	100,624	86,579	110,450	-7,660	128,609	17,835	111,326	62,903	120,739	837,728	76,157	46,095
29	61,117	70,541	50,249	82,072	67,001	31,580	112,068	139,845	30,525	85,320	37,350	45,414	751,966	68,361	34,789
30	58,977	98,437	117,346	-36,566	130,399	17,385	77,066	153,769	59,513	15,499	112,570	87,668	833,084	75,735	57,213
31	31,329	145,186	54,366	-6,226	156,783	71,601	36,299	88,234	58,537	98,849	-2,311	131,745	833,064	75,733	55,094
32	111,409	-19,408	94,903	69,088	54,382	88,524	13,027	79,653	22,041	140,216	74,721	118,871	736,019	66,911	46,986
33	69,060	64,568	37,334	92,081	77,625	79,423	49,653	58,177	58,152	148,640	121,882	34,373	821,908	74,719	35,108
34	71,977	88,122	72,499	16,144	87,941	73,504	88,654	41,433	51,358	76,774	58,715	116,197	771,341	70,122	27,181
35	14,605	159,709	21,451	105,219	23,933	91,884	90,852	38,101	109,968	40,388	79,916	107,147	868,566	78,961	43,322
mean	70,669	68,920	62,948	62,640	76,289	77,631	55,398	76,904	61,501	88,700	60,488	82,241			
std. dev	27,268	50,769	44,311	48,685	39,788	48,168	55,303	50,076	39,814	43,899	52,357	42,414			

Gross profit using the full absorption costing method
Inventory reduction policy: 50% reduction over 12 reporting periods

Month Series (yr)	Jan	Feb	Mar	Apr	May	Jun	Jul	Aug	Sep	Oct	Nov	Dec	mean	std.dev.
1	896770	992367	930203	831173	862143	853876	748567	722517	585704	567155	496402	520320	737312	172524
2	917933	996044	943142	889149	759913	820896	791049	749260	666652	572353	564882	392129	740497	179963
3	953063	855244	857820	840253	799225	765085	621704	788009	664428	633580	475276	520882	711046	135483
4	1057753	982539	905230	863159	749009	771612	735584	673259	577794	649090	502528	563830	724876	150445
5	1029572	981012	929077	874255	839869	852439	604273	630001	633399	618338	480997	448188	717441	183794
6	1044636	1021367	893171	888795	868806	847633	736528	743710	639688	526480	602289	510405	752625	166898
7	968027	1002169	859820	802790	807764	862603	822690	640822	678145	705160	512491	540720	748652	147993
8	1031223	989703	959466	792136	862404	766244	745777	671041	631095	596242	507330	610263	739245	154007
9	1017621	999376	1013644	859944	847788	796728	781155	748583	630134	553751	580873	496202	755289	173809
10	1092774	935133	957813	940508	811141	797816	689611	714410	700331	617130	518122	584432	751495	150323
11	975740	943790	919401	902972	778305	776678	722780	690852	627599	661489	654010	532990	746442	132056
12	1040519	938341	902140	876782	863506	749167	820078	745091	655317	629472	561516	510575	741643	142739
13	1043887	980813	915228	954443	851835	823211	826168	770593	601031	703124	565291	536845	774772	155122
14	985660	990072	896817	925597	840849	832637	727159	692213	730318	690209	611382	545688	771240	137573
15	1026882	989951	888619	910788	920546	750603	680744	730788	605133	556849	596461	550591	743734	160654
16	1044624	1042301	909945	874197	886007	702784	732431	658642	661859	642861	621967	474113	747919	163472
17	1059853	932724	935429	963919	856149	766607	797072	713724	689770	632125	493671	502351	753049	165246
18	1061495	832970	926369	825163	838481	897487	668060	821328	675022	645299	532201	586707	749917	132555
19	956837	981573	865255	894532	799488	864833	702712	655120	675042	623248	522406	478451	732969	160843
20	913509	1016502	843053	936627	794698	863558	766932	679191	672423	516216	553851	593127	748743	160762
21	1002614	992726	857886	758293	872782	820157	761737	667555	667985	621786	624795	519299	742273	137464
22	1069197	929041	949080	819584	716856	790080	810945	673595	668662	604349	581944	544015	735286	135981
23	1021071	927342	883411	802282	754353	821480	678607	621826	667675	687794	596045	473029	719391	133966
24	1093624	1012121	826869	893494	876674	804243	767056	749330	665555	562724	591213	565737	755920	146798
25	1007061	970439	938076	819644	863682	784401	729893	675878	655597	738301	561237	561923	754461	137352
26	1002880	1045606	947496	875048	885551	890326	689377	707744	661055	644520	620459	568172	775941	157171
27	1029504	969471	920293	836065	899236	677816	828417	644181	616526	685855	614172	510245	745662	150684
28	1030508	885954	870801	849628	849176	840992	693023	701624	612228	617857	540568	558024	729079	133809
29	993087	982666	930976	894949	864306	683825	707460	758246	648832	656162	551055	523494	745634	153926
30	938267	924301	1016840	841108	857280	749357	653856	700633	704466	556528	549304	548552	736566	158573
31	943533	983516	948990	820795	872273	816241	765988	722797	663899	672593	507790	580449	759576	148082
32	1105320	945466	952131	885210	848250	849900	708692	686772	637668	599824	530156	559362	745766	155670
33	999377	969285	916165	864729	835570	761164	680607	610498	605491	576580	599559	518516	721651	154569
34	965692	984818	952243	861713	816208	792736	778509	661178	634258	548120	465813	553133	731703	171296
35	934693	1016944	862151	895043	824964	783430	761363	670720	671373	552499	506985	534104	734507	163169
mean	1007280	969840	915001	867565	836434	800818	733030	699764	650919	619019	554144	531910		
std. dev	53711	47004	43785	47480	45598	53568	55353	48750	33894	55289	49373	43976		

Appendix 3

Simulation Data

Dataset 3 — Inventory Reduction Policy 3 — Aggressive-Reduction; 50 Percent Reduction in On-Hand Finished Goods Inventory Levels over a 6-Month Period and No Further Reduction through the Remainder of the Evaluation Period

Finished goods inventory trends

Inventory reduction policy: 50% reduction over initial 6 reporting periods and no further reductions

Percent	Jan	Feb	Mar	Apr	May	Jun	Jul	Aug	Sep	Oct	Nov	Dec	sum	mean	std. dev.
Series (yr)															
1	-1.09%	27.88%	3.60%	1.32%	19.46%	8.69%	16.90%	21.90%	6.93%	19.12%	19.81%	26.28%	170.80%	14.23%	9.90%
2	0.51%	23.91%	8.51%	3.50%	0.75%	27.90%	16.88%	17.83%	15.02%	12.70%	26.85%	6.07%	160.44%	13.37%	9.72%
3	4.31%	6.51%	16.16%	9.92%	0.87%	16.78%	12.07%	49.56%	8.64%	20.82%	6.45%	26.71%	178.81%	14.90%	13.16%
4	11.72%	8.97%	3.07%	3.42%	6.89%	18.70%	13.97%	18.93%	13.10%	34.54%	7.17%	40.73%	181.23%	15.10%	11.79%
5	12.18%	5.64%	11.89%	2.42%	10.06%	12.77%	-4.88%	28.58%	21.31%	40.26%	6.62%	12.58%	159.43%	13.29%	12.03%
6	12.61%	9.09%	2.16%	8.93%	8.07%	19.16%	7.38%	28.90%	6.61%	14.74%	38.82%	9.60%	166.07%	13.84%	10.49%
7	-1.00%	30.92%	-9.68%	13.98%	8.54%	30.38%	14.33%	3.78%	30.66%	33.62%	0.37%	28.65%	184.55%	15.38%	15.12%
8	15.03%	2.09%	17.92%	-11.48%	24.73%	3.86%	25.07%	7.78%	25.07%	20.03%	15.97%	43.20%	189.29%	15.77%	14.03%
9	10.93%	11.78%	13.78%	-7.61%	13.68%	5.07%	29.41%	17.96%	9.95%	13.46%	33.13%	15.90%	167.43%	13.95%	10.45%
10	18.39%	-3.83%	22.25%	-2.27%	4.04%	12.16%	11.11%	32.39%	24.61%	7.15%	14.55%	36.14%	176.69%	14.72%	12.66%
11	7.09%	10.23%	5.89%	12.67%	3.73%	11.58%	17.69%	18.37%	21.86%	28.49%	28.45%	8.90%	174.95%	14.58%	8.40%
12	10.71%	4.52%	3.69%	11.40%	14.28%	-1.72%	26.30%	30.49%	21.94%	23.71%	15.47%	16.21%	167.01%	13.92%	9.48%
13	15.88%	2.24%	9.01%	13.56%	5.47%	2.42%	33.27%	12.91%	3.36%	45.80%	6.97%	22.81%	173.72%	14.48%	13.47%
14	4.11%	14.90%	1.37%	22.14%	3.74%	10.02%	11.12%	26.26%	23.93%	24.53%	13.42%	13.92%	169.45%	14.12%	8.60%
15	10.37%	11.77%	-1.48%	19.10%	12.36%	-9.95%	19.27%	34.29%	6.58%	19.14%	27.60%	30.25%	179.30%	14.94%	12.86%
16	15.63%	11.74%	-8.34%	12.38%	16.09%	-6.19%	33.18%	10.29%	24.66%	27.64%	21.37%	6.78%	165.24%	13.77%	12.46%
17	20.39%	-4.60%	12.65%	21.86%	-3.95%	3.79%	29.82%	8.09%	26.68%	17.50%	9.34%	21.35%	162.94%	13.58%	11.32%
18	11.95%	-6.89%	36.58%	-6.16%	14.82%	24.82%	-1.74%	64.16%	0.83%	20.74%	11.33%	34.22%	204.64%	17.05%	20.80%
19	3.75%	18.02%	-0.22%	19.63%	3.68%	18.63%	4.28%	19.38%	30.37%	23.80%	11.20%	18.80%	171.32%	14.28%	9.54%
20	-1.16%	31.94%	-3.47%	22.64%	-4.01%	25.06%	12.27%	14.41%	22.73%	8.98%	29.94%	34.83%	194.15%	16.18%	13.86%
21	10.08%	11.63%	-2.71%	0.41%	36.61%	2.75%	19.86%	13.40%	26.33%	14.15%	29.93%	12.72%	174.08%	14.51%	11.82%
22	19.08%	-8.91%	20.66%	2.48%	5.48%	16.14%	32.97%	8.43%	25.23%	13.89%	19.08%	23.19%	178.82%	14.90%	11.48%
23	13.12%	0.33%	10.87%	3.48%	10.81%	20.61%	4.95%	16.76%	32.87%	37.36%	10.54%	10.97%	172.68%	14.39%	11.17%
24	19.45%	-0.65%	-4.32%	21.99%	16.92%	2.27%	20.88%	20.21%	33.94%	11.83%	35.56%	17.11%	175.18%	14.60%	11.08%
25	8.72%	7.72%	12.89%	-2.69%	23.06%	4.58%	14.16%	22.87%	21.08%	38.25%	0.25%	35.14%	186.02%	15.50%	12.94%
26	10.25%	15.61%	-1.91%	9.92%	11.61%	13.28%	2.42%	25.54%	17.21%	31.72%	16.93%	19.78%	172.35%	14.36%	9.17%
27	10.36%	3.27%	12.81%	5.26%	18.51%	-11.98%	52.41%	5.12%	20.09%	45.66%	5.23%	15.02%	181.76%	15.15%	17.98%
28	10.74%	-0.88%	10.38%	14.67%	10.16%	17.81%	5.39%	28.29%	8.62%	28.15%	17.10%	29.72%	180.15%	15.01%	9.66%
29	6.34%	10.97%	3.22%	11.86%	9.87%	-1.33%	28.81%	34.98%	9.87%	27.61%	12.44%	12.73%	167.36%	13.95%	10.90%
30	5.20%	13.33%	21.13%	-10.04%	21.79%	-1.61%	16.42%	39.98%	18.29%	8.36%	24.40%	23.48%	180.74%	15.06%	13.23%
31	0.49%	23.56%	6.28%	-4.60%	28.06%	7.75%	15.82%	21.32%	18.27%	30.64%	2.80%	34.71%	185.11%	15.43%	12.79%
32	22.26%	-7.40%	13.90%	8.77%	5.00%	13.40%	8.99%	17.31%	16.54%	26.82%	18.37%	30.38%	174.34%	14.53%	10.12%
33	8.53%	7.67%	3.07%	11.77%	8.07%	10.68%	12.54%	15.25%	11.99%	28.73%	37.59%	12.89%	168.78%	14.07%	9.64%
34	5.78%	16.83%	8.79%	-1.33%	10.87%	10.74%	25.14%	10.71%	16.52%	15.94%	13.02%	33.91%	166.93%	13.91%	9.05%
35	-3.05%	30.92%	-2.71%	18.91%	-1.32%	14.30%	22.93%	13.01%	24.83%	12.38%	21.78%	24.86%	176.83%	14.74%	11.63%
mean	9.42%	9.74%	7.36%	7.49%	10.82%	10.10%	17.47%	21.70%	17.62%	23.66%	17.43%	22.59%			
std. dev	6.65%	11.06%	9.72%	9.73%	9.04%	10.26%	11.59%	12.65%	8.29%	10.49%	10.60%	10.25%			

Finished goods inventory trends
Inventory reduction policy: 50% reduction over initial 6 reporting periods and no further reductions

Dollars Series (yr)	Jan	Feb	Mar	Apr	May	Jun	Jul	Aug	Sep	Oct	Nov	Dec	sum	mean	std. dev.
1	-8,193	160,448	21,582	8,841	110,788	46,120	102,565	128,154	48,699	128,242	139,761	162,960	1,049,968	87,497	60,855
2	3,679	136,627	49,714	20,872	5,303	159,657	93,657	98,366	90,304	84,377	165,756	47,397	955,710	79,642	55,950
3	29,252	48,648	105,088	61,703	5,720	107,770	91,573	224,914	52,185	122,365	47,196	158,796	1,055,211	87,934	61,084
4	64,451	52,858	19,409	21,517	49,370	118,486	87,163	122,438	93,230	195,738	50,025	230,808	1,105,492	92,124	65,913
5	71,139	33,285	71,498	14,787	60,592	68,094	-38,416	178,633	124,952	235,811	45,010	85,525	950,912	79,243	72,864
6	71,289	49,103	13,934	53,254	45,778	103,234	45,998	161,569	41,975	106,347	222,102	59,825	974,408	81,201	59,049
7	-6,638	174,619	-66,594	98,329	54,925	158,022	73,804	26,026	174,247	167,352	2,545	170,476	1,027,112	85,593	84,356
8	87,483	12,077	100,875	-82,273	142,390	24,747	153,404	50,553	159,561	126,686	110,380	219,337	1,105,219	92,102	80,751
9	65,482	66,732	68,018	-48,135	81,140	30,588	166,787	99,268	64,384	92,578	198,408	103,343	988,592	82,383	61,934
10	92,876	-24,810	125,631	-12,065	25,794	73,051	75,690	193,009	137,405	43,498	98,758	194,953	1,023,789	85,316	70,929
11	46,185	65,020	36,073	73,284	25,378	72,662	113,221	111,858	142,124	157,755	144,458	53,806	1,041,823	86,819	45,414
12	61,187	29,113	23,406	69,670	81,891	-11,369	167,361	170,003	73,509	140,745	96,587	102,453	1,004,556	83,713	56,152
13	89,926	13,210	55,644	69,834	32,159	13,774	172,617	67,811	22,942	228,878	43,154	136,853	946,803	78,900	67,859
14	26,277	86,091	8,772	121,746	55,916	55,916	70,605	163,829	124,872	126,781	75,284	81,813	964,516	80,376	47,638
15	60,932	66,351	-9,614	108,613	62,144	-65,682	133,561	197,237	44,634	127,484	159,806	175,913	1,061,378	88,448	77,326
16	88,297	60,267	-52,111	76,103	87,785	-44,523	193,980	68,528	149,778	159,409	117,123	45,971	950,606	79,217	74,051
17	111,418	-29,906	75,020	109,964	-23,012	24,253	163,102	47,852	152,844	103,135	66,140	137,147	937,958	78,163	63,894
18	64,957	-53,362	205,478	-41,635	87,576	118,384	-12,318	279,433	4,886	118,923	74,803	183,804	1,030,929	85,911	102,655
19	25,279	105,818	-1,480	114,536	24,017	96,217	28,411	129,931	179,235	143,158	75,348	126,402	1,046,871	87,239	56,750
20	-8,470	171,348	-24,571	119,691	-26,431	130,056	71,730	92,190	135,088	65,958	189,402	184,223	1,100,215	91,685	78,135
21	62,379	66,860	-18,711	3,057	203,279	15,725	117,315	87,701	151,592	85,424	162,970	78,990	1,016,581	84,715	66,538
22	102,077	-58,306	118,950	16,907	39,791	94,686	174,950	54,551	154,949	86,728	114,026	136,964	1,036,224	86,352	64,799
23	78,109	2,172	71,548	24,175	75,779	117,841	34,475	119,199	196,881	194,521	61,204	74,522	1,050,425	87,535	60,892
24	97,959	-3,588	-31,328	129,810	93,653	13,460	121,973	111,555	84,044	80,075	208,678	96,335	1,002,628	83,552	64,839
25	53,391	46,629	76,141	-18,211	130,605	28,314	89,512	147,261	129,640	174,900	1,564	199,645	1,059,391	88,283	69,047
26	63,311	79,487	-11,063	60,881	63,419	64,425	16,481	154,310	104,683	182,258	93,081	110,877	982,149	81,846	53,224
27	60,494	19,786	77,704	34,810	97,736	-89,985	264,565	34,965	133,377	238,185	29,182	94,960	995,780	82,982	96,260
28	62,584	-6,224	69,829	92,602	60,087	97,574	36,449	172,776	57,727	170,942	111,055	170,235	1,095,636	91,303	56,849
29	39,950	64,533	19,260	69,763	56,433	-9,928	182,840	189,465	61,631	154,589	79,128	78,297	985,962	82,163	62,295
30	36,277	85,853	103,813	-65,818	126,646	-10,624	119,228	227,286	99,375	57,053	155,589	137,389	1,072,067	89,339	77,612
31	3,364	138,345	36,269	-31,271	157,964	44,805	92,689	124,957	110,595	165,265	19,296	189,058	1,051,334	87,611	71,452
32	109,074	-46,912	79,583	52,677	29,640	71,846	57,098	106,286	100,127	169,081	121,895	173,327	1,023,722	85,310	60,290
33	53,079	46,442	18,961	73,686	48,289	69,123	86,883	107,433	76,690	183,226	213,301	80,199	1,057,312	88,109	56,558
34	38,429	95,196	50,241	-8,357	68,787	64,946	143,267	70,902	105,011	110,948	96,816	188,379	1,024,565	85,380	50,771
35	-21,397	168,458	-18,582	111,345	-8,210	86,714	135,834	84,585	147,938	85,410	146,543	149,961	1,068,600	89,050	69,253
mean	53,595	54,922	41,954	42,991	62,850	55,382	103,659	125,852	106,603	137,538	106,754	132,027			
std dev	35,488	63,593	56,575	57,710	50,471	59,064	63,050	59,398	47,511	50,207	60,582	52,444			

Finished goods inventory trends

Inventory reduction policy: 50% reduction over initial 6 reporting periods and no further reductions

Percent Series (yr)	Jan	Feb	Mar	Apr	May	Jun	Jul	Aug	Sep	Oct	Nov	Dec	sum	mean	std. dev.
1	-2.80%	25.52%	1.60%	-0.15%	17.75%	7.02%	15.59%	20.50%	5.96%	18.07%	18.85%	25.06%	152.97%	12.75%	9.93%
2	-1.30%	21.53%	6.43%	1.70%	-0.40%	26.44%	15.33%	16.27%	13.68%	11.60%	25.61%	5.32%	143.51%	13.05%	9.17%
3	2.30%	4.97%	14.45%	8.25%	-0.46%	15.61%	11.30%	47.63%	7.31%	19.43%	5.57%	25.47%	159.53%	14.50%	13.19%
4	8.96%	6.69%	1.24%	1.78%	5.78%	17.50%	12.73%	17.77%	12.16%	33.10%	6.18%	39.25%	154.19%	14.02%	12.36%
5	9.65%	3.37%	9.90%	0.70%	8.51%	11.11%	-5.61%	27.61%	20.22%	39.02%	5.71%	11.66%	132.18%	12.02%	12.69%
6	9.95%	6.50%	0.39%	7.14%	6.35%	17.53%	6.15%	27.37%	5.41%	13.83%	37.39%	8.39%	136.44%	12.40%	11.07%
7	-3.10%	28.49%	-11.27%	12.64%	7.17%	28.65%	12.57%	2.77%	29.24%	31.76%	-0.65%	27.29%	168.64%	15.33%	14.70%
8	12.49%	-0.26%	15.71%	-12.77%	23.05%	2.68%	23.78%	6.64%	23.92%	18.86%	14.97%	41.39%	157.98%	14.36%	14.68%
9	8.49%	9.36%	11.09%	-9.22%	12.08%	3.74%	27.92%	16.40%	8.79%	12.46%	31.80%	14.76%	139.19%	12.65%	10.97%
10	15.27%	-5.79%	20.06%	-4.44%	2.65%	10.82%	10.09%	31.05%	23.08%	5.84%	13.51%	34.54%	141.41%	12.86%	13.30%
11	4.94%	8.21%	3.96%	10.78%	2.50%	10.35%	16.51%	17.12%	20.73%	26.94%	26.65%	7.58%	151.31%	13.76%	8.48%
12	8.10%	2.54%	1.87%	9.68%	12.60%	-2.82%	25.10%	28.95%	10.67%	26.34%	14.23%	14.99%	140.15%	12.74%	9.97%
13	13.23%	-0.03%	7.10%	11.29%	3.85%	0.94%	31.53%	11.21%	2.33%	44.00%	5.71%	21.47%	139.41%	12.67%	14.08%
14	1.90%	12.55%	-0.42%	20.09%	2.19%	8.49%	9.92%	25.02%	22.21%	22.78%	11.90%	12.53%	147.25%	13.39%	8.38%
15	7.86%	-9.35%	-3.22%	17.16%	10.27%	-11.06%	18.27%	32.86%	5.53%	18.10%	26.20%	28.83%	152.28%	13.84%	13.42%
16	12.97%	8.95%	-10.21%	10.68%	14.26%	-7.11%	31.84%	9.20%	23.35%	26.19%	19.79%	5.73%	132.67%	12.06%	13.06%
17	17.60%	-6.55%	10.61%	19.51%	-5.59%	2.61%	28.24%	6.75%	25.25%	16.12%	8.39%	20.21%	125.55%	11.41%	11.66%
18	9.14%	-8.33%	34.41%	-7.61%	13.22%	22.82%	-2.69%	61.97%	-0.55%	19.28%	10.22%	32.58%	175.32%	15.94%	21.44%
19	1.72%	15.73%	-1.83%	17.77%	2.34%	16.88%	3.18%	18.31%	28.99%	22.46%	10.14%	17.76%	151.72%	13.79%	9.34%
20	-2.95%	29.32%	-4.98%	20.46%	-5.32%	23.32%	10.86%	13.23%	21.37%	8.11%	28.76%	33.15%	178.28%	16.21%	13.14%
21	7.76%	9.27%	-4.29%	-0.79%	34.83%	1.28%	18.48%	12.27%	23.91%	12.83%	28.33%	11.46%	147.57%	13.42%	12.26%
22	16.21%	-10.84%	18.53%	1.06%	4.42%	14.74%	31.30%	7.27%	24.99%	12.65%	17.73%	21.81%	143.66%	13.06%	11.96%
23	10.66%	-1.59%	9.16%	2.11%	9.65%	19.15%	3.96%	15.86%	31.58%	35.64%	9.12%	9.93%	144.57%	13.14%	11.69%
24	16.32%	-3.16%	-5.77%	20.16%	15.13%	0.90%	19.47%	18.65%	12.61%	10.78%	34.17%	15.60%	138.54%	12.59%	11.61%
25	6.36%	5.52%	10.84%	-4.12%	21.33%	3.31%	12.96%	21.70%	19.80%	36.11%	-0.99%	33.66%	160.12%	14.56%	13.30%
26	7.92%	12.78%	-4.03%	8.21%	9.78%	11.34%	1.38%	24.24%	15.91%	30.26%	15.37%	18.28%	143.52%	13.05%	9.63%
27	7.83%	1.08%	10.85%	3.76%	16.57%	-12.82%	50.69%	4.09%	19.00%	43.95%	3.70%	13.81%	154.68%	14.06%	18.65%
28	8.20%	-2.57%	8.73%	13.04%	8.56%	16.22%	4.33%	27.03%	7.55%	26.85%	15.95%	28.28%	153.97%	14.00%	10.08%
29	4.08%	8.69%	1.21%	10.02%	8.17%	-2.18%	27.68%	33.36%	8.63%	26.09%	11.24%	11.46%	144.37%	13.12%	11.16%
30	3.27%	11.35%	18.42%	-11.56%	20.14%	-2.71%	15.52%	38.64%	16.77%	7.34%	23.22%	22.08%	159.20%	14.47%	13.44%
31	-1.47%	21.27%	4.16%	-6.02%	26.31%	6.32%	14.42%	19.92%	16.95%	29.01%	1.79%	33.12%	167.24%	15.20%	12.37%
32	19.01%	-9.44%	11.75%	7.00%	3.41%	11.75%	7.86%	16.10%	15.31%	25.60%	17.29%	28.91%	135.53%	12.32%	10.49%
33	6.23%	5.49%	1.16%	10.12%	6.50%	9.53%	11.57%	14.40%	11.04%	27.73%	36.17%	11.64%	145.35%	13.21%	10.11%
34	3.70%	14.41%	6.64%	-2.96%	9.45%	9.42%	23.67%	9.61%	15.38%	14.95%	12.20%	32.50%	145.27%	13.21%	9.15%
35	-4.95%	28.36%	-4.32%	17.07%	-2.78%	12.98%	21.56%	11.86%	23.49%	11.37%	20.78%	23.53%	163.91%	14.90%	10.58%
mean	7.02%	7.51%	5.43%	5.79%	9.26%	8.71%	16.21%	20.39%	16.36%	22.33%	16.20%	21.26%			
std. dev	6.28%	10.88%	9.54%	9.56%	8.90%	10.06%	11.41%	12.45%	8.20%	10.27%	10.49%	10.08%			

Finished goods inventory trends
Inventory reduction policy: 50% reduction over initial 6 reporting periods and no further reductions

Dollars Series (yr)	Jan	Feb	Mar	Apr	May	Jun	Jul	Aug	Sep	Oct	Nov	Dec	sum	mean	std. dev.
1	-20,989	146,861	9,597	-1,003	101,068	37,247	94,615	119,977	41,885	121,187	132,975	155,388	938,809	78,234	61,697
2	-9,435	122,997	37,535	10,158	-2,819	151,278	85,069	89,747	82,277	77,106	158,080	41,523	852,949	77,541	53,023
3	15,611	37,130	93,964	51,344	-2,992	100,229	85,705	216,127	44,191	114,175	40,726	151,449	932,047	84,732	61,290
4	49,240	39,431	7,800	11,192	41,411	110,846	79,407	114,959	86,535	187,627	43,147	222,396	944,751	85,886	69,380
5	56,351	19,881	59,530	4,262	51,271	59,242	-44,202	172,547	118,566	228,526	38,787	79,285	787,695	71,609	77,129
6	56,275	35,094	2,505	42,544	36,023	94,454	38,297	153,033	34,351	99,764	213,903	52,312	802,280	72,935	62,660
7	-20,503	160,897	-77,522	88,910	46,085	149,018	64,741	19,033	166,144	158,088	-4,483	162,365	933,277	84,843	82,754
8	72,670	-1,492	88,451	-91,533	132,730	17,187	145,496	43,107	152,206	119,288	103,490	210,183	919,114	83,556	85,223
9	50,874	53,052	54,761	-58,308	71,700	22,572	158,347	90,658	56,904	85,678	190,409	95,900	821,673	74,698	65,430
10	77,140	-37,526	113,230	-23,550	16,904	65,018	68,736	184,985	128,872	35,555	91,646	186,325	830,194	75,472	75,215
11	32,204	52,160	24,250	62,362	16,981	64,946	105,657	104,251	134,755	149,146	135,307	45,811	895,627	81,421	46,501
12	46,234	16,349	11,842	59,141	72,215	-18,672	159,747	161,446	65,682	132,617	88,824	94,794	843,985	76,726	59,223
13	74,923	-191	43,883	58,140	22,657	5,360	163,594	58,872	15,899	219,869	35,335	128,801	752,218	68,383	71,464
14	12,148	72,540	-2,712	110,485	13,194	47,361	62,976	156,066	115,889	117,741	66,773	73,627	833,940	75,813	47,080
15	46,184	52,668	-20,975	97,574	51,612	-73,007	126,627	189,028	37,529	120,551	151,698	167,672	900,979	81,907	81,096
16	73,283	45,943	-63,792	65,613	77,772	-51,130	186,135	61,268	141,841	151,079	108,453	38,859	762,040	69,276	78,085
17	96,175	-42,586	62,957	98,128	-32,577	16,689	154,424	39,898	144,640	94,967	59,395	129,819	725,752	65,977	66,799
18	49,689	-64,545	193,292	-51,389	78,129	108,856	-19,061	269,887	-3,236	110,557	67,480	175,010	864,980	78,635	107,109
19	11,582	92,376	-12,491	103,673	15,299	87,171	21,148	122,723	171,081	135,123	68,172	119,362	923,637	83,967	56,254
20	-21,517	157,297	-35,248	108,176	-35,075	121,038	63,504	84,622	126,974	59,529	181,987	175,326	1,008,129	91,648	74,761
21	47,996	53,280	-29,611	-5,884	193,385	7,357	109,167	80,307	143,544	77,411	154,258	71,200	854,414	77,674	69,761
22	86,644	-70,930	106,682	7,236	32,106	86,484	166,064	47,066	147,059	78,977	105,957	128,804	835,504	75,955	68,548
23	63,449	-10,428	60,265	14,640	67,630	109,453	27,582	112,807	189,176	185,595	52,923	67,427	877,069	79,734	64,532
24	82,210	-17,459	-41,807	119,027	83,738	5,331	113,745	102,934	76,033	72,948	200,514	87,849	802,853	72,987	68,718
25	38,940	33,383	64,038	-27,937	120,841	20,482	81,888	139,743	121,778	165,139	-6,195	191,231	904,390	82,217	71,836
26	48,923	65,114	-23,307	50,378	53,412	55,003	9,419	146,461	96,739	173,904	84,500	102,470	814,092	74,008	56,330
27	45,706	6,555	65,795	24,892	87,522	-96,218	255,849	27,922	126,126	229,267	20,630	87,306	835,645	75,968	100,591
28	47,781	-18,202	58,736	82,317	50,626	88,893	29,332	165,044	50,515	163,042	103,606	161,983	935,892	85,081	59,668
29	25,709	51,104	7,264	58,961	46,745	-16,251	175,656	180,711	53,871	146,060	71,522	70,479	846,122	76,920	64,293
30	22,858	73,093	90,529	-75,811	148,156	-17,930	112,698	219,626	91,129	50,063	148,058	180,355	937,677	85,243	79,831
31	-10,134	124,903	24,002	-40,960	20,193	36,496	84,477	116,734	102,608	156,490	12,339	180,566	945,599	85,964	69,506
32	93,150	-59,783	67,270	42,022	38,909	63,032	49,876	98,804	92,684	161,399	114,722	164,937	815,155	74,105	64,104
33	38,744	33,213	7,187	63,337	59,821	61,640	80,172	101,428	70,636	176,832	205,263	72,422	911,039	82,822	59,479
34	24,599	81,533	37,926	-18,660	-17,308	56,955	134,867	63,604	97,760	104,059	90,725	180,566	889,156	80,832	51,806
35	-34,762	154,515	-29,546	100,543	53,555	78,754	127,691	77,143	139,939	78,437	139,777	141,961	991,905	90,173	62,926
mean	39,142	41,664	30,179	32,572	50,153	47,291	95,984	118,073	98,931	129,651	99,163	124,124			
std dev	34,754	63,192	56,199	57,301		58,522	62,581	59,092	47,332	49,784	60,346	51,997			

Finished goods inventory trends
Inventory reduction policy: 50% reduction over initial 6 reporting periods and no further reductions

Percent Series (yr)	Jan	Feb	Mar	Apr	May	Jun	Jul	Aug	Sep	Oct	Nov	Dec	sum	mean	std. dev.
1	24.06%	47.46%	27.11%	26.12%	38.26%	33.56%	37.82%	41.41%	30.22%	39.26%	39.36%	44.58%	429.22%	35.77%	7.52%
2	24.74%	44.15%	31.20%	27.57%	25.42%	45.99%	36.63%	38.94%	35.71%	35.22%	45.49%	29.71%	36.00%	396.04%	7.15%
3	28.29%	29.94%	37.95%	31.80%	24.47%	39.27%	33.77%	62.79%	31.97%	40.41%	29.28%	45.19%	36.99%	406.84%	10.39%
4	32.78%	32.10%	27.13%	28.71%	29.63%	39.19%	35.03%	39.76%	33.83%	50.66%	30.66%	55.97%	36.61%	402.66%	9.25%
5	34.13%	29.72%	34.11%	26.11%	31.67%	36.54%	20.50%	47.17%	42.51%	55.59%	29.50%	34.62%	35.27%	388.02%	9.95%
6	34.41%	32.12%	26.41%	31.39%	31.54%	40.75%	30.11%	47.23%	29.77%	55.74%	55.21%	32.53%	35.71%	392.81%	8.66%
7	24.14%	49.23%	17.04%	35.56%	31.11%	48.64%	35.28%	27.89%	48.06%	50.36%	24.91%	46.86%	37.72%	414.94%	11.59%
8	37.71%	25.46%	40.04%	15.83%	43.46%	27.80%	43.95%	30.91%	44.27%	40.57%	36.37%	58.35%	37.00%	407.02%	11.51%
9	33.40%	34.06%	36.19%	18.18%	35.33%	28.02%	47.79%	38.79%	33.16%	34.70%	50.24%	36.96%	35.77%	393.43%	8.63%
10	38.82%	22.16%	42.24%	22.40%	28.07%	34.64%	32.72%	50.30%	44.03%	31.03%	36.04%	52.13%	35.98%	395.75%	10.22%
11	30.94%	32.80%	29.26%	34.49%	27.69%	32.78%	38.74%	39.02%	41.09%	46.82%	47.54%	30.64%	36.44%	400.86%	6.76%
12	33.84%	28.21%	27.16%	33.51%	35.44%	23.68%	44.27%	49.71%	32.99%	43.09%	36.82%	37.79%	35.70%	392.68%	7.84%
13	37.40%	26.03%	32.04%	35.35%	28.81%	26.54%	49.95%	36.47%	27.28%	60.34%	29.88%	42.28%	35.91%	394.97%	10.94%
14	27.20%	36.27%	26.45%	41.75%	28.58%	32.89%	32.34%	45.77%	42.51%	44.18%	34.46%	35.02%	36.38%	400.23%	6.40%
15	32.73%	34.46%	24.05%	39.63%	33.91%	17.25%	38.83%	51.28%	29.96%	39.84%	46.15%	46.99%	36.58%	402.36%	10.13%
16	37.20%	34.11%	18.34%	33.68%	38.04%	20.60%	49.09%	33.10%	43.26%	46.23%	41.11%	29.70%	35.21%	387.27%	9.79%
17	40.45%	21.96%	33.93%	41.39%	22.05%	28.06%	48.04%	30.76%	45.29%	38.03%	31.76%	41.56%	34.80%	382.82%	8.85%
18	33.98%	20.36%	52.80%	20.36%	36.08%	43.09%	24.35%	74.68%	25.32%	41.02%	33.61%	51.62%	38.48%	423.29%	16.66%
19	28.00%	38.46%	25.29%	40.35%	27.76%	39.40%	27.78%	40.00%	47.01%	33.55%	33.25%	39.32%	36.56%	402.16%	7.04%
20	23.15%	50.43%	22.43%	41.90%	21.50%	44.51%	34.02%	36.44%	41.90%	31.35%	47.52%	51.52%	38.50%	423.53%	10.37%
21	32.27%	34.47%	23.63%	24.69%	51.89%	27.27%	39.64%	35.48%	44.11%	34.65%	47.76%	35.34%	36.27%	398.93%	9.12%
22	40.16%	17.77%	40.93%	27.88%	28.47%	36.94%	50.61%	31.86%	44.54%	35.92%	38.79%	42.01%	35.97%	395.72%	9.10%
23	35.38%	24.04%	34.26%	26.21%	32.96%	40.84%	28.27%	37.70%	50.23%	53.78%	31.63%	34.48%	35.85%	394.40%	9.37%
24	39.69%	24.14%	21.61%	41.71%	38.19%	27.19%	41.29%	39.40%	35.67%	34.36%	51.84%	38.29%	35.79%	393.70%	8.72%
25	31.85%	31.58%	36.26%	22.25%	42.68%	29.24%	34.72%	42.24%	41.10%	52.77%	25.00%	52.29%	37.28%	410.13%	10.07%
26	32.40%	38.22%	22.79%	32.01%	34.09%	35.52%	26.93%	44.30%	37.83%	50.31%	36.99%	40.47%	36.31%	399.45%	7.61%
27	33.09%	27.38%	34.04%	29.32%	38.65%	16.16%	64.95%	28.66%	39.55%	61.03%	27.95%	37.24%	36.81%	404.92%	14.54%
28	34.22%	24.14%	32.87%	35.86%	32.44%	38.35%	28.72%	46.25%	32.34%	45.56%	38.18%	48.28%	36.63%	402.98%	7.63%
29	30.31%	32.57%	27.48%	34.98%	31.40%	24.16%	46.18%	51.91%	32.53%	44.84%	34.81%	35.34%	36.02%	396.19%	8.34%
30	29.18%	35.35%	42.65%	17.01%	41.00%	23.32%	38.07%	54.99%	39.27%	30.86%	44.01%	42.32%	37.17%	408.86%	10.40%
31	25.28%	43.52%	29.92%	20.36%	46.26%	31.49%	36.32%	41.57%	38.46%	48.04%	27.33%	51.84%	37.74%	415.12%	9.69%
32	41.68%	19.36%	35.83%	32.04%	28.92%	34.20%	32.48%	38.14%	36.62%	45.76%	38.42%	48.90%	35.51%	390.66%	7.93%
33	31.47%	30.51%	27.44%	34.79%	30.59%	33.61%	35.05%	35.77%	32.75%	47.29%	52.40%	35.00%	35.93%	395.20%	7.41%
34	30.26%	36.87%	32.86%	22.50%	34.49%	32.65%	43.34%	34.39%	36.23%	36.51%	34.50%	50.88%	35.93%	395.23%	6.98%
35	22.12%	49.29%	22.38%	38.91%	24.16%	35.43%	42.23%	33.83%	44.49%	34.95%	40.61%	43.94%	37.29%	410.21%	8.33%
mean	32.19%	32.53%	30.75%	30.47%	33.00%	32.84%	37.99%	41.68%	38.17%	42.99%	37.98%	42.29%			
std. dev	5.23%	8.76%	7.66%	7.62%	6.81%	7.87%	8.87%	9.74%	6.34%	8.09%	8.20%	7.84%			

Finished goods inventory trends
Inventory reduction policy: 50% reduction over initial 6 reporting periods and no further reductions

Dollars Series (yr)	Jan	Feb	Mar	Apr	May	Jun	Jul	Aug	Sep	Oct	Nov	Dec	sum	mean	std. dev.
1	180,334	273,161	162,444	174,875	217,797	178,137	229,565	242,364	212,268	263,317	277,631	276,377	2,688,270	224,023	43,000
2	179,155	252,250	182,182	164,461	178,976	263,143	203,267	214,854	214,733	234,053	280,845	231,839	2,420,602	220,055	36,706
3	192,179	223,727	246,786	197,806	160,093	252,152	256,204	284,919	193,194	237,474	214,213	268,673	2,535,242	230,477	36,866
4	180,237	189,116	171,237	180,586	212,189	248,261	218,511	257,191	240,734	287,117	213,958	317,116	2,536,017	230,547	45,066
5	199,242	175,491	205,119	159,786	190,827	194,753	161,356	294,770	249,259	325,595	200,487	235,382	2,392,827	217,530	53,761
6	194,575	173,456	170,404	187,081	178,984	219,586	187,609	264,082	189,165	257,841	315,843	202,724	2,346,775	213,343	46,652
7	159,516	278,046	117,218	250,141	200,051	252,960	181,696	191,883	273,091	250,680	170,504	278,802	2,445,072	222,279	53,098
8	219,424	146,814	225,428	113,467	250,281	278,047	268,884	200,785	281,720	256,626	251,348	296,305	2,469,705	224,519	58,226
9	200,079	193,004	178,648	115,006	209,601	168,937	271,055	214,450	214,619	238,682	300,863	240,174	2,345,039	213,185	50,625
10	196,078	143,634	238,480	118,918	179,387	208,058	222,860	299,666	245,863	188,772	244,556	281,218	2,371,413	215,583	55,062
11	201,485	208,365	179,169	199,580	188,301	205,708	247,939	237,613	267,157	259,230	241,395	185,168	2,419,624	219,966	31,549
12	193,229	181,666	172,362	204,719	203,190	156,566	281,738	277,184	203,077	255,724	229,832	238,929	2,404,988	218,635	41,662
13	211,781	153,533	197,979	182,011	169,441	151,191	259,117	191,495	186,026	301,540	184,904	253,636	2,230,871	202,806	47,848
14	173,828	209,583	169,573	229,650	172,170	183,593	205,342	285,506	221,828	228,405	193,309	205,819	2,304,777	209,525	32,625
15	192,315	194,188	156,645	225,404	170,464	113,873	269,156	294,973	203,338	265,359	267,168	273,301	2,433,870	221,261	58,178
16	210,118	175,166	114,629	207,016	207,484	148,190	287,035	220,302	262,742	266,655	225,319	201,450	2,315,989	210,544	51,460
17	221,035	142,795	201,248	208,206	128,562	179,558	262,717	181,870	259,410	224,110	224,827	266,889	2,280,192	207,290	46,628
18	184,757	157,789	296,609	137,488	213,184	205,539	172,287	325,270	149,560	235,279	221,931	277,299	2,392,235	217,476	62,107
19	188,943	225,839	172,207	235,448	181,293	203,485	184,566	268,111	277,462	261,946	223,665	264,326	2,498,348	227,123	37,920
20	168,796	270,535	158,831	221,549	141,763	231,033	198,865	233,101	248,991	230,248	300,673	272,508	2,508,097	228,009	47,607
21	199,661	198,214	163,021	182,709	288,118	156,158	234,197	232,290	264,803	209,127	260,014	219,460	2,408,109	218,919	42,302
22	214,688	116,259	235,582	190,369	206,845	216,731	268,529	206,203	262,142	224,340	231,827	248,073	2,406,902	218,809	41,616
23	210,652	158,135	225,498	181,896	231,065	233,470	196,707	268,133	300,888	280,046	183,612	234,156	2,493,606	226,691	44,332
24	199,908	153,219	156,595	246,262	211,428	161,344	241,184	217,477	215,046	232,490	304,244	215,619	2,334,908	212,264	47,800
25	194,940	190,834	214,249	150,805	241,740	180,715	219,478	271,969	252,800	241,319	155,868	297,131	2,416,907	219,719	46,883
26	200,145	194,664	131,706	196,465	186,219	172,312	183,689	267,662	230,050	289,108	203,404	226,835	2,282,113	207,465	44,122
27	193,274	165,453	206,432	194,179	204,115	121,335	327,851	195,849	262,585	318,336	155,817	235,420	2,387,372	217,034	64,631
28	199,350	170,989	221,016	226,391	191,846	210,123	194,368	282,441	216,498	276,668	247,966	276,569	2,514,876	228,625	37,785
29	190,870	191,635	164,541	205,773	179,606	179,711	293,024	281,190	203,119	251,016	221,399	217,374	2,388,388	217,126	41,928
30	203,754	227,665	209,555	111,539	238,277	154,341	276,452	312,619	213,326	210,590	280,699	247,601	2,482,664	225,697	57,065
31	174,826	255,559	172,648	138,545	260,445	181,956	212,742	243,660	232,849	259,157	188,536	282,328	2,428,425	220,766	45,171
32	204,198	122,642	205,175	192,322	171,472	183,394	206,175	234,137	221,733	288,435	254,960	279,032	2,359,476	214,498	48,591
33	195,832	184,746	169,397	217,693	183,177	217,414	242,814	251,999	209,503	301,562	297,337	217,849	2,493,491	226,681	43,558
34	201,264	208,592	187,780	141,688	218,230	197,442	246,985	227,609	230,326	254,112	256,490	282,664	2,451,919	222,902	38,775
35	155,392	268,562	153,192	229,143	150,279	214,912	250,113	219,992	265,040	241,099	273,194	265,090	2,530,616	230,056	43,500
mean	193,882	193,009	186,674	186,256	197,626	192,118	233,259	248,389	233,570	255,602	237,104	251,804			
std. dev	15,327	43,656	37,528	38,785	33,447	35,990	39,711	37,807	32,742	30,742	43,314	31,865			

Finished goods inventory trends

Inventory reduction policy: 50% reduction over initial 6 reporting periods and no further reductions

Percent	Jan	Feb	Mar	Apr	May	Jun	Jul	Aug	Sep	Oct	Nov	Dec	sum	mean	std. dev.
Series (yr)															
1	5.32%	22.91%	3.80%	5.58%	14.12%	7.83%	15.47%	18.19%	11.07%	19.17%	20.29%	22.76%	166.51%	13.88%	7.00%
2	5.50%	19.68%	7.50%	4.62%	6.34%	22.47%	12.34%	14.51%	13.39%	15.14%	23.81%	12.79%	158.09%	13.17%	6.46%
3	7.16%	11.01%	16.26%	9.25%	3.28%	17.86%	15.87%	32.22%	9.15%	16.91%	10.64%	22.10%	171.70%	14.31%	7.73%
4	7.03%	8.37%	5.27%	6.98%	10.87%	18.03%	13.53%	19.07%	15.13%	26.93%	11.57%	32.18%	174.96%	14.58%	8.30%
5	10.00%	6.10%	11.15%	3.79%	9.20%	11.22%	3.75%	26.02%	19.92%	32.82%	10.03%	15.16%	159.15%	13.26%	8.90%
6	10.27%	7.02%	5.80%	9.20%	8.41%	16.57%	9.37%	23.97%	9.45%	17.98%	32.53%	11.83%	162.41%	13.53%	7.94%
7	3.43%	25.03%	-2.43%	16.74%	10.61%	23.26%	9.64%	9.00%	24.99%	23.79%	5.92%	24.83%	174.81%	14.57%	9.76%
8	13.71%	1.46%	15.66%	-2.88%	20.11%	7.13%	22.25%	10.55%	23.50%	19.67%	17.31%	31.97%	180.46%	15.04%	9.78%
9	10.75%	10.28%	8.98%	-2.57%	13.33%	6.61%	24.96%	15.33%	13.30%	16.10%	28.69%	17.18%	162.94%	13.58%	8.14%
10	11.79%	1.56%	18.65%	-2.52%	7.78%	13.19%	13.96%	28.67%	20.87%	9.87%	17.19%	28.13%	169.14%	14.09%	9.45%
11	9.82%	11.33%	7.15%	11.25%	8.29%	11.86%	18.25%	17.48%	20.95%	22.95%	21.41%	8.87%	169.62%	14.14%	5.69%
12	9.57%	7.04%	5.86%	11.55%	12.19%	3.88%	23.65%	26.01%	11.64%	20.89%	15.78%	17.03%	165.10%	13.76%	7.06%
13	14.20%	4.03%	11.30%	10.48%	7.41%	4.63%	25.78%	12.60%	9.18%	35.25%	9.81%	21.54%	166.21%	13.85%	9.24%
14	6.54%	13.53%	6.27%	18.27%	7.46%	10.24%	12.57%	25.63%	18.20%	19.63%	11.93%	13.57%	163.86%	13.66%	5.88%
15	9.31%	10.22%	3.44%	16.08%	7.37%	-2.48%	20.10%	28.49%	10.81%	20.35%	23.52%	24.44%	171.65%	14.30%	9.36%
16	13.00%	7.62%	-3.00%	12.18%	13.90%	2.77%	26.94%	13.72%	21.92%	23.69%	17.33%	10.71%	160.78%	13.40%	8.54%
17	15.60%	1.47%	11.57%	15.07%	-0.27%	8.04%	24.41%	9.02%	22.81%	16.19%	13.78%	21.64%	159.32%	13.28%	7.82%
18	8.91%	3.29%	29.08%	0.99%	13.99%	15.71%	6.29%	44.69%	3.45%	18.46%	14.16%	27.45%	186.45%	15.54%	12.88%
19	7.04%	14.42%	4.91%	16.59%	6.86%	12.91%	7.46%	19.86%	23.98%	20.97%	13.19%	19.27%	167.48%	13.96%	6.35%
20	4.32%	24.65%	3.38%	16.23%	1.35%	18.84%	11.36%	15.83%	19.63%	13.56%	26.72%	26.35%	182.22%	15.19%	8.78%
21	9.97%	10.62%	4.14%	6.78%	27.85%	4.23%	17.34%	15.48%	22.18%	12.85%	23.46%	14.18%	169.08%	14.09%	7.60%
22	14.10%	-3.10%	17.26%	8.31%	10.35%	14.42%	25.58%	11.55%	22.14%	14.83%	16.70%	19.64%	171.77%	14.31%	7.35%
23	11.38%	2.63%	13.06%	6.36%	13.51%	16.94%	8.85%	18.77%	27.54%	27.44%	4.55%	14.55%	169.15%	14.10%	7.70%
24	12.81%	-0.05%	3.66%	19.62%	14.79%	5.66%	19.40%	16.17%	14.50%	15.62%	30.07%	15.54%	167.79%	13.98%	8.01%
25	9.56%	9.21%	13.57%	2.82%	19.42%	8.24%	14.22%	22.13%	19.99%	23.97%	4.19%	29.35%	176.69%	14.72%	8.30%
26	11.11%	12.40%	0.40%	11.21%	10.81%	9.43%	8.72%	23.62%	17.26%	28.47%	14.13%	18.07%	165.63%	13.80%	7.33%
27	9.51%	4.84%	11.80%	9.26%	13.43%	-1.05%	38.87%	9.64%	19.94%	35.75%	4.36%	16.58%	172.92%	14.41%	12.06%
28	9.89%	4.53%	12.34%	14.12%	9.38%	13.60%	8.91%	24.20%	12.30%	23.36%	17.49%	24.68%	174.81%	14.57%	6.56%
29	8.47%	9.34%	4.89%	12.19%	8.16%	6.74%	25.62%	27.54%	11.54%	21.30%	14.23%	14.03%	164.03%	13.67%	7.40%
30	9.15%	13.73%	14.21%	-3.80%	17.59%	3.11%	19.76%	31.40%	14.47%	11.30%	23.00%	19.30%	173.21%	14.43%	9.16%
31	5.74%	20.52%	6.71%	1.06%	22.91%	9.00%	14.15%	19.41%	17.05%	23.86%	8.69%	27.90%	176.99%	14.75%	8.46%
32	13.86%	-1.67%	12.66%	10.21%	7.02%	10.11%	12.38%	17.31%	15.51%	25.44%	19.20%	26.33%	168.35%	14.03%	7.70%
33	8.73%	7.32%	4.93%	12.81%	7.79%	12.79%	15.72%	16.87%	11.92%	26.34%	28.57%	13.32%	167.12%	13.67%	7.24%
34	9.17%	12.11%	8.58%	0.79%	13.09%	10.42%	19.68%	14.19%	15.20%	17.36%	16.68%	26.72%	164.00%	13.93%	6.45%
35	2.24%	23.56%	2.33%	15.64%	2.40%	13.30%	19.54%	13.27%	21.95%	15.64%	20.83%	21.68%	172.38%	14.37%	8.00%
mean	9.40%	9.63%	8.60%	8.69%	10.89%	10.50%	16.76%	19.78%	16.77%	20.97%	17.01%	20.33%			
std. dev	3.19%	7.51%	6.43%	6.55%	5.90%	6.10%	7.39%	7.79%	5.57%	6.31%	7.35%	6.33%			

Finished goods inventory trends

Inventory reduction policy: 50% reduction over initial 6 reporting periods and no further reductions

Dollars Series (yr)	Jan	Feb	Mar	Apr	May	Jun	Jul	Aug	Sep	Oct	Nov	Dec	sum	mean	std. dev.
1	39,840	131,876	22,762	37,332	80,379	41,565	93,916	106,490	77,756	128,564	143,147	141,107	1,044,734	87,061	43,963
2	39,850	112,429	43,812	27,556	44,663	128,573	68,488	80,043	80,514	100,591	146,977	99,774	973,271	81,106	37,840
3	48,614	82,285	105,737	57,523	21,457	114,686	120,411	146,207	55,275	99,360	77,819	131,401	1,060,776	88,398	37,648
4	38,657	49,320	33,258	43,893	77,862	114,252	84,386	123,343	107,670	152,638	80,711	182,336	1,088,325	90,694	47,056
5	58,376	36,009	67,074	23,184	55,428	59,823	29,492	162,606	116,795	192,233	68,187	103,063	972,270	81,023	52,909
6	58,045	37,930	37,458	54,856	47,713	89,290	58,393	134,030	60,026	129,742	186,128	73,696	967,308	80,609	46,103
7	22,671	141,345	-16,690	117,742	68,232	120,976	49,654	61,910	142,009	118,437	40,497	147,711	1,014,494	84,541	54,028
8	79,792	8,427	88,186	-20,611	115,803	45,669	136,156	68,520	149,547	124,409	119,639	162,332	1,077,869	89,822	56,455
9	64,401	58,255	44,321	-16,237	79,092	39,851	141,546	84,771	86,069	110,712	171,795	111,661	976,237	81,353	49,599
10	59,537	10,113	105,274	-13,372	49,692	79,221	95,101	170,838	116,525	60,024	116,639	151,785	1,001,379	83,448	54,058
11	63,957	71,958	43,799	65,111	56,355	74,445	116,827	106,459	136,241	127,074	108,697	53,626	1,024,549	85,379	31,697
12	54,676	45,302	37,198	70,590	69,913	25,663	150,522	145,027	71,649	123,995	98,468	107,670	1,000,673	83,389	41,556
13	80,401	23,754	69,841	53,940	43,562	26,400	133,716	66,178	62,605	176,155	60,707	129,206	926,465	77,205	46,193
14	41,825	78,159	40,215	100,515	44,960	57,164	79,839	159,869	94,972	101,492	66,925	79,760	945,696	78,808	33,619
15	54,670	57,608	22,387	91,468	37,036	-16,349	139,326	163,868	73,336	135,530	136,163	142,163	1,037,207	86,434	57,149
16	73,420	39,159	-18,736	74,842	75,787	19,898	157,505	91,358	133,121	136,641	94,965	72,654	950,614	79,218	50,049
17	85,231	9,553	68,623	75,808	-1,565	51,432	133,477	53,355	130,644	95,381	97,520	138,999	938,459	78,205	55,454
18	48,417	25,532	163,330	6,660	82,664	74,938	44,471	194,651	20,365	105,840	93,534	147,432	1,007,856	83,988	59,919
19	47,498	84,650	33,449	96,838	44,829	66,691	49,555	133,156	141,561	126,164	88,741	129,538	1,042,671	86,889	38,820
20	31,518	132,254	23,922	85,804	8,889	97,783	66,408	101,302	116,646	99,588	169,027	139,381	1,072,522	89,377	48,984
21	61,697	61,053	28,540	50,187	154,644	24,210	102,469	101,316	133,175	77,534	127,721	88,090	1,010,637	84,220	41,382
22	75,357	-20,313	99,366	56,750	75,212	84,581	135,695	74,770	130,304	92,641	99,810	115,965	1,020,137	85,011	40,730
23	67,763	17,307	85,987	44,133	94,688	96,854	113,328	133,513	87,407	142,892	47,103	98,832	1,055,613	87,968	43,644
24	64,531	-280	26,487	115,351	81,885	33,587	89,901	89,228	122,986	105,735	176,452	87,506	981,717	81,810	46,927
25	58,538	55,636	80,194	19,127	110,024	50,931	59,484	142,498	104,965	109,605	26,156	166,764	1,032,361	86,030	45,950
26	68,616	63,149	2,320	68,821	59,071	45,749	196,179	142,673	132,377	163,612	77,682	101,287	957,430	79,786	43,280
27	55,530	29,266	71,567	61,305	70,945	-7,854	60,326	65,850	82,361	186,461	24,308	104,810	990,744	82,562	62,382
28	57,622	32,085	82,997	89,181	55,460	74,518	162,569	147,784	72,087	141,842	113,592	141,392	1,079,160	89,930	38,196
29	53,358	54,934	29,273	71,700	46,647	50,117	143,452	149,164	78,611	119,216	90,521	86,285	985,871	82,156	41,868
30	63,866	88,435	69,801	-24,925	102,224	20,565	82,876	178,488	103,209	77,129	146,697	112,903	1,057,246	88,104	55,555
31	39,674	120,464	38,728	7,202	128,984	51,993	78,570	113,784	93,908	128,728	59,925	151,971	1,027,538	85,628	45,443
32	67,891	-10,611	72,479	61,284	41,642	54,197	108,925	106,272	76,272	160,371	127,404	150,259	1,003,666	83,639	47,931
33	54,320	44,341	30,446	80,168	46,621	82,754	112,164	118,817	96,654	167,990	162,122	82,895	1,055,673	87,973	47,311
34	61,012	68,508	49,043	4,964	82,843	63,029	115,708	93,889	130,777	120,801	123,977	148,429	1,025,314	85,443	39,090
35	15,765	128,356	15,965	92,077	14,919	80,689	102,069	86,288	102,382	124,200	140,166	130,827	1,059,399	88,283	47,669
mean	55,912	56,236	51,384	52,322	33,123	34,300	39,659	37,255	32,107	30,612	42,841	31,013			
std. dev	15,631	42,354	36,922	38,732											

Finished goods inventory trends

Inventory reduction policy: 50% reduction over initial 6 reporting periods and no further reductions

Percent Series (yr)	Jan	Feb	Mar	Apr	May	Jun	Jul	Aug	Sep	Oct	Nov	Dec	sum	mean	std. dev.
1	-0.98%	28.69%	3.00%	1.41%	18.08%	11.75%	16.08%	21.35%	7.13%	18.91%	19.12%	25.59%	170.14%	14.18%	9.68%
2	0.03%	24.92%	8.32%	3.69%	0.89%	27.00%	15.88%	19.37%	14.45%	13.65%	26.94%	6.40%	161.53%	13.46%	9.76%
3	4.61%	6.71%	16.52%	8.73%	0.52%	18.68%	11.32%	49.32%	9.47%	20.17%	5.68%	26.80%	178.53%	14.88%	13.20%
4	10.70%	9.63%	3.24%	5.14%	5.77%	18.68%	13.54%	19.74%	12.34%	33.61%	8.58%	40.24%	181.22%	15.10%	11.43%
5	11.84%	6.14%	11.45%	2.53%	8.95%	15.81%	-5.88%	28.21%	23.12%	39.77%	5.81%	13.36%	161.11%	13.43%	12.22%
6	12.39%	9.87%	1.55%	9.11%	8.35%	19.71%	6.88%	29.01%	6.83%	14.18%	38.83%	10.33%	167.05%	13.92%	10.53%
7	-0.59%	31.14%	-10.21%	13.81%	8.53%	30.77%	13.52%	4.17%	30.42%	33.69%	0.58%	28.84%	184.66%	15.39%	15.18%
8	16.36%	0.11%	19.30%	-11.65%	24.30%	3.75%	24.88%	8.43%	24.95%	20.63%	15.06%	43.30%	189.42%	15.78%	14.24%
9	10.88%	11.60%	14.98%	-8.22%	13.36%	4.46%	30.49%	18.01%	10.72%	13.12%	32.84%	15.65%	167.90%	13.99%	10.70%
10	17.94%	-3.59%	22.75%	-3.06%	4.13%	12.61%	10.55%	33.26%	24.66%	8.25%	14.25%	34.84%	176.57%	14.71%	12.61%
11	7.77%	9.84%	5.71%	12.79%	3.66%	10.47%	18.24%	19.09%	21.30%	29.01%	29.32%	7.56%	174.75%	14.56%	8.74%
12	11.63%	3.78%	3.62%	11.59%	13.92%	-1.06%	25.25%	32.03%	10.74%	23.87%	15.96%	16.29%	167.62%	13.97%	9.63%
13	16.14%	1.13%	9.86%	13.19%	5.16%	2.60%	32.82%	15.79%	2.92%	45.20%	6.60%	22.84%	174.26%	14.52%	13.41%
14	3.26%	15.61%	2.18%	21.80%	4.32%	10.15%	9.70%	26.96%	23.87%	24.76%	12.68%	14.01%	169.31%	14.11%	8.68%
15	9.75%	12.65%	-1.16%	18.71%	11.83%	-9.33%	18.59%	34.35%	7.01%	19.76%	27.86%	28.80%	178.82%	14.90%	12.58%
16	16.26%	11.38%	-8.25%	11.31%	17.50%	-5.70%	31.64%	11.54%	23.89%	28.09%	21.38%	6.44%	165.48%	13.79%	12.21%
17	19.86%	-3.67%	11.56%	21.26%	-3.05%	4.29%	29.47%	7.96%	26.85%	17.55%	9.56%	21.76%	163.41%	13.62%	10.96%
18	12.24%	-6.07%	35.23%	-6.10%	15.06%	23.75%	-0.17%	63.91%	0.20%	20.69%	11.45%	34.23%	204.42%	17.04%	20.42%
19	3.83%	17.68%	0.78%	19.69%	3.42%	18.34%	3.97%	20.11%	28.67%	24.57%	11.42%	18.74%	171.22%	14.27%	9.28%
20	-1.72%	33.46%	-3.73%	22.11%	-3.90%	25.10%	12.16%	15.20%	22.01%	8.95%	29.83%	34.65%	194.12%	16.18%	14.03%
21	9.45%	12.62%	-1.67%	-0.05%	34.90%	3.68%	19.49%	14.06%	25.41%	12.96%	30.40%	13.81%	175.07%	14.59%	11.42%
22	19.36%	-8.93%	20.48%	3.64%	4.24%	16.06%	33.40%	9.31%	25.29%	14.42%	18.37%	22.54%	178.17%	14.85%	11.33%
23	13.63%	-1.13%	12.74%	2.12%	10.92%	21.33%	4.70%	17.40%	32.73%	37.64%	9.19%	12.57%	173.84%	14.49%	11.54%
24	18.93%	-0.97%	-3.67%	21.79%	17.33%	2.51%	21.14%	18.97%	14.78%	12.17%	34.83%	17.61%	175.42%	14.62%	10.81%
25	9.28%	8.63%	13.23%	-4.01%	23.72%	4.51%	13.11%	22.70%	21.81%	36.37%	1.01%	35.72%	186.08%	15.51%	12.83%
26	9.76%	17.45%	-3.40%	10.23%	12.09%	13.33%	2.61%	25.64%	16.85%	32.54%	15.18%	20.91%	173.19%	14.43%	9.61%
27	10.41%	3.22%	12.34%	5.57%	18.20%	-10.76%	51.71%	4.91%	20.17%	46.09%	4.31%	16.41%	182.57%	15.21%	17.81%
28	12.26%	-1.69%	11.03%	13.61%	9.79%	17.89%	4.92%	28.16%	10.49%	26.80%	17.27%	30.16%	180.68%	15.06%	9.58%
29	7.09%	9.86%	3.75%	13.38%	7.77%	-0.58%	27.86%	35.19%	10.12%	26.28%	13.09%	14.40%	168.19%	14.02%	10.57%
30	5.62%	12.91%	23.07%	-10.73%	20.52%	-1.61%	17.87%	38.69%	18.88%	7.77%	24.76%	23.01%	180.76%	15.06%	13.22%
31	0.61%	24.13%	5.91%	-5.41%	28.30%	8.46%	15.25%	21.78%	17.73%	30.01%	3.68%	34.93%	185.40%	15.45%	12.83%
32	21.58%	-6.56%	13.60%	9.30%	5.46%	11.03%	10.39%	17.37%	16.17%	27.90%	17.26%	31.47%	174.95%	14.58%	10.08%
33	8.72%	7.53%	3.77%	12.72%	6.84%	11.02%	12.78%	13.95%	11.46%	29.39%	36.24%	13.95%	168.37%	14.03%	9.42%
34	7.01%	14.99%	10.59%	-3.37%	12.91%	9.66%	24.13%	12.50%	14.89%	16.07%	13.01%	34.59%	166.99%	13.92%	9.14%
35	-3.02%	31.46%	-2.99%	18.29%	-0.85%	14.10%	23.17%	12.40%	25.54%	13.41%	20.10%	25.51%	177.11%	14.76%	11.70%
mean	9.51%	9.84%	7.58%	7.28%	10.66%	10.36%	17.18%	22.02%	17.54%	23.66%	17.21%	22.82%			
std. dev	6.62%	11.33%	9.80%	9.84%	8.87%	10.08%	11.49%	12.42%	8.18%	10.33%	10.52%	10.05%			

Finished goods inventory trends

Inventory reduction policy: 50% reduction over initial 6 reporting periods and no further reductions

Dollars	Jan	Feb	Mar	Apr	May	Jun	Jul	Aug	Sep	Oct	Nov	Dec	sum	mean	std. dev.
Series (yr)															
1	-7,351	165,135	17,956	9,456	102,929	62,373	97,605	124,981	50,102	126,817	134,841	158,687	1,043,532	86,961	59,220
2	203	142,353	48,583	22,003	6,256	154,505	88,101	106,901	86,902	90,693	166,324	49,954	962,734	80,228	56,325
3	31,307	50,139	107,408	54,289	3,395	119,986	85,890	223,800	57,258	118,505	41,556	159,341	1,052,874	87,740	61,724
4	58,803	56,745	20,482	32,341	41,317	118,351	84,460	127,687	87,833	190,495	59,887	227,991	1,106,392	92,199	63,858
5	69,134	36,253	68,854	15,505	53,938	84,276	-46,325	176,282	135,568	232,955	39,517	90,803	956,760	79,730	74,149
6	70,079	53,312	10,032	54,296	47,364	106,207	42,893	162,177	43,376	102,296	222,134	64,396	978,563	81,547	59,164
7	-3,910	175,859	-70,226	97,120	54,842	160,045	69,632	28,661	172,882	167,719	3,960	171,585	1,028,169	85,681	84,734
8	95,197	624	108,644	-83,521	139,936	23,988	152,203	54,771	158,770	130,515	104,096	219,888	1,105,113	92,093	81,921
9	65,155	65,736	73,946	-51,998	79,272	26,906	172,908	99,581	69,402	90,253	196,674	101,728	989,562	82,463	63,208
10	90,589	-23,292	128,404	-16,253	26,361	75,760	71,824	198,193	137,711	50,199	96,668	187,945	1,024,110	85,342	70,792
11	50,586	62,520	34,987	73,986	24,888	65,682	116,749	116,253	138,464	160,617	148,870	45,707	1,039,311	86,609	47,148
12	66,445	24,314	22,994	70,789	79,829	-7,025	160,699	178,623	66,110	141,648	99,636	102,954	1,007,017	83,918	56,531
13	91,356	6,686	60,927	67,926	30,373	14,832	170,258	82,897	19,904	225,863	40,853	137,031	948,906	79,076	67,783
14	20,855	90,220	13,971	119,931	26,007	56,632	61,586	168,197	124,543	128,006	71,161	82,314	963,423	80,285	48,154
15	57,274	71,303	-7,583	106,426	59,471	-61,612	128,887	197,582	47,601	131,572	161,293	167,485	1,059,699	88,308	75,556
16	91,821	58,420	-51,561	69,502	95,462	-40,984	185,016	76,803	145,116	162,002	117,175	43,699	952,473	79,373	72,361
17	108,557	-23,862	68,556	106,953	-17,783	27,460	161,177	47,081	153,806	103,415	67,646	139,754	942,760	78,563	61,901
18	66,544	-47,060	197,934	-41,200	88,999	113,278	-1,170	278,335	1,197	118,668	75,601	183,846	1,034,972	86,248	100,035
19	25,868	103,814	5,332	114,900	22,323	94,732	26,364	134,811	169,206	147,764	76,831	125,990	1,047,935	87,328	55,388
20	-12,508	179,504	-26,435	116,901	-25,728	130,287	71,083	97,234	130,795	65,731	188,733	183,264	1,098,860	91,572	79,141
21	58,459	72,592	-11,500	-336	193,769	21,078	115,130	92,051	152,564	78,189	165,489	85,794	1,023,279	85,273	64,256
22	103,490	-58,445	117,875	24,843	30,816	94,200	177,192	60,240	148,854	90,060	109,812	133,125	1,032,062	86,005	63,799
23	81,121	-7,423	83,832	14,721	76,551	121,940	32,741	123,770	199,077	195,989	53,357	85,370	1,058,018	88,168	63,746
24	95,369	-5,363	-26,575	128,656	95,925	14,923	123,514	104,672	89,077	82,366	204,386	99,153	1,006,103	83,842	63,238
25	56,798	52,170	78,190	-27,157	134,368	27,873	82,845	146,140	134,160	166,323	6,296	202,948	1,060,953	88,413	69,373
26	60,257	88,880	-19,677	62,803	66,040	64,654	17,803	154,874	102,502	186,984	83,488	117,216	985,826	82,152	55,513
27	60,796	19,452	74,827	36,910	96,129	-80,756	261,012	33,524	133,893	240,402	24,004	103,725	1,003,919	83,660	94,925
28	71,448	-11,986	74,139	85,948	57,882	98,028	33,269	171,980	70,195	162,772	112,142	172,778	1,098,594	91,549	56,448
29	44,630	57,997	22,444	78,678	44,420	-4,319	176,795	190,632	63,218	147,118	83,239	88,539	993,390	82,783	60,160
30	39,241	83,158	113,368	-70,368	119,241	-10,650	129,754	219,943	102,543	53,023	157,894	134,648	1,071,792	89,316	77,729
31	4,216	141,703	34,092	-36,787	159,352	48,902	89,359	127,669	107,330	161,906	25,409	190,215	1,053,366	87,780	71,844
32	105,719	-41,541	77,869	55,839	32,347	59,150	65,927	106,600	97,902	175,881	114,511	179,575	1,029,780	85,815	60,187
33	54,253	45,620	23,284	79,589	40,961	71,264	88,546	98,303	73,285	187,418	205,644	86,809	1,054,977	87,915	55,379
34	46,597	84,819	60,501	-21,208	81,713	58,410	137,258	82,723	94,686	111,817	96,730	192,155	1,026,477	85,539	51,581
35	-21,249	171,385	-20,496	107,726	-5,316	85,523	137,258	80,626	152,171	92,496	135,243	153,914	1,069,281	89,107	69,376
mean	54,204	55,478	43,297	41,692	61,819	57,026	101,958	127,844	106,142	137,671	105,460	133,438			
std. dev	35,619	64,876	56,906	58,601	49,568	57,780	62,600	58,011	46,753	49,619	59,863	51,158			

Finished goods inventory trends

Inventory reduction policy: 50% reduction over initial 6 reporting periods and no further reductions

Percent Series (yr)	Jan	Feb	Mar	Apr	May	Jun	Jul	Aug	Sep	Oct	Nov	Dec	sum	mean	std. dev.
1	-2.69%	26.33%	1.00%	-0.06%	16.37%	10.08%	14.77%	19.96%	6.16%	17.86%	18.15%	24.37%	152.31%	12.69%	9.70%
2	-1.78%	22.53%	6.24%	1.89%	-0.27%	25.54%	14.33%	17.80%	13.12%	12.55%	25.70%	5.65%	143.30%	11.94%	9.72%
3	2.60%	5.17%	14.81%	7.06%	-0.81%	17.51%	10.55%	47.38%	8.15%	18.77%	4.80%	25.57%	161.55%	13.46%	13.10%
4	7.93%	7.35%	1.41%	3.50%	4.66%	17.48%	12.30%	18.58%	11.40%	32.18%	7.60%	38.75%	163.13%	13.59%	11.53%
5	9.31%	3.87%	9.46%	0.81%	7.40%	14.15%	-6.62%	27.23%	22.03%	38.53%	4.90%	12.44%	143.51%	11.96%	12.30%
6	9.74%	7.28%	-0.22%	7.31%	6.63%	18.08%	5.65%	27.48%	5.63%	13.27%	37.40%	9.13%	147.37%	12.28%	10.61%
7	-2.69%	28.71%	-11.80%	12.47%	7.15%	29.04%	11.76%	3.15%	29.00%	31.83%	-0.45%	27.48%	165.65%	13.80%	15.05%
8	13.81%	-2.24%	17.09%	-12.94%	22.62%	2.57%	23.58%	7.28%	23.79%	19.47%	14.07%	41.50%	170.60%	14.22%	14.22%
9	8.44%	9.19%	12.29%	-9.83%	11.77%	3.13%	29.00%	16.46%	9.57%	12.12%	31.51%	14.51%	148.15%	12.35%	10.77%
10	14.82%	-5.56%	20.55%	-5.22%	2.73%	11.27%	9.52%	31.92%	23.13%	6.95%	13.20%	33.24%	156.55%	13.05%	12.66%
11	5.62%	7.82%	3.78%	10.90%	2.42%	9.24%	17.06%	17.84%	20.16%	27.46%	27.51%	6.24%	156.06%	13.00%	8.81%
12	9.02%	1.79%	1.80%	9.86%	12.24%	-2.17%	24.05%	30.50%	9.47%	22.50%	14.72%	15.07%	148.85%	12.40%	9.73%
13	13.49%	-1.14%	7.96%	10.92%	3.55%	1.13%	31.08%	14.08%	1.89%	43.40%	5.34%	21.50%	153.19%	12.77%	13.37%
14	1.05%	13.27%	0.39%	19.76%	2.77%	8.61%	8.50%	25.72%	22.15%	23.01%	11.17%	12.61%	149.00%	12.42%	8.72%
15	7.24%	10.22%	-2.91%	16.77%	9.74%	-10.44%	17.59%	32.92%	5.97%	18.71%	26.46%	27.38%	159.65%	13.30%	12.63%
16	13.60%	8.59%	-10.12%	9.60%	15.67%	-6.62%	30.30%	10.45%	22.59%	26.64%	19.80%	5.39%	145.89%	12.16%	12.20%
17	17.08%	-5.62%	9.52%	18.91%	-4.69%	3.11%	27.88%	6.62%	25.42%	16.16%	8.60%	20.62%	143.62%	11.97%	10.92%
18	9.43%	-7.51%	33.06%	-7.54%	13.46%	21.75%	-1.12%	61.71%	-1.17%	19.23%	10.34%	32.59%	184.23%	15.35%	20.16%
19	1.80%	15.39%	-0.83%	17.83%	2.08%	16.59%	2.87%	19.04%	27.29%	23.23%	10.36%	17.70%	153.34%	12.78%	9.31%
20	-3.51%	30.84%	-5.24%	19.93%	-5.21%	23.36%	10.75%	14.02%	20.65%	8.07%	28.66%	32.97%	175.29%	14.61%	13.86%
21	7.12%	10.26%	-3.25%	-1.25%	33.12%	2.22%	18.11%	12.93%	24.07%	11.63%	28.80%	12.56%	156.32%	13.03%	11.40%
22	16.48%	-10.86%	18.35%	2.22%	3.18%	14.66%	31.72%	8.15%	23.95%	13.18%	17.02%	21.16%	159.22%	13.27%	11.29%
23	11.16%	-3.04%	11.02%	0.75%	9.76%	19.86%	3.71%	16.50%	31.44%	35.93%	7.76%	11.53%	156.39%	13.03%	11.54%
24	15.81%	-3.49%	-5.11%	19.96%	15.54%	1.14%	19.74%	17.40%	13.45%	11.12%	33.44%	16.10%	155.10%	12.92%	10.87%
25	6.92%	6.44%	11.19%	-5.44%	22.00%	3.24%	11.90%	21.53%	20.53%	34.24%	-0.23%	34.24%	166.54%	13.88%	12.79%
26	7.43%	14.63%	-5.52%	8.52%	10.26%	11.39%	1.57%	24.34%	15.55%	31.08%	13.62%	19.41%	152.28%	12.69%	9.72%
27	7.88%	1.03%	10.37%	4.08%	16.27%	-11.59%	49.98%	3.88%	19.07%	44.38%	2.77%	15.20%	163.32%	13.61%	17.71%
28	9.72%	-3.38%	9.38%	11.98%	8.19%	16.31%	3.86%	26.90%	9.41%	25.50%	16.12%	28.72%	162.70%	13.56%	9.66%
29	4.83%	7.57%	1.74%	11.54%	6.07%	-1.43%	26.73%	33.58%	8.88%	24.76%	11.89%	13.12%	149.28%	12.44%	10.64%
30	3.70%	10.93%	20.37%	-12.26%	18.87%	-2.71%	16.97%	37.34%	17.36%	6.75%	23.58%	21.61%	162.50%	13.54%	13.19%
31	-1.34%	21.84%	3.78%	-6.83%	26.56%	7.02%	13.85%	20.38%	16.41%	28.39%	2.67%	33.33%	166.07%	13.84%	12.78%
32	18.33%	-8.59%	11.45%	7.53%	3.86%	9.39%	9.25%	16.15%	14.94%	26.68%	16.17%	30.00%	155.16%	12.93%	10.17%
33	6.41%	5.35%	1.86%	11.06%	5.27%	9.86%	11.81%	13.10%	10.51%	28.39%	34.82%	12.70%	151.16%	12.60%	9.62%
34	4.93%	12.58%	8.43%	5.00%	11.50%	8.34%	22.66%	11.40%	13.75%	15.08%	12.19%	33.18%	149.03%	12.42%	9.24%
35	-4.93%	28.90%	-4.60%	16.46%	-2.32%	12.79%	21.80%	11.25%	24.20%	12.40%	19.10%	24.18%	159.24%	13.27%	11.67%
mean	7.11%	7.61%	5.65%	5.58%	9.10%	8.97%	15.93%	20.71%	16.28%	22.33%	15.99%	21.48%			
std. dev	6.26%	11.15%	9.62%	9.67%	8.74%	9.88%	11.31%	12.22%	8.09%	10.12%	10.41%	9.88%			

Finished goods inventory trends

Inventory reduction policy: 50% reduction over initial 6 reporting periods and no further reductions

Dollars	Jan	Feb	Mar	Apr	May	Jun	Jul	Aug	Sep	Oct	Nov	Dec	sum	mean	std. dev.
Series (yr)															
1	-20,147	151,549	5,971	-389	93,209	53,500	89,655	116,805	43,289	119,763	128,054	151,115	932,373	77,698	60,036
2	-12,911	128,723	36,404	11,289	-1,866	146,126	79,513	98,238	78,874	83,421	158,647	44,080	850,539	70,878	56,830
3	17,667	38,621	96,283	43,930	-5,317	112,444	80,021	215,013	49,264	110,315	35,087	151,993	945,321	78,777	62,355
4	43,592	43,318	8,872	22,016	33,358	110,711	76,704	120,208	81,138	182,384	53,008	219,580	994,891	82,908	64,970
5	54,345	22,848	56,887	4,980	44,616	75,424	-52,111	170,195	129,182	225,671	84,562	33,295	849,894	70,825	74,942
6	55,065	39,303	-1,397	43,586	37,608	97,427	35,192	153,641	35,753	95,713	213,935	56,883	862,709	71,892	60,038
7	-17,775	162,138	-81,154	87,701	46,002	151,040	60,569	21,668	164,780	158,455	-3,068	163,475	913,831	76,153	84,935
8	80,384	-12,964	96,221	-92,780	130,276	16,429	144,295	47,325	151,416	123,117	97,206	210,734	991,679	82,640	82,456
9	50,546	52,056	60,689	-62,171	69,832	18,890	164,468	90,971	61,922	83,353	188,675	94,285	873,516	72,793	64,000
10	74,853	-36,009	116,003	-27,738	17,471	67,727	64,870	190,169	129,178	42,255	89,556	179,318	907,655	75,638	71,595
11	36,606	49,660	23,164	63,065	16,490	57,966	109,185	108,647	131,095	152,008	139,720	37,712	925,319	77,110	48,206
12	51,493	11,549	11,431	60,260	70,153	153,084	-14,328	170,066	58,283	133,519	91,873	95,295	892,680	74,390	57,502
13	76,353	-6,715	49,167	56,232	20,870	6,418	161,235	73,958	12,861	216,855	33,033	128,978	829,245	69,104	68,098
14	6,725	76,669	2,487	108,669	16,671	48,077	53,956	160,434	115,560	118,967	62,650	74,129	844,994	70,416	48,994
15	42,526	57,620	-18,944	95,387	48,939	-68,937	121,954	189,374	40,496	124,639	153,185	159,244	945,484	78,790	76,261
16	76,807	44,096	-63,241	59,012	85,449	-47,591	177,171	69,543	137,178	153,672	108,505	36,588	837,190	69,766	72,773
17	93,314	-36,542	56,493	95,117	-27,348	19,896	152,499	39,127	145,602	95,247	60,901	132,426	826,730	68,894	62,357
18	51,277	-58,244	185,748	-50,955	79,552	103,750	-7,913	268,789	-6,925	110,302	68,277	175,052	918,712	76,559	99,867
19	12,170	90,372	-5,678	104,038	13,605	85,686	19,101	127,604	161,052	139,729	69,655	118,950	936,284	78,024	56,211
20	-25,555	165,454	-37,113	105,386	-34,372	121,268	62,856	89,666	122,680	59,301	181,318	174,367	985,256	82,105	79,397
21	44,076	59,012	-22,400	-9,278	183,876	12,710	106,982	84,657	144,516	70,176	156,777	78,004	909,107	75,759	64,805
22	88,108	-71,070	105,607	15,172	23,131	85,998	168,306	52,755	140,964	82,308	101,742	124,965	917,987	76,499	64,403
23	66,460	-20,022	72,549	5,186	68,402	113,552	25,848	117,378	188,342	187,063	45,076	78,275	948,110	79,009	64,556
24	79,620	-19,234	-37,054	117,873	86,010	6,793	115,286	96,052	81,065	75,238	196,221	90,667	888,539	74,045	64,032
25	42,347	38,924	66,087	-36,884	124,604	20,042	75,221	138,621	126,298	156,562	-1,463	194,534	944,893	78,741	69,899
26	45,869	74,507	-31,922	52,300	56,033	55,232	10,741	147,026	94,558	178,630	74,908	108,810	866,692	72,224	56,437
27	46,009	6,221	62,917	26,992	85,915	-86,989	252,297	26,481	126,641	231,484	15,451	96,071	889,490	74,124	95,014
28	56,646	-23,965	63,045	75,662	48,421	89,348	26,151	164,249	62,983	154,872	104,693	164,526	986,631	82,219	57,472
29	30,389	44,568	10,448	67,877	34,732	-10,642	169,611	181,878	55,458	138,589	75,633	80,720	879,259	73,272	60,967
30	25,823	70,398	100,083	-80,362	109,658	-17,956	123,224	212,282	94,297	46,033	150,362	126,420	960,261	80,022	78,307
31	-9,282	128,261	21,825	-46,476	149,545	40,593	81,147	119,447	99,344	153,130	18,452	181,512	937,498	78,125	72,237
32	89,795	-54,412	65,555	45,184	22,899	50,335	58,705	92,298	90,460	168,200	107,339	171,185	914,363	76,197	61,289
33	39,918	32,392	11,509	69,241	31,582	63,781	81,834	75,425	67,232	181,024	197,606	79,031	947,448	78,954	56,913
34	32,767	71,156	48,186	-31,511	72,747	50,420	129,129	73,185	87,436	104,928	128,477	184,342	915,663	76,305	52,770
35	-34,614	157,442	-31,460	96,923	-14,414	77,562	129,116	120,066	144,172	85,522	81,595	145,914	957,824	79,819	70,107
mean	39,750	42,220	31,522	31,272	52,524	48,934	94,283	120,066	98,470	129,784	97,869	125,535			
std. dev	34,897	64,475	56,533	58,194	49,237	57,240	62,132	57,687	46,579	49,209	59,624	50,716			

Finished goods inventory trends
Inventory reduction policy: 50% reduction over initial 6 reporting periods and no further reductions

Percent Series (yr)	Jan	Feb	Mar	Apr	May	Jun	Jul	Aug	Sep	Oct	Nov	Dec	sum	mean	std. dev.
1	36.64%	57.25%	38.87%	38.52%	47.66%	46.00%	48.28%	51.16%	41.87%	49.33%	49.13%	53.72%	558.43%	46.54%	6.40%
2	36.86%	54.27%	42.55%	39.61%	37.76%	55.03%	46.51%	49.50%	46.06%	46.48%	54.81%	41.53%	550.97%	45.91%	6.50%
3	40.28%	41.66%	48.84%	42.74%	36.27%	50.51%	44.63%	69.40%	43.63%	50.21%	40.69%	54.45%	563.31%	46.94%	8.77%
4	43.31%	43.67%	39.15%	41.36%	41.00%	49.43%	45.55%	50.17%	44.19%	58.76%	42.41%	63.58%	562.59%	46.88%	7.47%
5	45.10%	41.76%	45.22%	37.96%	42.48%	48.42%	33.18%	56.46%	53.14%	63.26%	40.94%	45.64%	553.55%	46.13%	8.26%
6	45.31%	43.64%	36.53%	42.62%	43.28%	51.55%	41.47%	56.40%	41.36%	46.24%	63.40%	44.00%	557.80%	46.48%	7.17%
7	36.71%	58.39%	30.41%	46.35%	42.39%	57.76%	45.76%	39.94%	56.75%	58.73%	37.17%	55.97%	566.34%	47.19%	10.04%
8	49.05%	37.14%	51.11%	29.48%	52.83%	39.77%	53.38%	42.47%	53.87%	50.85%	46.57%	65.93%	572.45%	47.70%	9.47%
9	44.63%	45.20%	47.40%	31.07%	46.15%	39.50%	56.99%	49.21%	44.77%	45.32%	58.79%	47.49%	556.52%	46.38%	7.18%
10	49.04%	35.16%	52.24%	34.73%	40.09%	45.87%	43.52%	59.25%	53.74%	42.97%	46.79%	60.12%	563.51%	46.96%	8.35%
11	42.86%	44.08%	40.94%	45.41%	39.67%	43.38%	49.26%	49.35%	50.71%	55.99%	57.08%	41.51%	560.22%	46.68%	5.78%
12	45.40%	40.06%	38.90%	44.56%	46.02%	36.39%	53.26%	59.32%	43.52%	52.77%	47.50%	48.59%	556.26%	46.36%	6.54%
13	48.17%	37.92%	43.56%	46.24%	40.49%	38.60%	58.28%	48.25%	39.23%	67.61%	41.34%	52.01%	561.70%	46.81%	8.94%
14	38.74%	46.96%	39.00%	51.56%	41.00%	44.33%	42.95%	55.52%	51.80%	54.01%	44.97%	45.57%	556.42%	46.37%	5.71%
15	43.92%	45.80%	36.82%	49.90%	44.69%	30.85%	48.61%	59.77%	41.66%	50.20%	55.42%	55.36%	562.99%	46.92%	8.17%
16	47.98%	45.29%	31.68%	44.33%	49.01%	34.00%	57.05%	44.50%	52.56%	55.53%	50.98%	41.16%	554.09%	46.17%	7.81%
17	50.48%	35.24%	44.57%	51.16%	35.04%	40.19%	57.14%	42.09%	54.59%	48.30%	42.97%	51.66%	553.43%	46.12%	7.25%
18	45.00%	33.98%	60.91%	33.62%	46.71%	52.22%	37.39%	79.95%	37.57%	51.17%	44.75%	60.33%	583.59%	48.63%	13.51%
19	40.13%	48.68%	38.04%	50.71%	39.80%	49.78%	39.53%	50.30%	55.33%	53.42%	44.28%	49.58%	559.58%	46.63%	5.98%
20	35.31%	59.68%	35.39%	51.54%	34.25%	54.23%	44.90%	47.45%	51.49%	42.54%	56.32%	59.87%	572.94%	47.75%	9.33%
21	43.37%	45.89%	36.80%	36.82%	59.53%	39.54%	49.53%	46.52%	53.53%	44.90%	56.67%	46.65%	559.76%	46.65%	7.26%
22	50.69%	31.11%	51.06%	40.59%	39.96%	47.35%	59.43%	43.58%	53.65%	46.94%	48.65%	51.41%	564.41%	47.03%	7.42%
23	46.52%	35.90%	45.96%	37.57%	44.03%	50.95%	39.92%	48.17%	58.91%	62.00%	42.17%	46.24%	558.33%	46.53%	7.85%
24	49.81%	36.54%	34.58%	51.57%	48.83%	39.65%	51.49%	49.00%	46.54%	45.62%	59.98%	48.88%	562.49%	46.87%	7.06%
25	43.41%	43.51%	47.95%	34.72%	52.48%	41.57%	45.00%	51.92%	51.11%	60.03%	37.37%	60.87%	569.97%	47.50%	8.16%
26	43.48%	49.53%	35.14%	43.05%	45.33%	46.64%	39.18%	53.69%	48.13%	59.61%	47.02%	50.82%	561.61%	46.80%	6.45%
27	44.46%	39.43%	44.65%	41.35%	48.72%	30.23%	71.22%	40.44%	49.28%	68.71%	39.30%	48.35%	566.14%	47.18%	11.88%
28	45.95%	36.66%	44.11%	46.45%	43.58%	48.62%	40.39%	55.23%	44.20%	54.26%	48.72%	57.56%	565.72%	47.14%	6.16%
29	42.29%	43.37%	39.61%	46.54%	42.17%	36.91%	54.86%	60.38%	43.86%	53.45%	45.99%	56.07%	556.07%	46.34%	6.77%
30	41.18%	46.36%	53.41%	30.54%	50.61%	35.78%	48.90%	62.50%	49.76%	42.11%	53.82%	51.74%	566.69%	47.22%	8.68%
31	37.68%	53.51%	41.73%	32.84%	55.36%	43.36%	46.57%	51.70%	48.56%	56.74%	39.60%	60.40%	568.04%	47.34%	8.49%
32	51.38%	32.74%	46.79%	43.67%	40.88%	44.60%	44.22%	44.24%	46.66%	55.23%	48.45%	58.17%	561.33%	46.78%	6.16%
33	42.94%	41.93%	39.62%	46.29%	41.86%	45.07%	46.31%	46.03%	43.17%	56.60%	59.80%	46.06%	555.68%	46.31%	6.61%
34	42.51%	46.89%	44.90%	34.41%	46.30%	43.61%	52.44%	46.23%	46.09%	46.80%	45.27%	59.41%	554.85%	46.24%	5.99%
35	34.70%	58.48%	34.92%	48.91%	36.90%	46.00%	48.26%	51.67%	54.32%	46.24%	50.02%	53.48%	560.07%	46.67%	5.85%
mean	43.58%	43.93%	42.44%	41.97%	44.09%	44.22%	48.26%	51.67%	48.45%	52.65%	50.02%	52.14%	560.07%	46.67%	7.81%
std. dev	4.55%	7.63%	6.66%	6.59%	5.73%	6.71%	7.54%	8.30%	5.40%	6.92%	7.02%	6.66%			

Finished goods inventory trends
Inventory reduction policy: 50% reduction over initial 6 reporting periods and no further reductions

Dollars	Jan	Feb	Mar	Apr	May	Jun	Jul	Aug	Sep	Oct	Nov	Dec	sum	mean	std. dev.
Series (yr)															
1	274,597	329,517	232,875	257,891	271,302	244,145	293,065	299,470	294,053	330,854	346,566	333,086	3,507,421	292,285	37,323
2	266,893	310,061	248,416	236,256	265,812	314,886	258,071	273,097	276,947	308,891	338,389	324,059	3,421,780	285,148	32,766
3	273,642	311,267	317,635	265,858	237,279	324,342	338,519	314,921	263,699	295,029	297,722	323,711	3,563,624	296,969	30,646
4	238,129	257,245	247,151	260,121	293,599	313,148	284,186	324,567	314,486	333,015	295,925	360,270	3,521,842	293,487	37,594
5	263,294	246,594	271,930	232,286	255,945	258,082	261,242	352,838	311,647	370,487	278,226	310,310	3,412,882	284,407	42,992
6	256,217	235,632	248,638	253,995	245,587	277,762	258,415	315,339	262,761	333,588	362,714	274,174	3,324,821	277,068	39,358
7	242,592	329,760	209,124	326,046	272,615	300,429	235,643	274,811	322,514	292,344	254,484	332,965	3,393,326	282,777	41,351
8	285,394	214,183	287,705	211,337	304,227	254,698	326,624	275,900	342,800	321,595	321,832	334,789	3,481,083	290,090	44,473
9	267,378	256,140	233,963	196,576	273,832	238,112	323,190	272,041	289,736	311,734	352,091	308,589	3,323,381	276,948	43,205
10	247,679	227,856	294,904	184,409	256,183	275,562	296,445	352,995	300,092	261,409	317,455	324,350	3,339,342	278,278	46,115
11	279,135	280,037	250,717	262,728	269,762	272,231	315,297	300,490	329,674	309,967	289,863	250,850	3,410,752	284,229	25,380
12	259,250	257,943	246,841	272,244	263,839	240,534	338,926	330,775	267,860	313,214	296,454	307,167	3,395,048	282,921	33,170
13	272,708	223,694	269,146	238,099	238,082	219,899	302,366	253,336	267,567	337,872	255,779	312,027	3,190,577	265,881	36,183
14	247,603	271,329	249,973	283,602	246,990	247,431	272,710	346,345	270,306	279,217	252,321	267,822	3,235,649	269,637	27,576
15	258,006	258,106	239,775	283,800	224,625	203,603	336,954	343,841	282,689	334,297	320,849	321,995	3,408,587	284,049	47,675
16	271,028	232,616	197,999	272,472	267,334	244,546	333,562	296,189	319,224	320,278	279,418	279,190	3,313,857	276,155	38,893
17	275,843	229,145	264,362	257,327	204,349	257,211	312,524	248,879	312,693	284,598	304,170	331,760	3,282,861	273,572	37,524
18	244,658	263,364	342,175	227,049	275,988	249,117	264,590	348,188	221,897	293,457	295,495	324,046	3,350,024	279,169	42,406
19	270,775	285,850	259,051	295,904	259,932	257,118	262,643	337,201	326,575	321,340	297,823	333,288	3,507,501	292,292	30,944
20	257,429	320,128	250,531	272,479	225,860	281,521	262,432	303,557	305,942	312,393	356,308	316,651	3,465,232	288,769	36,690
21	268,302	263,890	253,887	272,534	330,537	226,375	292,638	304,584	321,408	270,979	308,536	289,695	3,403,365	283,614	29,963
22	271,018	203,542	293,899	277,100	290,372	277,754	315,318	282,029	315,739	293,147	290,728	303,628	3,414,273	284,523	29,186
23	276,923	236,116	302,474	260,757	308,708	291,284	277,823	342,601	352,891	322,808	244,817	313,973	3,531,174	294,265	36,658
24	250,882	201,623	250,556	304,488	270,316	235,286	300,789	270,438	280,547	308,697	352,027	275,261	3,300,909	275,076	39,101
25	265,715	262,937	283,303	235,314	297,308	256,916	284,460	334,323	314,380	274,528	233,019	345,874	3,388,076	282,340	35,674
26	268,562	252,252	203,090	264,257	247,619	226,256	267,292	324,338	292,734	342,532	258,566	284,814	3,232,313	269,359	38,523
27	259,663	238,286	270,796	273,864	257,305	226,995	359,494	276,292	327,189	358,411	219,135	305,650	3,373,079	281,090	47,345
28	267,733	259,596	296,609	293,286	257,726	266,398	273,328	337,274	295,884	329,530	316,422	329,736	3,523,521	293,627	29,081
29	266,331	255,185	237,181	273,778	241,193	274,531	348,117	327,052	273,863	299,230	292,534	286,913	3,375,907	281,326	32,552
30	287,493	298,571	262,426	200,218	294,092	236,823	355,065	355,285	270,302	287,358	343,254	302,707	3,493,594	291,133	46,337
31	260,556	314,167	240,838	223,453	311,686	250,531	272,769	303,012	293,977	306,103	273,156	328,963	3,379,209	281,601	33,058
32	251,759	207,420	267,971	262,145	242,388	239,168	280,713	298,063	282,536	348,112	321,492	331,884	3,333,650	277,804	41,494
33	257,209	253,899	244,615	289,697	250,621	291,560	320,779	324,282	276,166	360,897	339,355	286,675	3,505,754	292,146	37,134
34	282,681	265,291	256,549	216,711	292,952	263,689	298,845	305,963	292,984	325,693	336,561	330,044	3,467,963	288,997	34,681
35	243,787	318,614	239,079	288,041	229,524	279,012	307,253	287,696	323,590	318,943	336,520	322,654	3,494,714	291,226	36,694
mean	264,025	262,053	259,034	257,889	265,014	260,486	298,060	309,658	297,067	314,644	302,286	311,702			
std. dev	12,571	36,339	30,374	32,164	27,965	28,277	31,873	30,191	27,255	25,993	37,621	24,347			

Finished goods inventory trends

Inventory reduction policy: 50% reduction over initial 6 reporting periods and no further reductions

Percent Series (yr)	Jan	Feb	Mar	Apr	May	Jun	Jul	Aug	Sep	Oct	Nov	Dec	sum	mean	std. dev.
1	4.66%	23.62%	6.57%	6.77%	16.63%	13.11%	16.07%	19.29%	10.61%	18.26%	18.41%	22.68%	176.67%	14.72%	6.36%
2	5.26%	21.07%	10.02%	7.63%	6.47%	23.22%	13.68%	17.85%	14.95%	14.95%	22.99%	10.32%	170.42%	14.20%	6.31%
3	7.89%	9.68%	16.30%	11.08%	5.83%	18.23%	13.40%	37.16%	11.61%	18.60%	10.00%	33.27%	183.06%	15.25%	8.53%
4	11.22%	11.12%	7.19%	8.87%	9.56%	17.81%	14.58%	18.61%	13.77%	27.66%	11.48%	31.68%	183.57%	15.30%	7.57%
5	12.28%	8.88%	12.57%	6.43%	11.48%	15.59%	2.58%	24.67%	20.78%	31.02%	10.00%	14.57%	170.85%	14.24%	7.94%
6	12.43%	10.64%	6.41%	10.92%	11.23%	18.31%	9.87%	24.20%	10.05%	15.36%	31.01%	12.24%	172.66%	14.39%	6.98%
7	4.55%	24.80%	-1.12%	14.69%	11.18%	25.16%	14.05%	8.76%	25.31%	26.55%	6.23%	24.46%	184.63%	15.39%	9.66%
8	15.04%	4.94%	17.39%	-1.96%	21.15%	8.39%	21.78%	11.32%	22.15%	18.96%	15.55%	33.56%	188.27%	15.69%	9.25%
9	11.71%	12.26%	13.69%	-0.20%	14.52%	8.69%	25.04%	17.21%	12.81%	14.26%	27.03%	15.96%	172.96%	14.41%	7.03%
10	15.72%	2.85%	19.19%	3.00%	8.48%	13.92%	12.62%	27.10%	21.32%	10.90%	15.26%	28.21%	178.56%	14.88%	8.18%
11	9.89%	11.41%	8.83%	13.33%	8.12%	12.68%	17.92%	17.95%	19.52%	24.20%	24.09%	10.39%	178.33%	14.86%	5.71%
12	12.01%	7.61%	7.36%	12.85%	14.37%	5.18%	22.26%	26.46%	12.34%	21.19%	15.99%	16.73%	174.34%	14.53%	6.43%
13	14.81%	5.67%	11.24%	13.71%	8.61%	7.31%	26.43%	15.22%	7.73%	34.77%	9.81%	20.39%	175.70%	14.64%	8.69%
14	6.97%	14.69%	6.80%	18.96%	8.42%	11.99%	12.03%	23.43%	20.19%	21.55%	13.53%	14.51%	173.08%	14.42%	5.62%
15	11.20%	12.58%	4.48%	17.26%	12.48%	-0.21%	18.00%	28.02%	10.54%	18.71%	23.50%	23.84%	180.41%	15.03%	8.18%
16	14.58%	11.83%	-0.19%	12.87%	16.45%	2.40%	26.06%	13.23%	21.35%	23.63%	19.12%	10.18%	171.52%	14.29%	7.87%
17	17.15%	2.66%	12.61%	18.64%	3.24%	8.57%	24.87%	10.75%	22.82%	16.75%	11.98%	20.17%	170.22%	14.19%	7.15%
18	11.99%	1.79%	27.86%	1.72%	14.93%	20.39%	5.74%	46.30%	5.71%	19.11%	13.22%	27.71%	196.48%	16.37%	13.02%
19	7.66%	16.10%	5.80%	17.93%	7.82%	17.43%	8.37%	18.88%	24.22%	21.55%	13.05%	18.23%	177.02%	14.75%	6.08%
20	3.98%	26.24%	3.21%	19.12%	3.03%	22.00%	13.30%	15.64%	19.89%	11.71%	24.98%	27.92%	191.01%	15.92%	9.00%
21	10.97%	12.78%	4.29%	5.70%	27.96%	7.92%	18.15%	15.01%	21.87%	14.26%	25.11%	14.71%	178.74%	14.90%	7.39%
22	16.86%	-0.85%	18.39%	7.90%	8.70%	16.11%	27.06%	11.56%	22.00%	15.17%	11.30%	20.31%	180.69%	15.06%	7.37%
23	13.34%	4.49%	13.47%	6.84%	13.17%	19.37%	9.20%	17.18%	27.15%	29.43%	17.49%	14.35%	179.27%	14.94%	7.47%
24	16.36%	4.12%	2.96%	19.52%	16.25%	7.46%	19.12%	17.56%	15.04%	14.04%	28.05%	16.88%	177.37%	14.78%	7.02%
25	10.53%	10.43%	14.08%	2.91%	20.16%	9.19%	14.09%	20.63%	19.56%	28.59%	6.43%	28.58%	185.19%	15.43%	8.21%
26	11.02%	15.56%	2.94%	11.38%	13.23%	13.99%	7.63%	22.11%	16.72%	26.72%	15.38%	18.72%	175.40%	14.62%	6.30%
27	11.43%	6.99%	12.75%	9.41%	16.72%	-0.87%	38.82%	9.15%	18.44%	35.56%	8.12%	16.34%	182.87%	15.24%	11.49%
28	12.29%	4.38%	12.03%	14.58%	11.95%	16.80%	9.39%	23.84%	12.57%	22.99%	17.20%	25.12%	183.15%	15.26%	6.23%
29	9.38%	11.18%	7.54%	13.68%	10.51%	5.67%	23.87%	28.30%	12.28%	22.36%	14.49%	14.84%	174.11%	14.51%	6.91%
30	8.65%	13.71%	19.06%	-1.40%	18.71%	4.86%	17.38%	30.76%	17.66%	10.96%	22.08%	20.30%	182.76%	15.23%	8.52%
31	5.55%	20.29%	8.99%	1.95%	23.51%	11.18%	15.25%	19.87%	17.14%	24.90%	8.25%	28.10%	185.00%	15.42%	8.27%
32	17.95%	0.46%	14.20%	11.06%	8.73%	13.22%	12.49%	17.00%	15.92%	23.43%	17.30%	25.78%	177.62%	14.80%	6.62%
33	10.30%	9.75%	7.59%	13.57%	10.10%	13.02%	14.45%	15.33%	13.31%	24.99%	28.79%	14.93%	176.15%	14.68%	6.23%
34	9.45%	14.41%	11.56%	3.31%	13.96%	12.01%	21.10%	14.09%	15.34%	16.30%	14.71%	27.89%	174.15%	14.51%	5.98%
35	3.08%	25.11%	3.21%	17.14%	5.43%	14.61%	20.43%	13.67%	22.58%	14.51%	19.13%	22.13%	181.04%	15.09%	7.61%
mean	10.80%	11.24%	9.98%	10.03%	12.37%	12.42%	16.83%	19.95%	17.01%	20.97%	16.89%	20.46%			
std. dev	3.96%	7.20%	6.19%	6.25%	5.58%	6.37%	7.28%	7.91%	5.26%	6.50%	6.72%	6.40%			

Finished goods inventory trends

Inventory reduction policy: 50% reduction over initial 6 reporting periods and no further reductions

Dollars Series (yr)	Jan	Feb	Mar	Apr	May	Jun	Jul	Aug	Sep	Oct	Nov	Dec	sum	mean	std. dev.
1	34,928	135,945	39,384	45,329	94,681	69,576	97,530	112,915	74,491	122,455	129,864	140,599	1,097,697	91,475	38,304
2	38,059	120,399	58,529	45,490	45,580	132,867	87,021	98,497	89,919	99,348	141,940	80,499	1,038,149	86,512	34,660
3	53,572	72,307	106,006	68,928	38,159	117,059	101,669	168,644	70,191	109,284	73,175	138,340	1,117,335	93,111	37,355
4	61,704	65,530	45,416	55,791	68,491	112,814	90,978	120,396	97,973	156,780	80,097	179,523	1,135,492	94,624	41,390
5	71,715	52,441	75,600	39,343	69,158	83,108	20,272	154,171	121,853	181,688	67,971	99,063	1,036,382	86,365	46,525
6	70,267	57,433	41,365	65,060	63,748	98,653	61,526	135,312	63,844	110,819	76,277	177,380	1,021,684	85,140	38,991
7	30,052	140,061	-7,715	103,317	71,930	130,861	72,334	60,295	143,845	132,191	42,649	145,533	1,065,354	88,779	51,349
8	87,547	28,493	97,878	-14,037	121,778	53,726	133,275	73,524	140,934	119,908	107,469	170,417	1,120,911	93,409	51,580
9	70,172	69,445	67,552	-1,278	86,121	52,367	141,984	95,144	82,914	82,065	103,733	177,864	1,028,083	85,674	41,621
10	79,410	18,457	108,340	15,907	54,205	83,588	85,946	161,436	119,064	66,297	103,558	152,194	1,048,401	87,367	45,601
11	64,387	72,499	54,061	77,113	55,210	79,597	114,697	109,289	126,915	133,993	122,345	62,804	1,072,908	89,409	29,849
12	68,599	48,989	46,693	78,507	82,391	34,232	141,668	147,563	75,929	125,768	99,784	105,778	1,055,900	87,992	37,016
13	83,875	33,440	69,429	70,612	50,621	41,660	137,124	79,904	52,733	173,727	60,698	122,304	976,126	81,344	42,263
14	44,566	84,884	43,602	104,292	50,753	66,907	76,398	146,178	105,349	111,377	75,895	85,299	995,500	82,958	30,422
15	65,783	70,920	29,198	98,138	62,755	-1,394	124,733	161,200	71,555	124,625	136,041	138,675	1,082,228	90,186	48,722
16	82,346	60,778	-1,187	79,088	89,719	17,286	152,347	88,040	129,674	136,325	104,802	69,041	1,008,259	84,022	45,201
17	93,701	17,303	74,778	93,774	18,903	54,876	136,041	63,586	130,697	98,674	84,828	129,562	996,725	83,060	39,768
18	65,178	13,854	156,506	11,647	88,217	97,274	40,645	201,647	33,716	109,576	87,334	148,854	1,054,449	87,871	59,468
19	51,677	94,548	39,481	104,655	51,059	90,005	55,590	126,553	142,921	129,629	87,755	122,524	1,096,397	91,366	35,297
20	28,993	140,737	22,757	101,102	19,980	114,174	77,746	100,054	118,189	86,030	158,056	147,660	1,115,477	92,956	47,997
21	67,884	73,505	29,623	42,205	155,238	45,352	107,205	98,249	131,324	86,087	136,721	91,359	1,064,751	88,729	39,535
22	90,160	-5,589	105,845	53,952	63,190	94,506	143,561	74,824	129,451	94,744	104,550	119,938	1,069,131	89,094	39,546
23	79,415	29,502	88,666	47,455	92,342	110,735	63,990	122,169	162,649	153,222	65,574	97,441	1,113,161	92,763	39,961
24	82,400	22,756	21,472	115,240	89,944	44,253	111,691	96,921	90,669	95,024	164,638	95,037	1,030,044	85,837	40,382
25	64,478	62,998	83,206	19,714	114,196	56,799	89,067	132,847	120,334	130,748	40,124	162,367	1,076,876	89,740	42,848
26	68,082	79,233	16,967	65,872	72,294	67,853	52,020	133,593	101,673	153,569	84,571	104,909	1,004,637	83,720	36,229
27	66,762	42,245	77,344	62,355	88,328	-6,523	195,954	62,524	122,437	185,498	45,260	103,255	1,045,440	87,120	58,228
28	71,616	31,014	80,926	92,076	70,677	92,058	63,537	145,592	84,138	139,627	111,718	143,923	1,126,903	93,909	35,375
29	59,054	65,796	45,170	80,455	60,117	42,207	151,504	153,313	76,663	125,179	92,135	91,298	1,042,890	86,908	38,043
30	60,394	88,334	93,662	-9,148	108,756	32,162	126,229	174,865	95,964	74,781	140,844	118,756	1,105,601	92,133	49,137
31	38,384	119,144	51,902	13,284	132,362	64,606	89,334	116,466	103,788	134,321	56,945	153,038	1,073,574	89,464	43,909
32	87,932	2,933	81,334	66,394	51,782	70,917	79,272	104,757	96,422	147,695	114,812	147,095	1,051,346	87,612	39,945
33	64,068	59,028	46,855	84,913	60,498	84,265	100,072	108,139	85,125	159,330	163,402	92,923	1,108,617	92,385	36,941
34	62,856	81,545	66,052	20,870	88,325	72,641	120,248	93,267	97,545	113,464	109,334	154,946	1,081,093	90,091	33,831
35	21,617	136,779	21,951	100,936	33,772	88,639	121,007	88,899	134,537	100,108	128,725	133,547	1,110,527	92,544	43,844
mean	63,761	65,362	59,390	60,096	73,294	71,135	101,835	117,451	103,584	123,427	104,653	120,815			
std. dev	18,414	39,685	34,446	35,683	29,952	34,145	37,344	35,078	29,225	29,025	37,373	30,499			

Finished goods inventory trends

Inventory reduction policy: 50% reduction over initial 6 reporting periods and no further reductions

Percent Series (yr)	Jan	Feb	Mar	Apr	May	Jun	Jul	Aug	Sep	Oct	Nov	Dec	sum	mean	std. dev.
1	-0.25%	23.99%	2.26%	1.68%	14.99%	7.28%	16.67%	22.03%	10.02%	19.27%	18.72%	18.19%	154.85%	12.90%	8.42%
2	1.49%	18.84%	8.96%	3.05%	0.92%	20.46%	16.78%	19.47%	14.68%	14.47%	25.06%	10.28%	154.44%	12.87%	7.96%
3	3.31%	7.74%	12.38%	8.25%	0.63%	15.42%	12.92%	33.34%	19.93%	18.68%	7.79%	13.45%	153.84%	12.82%	8.66%
4	10.71%	8.27%	0.61%	4.98%	3.48%	16.72%	16.02%	17.07%	14.24%	21.93%	19.69%	34.51%	168.24%	14.02%	9.30%
5	9.21%	5.08%	10.66%	1.46%	6.51%	15.74%	-2.66%	16.80%	13.54%	53.01%	11.31%	11.08%	151.74%	12.64%	13.92%
6	12.61%	6.42%	-0.18%	8.43%	7.23%	17.45%	5.64%	30.88%	8.67%	14.38%	30.27%	14.31%	156.12%	13.01%	9.46%
7	-0.60%	27.34%	-8.42%	12.60%	5.56%	26.10%	13.91%	7.78%	25.46%	34.74%	2.72%	28.72%	175.91%	14.66%	13.66%
8	13.92%	-0.69%	15.31%	-8.68%	22.00%	1.90%	25.84%	8.69%	20.98%	19.44%	19.61%	40.31%	178.63%	14.89%	13.15%
9	9.11%	11.15%	9.31%	-5.19%	11.23%	3.04%	19.10%	17.42%	13.12%	14.35%	29.55%	26.80%	158.98%	13.25%	9.69%
10	13.27%	-1.21%	17.61%	-2.54%	4.40%	10.47%	10.45%	31.05%	25.08%	11.57%	14.55%	31.02%	165.74%	13.81%	11.06%
11	5.68%	9.13%	6.66%	9.87%	2.02%	10.35%	17.11%	18.52%	20.99%	29.96%	27.73%	8.00%	166.01%	13.83%	8.94%
12	10.04%	4.06%	1.99%	9.33%	9.79%	0.54%	25.99%	29.27%	12.32%	24.40%	15.64%	17.85%	161.20%	13.43%	9.44%
13	12.77%	2.40%	6.45%	13.79%	4.09%	2.86%	31.39%	12.70%	5.01%	42.80%	9.31%	22.62%	166.17%	13.85%	12.53%
14	3.42%	12.64%	3.04%	15.52%	4.89%	9.02%	11.97%	24.88%	23.51%	25.05%	11.45%	16.36%	161.75%	13.48%	7.91%
15	8.47%	9.73%	-0.24%	15.21%	8.74%	-6.46%	19.16%	25.39%	14.85%	16.32%	27.57%	28.39%	167.11%	13.93%	10.67%
16	12.68%	10.68%	-7.07%	9.93%	14.31%	-5.89%	32.52%	11.76%	23.37%	27.15%	19.45%	10.05%	158.95%	13.25%	11.74%
17	17.03%	-3.13%	9.57%	18.44%	-3.55%	3.38%	29.15%	6.71%	27.27%	16.95%	12.62%	19.06%	153.51%	12.79%	10.62%
18	9.46%	-3.70%	29.30%	-5.82%	12.74%	22.04%	1.18%	57.69%	2.12%	21.52%	13.23%	32.38%	192.14%	16.01%	18.06%
19	3.34%	13.36%	1.33%	18.09%	2.44%	15.54%	4.21%	21.94%	27.12%	24.17%	13.13%	17.15%	161.82%	13.48%	8.89%
20	-0.64%	27.37%	-3.25%	19.28%	-1.97%	18.65%	13.59%	15.47%	23.08%	10.02%	22.69%	39.35%	183.65%	15.30%	12.77%
21	8.08%	7.12%	1.66%	1.27%	28.34%	4.00%	17.13%	16.21%	24.92%	15.32%	26.97%	13.60%	164.61%	13.72%	9.56%
22	14.80%	-6.94%	17.43%	2.67%	5.01%	12.88%	33.44%	8.96%	25.17%	15.45%	19.06%	21.10%	169.02%	14.09%	10.73%
23	11.79%	-1.17%	10.97%	1.82%	10.45%	16.05%	8.43%	9.74%	31.10%	42.20%	14.26%	12.17%	167.81%	13.98%	11.87%
24	15.66%	-1.03%	-2.83%	19.61%	13.78%	2.72%	20.16%	18.11%	14.55%	15.49%	31.26%	19.41%	166.90%	13.91%	9.79%
25	7.65%	7.51%	12.81%	-4.81%	20.14%	3.50%	14.95%	21.40%	21.49%	36.73%	2.83%	30.78%	174.99%	14.58%	12.12%
26	10.31%	12.33%	-2.54%	7.75%	10.39%	9.88%	6.19%	24.84%	16.97%	32.22%	16.41%	17.37%	162.12%	13.51%	9.16%
27	8.42%	3.34%	9.20%	5.87%	15.25%	-8.24%	38.35%	12.87%	19.71%	38.83%	9.18%	18.28%	171.06%	14.25%	13.53%
28	9.08%	-0.19%	8.29%	11.73%	10.29%	15.25%	6.19%	23.93%	14.61%	25.12%	18.10%	26.50%	168.91%	14.08%	8.18%
29	5.89%	8.05%	4.15%	9.64%	7.34%	0.38%	25.30%	35.15%	12.51%	23.94%	13.26%	14.00%	159.60%	13.30%	10.08%
30	4.81%	11.46%	18.85%	-9.65%	18.02%	-1.65%	17.37%	35.84%	19.75%	9.22%	25.05%	23.14%	172.23%	14.35%	12.37%
31	0.88%	20.70%	4.99%	-4.88%	23.34%	7.68%	14.84%	23.65%	17.64%	27.47%	6.45%	33.01%	175.78%	14.65%	11.61%
32	18.13%	-6.82%	12.16%	7.23%	4.89%	11.57%	8.57%	18.24%	12.84%	31.66%	18.47%	29.16%	166.10%	13.84%	10.44%
33	7.12%	6.67%	1.77%	10.45%	8.57%	7.90%	14.36%	13.81%	1.86%	23.85%	39.99%	26.49%	162.84%	13.57%	11.30%
34	7.03%	11.36%	8.16%	-1.66%	9.71%	7.56%	24.52%	13.79%	13.50%	18.76%	6.96%	23.25%	142.93%	11.91%	7.46%
35	-1.62%	24.98%	-0.88%	13.39%	-0.43%	13.57%	20.81%	13.57%	21.71%	17.11%	17.69%	26.21%	166.11%	13.84%	9.79%
mean	8.09%	8.20%	6.30%	6.23%	9.01%	8.79%	17.15%	20.54%	17.53%	23.82%	18.89%	21.84%			
std. dev	5.27%	9.18%	7.96%	8.24%	7.37%	8.33%	9.76%	10.22%	7.12%	10.20%	8.63%	8.55%			

Finished goods inventory trends
Inventory reduction policy: 50% reduction over initial 6 reporting periods and no further reductions

Dollars / Series (yr)	Jan	Feb	Mar	Apr	May	Jun	Jul	Aug	Sep	Oct	Nov	Dec	sum	mean	std. dev.
1	-1,869	138,073	13,569	11,226	85,313	38,627	101,207	128,952	70,397	129,264	132,019	112,784	959,563	79,964	52,314
2	10,790	107,620	52,291	18,201	6,450	117,048	93,092	107,405	88,265	96,189	154,694	80,223	932,268	77,689	46,407
3	22,497	57,815	80,516	51,322	4,117	98,993	98,030	151,301	120,455	109,771	56,995	79,932	931,746	77,646	41,708
4	58,863	48,711	3,822	31,315	24,943	105,952	99,969	110,404	101,357	124,270	137,425	195,559	1,042,589	86,882	54,877
5	53,744	30,017	64,082	8,361	39,211	83,888	-20,979	105,024	79,412	310,485	76,871	75,348	906,064	75,505	81,966
6	71,297	34,666	-1,132	50,255	41,004	94,027	35,123	172,648	55,104	103,754	18,614	89,207	919,111	76,593	53,700
7	-3,942	154,426	-57,919	88,547	35,748	135,738	71,628	53,537	144,670	172,947	135,537	170,839	984,934	82,078	75,261
8	80,981	-3,994	86,193	-62,199	126,694	12,154	158,127	56,445	133,496	122,959	98,742	204,660	1,051,055	87,588	75,917
9	54,600	63,199	45,967	-32,865	66,627	18,321	165,020	96,297	84,906	98,672	176,937	109,181	946,862	78,905	57,925
10	67,033	-7,845	99,410	-13,461	28,144	62,909	71,205	185,012	140,037	70,388	98,742	167,361	968,935	80,745	62,345
11	37,012	57,979	40,808	57,093	13,721	64,963	109,517	112,803	136,456	165,845	140,792	48,328	985,316	82,110	48,769
12	57,330	26,137	12,625	56,976	56,144	3,588	165,390	163,211	75,815	144,801	97,606	112,836	972,458	81,038	56,165
13	72,321	14,149	39,830	70,986	24,056	16,264	162,847	66,673	34,160	213,870	57,591	135,687	908,434	75,703	63,049
14	21,851	73,046	19,477	85,343	29,452	50,360	76,015	155,173	122,683	129,511	64,253	96,144	923,308	76,942	43,580
15	49,778	54,843	-1,558	86,493	43,909	-42,355	132,781	146,049	100,745	108,687	159,594	165,108	1,003,778	83,648	64,952
16	71,625	54,854	-44,188	61,344	78,066	-42,658	190,155	78,290	141,924	156,597	106,574	68,193	920,776	76,731	70,075
17	93,090	-20,323	56,787	92,745	-20,681	21,634	159,412	39,687	156,216	99,846	89,321	122,424	890,158	74,180	60,374
18	51,456	-28,650	164,585	-39,331	75,276	105,140	8,384	251,269	12,541	123,396	87,337	173,933	985,336	82,111	87,588
19	22,511	78,456	9,081	105,594	15,905	80,267	27,955	147,069	160,075	145,391	88,288	115,306	995,899	82,992	54,107
20	-4,636	146,848	-23,011	101,922	-12,958	96,795	79,423	98,973	137,170	73,560	143,571	208,154	1,045,811	87,151	70,819
21	49,970	40,949	11,426	9,405	157,328	-77,093	201,201	106,143	149,616	92,451	146,820	84,479	972,695	81,058	53,900
22	79,138	-45,413	100,341	18,207	36,368	75,573	177,401	57,988	148,129	96,497	113,928	124,597	982,753	81,896	60,202
23	70,209	-7,727	72,224	12,611	73,252	91,730	58,672	69,277	186,306	219,749	82,788	82,652	1,011,744	84,312	63,079
24	78,869	-5,675	-20,512	115,768	76,276	16,167	117,731	99,961	87,695	104,849	183,472	109,329	963,930	80,327	57,900
25	46,817	45,359	75,680	-32,575	114,072	21,643	94,509	137,820	132,209	167,982	17,628	174,893	996,038	83,003	64,924
26	63,668	62,774	-14,698	47,574	56,750	47,927	34,043	150,063	103,203	185,177	90,207	104,132	930,820	77,568	53,419
27	49,154	20,167	55,822	38,890	80,540	-61,844	193,565	87,930	130,843	202,524	51,198	115,575	964,366	80,364	73,594
28	52,883	-1,355	55,774	74,077	60,881	83,572	41,879	146,150	97,807	152,544	117,580	151,813	1,033,606	86,134	48,506
29	37,082	47,364	24,862	56,712	41,981	2,863	160,563	190,289	78,105	133,990	84,374	86,114	944,301	78,692	56,804
30	33,570	73,840	92,632	-63,271	104,735	-10,892	126,120	203,751	107,318	62,943	159,781	135,371	1,025,899	85,492	73,423
31	6,088	121,518	28,792	-33,183	131,405	44,383	86,923	138,611	106,814	148,212	44,518	179,794	1,003,876	83,656	64,977
32	88,846	-43,211	69,621	43,392	28,995	62,073	54,419	111,953	77,768	199,565	122,560	166,376	982,358	81,863	63,844
33	44,297	40,385	10,942	65,413	51,297	51,088	99,507	97,286	11,871	152,111	226,925	164,858	1,015,980	84,665	66,424
34	46,746	64,260	46,629	-10,481	61,416	45,710	139,755	91,229	85,829	130,557	51,734	129,186	882,571	73,548	43,881
35	-11,349	136,080	-6,029	78,843	-2,656	82,315	123,237	88,285	129,326	118,027	127,064	150,891	1,014,036	84,503	59,194
mean	46,352	46,553	36,136	35,761	52,394	48,482	102,681	120,085	106,535	139,068	109,043	128,322			
std dev	28,077	52,561	46,172	49,032	41,273	47,461	53,348	47,119	40,559	49,784	48,673	42,099			

Finished goods inventory trends

Inventory reduction policy: 50% reduction over initial 6 reporting periods and no further reductions

Percent Series (yr)	Jan	Feb	Mar	Apr	May	Jun	Jul	Aug	Sep	Oct	Nov	Dec	sum	mean	std. dev.
1	-1.96%	21.63%	0.26%	0.2%	13.28%	5.61%	15.36%	20.63%	9.05%	18.22%	17.75%	16.97%	137.02%	11.42%	8.50%
2	-0.32%	16.45%	6.87%	1.26%	-0.24%	18.99%	15.23%	17.90%	13.34%	13.38%	23.81%	9.53%	136.21%	11.35%	7.99%
3	1.30%	6.20%	10.67%	6.59%	-0.70%	14.24%	12.15%	31.40%	18.61%	17.29%	6.91%	12.21%	136.86%	11.40%	8.61%
4	7.94%	5.99%	-1.23%	3.34%	2.37%	15.52%	14.78%	15.91%	13.30%	20.49%	18.71%	33.03%	150.15%	12.51%	9.48%
5	6.67%	2.81%	8.67%	-0.26%	4.96%	14.08%	-3.40%	15.83%	12.45%	51.77%	10.40%	10.16%	134.14%	11.18%	14.01%
6	9.95%	3.83%	-1.95%	6.63%	5.51%	15.82%	4.40%	29.35%	7.47%	13.47%	28.83%	13.11%	136.44%	11.37%	9.59%
7	-2.69%	24.91%	-10.01%	11.26%	4.18%	24.37%	12.15%	6.77%	24.03%	32.88%	1.69%	27.35%	156.90%	13.07%	13.54%
8	11.37%	-3.05%	13.10%	-9.97%	20.32%	0.72%	24.55%	7.54%	19.82%	18.27%	18.61%	38.50%	159.81%	13.32%	13.18%
9	6.68%	8.74%	6.63%	-6.80%	9.64%	1.71%	27.61%	15.86%	11.96%	13.34%	28.21%	15.66%	139.23%	11.60%	9.85%
10	10.16%	-3.17%	15.41%	-4.70%	3.01%	9.14%	9.43%	29.71%	23.55%	10.26%	13.50%	29.42%	145.73%	12.14%	11.18%
11	3.54%	7.10%	4.73%	7.98%	0.78%	9.12%	15.93%	17.29%	19.85%	28.40%	25.92%	6.67%	147.31%	12.28%	9.01%
12	7.42%	2.08%	0.17%	7.60%	8.10%	-0.56%	24.79%	27.73%	11.05%	23.03%	14.39%	16.64%	142.44%	11.87%	9.59%
13	10.12%	0.13%	4.54%	11.52%	2.47%	1.38%	29.65%	11.00%	3.98%	41.00%	8.04%	21.28%	145.10%	12.09%	12.52%
14	1.21%	10.30%	1.25%	13.47%	3.34%	7.49%	10.77%	23.63%	21.79%	23.31%	9.94%	14.97%	141.45%	11.79%	8.01%
15	5.96%	7.30%	-1.98%	13.27%	6.64%	-7.57%	18.16%	23.96%	13.80%	15.28%	26.17%	26.97%	147.95%	12.33%	10.81%
16	10.02%	7.89%	-8.94%	8.23%	12.48%	-6.81%	31.18%	10.67%	22.06%	25.71%	17.86%	9.01%	139.36%	11.61%	11.79%
17	14.25%	-5.08%	7.54%	16.09%	-5.19%	2.20%	27.56%	5.37%	25.84%	15.56%	11.67%	17.92%	133.72%	11.14%	10.62%
18	6.66%	-5.14%	27.13%	-7.27%	11.14%	20.04%	0.23%	55.50%	0.75%	20.06%	12.12%	30.74%	171.96%	14.33%	17.83%
19	1.31%	11.07%	-0.28%	16.25%	1.10%	13.79%	3.11%	20.86%	25.74%	22.84%	12.06%	16.11%	143.94%	11.99%	8.98%
20	-2.43%	24.75%	-4.76%	17.10%	-3.28%	16.91%	12.18%	14.29%	21.72%	9.14%	21.52%	37.67%	164.82%	13.74%	12.64%
21	5.75%	4.76%	0.08%	0.06%	26.55%	2.54%	15.75%	15.08%	23.58%	13.99%	25.37%	12.35%	145.86%	12.16%	9.62%
22	11.93%	-8.87%	15.30%	1.25%	3.95%	11.48%	31.76%	7.80%	23.83%	14.21%	17.71%	19.72%	150.07%	12.51%	10.74%
23	9.33%	-3.09%	9.26%	0.4%	9.29%	14.58%	7.44%	8.84%	29.81%	40.49%	12.83%	11.13%	150.35%	12.53%	11.86%
24	12.53%	-3.54%	-4.28%	17.78%	11.99%	1.35%	18.75%	16.55%	13.22%	14.44%	29.87%	17.91%	146.57%	12.21%	9.91%
25	5.29%	5.31%	10.76%	-6.2%	18.41%	2.24%	13.75%	20.24%	20.21%	34.60%	1.58%	29.30%	155.45%	12.95%	12.08%
26	7.98%	9.50%	-4.66%	6.04%	8.56%	7.94%	3.96%	23.54%	15.66%	30.77%	14.84%	17.08%	141.21%	11.77%	9.35%
27	5.88%	1.15%	7.24%	4.37%	13.32%	-9.07%	36.62%	11.84%	18.61%	37.12%	7.65%	17.07%	151.81%	12.65%	13.49%
28	6.54%	-1.88%	6.64%	10.10%	8.69%	13.67%	5.14%	22.67%	13.53%	23.82%	16.96%	25.06%	150.93%	12.58%	8.33%
29	3.63%	5.77%	2.15%	7.81%	5.65%	-0.47%	24.17%	33.51%	11.27%	22.41%	12.07%	12.73%	140.69%	11.72%	10.17%
30	2.89%	9.48%	16.15%	-11.17%	16.37%	-2.75%	16.47%	34.50%	18.24%	8.20%	23.87%	21.73%	153.97%	12.83%	12.38%
31	-1.07%	18.41%	2.86%	-6.30%	21.60%	6.24%	13.44%	22.25%	16.33%	25.85%	5.44%	31.42%	156.45%	13.04%	11.60%
32	14.88%	-8.85%	10.01%	5.45%	3.30%	9.93%	7.43%	17.02%	11.61%	30.44%	17.39%	27.69%	146.31%	12.19%	10.58%
33	4.82%	4.48%	-0.13%	8.80%	7.00%	6.74%	13.40%	12.96%	0.91%	22.85%	38.57%	25.24%	145.63%	12.14%	11.45%
34	4.95%	8.94%	6.01%	-3.30%	8.29%	6.24%	23.05%	12.43%	12.36%	16.10%	6.14%	23.68%	124.97%	10.41%	7.59%
35	-3.52%	22.42%	-2.48%	11.55%	-1.89%	12.26%	19.43%	19.23%	20.37%	22.48%	17.68%	10.70%	148.23%	12.35%	9.84%
mean	5.68%	5.96%	4.36%	4.55%	7.46%	7.40%	15.90%	19.42%	16.28%	22.48%	16.47%	20.51%			
std dev	4.91%	9.01%	7.79%	8.07%	7.24%	8.12%	9.58%	10.02%	7.02%	10.01%	8.53%	8.37%			

Finished goods inventory trends

Inventory reduction policy: 50% reduction over initial 6 reporting periods and no further reductions

Dollars	Jan	Feb	Mar	Apr	May	Jun	Jul	Aug	Sep	Oct	Nov	Dec	sum	mean	std. dev.
Series (yr)															
1	-14,665	124,487	1,585	1,381	75,593	29,753	93,256	120,776	63,584	122,209	125,232	105,212	848,404	70,700	53,384
2	-2,324	93,991	40,112	7,487	-1,672	108,669	84,504	98,785	80,237	88,917	147,017	74,349	820,073	68,339	47,347
3	8,856	46,298	69,391	40,962	-4,595	91,451	92,162	142,514	112,461	101,581	50,526	72,585	824,193	68,683	42,729
4	43,652	35,283	-7,788	20,990	16,984	98,313	92,213	102,924	94,662	116,160	130,547	187,148	931,088	77,591	56,391
5	38,956	16,612	52,114	-1,565	29,889	75,036	-26,765	98,938	73,025	303,201	70,648	69,108	799,198	66,600	82,762
6	56,283	20,656	-12,561	39,546	31,249	85,247	27,423	164,112	47,480	97,170	164,959	81,695	803,258	66,938	54,820
7	-17,807	140,704	-68,848	79,228	26,909	126,733	62,566	46,544	136,567	163,683	11,586	162,728	870,595	72,550	75,615
8	66,168	-17,563	73,769	-71,458	117,035	4,595	150,219	48,999	126,142	115,561	128,647	195,506	937,620	78,135	76,692
9	39,991	49,519	32,710	-43,038	57,187	10,305	156,581	87,687	77,426	91,771	168,939	101,738	830,816	69,235	59,040
10	51,297	-20,561	87,010	-24,946	19,254	54,876	64,251	176,988	131,504	62,445	91,630	158,734	852,481	71,040	63,466
11	23,031	45,119	28,985	46,171	5,323	57,248	101,953	105,196	129,087	157,236	131,642	40,333	871,323	72,610	49,891
12	42,377	13,373	1,062	46,447	46,468	-3,715	157,776	154,654	67,988	136,673	89,842	105,177	858,121	71,510	57,357
13	57,318	748	28,070	59,292	14,554	7,850	153,824	57,733	27,117	204,862	49,771	127,635	788,773	65,731	63,591
14	7,722	59,496	7,993	74,082	20,116	41,805	68,386	147,409	113,700	120,471	55,742	87,959	804,879	67,073	44,730
15	35,031	41,160	-12,919	75,454	33,378	-49,975	125,848	137,841	93,640	101,754	151,486	156,867	889,563	74,130	66,034
16	56,611	40,530	-55,869	50,554	68,052	-48,963	182,309	71,029	133,986	148,268	97,904	61,081	805,493	67,124	70,722
17	77,848	-33,003	44,724	80,909	-30,247	14,069	150,734	31,733	148,012	91,678	82,575	115,096	774,127	64,511	61,033
18	36,189	-39,834	152,400	-49,086	65,829	95,612	1,641	241,723	4,419	115,030	80,014	165,139	869,076	72,423	87,606
19	8,814	65,014	-1,929	94,732	7,187	71,221	20,692	139,862	151,922	137,356	81,112	108,266	884,248	73,687	55,174
20	-17,684	132,798	-33,688	90,407	-21,602	87,776	71,197	91,405	129,056	67,131	136,156	199,257	932,207	77,684	71,247
21	35,586	27,369	526	464	147,434	14,541	93,053	98,749	141,568	84,437	138,107	76,690	858,524	71,544	54,837
22	63,755	-58,037	88,073	8,536	28,683	67,371	168,515	50,504	140,239	88,745	105,859	116,437	868,678	72,390	61,048
23	55,549	-20,326	60,941	3,076	65,104	83,343	51,779	62,885	178,600	210,823	74,507	75,557	901,837	75,153	63,868
24	63,120	-19,546	-30,992	104,985	66,361	8,038	109,503	91,340	79,684	97,721	175,307	100,843	846,365	70,530	58,974
25	32,367	32,114	63,577	-42,302	104,308	13,812	86,885	130,301	124,347	158,221	9,869	166,479	879,977	73,331	65,566
26	49,280	48,401	-26,942	37,071	46,743	38,505	26,980	142,215	95,260	176,823	81,626	95,725	811,686	67,640	54,569
27	34,367	6,936	43,913	28,972	70,326	-68,077	184,849	80,887	123,592	193,605	42,645	107,922	849,937	70,828	74,047
28	38,081	-13,333	44,681	63,792	51,420	74,892	34,762	138,419	90,596	144,643	110,131	143,561	921,644	76,804	49,906
29	22,842	33,935	12,866	45,911	32,293	-3,460	153,380	181,535	70,345	125,462	76,767	78,296	830,170	69,181	57,810
30	20,152	61,080	79,348	-73,265	95,152	-18,198	119,590	196,091	99,073	55,953	152,250	127,143	914,368	76,197	74,198
31	-7,409	108,076	16,526	-42,872	121,597	36,074	78,711	130,388	98,828	139,437	37,560	171,091	888,008	74,001	65,581
32	72,922	-56,082	57,307	32,737	19,548	53,259	47,198	104,471	70,326	191,883	218,887	157,985	866,941	72,245	65,077
33	29,962	27,156	-833	55,065	41,917	43,605	92,796	91,281	5,817	145,717	45,643	157,081	908,451	75,704	67,655
34	32,916	50,597	34,314	-20,784	52,450	37,719	131,355	83,931	78,578	123,668	120,298	121,372	771,761	64,313	45,100
35	-24,714	122,137	-16,993	68,040	-11,753	37,355	115,094	80,844	121,326	111,054	101,452	142,891	902,579	75,215	60,265
mean	31,898	33,294	24,361	25,342	43,099	40,391	95,006	112,306	98,863	131,181	101,452	120,420			
std dev	27,369	52,207	45,816	48,635	40,955	46,918	52,909	46,746	40,277	49,445	48,468	41,607			

Finished goods inventory trends

Inventory reduction policy: 50% reduction over initial 6 reporting periods and no further reductions

Month	Jan	Feb	Mar	Apr	May	Jun	Jul	Aug	Sep	Oct	Nov	Dec	mean	std.dev.
Series (yr)														
1	853079	905780	798954	656324	647999	591580	530041	545073	454233	470305	452424	504811	596138	146726
2	874241	908653	811928	714299	541474	558600	572523	574630	535180	484779	511777	391593	600494	151154
3	909371	767853	741659	690627	580786	502789	391223	585799	532957	546006	431298	489835	569166	121496
4	1014062	895148	773992	688310	530570	509316	517058	498629	446322	540711	458551	560762	583579	141809
5	985881	893621	797828	701678	621429	590143	385747	405774	425752	485638	414847	416049	558046	176655
6	1000945	933976	761958	713945	650366	585337	513373	569080	508217	438905	546630	500849	611149	144102
7	924336	914778	728570	627941	589300	600307	604164	466192	540151	617586	468513	540720	608929	125797
8	987532	904590	828253	617286	643965	503948	527250	496410	490301	493197	459333	610263	597709	146844
9	973930	911985	883813	678186	629324	534432	562629	573953	498663	460009	533278	496202	614770	152946
10	1049083	847742	826708	765659	592702	535519	463597	534924	568860	529056	474145	575156	610415	137282
11	932049	857337	788188	728123	559866	514381	504253	507096	491256	573915	610033	532990	606131	127073
12	996828	850950	770902	701932	645067	486871	507642	570461	521789	541898	517539	510575	602330	122896
13	1000196	893422	784015	779593	633495	560915	601552	595963	469559	600572	521314	536845	634295	130053
14	941969	903381	765604	750748	622409	570341	508633	517583	598847	602634	567405	545688	632116	123039
15	983191	912206	757406	735938	702106	488307	462218	547204	473661	462176	540547	549400	602834	150454
16	1000933	954910	778707	699347	667568	440488	523023	484012	529182	555287	577990	474113	607693	154871
17	1016162	845333	804216	789069	637709	504311	578546	530280	546933	544550	449694	488555	610836	138979
18	1017804	745579	812373	650313	629788	635191	449534	636368	541466	557725	488223	586274	612076	105455
19	913146	896130	734042	724179	581148	603073	484186	480490	543570	535674	478428	469338	593660	137067
20	869817	936700	711840	767654	576258	601262	548406	504561	540952	428642	494352	593127	609432	144706
21	958923	905335	726673	596083	659569	557861	543211	492924	536514	534212	580818	519299	604773	120122
22	1025506	841649	817866	644734	512327	546820	592419	498965	525996	516775	537967	544015	598139	121651
23	977380	839951	752197	635665	543247	559184	459541	426131	513720	595056	552068	473029	577254	125321
24	1049933	924730	698652	718861	660988	541947	548530	574700	534083	475149	544313	565737	617063	126765
25	963370	883048	806863	648412	650952	522105	508284	501248	524126	650727	517259	560948	615816	128852
26	959189	958215	816283	700199	667112	628141	470851	523212	529584	556946	572060	560458	634823	144508
27	985813	882080	793969	661216	680934	415520	581053	469551	483431	594565	570194	510245	603887	141879
28	986816	798563	739588	685686	630737	578696	474497	515430	480756	526690	496591	550126	588851	110437
29	949396	895275	799762	720099	645867	421529	478921	583616	517361	568588	507077	521221	605392	145855
30	894576	850643	885627	666259	638841	487061	435330	510700	549699	466006	502111	548552	594621	151837
31	899842	896125	817777	645946	653834	553945	547462	548166	532428	585018	463812	580181	620427	129164
32	1061629	858075	820918	710361	629811	587604	481460	498796	496159	512101	478183	559362	602985	137049
33	955686	881894	784951	689880	625310	498868	447431	400342	403553	426312	535883	518516	564813	161755
34	922001	910858	821030	686863	597744	532718	559983	486548	483369	459257	406107	520897	587761	157370
35	891002	929553	730938	720193	606525	530677	542837	496090	533301	464924	451070	533342	594495	144255
mean	963589	883888	784973	694617	619632	539422	511640	518597	511484	525774	506052	526831		
std. dev	53711	47262	43444	46296	44632	53497	55653	52478	40217	57964	50621	46603		

Appendix 4

Simulation Data

Dataset 4 — Sample Income Statements Utilizing the Mean Values of the 35-Replication Datasets under Each Accounting System and 25 Percent Sales Stochasticity

Sample full-absorption income statement: 25% sales stochasity and 50% finished goods inventory reduction over first 6 periods with no further reductions

	Jan	Feb	Mar	Apr	May	Jun	Jul	Aug	Sep	Oct	Nov	Dec
COGM cogm	563684.9167	437742.3333	549173.5167	472252.6667	498864.4833	486921.95	474978.1167	521725.8167	477914.0333	552890.95	539974.3167	483711.6
COGS +/- fgi	-160274.3	61375.9	-154017	-5293.16667	-131439.783	-32910.5833	18513.58333	-44050.7	30132.28333	-51511.5833	13717.46667	30333.75
cogs	723959.2167	376366.4333	703190.5167	477545.8333	630304.2667	519832.5333	456464.5333	565776.5167	447781.75	604402.5333	526256.85	453377.85
Sales	702562.2083	544824.2917	684608.7708	588891.2708	622094.1042	606546.5625	592298.0833	650361.0833	595720.2292	689813	672800.0833	603338.8125
less COGS	723959.2167	376366.4333	703190.5167	477545.8333	630304.2667	519832.5333	456464.5333	565776.5167	447781.75	604402.5333	526256.85	453377.85
GP	-21397.0083	168457.8583	-18581.7458	111345.4375	-8210.1625	86714.02917	135833.55	84584.56667	147938.4792	85410.46667	146543.2333	149960.9625
GP%	-0.03045568	0.309196673	-0.02714214	0.189076393	-0.01319762	0.142963516	0.229333091	0.130057854	0.248335497	0.123816841	0.217810962	0.248551824
Interest Expense	13365.023	13943.29525	10964.069	10802.8965	9097.87725	7960.15475	8142.55975	7441.34425	7999.50975	6973.86725	6766.043	8000.13425
Net Profit	-34762.0313	154514.5631	-29545.8148	100542.541	-17308.0398	78753.87442	127690.9903	77143.22242	139938.9694	78436.59942	139777.1903	141960.8283
NP%	-0.04947894	0.283604394	-0.04315723	0.170731926	-0.02782222	0.129839784	0.215585689	0.118615988	0.234907197	0.113707047	0.207754419	0.235292054

Sample full-absorption income statement: 25% sales stochasity and 50% finished goods inventory reduction over first 6 periods with no further reductions

	Jan	Feb	Mar	Apr	May	Jun	Jul	Aug	Sep	Oct	Nov	Dec
COGM												
cogm	424481.6389	325814.1111	411731.1722	354717.5556	374428.1611	365313.9833	356242.7056	394155.2722	357211.3444	411650.3167	405961.4389	362973.8667
COGS												
+/- fgi	-122688.1	49551.96667	-119685.667	-5031.05556	-97386.5944	-26320.1944	14057.86111	-36213.5667	26530.76111	-37063.8611	6355.822222	24724.58333
cogs	547169.7389	276262.1444	531416.8389	359748.6111	471814.7556	391634.1778	342184.8444	430368.8389	330680.5833	448714.1778	399605.6167	338249.2833
Sales	702562.2083	544824.2917	684608.7708	588891.2708	622094.1042	606546.5625	592298.0833	650361.0833	595720.2292	689813	672800.0833	603338.8125
less COGS	547169.7389	276262.1444	531416.8389	359748.6111	471814.7556	391634.1778	342184.8444	430368.8389	330680.5833	448714.1778	399605.6167	338249.2833
GP	155392.4694	268562.1472	153191.9319	229142.6597	150279.3486	214912.3847	250113.2389	219992.2444	265039.6458	241098.8222	273194.4667	265089.5292
GP%	0.221179659	0.492933504	0.223765658	0.389108603	0.241570122	0.35432133	0.422275955	0.338261698	0.444906238	0.349513306	0.406055935	0.43937092
Fixed	126262.7611	126262.7611	126262.7611	126262.7611	126262.7611	126262.7611	126262.7611	126262.7611	126262.7611	126262.7611	126262.7611	126262.7611
Interest Expense	13365.023	13943.29525	10964.069	10802.8965	9097.87725	7960.15475	8142.55975	7441.34425	7999.50975	6973.86725	6766.043	8000.13425
Net Profit	15764.68533	128356.0909	15965.10183	92077.00211	14918.71025	80689.46886	115707.918	86288.13908	130777.375	107862.1939	140165.6626	130826.6338
NP%	0.022438846	0.235591718	0.023320037	0.156356541	0.023981436	0.133030956	0.1953542	0.132677279	0.219528175	0.156364397	0.208331815	0.216837755

Sample full-absorption income statement: 25% sales stochasity and 50% finished goods inventory reduction over first 6 periods with no further reductions

	Jan	Feb	Mar	Apr	May	Jun	Jul	Aug	Sep	Oct	Nov	Dec
COGM												
cogm	563684.9167	437742.3333	549173.5167	472252.6667	498864.4833	486921.95	474978.1167	521725.8167	477914.0333	552890.95	539974.3167	483711.6
COGS												
+/- fgi	-160126.447	64303.02222	-155931.611	-8912.79167	-128545.553	-34102.0556	19938.48611	-48009.0944	34365.275	-44425.8194	2416.905556	34287.02778
cogs	723811.3639	373439.3111	705105.1278	481165.4583	627410.0361	521024.0056	455039.6306	569734.9111	443548.7583	597316.7694	537557.4111	449424.5722
Sales	702562.2083	544824.2917	684608.7708	588891.2708	622094.1042	606546.5625	592298.0833	650361.0833	595720.2292	689813	672800.0833	603338.8125
less COGS	723811.3639	373439.3111	705105.1278	481165.4583	627410.0361	521024.0056	455039.6306	569734.9111	443548.7583	597316.7694	537557.4111	449424.5722
GP	-21249.1556	171384.9806	-20496.3569	107725.8125	-5315.93194	85522.55694	137258.4528	80626.17222	152171.4708	92496.23056	135242.6722	153914.2403
GP%	-0.03024523	0.314569272	-0.02993879	0.182929885	-0.00854522	0.140999162	0.23173881	0.123971397	0.255441167	0.134088848	0.201014648	0.255104159
Interest Expense	13365.023	13943.29525	10964.069	10802.8965	9097.87725	7960.15475	8142.55975	7441.34425	7999.50975	6973.86725	6766.043	8000.13425
Net Profit	-34614.1786	157441.6853	-31460.4259	96922.916	-14413.8092	77562.40219	129115.893	73184.82797	144171.9611	85522.36331	128476.6292	145914.106
NP%	-0.04926849	0.288976993	-0.04595388	0.164585418	-0.02316982	0.12787543	0.217991408	0.112529531	0.242012868	0.123979054	0.190958105	0.241844388

Sample full-absorption income statement: 25% sales stochasity and 50% finished goods inventory reduction over first 6 periods with no further reductions

	Jan	Feb	Mar	Apr	May	Jun	Jul	Aug	Sep	Oct	Nov	Dec
COGM												
cogm	354880	269850	343010	295950	312210	304510	296875	330370	296860	341030	338955	302605
COGS												
+/- fgi	-103895	43640	-102520	-4900	-80360	-23025	11830	-32295	24730	-29840	2675	21920
cogs	458775	226210	445530	300850	392570	327535	285045	362665	272130	370870	336280	280685
Sales	702562.2083	544824.2917	684608.7708	588891.2708	622094.1042	606546.5625	592298.0833	650361.0833	595720.2292	689813	672800.0833	603338.8125
less COGS	458775	226210	445530	300850	392570	327535	285045	362665	272130	370870	336280	280685
GP	243787.2083	318614.2917	239078.7708	288041.2708	229524.1042	279011.5625	307253.0833	287696.0833	323590.2292	318943	336520.0833	322653.8125
GP%	0.346997327	0.58480192	0.349219556	0.489124708	0.368953994	0.460000237	0.518747387	0.44236362	0.543191608	0.462361539	0.500178421	0.534780468
Fixed Costs												
Labor	69601.63889	55964.11111	68721.17222	58767.55556	62218.16111	60803.98333	59367.70556	63785.27222	60351.34444	70620.31667	67006.43889	60368.86667
Other OH	139203.2778	111928.2222	137442.3444	117535.1111	124436.3222	121607.9667	118735.4111	127570.5444	120702.6889	141240.6333	134012.8778	120737.7333
Interest Expense	13365.023	13943.29525	10964.069	10802.8965	9097.87725	7960.15475	8142.55975	7441.34425	7999.50975	6973.86725	6766.043	8000.13425
Net Profit	21617.26867	136778.6631	21951.18517	100935.7077	33771.74358	88639.45775	121007.4069	88898.92242	134536.6861	100108.1828	128734.7237	133547.0783
NP%	0.030769188	0.251050963	0.032063839	0.171399565	0.054287194	0.146137928	0.204301534	0.136691639	0.225838707	0.145123653	0.191341718	0.221346738

Sample full-absorption income statement: 25% sales stochasity and 50% finished goods inventory reduction over first 6 periods with no further reductions

	Jan	Feb	Mar	Apr	May	Jun	Jul	Aug	Sep	Oct	Nov	Dec
COGM												
cogm	563684.9167	437742.3333	549173.5167	472252.6667	498864.4833	486921.95	474978.1167	521725.8167	477914.0333	552890.95	539974.3167	483711.6
COGS												
+/- fgi	-150225.931	28998.05244	-141464.253	-37795.6212	-125885.188	-37309.8435	5916.828374	-40350.002	11519.69384	-18894.6434	-5761.44934	31264.25805
cogs	713910.8477	408744.2809	690637.7701	510048.2879	624749.6712	524231.7935	469061.2883	562075.8187	466394.3395	571785.5934	545735.766	452447.3419
Sales	702562.2083	544824.2917	684608.7708	588891.2708	622094.1042	606546.5625	592298.0833	650361.0833	595720.2292	689813	672800.0833	603338.8125
less COGS	713910.8477	408744.2809	690637.7701	510048.2879	624749.6712	524231.7935	469061.2883	562075.8187	466394.3395	571785.5934	545735.766	452447.3419
GP	-11348.6393	136080.0108	-6028.99923	78842.98292	-2655.56699	82314.76898	123236.795	88285.26468	129325.8897	118027.4066	127064.3173	150891.4706
GP%	-0.01615322	0.249768619	-0.00880649	0.133883769	-0.00426875	0.135710552	0.208065497	0.135748074	0.217091654	0.171100583	0.18885895	0.250094089
Interest Expense	13365.023	13943.29525	10964.069	10802.8965	9097.87725	7960.15475	8142.55975	7441.34425	7999.50975	6973.86725	6766.043	8000.13425
Net Profit	-24713.6623	122136.7155	-16993.0682	68040.08642	-11753.4442	74354.61423	115094.2353	80843.92043	121326.3799	111053.5393	120298.2743	142891.3363
NP%	-0.03517648	0.22417634	-0.02482158	0.115539302	-0.01889335	0.12258682	0.194318095	0.124306209	0.203663354	0.160990789	0.178802407	0.236834318

Index